Socioeconomic Shocks and Africa's Development Agenda

This book investigates how African countries respond to socioeconomic shocks, drawing out lessons to help to inform future policy and development efforts.

The challenges posed by the COVID-19 pandemic affected all sectors of the economy, exposing substantial structural weaknesses and complexities in supply chains and logistics across the African continent. This book examines the disruptive impact of the pandemic across Africa. However, it also goes beyond the current crisis to investigate how socioeconomic pressures in general impact commodity prices, national budgeting processes, food, business, energy sectors, education, health, and sanitation. Overall, the book presents evidence-based solutions and policy recommendations to enable readers to improve resilience and responses to future crises.

The insights provided by this book will be of interest to policymakers and development agencies, as well as to researchers of global development, politics, economics, business, and African studies.

Evans Osabuohien is Professor and Head of the Department of Economics and Development Studies, Covenant University, Ota, Nigeria. He is the Pioneer Chair at the Centre for Economic Policy and Development Research (CEPDeR) as well as the Pioneer Chair for Regional Centre of Expertise, Ogun State (RCE Ogun). Also, he is a Visiting Professor at Witten/Herdecke University, Germany, and Visiting Scholar at Eduardo Mondlane University, Maputo, Mozambique. He is a fellow of the Alexander von Humboldt Foundation and Swedish Institute, among others. In 2020, he was recognised as one of the six youngest professors in Nigeria. He has published five books and over 185 scholarly articles.

Gbadebo Odularu is affiliated with Virginia Military Institute (VMI), Bay Atlantic University (BAU), Socio-economic Research Applications and Projects (SERAP), and Nexford University (NXU), United States. He holds a PhD degree from the University of Sunderland, UK. He was a regional policies and markets analyst at the continental Forum for Agricultural Research in Africa (FARA) based in Accra, Ghana, and a visiting scholar at the Centre for the Study of African Economies (CSAE), University of Oxford, UK.

Daniel Ufua is Lecturer at the Department of Business Management and a Research Fellow at the Centre for Economic Research and Policy Development (CEPDeR), at Covenant University, Nigeria. He holds a PhD in Management from the University of Hull, UK. His research interest is on the application of systems thinking and management science where he has published several research papers.

Romanus Osabohien is Lecturer at the Department of Economics and Development Studies and a Research Fellow, Centre for Economic Policy and Development Research (CEPDeR), Covenant University, Ota, Nigeria. He holds a PhD in Economics with research focus on Social Security, Food Security, Agricultural and Development Economics. He is a reviewer and editorial board member for well-rated journals including *Heliyon Business and Economics* (Elsevier).

Routledge Studies in African Development

Responding to Mass Atrocities in Africa
Protection First and Justice Later
Raymond Kwun-Sun Lau

Politics in The Gambia and Guinea-Bissau
Precolonial Influence on the Postcolonial State
Mariama Khan

Engendering Democracy in Africa
Women, Politics and Development
Niamh Gaynor

Social Protection, Pastoralism and Resilience in Ethiopia
Lessons for Sub-Saharan Africa
Edited by Zeremariam Fre, Bereket Tsegay, Araya M. Teka, John Livingstone and Nicole Kenton

Sustainable Development in Post-Pandemic Africa
Effective Strategies for Resource Mobilization
Edited by Fred Olayele and Yiagadeesen Samy

Socioeconomic Shocks and Africa's Development Agenda
Lessons and Policy Directions in a Post-COVID-19 Era
Edited by Evans Osabuohien, Gbadebo Odularu, Daniel Ufua and Romanus Osabohien

Africa's Economic Partnership with China
An Holistic Analysis
Mussie Delelegn Arega

For more information about this series, please visit: www.routledge.com/Routledge-Studies-in-African-Development/book-series/RSAD

Socioeconomic Shocks and Africa's Development Agenda

Lessons and Policy Directions in a Post-COVID-19 Era

Edited by Evans Osabuohien, Gbadebo Odularu, Daniel Ufua and Romanus Osabohien

Routledge
Taylor & Francis Group
LONDON AND NEW YORK

First published 2023
by Routledge
4 Park Square, Milton Park, Abingdon, Oxon OX14 4RN

and by Routledge
605 Third Avenue, New York, NY 10158

Routledge is an imprint of the Taylor & Francis Group, an informa business

British Library Cataloguing-in-Publication Data
A catalogue record for this book is available from the British Library

Library of Congress Cataloging-in-Publication Data
Names: Osabuohien, Evans, 1979– editor. | Odularu, Gbadebo, editor. | Ufua, Daniel E., editor.
Title: Socioeconomic shocks and Africa's development agenda : lessons and policy directions in a post-Covid-19 era / edited by Evans Osabuohien, Gbadebo Odularu, Daniel E. Ufua, Romanus A. Osabohien.
Description: New York, NY : Routledge, 2023. | Series: Routledge studies in African development | Includes bibliographical references and index.
Identifiers: LCCN 2022021124 (print) | LCCN 2022021125 (ebook) | ISBN 9781032076935 (hardback) | ISBN 9781032076966 (paperback) | ISBN 9781003208358 (ebook)
Subjects: LCSH: Africa—Economic conditions—21st century. | Africa—Economic policy—21st century. | Economic development—Africa. | COVID-19 Pandemic, 2020—Economic aspects—Africa.
Classification: LCC HC800 .S6347 2023 (print) | LCC HC800 (ebook) | DDC 338.96—dc23/eng/20220817
LC record available at https://lccn.loc.gov/2022021124
LC ebook record available at https://lccn.loc.gov/2022021125

ISBN: 978-1-032-07693-5 (hbk)
ISBN: 978-1-032-07696-6 (pbk)
ISBN: 978-1-003-20835-8 (ebk)

DOI: 10.4324/9781003208358

Typeset in Goudy
by Apex CoVantage, LLC

Contents

Figures

Tables

Short Biography of Contributors

Editors

Gbadebo Odularu He is affiliated with Virginia Military Institute (VMI), Bay Atlantic University (BAU), Pan-African Scientific Research Council (PASRC), Socio-Economic Research Applications and Projects (SERAP), and Nexford University (NXU), which are all located in Washington D. C. He holds a PhD degree from the University of Sunderland, UK. He was formerly a regional policy and markets data scientist at the continental Forum for Agricultural Research in Africa (FARA), Accra, Ghana. In addition to his great passion for advancing frontiers of interdisciplinary knowledge, he currently collaborates with national, continental, and international partners and governments by deploying data visualisation and geospatial analytics to provide evidence-based policy tools for enhancing post-pandemic socioeconomic recoveries amongst vulnerable communities.

Romanus Osabohien He is a lecturer at the Department of Economics and Development Studies and a research fellow at Centre for Economic Policy and Development Research (CEPDeR), Covenant University, Ota, Nigeria. He is also a fellow of the Research Linkage Programme between Covenant University, Nigeria, and Witten/Herdecke University, Germany, funded by the Alexander von Humboldt Foundation (AvH). He is a research fellow at the International Institute of Tropical Agriculture (IITA) as well as a research fellow at ILMA University, Karachi, Pakistan. He holds master's and PhD degrees in economics from Covenant University, Nigeria. His main research focus is on social protection, food security, and agricultural and development economics. He has attended and presented research findings in both international and local conferences/workshops and has published peer-reviewed papers in rated journals. In addition, he is a reviewer and editorial board member for well-rated journals including *Heliyon Business and Economics* (Elsevier).

Evans Osabuohien He is a professor of economics and a head of department at Covenant University, Ota, Nigeria. In 2020, he was recognised as one of the six Youngest Professors in Nigeria. He pioneered the Centre for Economic Policy and Development Research (CEPDeR) as well as Regional Centre of

Expertise, Ogun State (RCE Ogun) at Covenant University. He is a Visiting Professor at Witten/Herdecke University, Germany, and Eduardo Mondlane University, Mozambique. He is a fellow of the Alexander von Humboldt Foundation and Swedish Institute, among others. He has published five books and over 185 scholarly articles. He is a member of numerous professional associations, a reviewer and editorial board member for many journals. In addition, he serves as a member of Board of Directors in several organisations as a way of making further impacts on humanity.

Daniel Ufua He is a lecturer at the Department of Business Management and a research fellow at Centre for Economic Policy and Development Research (CEPDeR), Covenant University, Ota, Ogun State, Nigeria. He holds master's and PhD degrees in management science from University of Hull, UK. His core research interest is on systems thinking, entrepreneurship, and general management. He has a preference for the use of systemic intervention and broad stakeholder engagement as a key methodology for his research practice. He has published several research materials on international outlets, some of which were done independently and others in collaboration with his colleagues and international scholars.

Contributors

Oluwayemisi Khadijat Adeleke Adeleke is a lecturer at the Department of Economics, Faculty of Social Sciences, Redeemer's University, Ede, Osun State, Nigeria. She is a member of the Research and Development Committee. She holds BSc, MSc and PhD degrees in economics through the Collaborative PhD programme of AERC and participated in the PhD internship programme of the AERC at the Nigerian Institute of Social and Economic Research (NISER). She is a reviewer to the *International Journal of Research and Innovation in Social Sciences* (*IJRISS*). She is an affiliate member of Association of Chartered Certified Accountants (ACCA) and a Facilitator for Accounting Technician Scheme in the Department of Accounting, Redeemers University. She has publications in the field of financial, macroeconomics, trade, and development economics.

Kingsley Chidera Adonike He is a postgraduate student in the Department of Economics, Nnamdi Azikiwe University, Awka, Nigeria. His research interest includes econometric analysis, development economics and international economics.

Omowumi Monisola Ajeigbe Ajeigbe is a lecturer at the Department of Economics, Faculty of Social Sciences, Redeemer's University, Ede, Osun State, Nigeria. She is the research and development coordinator and a managing editor of *Journal of Economics and Social Policy* at the same Department. She holds a BSc, MSc and PhD degrees in economics and a PGD in education. She is a reviewer to the *International Journal of Research and Innovation in Social Sciences* (*IJRISS*).

She is a facilitator and project supervisor at National Open University of Nigeria. She has publications in the field of financial, industrial, trade, labour, and development economics.

Khadijat Busola Amolegbe She is a lecturer at the University of Ilorin, Nigeria, and holds a PhD in agricultural economics from the same institution. She has held various research fellowship positions at international institutions such as the International Institute of Tropical Agriculture (IITA) and Nordic Africa Institute, Sweden. She was also a research fellow at Dyson School of Applied Economics and Management, Cornell University, under the Structural Transformation of African Agriculture and Rural Spaces (STAARS) fellowship programme. Her research areas are agricultural development economics, food security, and poverty and inequality issues in Sub-Saharan Africa, and she has published in peer-reviewed journal articles.

Sserunjogi Brian He is a research fellow in the macroeconomics department at the Economic Policy Research Centre. He holds a PhD in agricultural economics from Punjab Agricultural University, Ludhiana, India. He has a master's degree in agricultural economics from the University of Agricultural Sciences, Raichur, Karnataka, India, and a bachelor of science degree in agriculture from Makerere University. His research interest areas include macroeconomic analysis, public sector management, public expenditure analysis and local economic development, financial sector performance, and access to and use of financial services in Uganda. He is also interested in areas of agricultural finance, marketing, and rural development.

Francis Diawuo Darko He is a PhD student at the College of Humanities, Arts and Social Sciences, Flinders University, Australia. His PhD studies is funded by the Australian Government Research Training Programme Scholarship (AGRTPS). Francis has extensive research experience and interest in Household Solid Waste Management, Indigenous Knowledge and Resource Management, Human Geography Migration.

Hayelom Yrgaw Gereziher He obtained his MSc in development economics from Adigrat University, Adigrat, Ethiopia, in 2019 and is currently working as a lecturer of economics at Adigrat University, Ethiopia. He has published articles in several international peer reviewed journals and presented his research findings in international workshops and conferences. He has also recently secured research funding from UNU-WIDER.

Nora Francis Inyang She is a lecturer at the Department of Economics, University of Uyo. She has an MPhil in environmental economics, master's in development economics, post-graduate diploma in development economics, and a bachelor of agriculture in agricultural economics and extension. Nora has published in both national and international journals. Her recent publication is 'Nigerian Diversification Agenda and Economic Growth: The Role of Agriculture'. Nora has both industry and institutional work experience. She has worked as a research assistant at International Institute of Tropical Agriculture in the Cassava Enterprise Development Project (A USAID Sponsored Project). Aside her interest in research and writing, Nora is very sociable and enjoys family time with her husband and four children.

Rehema Kahunde She is currently a research analyst in the Macroeconomics Department at the Economic Policy Research Centre (EPRC). Rehema has read extensively on tax-related studies, tax structures of different countries and many public finance-related articles. She has also authored a paper titled "The Effect of the Quality of Governance on Tax Revenue in East Africa". Kahunde holds a MA degree in economics and a first-class bachelor's degree in development economics from Makerere University.

Gilles Quentin Kane He is a Cameroonian national. He is assistant lecturer at the University of Yaoundé II. He has won several research grant and fellowships positions such as European Investment Bank (EIB) – Global Development Network (GDN) Research Fellowship in Applied Development Finance, Partnership for Economic Policy (PEP) PMMA – Microeconomic analysis Research Grant, Collaborative PhD Programme of the AERC, and PhD Internship Program Scholarship of the United Nations University World Institute for Development Economics Research (UNU-WIDER) in Helsinki, Finland. He has provided consultancy services to the World Bank, GDN and SNV. His research interests include, but not limited to, food and nutrition security, gender issues, impact evaluation, and poverty issues in Sub-Saharan Africa. He has published peer-reviewed journal articles and is a reviewer for peer-reviewed journals such as *African Development Review, Applied Economics Letters, Telecommunications Policy, Review of Agricultural and Applied Economics, Brussels Economic Review*, and *Economie Rurale*.

Roseline Tapuwa Karambakuwa She is currently a postdoctoral research fellow and a lecturer at Nelson Mandela University, South Africa. Her fellowship is funded by the National Research Foundation (NRF) in South Africa. She holds a PhD in economics from Nelson Mandela University. Her research interests are in international economics, urban development, development economics, macroeconomics, and labour economics. She has published several research papers and presented at a number of local and international conferences. She is a former lecturer at Bindura University of Science Education in Zimbabwe.

Nicholas Kilimani He is formerly an Economist of the World Bank. He holds a PhD degree in economics from the University of Pretoria. He is a senior lecturer at the Department of Policy and Development Economics, School of Economics-Makerere University, and a senior research fellow at the Environment for Development Research Centre (EfD-Mak Centre) at Makerere University. He is a Fulbright Research Scholar at Rutgers State University in New Jersey, and a research associate at the Public Economics and Environmental Research Centre (PEERC), School of Economics, University of Johannesburg.

He is former guest researcher at the Nordic Africa Institute at Uppsala in Sweden. He is a peer reviewer for a number of reputed journals. His research interests are in the area of socioeconomic and environmental impacts of development policy where he has several publications.

Enoch Akwasi Kosoe He is a PhD candidate at the University for Development Studies and a lecturer at the Department of Environment and Resource Studies (DERS) of the SDD University of Business and Integrated Development Studies, Ghana. He holds MSc in environmental resource management from the Kwame Nkrumah University of Science and Technology, Ghana, and BA in integrated development studies from the University for Development Studies, Ghana. He is a member of the Ghana Geographical Association (GGA) and has a number of research articles published in reputable peer-reviewed journals and book chapters.

Paul Lakuma He is an established forecaster, economic model builder, and adviser with more than a decade of service to government and international organisations. He has advised the Finance Ministry in Uganda on macroeconomic and fiscal policy, fiscal institutions, and revenue administration. He has worked on the Domestic Resource Mobilization Strategy for the medium term for Uganda, where he authored numerous diagnostic papers to inform the reform process. Most recently, Lakuma has been involved in the conduct of several firm level surveys to establish the socioeconomic impact of COVID-19 on the productivity of Uganda's employees, firms, and industries. He holds an MSc in economics with distinction at the University of Essex, UK and a BA in social science from Makerere University Kampala (MUK) Uganda.

Chekwube Vitus Madichie He is a research fellow under the Management Scholar Academy of the Lagos Business School, Pan-Atlantic University, Lagos, Nigeria. He completed a master's degree in economics from Nnamdi Azikiwe University, Awka, with specialization in quantitative economics. His major research interests include, but not limited to, environmental and development economics, institutions, and entrepreneurship. He is proficient in many areas of economics, including theoretical/applied econometrics, macro-modelling and simulation, with particular expertise in the application of EViews, STATA, SPSS, Gretl, and Minitab for the analyses of both time-series and panel data. Chekwube is a highly motivated research scholar with in-depth teaching and research background and has several publications to his credit. Chekwube is the creator of the YouTube Digital Platform, ViData Solutions (link: www.youtube.com/c/chekwubemadichie), designed to teach heads-on econometric modelling and data analyses techniques to researchers around the world, with more than 35 videos in strategic areas.

Anne Chinonye Maduka She is a professor of economics teaching in the Department of Economics, Chukwuemeka Odumegwu Ojukwu University, Igbariam, Anambra State, Nigeria. She specialises in development economics with special interest in international, environmental, and monetary economics. She is a highly motivated, responsible, research minded, and hardworking scholar who has published several research articles and book chapters in development economics. She has served the university in various capacities, as a two-time head of economics department, associate dean, faculty of social sciences, chairman, and member of different committees in the university. In the course of her career as a lecturer, Anne has developed skills in teaching and research with which she has diligently transferred to her students through teaching and project supervision. Maduka discharges her duties with the fear of God and excellent spirit which is reflected in her good relationship with students and colleagues.

Elisa Saint Martin Elisa is a policy analyst for the Africa, Europe and Middle East Unit of the OECD Development Centre. In this position, she contributes to policy-oriented research and policy dialogue, notably through the flagship report *Africa's Development Dynamics* of the African Union Commission and the OECD Development Centre. Elisa holds a master's degree in international economics from University Paris Nanterre.

Amaka Gertrude Metu She is a lecturer at the Department of Economics, Nnamdi Azikiwe University, Awka Nigeria, where she earned a PhD (economics) in 2017. Her research interest focuses on the field of entrepreneurship and development studies particularly inclusive growth, institutions, and macroeconomic policies, published in both national and international journals. She is a member of professional associations such as Nigerian Economic Society, Association for the Advancement of African Women Economist (AAAWE), and African Finance and Economic Association (AFEA). She is a research fellow of Pan-African Scientific Research Council, associate fellow of the Centre for Migration Studies and Centre for Sustainable Development, Nnamdi Azikiwe University, Awka. She is currently a coordinator to postgraduate programmes of the Department of Economics Nnamdi Azikiwe University Awka.

Arthur Minsat He received his PhD from London School of Economics. Arthur heads the OECD Development Centre's Unit for Africa, Europe and Middle East, which produces *Africa's Development Dynamics* and Revenue Statistics in Africa, in partnership with the African Union. As lead economist, Arthur led the themes of the *African Economic Outlooks* (AEO). At UNDP in New York, Arthur researched for the flagship *Human Development Reports*. In Abidjan, he volunteered for the United Nations Operations in Côte d'Ivoire (ONUCI) during the electoral crisis. He taught at the LSE, King's College London and Sciences-Po. Arthur gained private sector experience at Wolters Kluwer.

Ronney Ncwadi He is currently a full professor of economics and a director of the School of Economics, Development and Tourism at Nelson Mandela University, South Africa. He holds a PhD in economics from Nelson Mandela University. His research interests are in public finance, international finance, macroeconomics, labour markets, policy analysis, development economics, and applied econometrics. He has published both in local and international journals and has presented papers at various academic conferences both in South Africa and abroad. He is a former director of the Macroeconomic Analysis Unit of the Eastern Cape Provincial Treasury between 2008 and 2010. He is a former associate professor and a deputy dean of the Faculty of Management and Commerce at Fort Hare University.

Franklin Nnaemeka Ngwu He is the director of Lagos Business School (LBS) Sustainability Centre and an associate professor of strategy, corporate governance, and risk management. He has a PhD in law and economics of banking regulation, MSc in economics, PGD in development economics from University of Manchester, UK, and MSc in comparative political economy from Cardiff University, UK. He has lectured at Glasgow School of Business and Society, Glasgow Caledonian University; School of Built Environment and Business, University of Salford; and Department of Economics and School of Law, University of Manchester, UK. He has a multi-disciplinary teaching and research interests, including business strategy and management, risk management and corporate governance, bank management and regulation, law and finance in emerging markets, corporate social responsibility, and development economics. He is the author of two corporate governance handbooks titled *Corporate Governance in Developing and Emerging Markets* (Routledge, 2016) and *Enhancing Board Effectiveness-Institutional, Regulatory and Functional Perspectives for Developing and Emerging Markets* (Routledge, 2019) and many other books published by Cambridge University Press.

John Bosco Nnyanzi He is a senior lecturer of economics at Makerere University. He received his doctorate in economics from Johannes Kepler University of Linz. He was also a visiting scholar at the University of Rwanda and a member of the American Economic Association, where he has attended international conferences on teaching economics and research. He was trade specialist for the Northern Corridor Integration Projects, 2017. His research interests include applied macroeconomics and microeconomics, development economics, risk-sharing, integration, and remittances. He is also a peer reviewer of, inter alia, the *African Journal of Economic and Management Sciences*, *African Development Review*, *Annals of Public and Cooperative Economics*, and *Journal of Economic Integration*.

Naser Yenus Nuru He received his PhD in economics from Luiss Guido Carli University, Rome, Italy, in 2018 and is currently working as assistant professor of economics at Adigrat University, Ethiopia. He has published articles in several international peer reviewed journals and presented his research findings in international workshops and conferences. He has recently secured research funding from UNU-WIDER and made a research visit to KU-Leuven, Belgium in May 2021.

Onyinye Ochuba She was in the Nigerian Banking industry for four years before venturing into academics. She has an MPhil in environmental economics and master's degree in monetary economics and disaster risk management and development studies. She currently undertakes research in areas of environmental economics and disaster risk management. Her research interest includes environmental quality, pollution with special interest in plastic pollution, agriculture and food security, disaster risk mitigation, gender studies and gender inclusion, and monetary economics. She has attended and presented papers in both local and international conferences with a number of scholarly publications in peer-review journals.

Oluwaseyi Ebenezer Olalere He obtained his PhD and MSc degrees in finance from the Universiti Malaysia Perlis, Malaysia with specific focus on corporate finance and banking and his BSc degree in finance from the University of Ilorin. His research interest revolves around emerging markets, corporate finance and banking and contemporary issues in finance. Most of his research focuses on emerging markets such as the ASEAN economies and emerging countries in Africa. He has widely published in a variety of journals indexed in Scopus and Web of Science core collections such as Asia-Pacific Social Science Review, Borsa Istanbul Review, Bank and Banks System, and Asian Finance and Economic Review. He has been involved in organisation of seminars and workshops and has also been a part of organising committee member of international conference. He is currently a visiting research fellow at the Centre for Africa-China Studies (CACS), University of Johannesburg, South Africa.

Flora Olubukola Olaniyi She is a graduate and master holder of Library, Archival and Information Studies (LARIS) from the University of Ibadan. She is a member of Library Registration Council of Nigeria (LRCN) and Nigeria Library Association (NLA). She has worked in a private, public, special and presently in an academic library as a librarian.

Mojeed Muhammed Ologundudu He is an associate professor and acting head of the Economics Department, Mountain Top University, Ogun State, Nigeria. He holds BSc (Ogun State University, 1990) MSc (University of Lagos, 1997), and a PhD (University of Bath, UK, 2016). In a quest for further knowledge in his cognate discipline, he completed another PhD in 2019 in business and applied economics from Olabisi Onabanjo University. Ologundudu has been involved in teaching and research activities for over a decade. He worked with Caleb University, Imota, as Lecturer II, McPherson University, Seriki-Sotayo, as Lecturer I before joining Mountain Top University as senior lecturer in 2017 and rose to the rank of associate professor in 2020. There he is also serving in various capacities among which include the acting director of academic planning, member Senate representative of Mountain Top University ceremony committee, chairman of the steering committee of the proposed department of Fine and Applied Arts, and member of several other committees. He has to his credit 25 published research articles in both local and international journals and has attended several academic conferences and workshops within and outside the country.

Olusola Joshua Olujobi He obtained his LLB degree from University of Ado-Ekiti in 2005 and BL degree from the Nigerian Law School. He was called to the

Nigerian Bar in 2007 as a Solicitor and Advocate of the Supreme Court of Nigeria. He had LLM at University of Lagos in 2012 and his PhD degree in jurisprudence and international law from University of Lagos. He became a Notary Public of the Federal Republic of Nigeria in 2014. He is an international legal consultant, a senior lecturer and the former sub-dean at Faculty of Law, Elizade University, Ilara-Mokin, Nigeria. He is currently a lecturer at the Department of Public and International Law, College of Law, Afe Babalola University, Ado Ekiti, Ekiti State, Nigeria. His experience is multi-disciplinary and spans the legal, regulatory, commercial, and contractual arena. He is a specialist on oil and gas law, recovery, and repatriation of assets derived from grand corruption to prior legitimate owners. He has widely published in both local and international journals. He is a member of numerous professional associations and a reviewer for many notable journals.

Olanrewaju Omosehin He holds a masters in agricultural technology from the Department of Agricultural and Resource Economics, Federal University of Technology, Akure, Ondo State, Nigeria and bachelor's degree in agricultural economics from Obafemi Awolowo University, Ile-Ife, Osun State. He also holds a mini-MBA from Tekedia Institute, Boston. He has some publications to his name with several others under review in a reputable journal. His research interest is focused on international trade, agribusiness management, agricultural economics, production economics, econometrics, welfare economics and policy analysis. He's a member of many professional bodies including International Food and Agribusiness Management Association.

Francis Chukwudi Onyedibe He is a postgraduate student in the Department of Economics, Nnamdi Azikiwe University, Awka, Nigeria. His research interest includes development studies and econometric analysis.

Wyclife Ong'Eta Wyclife holds a PhD from the United Nations-mandated University for Peace (UPEACE), Costa Rica. He is a lecturer at the School of Security, Diplomacy and Peace Studies at Kenyatta University and the executive director at Oasis Peace Web Organization in Kenya. He has over seven years of experience in teaching, research, and cross-border peacebuilding in Kenya, Uganda, and South Sudan in Africa. Chapter "Theorizing Somali Society: Hope Transformation and Development" is his recent contribution in a book. He published a chapter "A Theoretical Perspective of Religious Sect as the Root of Violent Extremism in Somalia" with Aalborg University Press. His other chapter focusing on "Resources, Climate Change and Implications to Positive Peace among the Pastoral Communities in Kenya" was published in *The Palgrave Handbook of Positive Peace* (Springer Publications). His personal philosophy: to touch more lives.

John Bosco Oryema He is a lecturer at the School of Economics, Makerere University. He earned a PhD in economics (University of South Florida), MSc in public policy (University College London), and a BA in Economics (Makerere University). His research interests broadly cover applied microeconomics, development economics, and applied microeconometrics. Some of his research is published in peer-reviewed journals such as *Journal of Forensic Economics* and *Journal of International Development and Global Public Health*. John has served as a visiting assistant of economics at Marshall University, West Virginia, USA.

Nathan Sunday He is currently a PhD candidate of economics at the University of Michigan, USA. He previously served as a research analyst in the Macroeconomics Department at Economic Policy Research Centre (EPRC). He holds a master's degree in economics and first-class bachelor of science with education in mathematics and economics from Makerere University. Nathan has extensive experience in enterprise-level analysis. His most recent firm-level research is analysis of "Gender and Firm Productivity in Africa: Examining the moderating role of business environment", a project that was funded by the African Economic Research Consortium (AERC). He was also a part of the EPRC team that conducts the Uganda business environment assessment quarterly. Nathan has researched and published papers about key development issues and has experience in policy analysis.

Maria Chinecherem Uzonwanne She is a senior lecturer in the Department of Economics, Nnamdi Azikiwe University, Awka, Nigeria. Her area of specialisation is development economics and monetary economics.

Ebenezer Lemven Wirba He holds a PhD in development economics from the University of Bamenda-Cameroon. He is a researcher with the African Economic Research Consortium (AERC), Council for the Development of Social Science Research in African (CODESRIA), Partnership for Economic Policy (PEP) and United Nations University World Institute for Development Economics Research (UNU-WIDER). Wirba has successfully undertook a course on policy impact evaluation co-organised by PEP and the Department of Economics, Universite' de Laval, Canada, in 2017. He is also graduate from National School of Administration and Magistracy (ENAM) where he studied legal metrology. Wirba has published papers in reputable peer-reviewed journals such as *Review of Development Economics*. His research interests are in food security, poverty, inequality, labour market issues, and impact evaluation.

Clement Olalekan Olaniyi He is currently a lecturer at the Department of Economics, Obafemi Awolowo University (OAU), Ile-Ife, Nigeria. Before his appointment in the University (OAU), he was one of the pioneer lecturers at the Department of Economics, Mountain Top University, Ibafo, Ogun State, Nigeria. He holds a PhD in economics from OAU. His research interests include financial economics, business economics, and industrial economics. He has published in a variety of journals indexed in the Web of Science core collections such as *Journal of Economic Studies*, *African Development Review*, *Economic Change and Restructuring*, *International Journal of Emerging Markets*, *Journal of Public Affairs*, *Global Business Review*, *International Journal of Business Performance Management*, *Global Journal of Emerging Market Economies*, and *Journal of Social and Economic Development*, among others.

Acknowledgement

In learning processes, the COVID-19 pandemic has made the world realise the effectiveness of online learning, teaching, and seminars that have made the world a more global village than ever. During the lockdown, while people, communities, and societies were seeking ways to cope with the pandemic, others were devising means for learning and expanding the frontiers of knowledge, which birthed this laudable book project. Thus, the editors thank God Almighty for the grace bestowed upon them throughout this book project.

The editors of this book appreciate the Management of Covenant University and Virginia Military Institute (VMI), and Bay Atlantic University, and Socio-Economic Research Applications and Projects (SERAP) for learning, teaching, and research platforms, which made this project a bit easy. Similarly, the contributions of faculty in the Department of Economics and Development Studies in conjunction with the fellows of Centre for Economic Policy and Development Research (CEPDeR), the Department of Business Management Covenant University, Ota, Nigeria, are highly acknowledged.

The editors appreciate the Alexander von Humboldt Foundation (AvH)'s Equipment Subsidy Grant [REF: 3.4–8151/19047] and Research Linkage Grant [REF 3.4–1147508-NGA-IP] awarded to CEPDeR, which were instrumental in the course of the project. The editors will not forget to appreciate the various platforms and avenues that publicised the call for chapters proposals. It is worth noting that a single volume was envisaged at the point of idea conceptualisation, but because of the quantum of quality proposals received, the idea culminated with two volumes.

The editors equally recognise the efforts of authors and reviewers who provided helpful comments for the improvement of submitted chapters considered in this edited volume. The editors appreciate the publishing team for the prompt response to clarifications and diverse supports. Finally, the editors gratefully appreciate the supports and encouragement from members of their families all through the development of this project.

Evans Osabuohien, Gbadebo Odularu,
Daniel Ufua, and Romanus Osabohien
June 2022

Foreword

The effects of the coronavirus (COVID-19) pandemic on the economies of Africa and Africa's development agenda are apparent. Not only has COVID-19 hampered the progress made in eliminating poverty and reducing income inequality, but it has also brought to bear serious socioeconomic challenges and important macroeconomic implications. The evidence so far indicates that this pandemic, like some others, has been detrimental not only to macroeconomic stability and economic growth but also to other socioeconomic outcomes such as poverty, welfare and livelihood, and human capital development.

The desire for sustainable economic growth and development requires systems that are capable of withstanding socioeconomic shocks. However, the COVID-19 pandemic has shown that Africa has serious structural weaknesses. This calls for better planning and designing of the health care systems, government tax and spending policies, as well as enhancing the social support systems so that the poor and vulnerable have equal access to opportunities and be protected at all times.

This timely and topical book provides policymakers with directions, recommendations and approaches to addressing future socioeconomic shocks. The chapters in the book are representative of a wide range of contemporary research on socioeconomic shocks and economic development from the African perspective, especially considering the effects of COVID-19.

Samuel Amponsah
Immediate Past-President and Board Chair,
African Finance and Economic Association

Introduction

Evans Osabuohien, Gbadebo Odularu, Daniel Ufua, and Romanus Osabohien

Background to the Book

The global impacts of the coronavirus (COVID-19) pandemic have further shown the level of Africa's structural fragilities with respect to weak response to socioeconomic shocks, coupled with the challenges associated with supply chain and logistics complexities across the entire continent (Osabuohien et al., 2022). The various ways of addressing the challenges posed by the COVID-19 pandemic are being pursued in the global community. However, countries in Africa have had a critical weakness with response to emerging socioeconomic challenges such as the effects of the COVID-19 pandemic (Odularu et al., in this volume). This edited book project puts a premium on exploring the social and economic challenges and the development of resilience to address identified complex challenges associated with the COVID-19.

The book adopts a critical view on current and prevailing trends regarding the socioeconomic effects of COVID-19. It broadly explores the nature and effects of non-health-related challenges and the attendant complexities. Also, it proffers workable solutions to socioeconomic shocks caused by COVID-19 and other social, political, and economic distortions in African countries. An in-depth understanding of the societal consequences of the challenges and policy space adopted by governments and non-governmental organisations (NGOs) to boost post-COVID-19 recovery is addressed. Thus, the book provides detailed suggestions of relevant approaches based on the context of African socioeconomic status by focusing on the engagement of systemic processes to boost the prospects for addressing socioeconomic shocks.

In essence, the edited book reflects on COVID-19 and associated events influencing the shifts towards the need for new policy directions in Africa. The future adaptations to heighten the responsibility are explored and recommendations are enunciated. Chapters in this edited book offer valuable insights into how the global pandemic affects socioeconomic outcomes such as poverty, supply chains, employment, income, welfare and livelihood, and human capital development. A variety of policy interventions and reflections on how to use propounded policies to mitigate future shocks are articulated in the chapters encapsulated in the

DOI: 10.4324/9781003208358-1

book. The chapters draw on a combination of conceptual arguments, global and country-level simulation models, in-country surveys, case studies, and expert opinions.

Organisation of the Book

Section 1: Socioeconomic Shocks and Economic Development

The section details the socio-cultural trends and their influence on economic activities and the African environment. A particular focus in this section is on agroforestry, price shocks and exchange rate variability, and their effect on African socioeconomic practices.

In Chapter 1, Enoch A. Kosoe and Francis Diawuo Darko assess the influence of socio-cultural, political, and economic factors on women's participation in agroforestry in Jaman South, Ghana. The chapter adopts a mixed-method approach. Questionnaire and multinomial regression are used in the study. The study highlights the social and cultural difficulty of women's considerable access to land for agroforestry practice. The chapter recommends the need for constituting women farmers to boost their chances of accessing financial credit. It also suggests further training of women extension officers to enhance women-friendly access to farmer extension services. Chapter 2, authored by Naser Yenus Nuru and Hayelom Yrgaw Gereziher, focuses on how coffee price shock transmits into the economy in Ethiopia. The study adopts a vector autoregressive model to explore the exogenous coffee price shock in the coffee product in the Ethiopian economy. The study finds a standard deviation shock in coffee price leads to about a 0.4 per cent increase in output. It highlights other factors, such as inflation, government spending money supply, and exchange rate, that also impact the coffee price shocks in Ethiopia.

In furtherance, Olanrewaju Omosehin and Evans Osabuohien, in Chapter 3, adopt unit root test using augmented Dickey–Fuller (ADF) test statistics on the times series data (1980 to 2018) to confirm the order of stationary of the variables. It also uses Johansen Cointegration to check the long-run relationship and Error Correction Model to check shock effect. The study establishes a linkage between exchange rate and palm oil export in the long run. The chapter concludes that the exchange rate can be stabilised to favour producers' prices and improve welfare.

Section 2: Resilience, Business and Value Chain Development

The section focuses on households and emerging socioeconomic shocks in the African continent. It brought to bear critical factors such as agricultural income level, value chain development, digital transformation, and the effects on non-health issues faced by the households, especially in the critical period of the COVID-19 pandemic.

Chapter 4 by Nicholas Kilimani, John Bosco Nnyanzi, and John Bosco Oryema examines the impact of climatic shocks on agricultural income, household food, and education expenditure in Uganda. The study applies Integrated Surveys on Agriculture (LSMS-ISA) data. Ordinary Least Squares estimation with fixed-effects and random-effects modelling. While the study highlights threats to household welfare and the possible mitigating remedies to such shocks, the findings show that rainfall shocks have significant adverse impacts on agricultural income, food consumption, and education expenditure. It also shows that modern agricultural technologies are crucial for agricultural income.

In Chapter 5, Onyinye Ochuba, Nora Francis Inyang, and Romanus Osabohien examine the role of information and communication technology (ICT) in the food supply chain occasioned by COVID-19. The authors establish that the food price hike was highest in 2020, attributed to high transportation costs, movement restrictions, disruption of supply chains, hoarding, inaccessibility of raw material, and low agricultural output. The study calls for more investment in ICT and agricultural ICT solutions to improve the agricultural value chain. Similarly, Chapter 6 by Arthur Minsat and Elisa Saint Martin investigates the scope of Africa's digital transformation before and after 2020. First, it analyses the state of Africa's digitalisation before 2020. Second, it analyses the impact of the COVID-19 crisis in accelerating Africa's digitalisation, since 2020 when COVID-19 hit the continent. The chapter also examines persisting challenges that the African continent faces in realising the benefits of digital transformation. The study draws policy recommendations to shape more resilient African economies.

In this section, Daniel Ufua, Olusola Joshua Olujobi, Romanus Osabohien, Evans Osabuohien, and Gbadebo Odularu in Chapter 7 adopt a conceptual approach to explore the critical non-health effects and the broad socioeconomic challenges related to the spread of the COVID-19 pandemic. The study emphasises the identification and engagement of relevant stakeholders in the intervention process to enhance commitment, prioritisation of issues through boundary critique, and joint development of a practical approach to address the non-health effects of COVID-19 at various stages of the research. The chapter concludes that effective implementation of systemic intervention can emancipate the affected stakeholders from the non-health effects of COVID-19, which can, in turn, support economic growth and development.

Section 3: Institutional Framework and Human Capital Development

This section focuses on human resource productivity in a critical, challenging period such as COVID-19, knowledge creation, and environmental development and human welfare practices during crisis periods. The section projects learning from an African perspective, focusing on small- and medium-sized enterprises (SMEs), stakeholder policy, and peaceful co-existence in Africa.

Chapter 8 by Brian Sserunjogi, Sunday Nathan, Paul Lakuma, and Rehama Kahunde explores the effects of COVID-19 on women and male-owned enterprises differently. It examines the pandemic's impact on employment and productivity and examines the gendered differences in coping mechanisms adopted between male and female SMEs. The findings reveal that more than five in every ten firms reported reducing their workers' wages overall. The study also finds that COVID-19 exacerbated the pre-existing gender productivity gap between female and male-owned enterprises. In this regard, while the COVID-19 pandemic led to a 32 per cent decline in sales per worker across all SME types, women's productivity reduced by as much as 38 per cent, compared to 29 per cent for the males. The chapter suggests that the government of Uganda should invest in digital infrastructure and create more awareness about the same to close the digital divide between male and female-owned firms.

In Chapter 9, Roseline Tapuwa Karambakuwa and Ronney Ncwadi focus on knowledge-based economy and communication technologies. The chapter notes that knowledge city and economic activities pertain to using brainpower, technology, and research to create high value-added products. The chapter adopts a literature review, gathering data on global best practice experiences to find out how other cities are developing their creative urban regions. The review shows that African cities can promote knowledge-based development and hence create knowledge cities by ensuring that people acquire technical knowledge that will enable them to innovate products and services.

Chapter 10 by Oluwayemisi Khadijat Adeleke and Omowumi Monisola Ajeigbe focuses on the key social and economic effects of COVID-19 and the supportive policies of selected government administrations in Sub-Saharan Africa (SSA). The authors adopt the panel vector autoregressive (PVAR) estimation technique with further robustness check through the impulse response function and variance decomposition. Part of their findings is that gross domestic products (GDP) growth rate, unemployment, and government debt show a positive trend to a Cholesky one standard deviation while inflation was positive but had a minimal impact. Similarly, the short- and long-run results reveal that COVID-19 has no effect on inflation and government debt. The chapter submits that government should pursue welfare policies that would reduce the negative effect of COVID-19 and facilitate measures to address the spread of COVID-19 among SSA countries to mitigate the issues of prolonged lockdown.

Chapter 11 authored by Wyclife Ong'Eta is based on a review that consulted reputable sources of information, including recent surveys and reports on the socioeconomic impact of COVID-19. The in-depth review situated within the qualitative paradigm is expected to guide policies, and legislation development to consolidate positive peace and development among people living in informal settlements in Kenya. The results revealed that increasing unemployment and loss of income had aggravated the wellbeing of people in slums.

Section 4: Services, Socioeconomic Shocks and Sustainable Development

In this section, chapters focus on crucial areas such as the disruptive effects of COVID-19 and the health challenges on humans, the critical effects of COVID-19 on the management of vital natural resources, as well as the inflationary shocks and key effects in the African economies. The section details national policy approaches to crisis management, the strength of the legal system in managing oil wealth, and explores the poverty levels and suggests emancipatory models across African countries.

Chapter 12, authored by Chekwube Vitus Madichie, Franklin Nnaemeka Ngwu, and Anne Chinonye Maduka, is focused on COVID-19 and poverty incidence in SSA drawing lessons from past pandemics. The authors underscore responses to both common and idiosyncratic shocks while permitting full cross-section heterogeneity of the response dynamics. Their results show that pandemic events will exert a significantly positive impact on poverty level in SSA, which implies that following the current COVID-19 pandemic, poverty rates in SSA region is expected to rise. However, the study reckons that the implementation of sound economic growth policies will serve as good insulators against future poverty incidence in the region.

Khadijat Busola Amolegbe, Ebenezer Lemven Wirba, and Gilles Quentin Kane in Chapter 13 examine household shocks and government policy initiatives in a critical socioeconomic period, such as COVID-19 lockdown in Africa. The chapter addresses the factors such as the effects of agricultural, financial, weather, health, and other shocks on Nigerian household welfare. It engages the Living Standards Measurement Survey (LSMS) for Nigeria and random effect models to understand these relationships. Whilst the study finds that agricultural and weather shocks negatively affect household welfare status, a key recommendation is that supportive government policies should be specifically targeted at mitigating the effects of these two categories of shocks.

In Chapter 14, Oluwaseyi Ebenezer Olalere uses discourse analysis from relevant materials to analyse the effects of COVID-19 and the challenges on the attainment of national policies and public service provisions. The author reveals that African countries have been affected by the coronavirus pandemic, and the effect was more severe for African regions than other regions. The chapter highlights the need for African authorities such as the health systems to be provided with significant investment funds to improve their capacity and functionality. The policymakers also need to bolster the fiscal stability of African countries and promote the efficient provision of public services amidst catastrophic health challenges.

Olusola Joshua Olujobi in Chapter 15 explores the challenges faced in the oil industry, such as crude oil theft in commercial quantity exported to neighbouring countries. This has occasioned the loss of revenues and environmental pollution due to oil spillage caused by crude oil thieves. The study adopts a conceptual legal research method using current literature using library-based doctrinal legal research techniques with primary and secondary sources of laws, case laws, and the provisions of the Petroleum Industry Act 2021. The study highlights the absence of specific oil and gas laws criminalising crude oil theft. It also advocates the need to redefine legal regimes on illegal oil refineries by inserting specifically illegal oil refineries in the Petroleum Industry Act to effectively criminalise crude oil theft and recommend remedial economic measures such as bailouts and tax reliefs for the vulnerable oil firm.

The sixteenth chapter, authored by Clement Olalekan Olaniyi and Mojeed Muhammed Ologundudu, explores remittance shocks and poverty reduction

Nexus in Nigeria using bootstrap simulation and asymmetric causality tests. The study provides asymmetric structure and nonlinearity into the causal relationship between remittances and poverty within the framework of bootstrap simulations with leverage adjustments. The findings reveal the dimensions of asymmetric structures in the causal nexus between remittance inflows and poverty. Vital information is revealed, which the prevalent symmetric approaches in extant studies could not divulge. The chapter concludes that remittance inflows to Nigeria is important particularly in catalysing and spurring changes in poverty level.

Chapter 17, contributed by Flora Olubukola Olaniyi, focuses on the teaching platforms adopted as coping strategies of teachers during the COVID-19 lockdown, using qualitative and quantitative approaches. The findings show that most schools used online teaching platforms, using messaging applications, while the virtual applications were sparingly used. The author affirms that teachers were able to cope with the rigour, although they lacked relevant training on how to apply online teaching platforms. The chapter concludes that if teachers are trained properly, they will do well in disseminating the knowledge, both online and on the ground to their students.

Finally, in Chapter 18, Maria Chinecherem Uzonwanne, Amaka Gertrude Metu, Kingsley Chidera Adonike and Francis Chukwudi Onyedibe explore the effect of COVID-19 pandemic on small- and medium-scale enterprises (SMEs) in Nigeria. Their findings show that SMEs in the hospitality, education and transport sectors were mostly affected by the COVID-19 pandemic, while the least affected SMEs are those in the information and communication technology (ICT) and e-commerce, food processing and agricultural sectors.

In conclusion, the book shows the various socioeconomic shocks occasioned by COIVD-19 and the possible effects on Africa's development agenda. The socioeconomic effects of COVID-19 in Africa and developing useful direction in addressing the identified effects are discussed. While the book covered a wide range of topics, it draws the attention of key stakeholders to the African socioeconomic outcomes to the broad need for the development of resilient structure needed to create reasonable respite to address future socioeconomic challenges including pandemics.

A suggestion for further studies is the need to focus on the development of African-based approaches that comprehensively reflect the current status of socioeconomic activities in Africa, with minimal reliance on foreign models that tend to be aliens to African socioeconomic realities.

References

Odularu, G.O.A., Osabuohien, E., Ufua, D., and Osabohien, R. (in this volume). Conclusion: Socioeconomic Shocks, Pandemic Responsiveness, and Platonic Policies Revisited. In Osabuohien, E., Odularu, G., Ufua, D., and Osabohien, R. (Eds.), *Socioeconomic Shocks and Africa's Development Agenda: Lessons and Policy Directions in a Post-COVID-19 Era*. Oxfordshire: Routledge (Taylor and Francis).

Osabuohien, E., Odularu, G., Ufua, D., and Osabohien, R. (2022). *COIVD-19 in the African Continent: Sustainable Development and Socioeconomic Shocks*. Bingley: Emerald Publishers Limited. https://doi.org/10.1108/978-1-80117-686-620221002

Section 1

Socioeconomic Shocks and Economic Development

1 Socioeconomic and Cultural Influence on Women's Participation in Agroforestry in Jaman South, Ghana

Enoch Akwasi Kosoe and Francis Diawuo Darko

Introduction

Agroforestry is the integrated approach of combining trees, tree crops and shrubs with crops and livestock on the same agricultural landscape. It combines agricultural and forestry technologies to create a more diverse, productive, profitable, healthy and sustainable land use system (Shiva & Aalok, 2014). Diawuo, Kosoe and Doke (2019) consider agroforestry as a practical solution to land degradation and climate change problems.

Agroforestry serves as both climate change adaptation and mitigation strategy because it has the potential of creating a carbon sink that removes carbon dioxide (CO_2) from the atmosphere, or the maintenance of existing carbon in the vegetation (Intergovernmental Panel on Climate Change, IPCC, 2012). The sustainable practice of agroforestry can therefore serve as an impetus to improved crop and livestock production, while providing a major source of cash income to households. Interestingly, agroforestry practices are less costly and more affordable and also inputs are readily available to small-holder farmers (Parwada, Gadzirayi, Muriritirwa & Mwenye, 2010).

Out of the millions of farmers practising agroforestry over the world, about 60–80% of them are women (Shiva & Aalok, 2014). Women participate in all farm management activities and are especially responsible for managing trees at the early stages of establishment (Diawuo et al., 2019; Kiptot, Franzel & Degrande, 2014). Put together, women throughout the developing world make huge contributions to agroforestry. Women in rural areas of developing countries take up the majority of the farm workload and grow and harvest most of the staple crops that their families feed on. Food security throughout the developing world depends primarily on women (Shiva & Aalok, 2014). Despite their significant contribution, women's full potentials are not optimised in agricultural production.

Studies (e.g. Aguilar, Carranza, Goldstein, Kilic & Oseni, 2015; Peterman, Behrman & Quisumbing, 2010) show that there exists a gap of 20% to 30% in agricultural productivity resulting from inadequate women's involvement. Women face various challenges that limit their capacities to achieve maximum production and agricultural development (Degrande & Arinloye, 2014). The Food and

DOI: 10.4324/9781003208358-3

Agricultural Organization (FAO, 2013) indicates that compared with men, women are frequently disadvantaged in their access to forest resources and economic opportunities. Women's opportunities in the agricultural sector are limited to low-return activities of little or no interest to men. Meanwhile, given the same access to resources (e.g. education, information, labour and farm inputs) as men, women could increase food production from 10% to 20% (FAO, 2013). Yet they own only a small fraction of the world's farmland and receive less than 10% of agricultural extension delivery (Shiva & Aalok, 2014).

Ghana, like most other Sub-Saharan countries, suffers the gender gap in development. Women in Ghana continuously face social inequalities that keep them behind in terms of development. Through their roles as farmers and labourers, women face more severe constraints than men in access to productive agroforestry resources (FAO, 2011) which affects their contributions to food security and household sustenance. The consensus is that gender inequalities in areas such as ownership and access to resources, land tenure systems, education, extension and financial credit have contributed to lower agricultural productivity and higher poverty levels of women (Kalovoto, Kimiti & Manono, 2020; Osabohien, Adeley & De Alwis, 2020). A study by Diawuo et al. (2019) among agroforestry women farmers in the Jaman South Municipality of Ghana shows that women participate in most agroforestry farm management activities, except the application of weedicides. Kalovoto et al. (2020) and Kiptot and Franzel (2012) report that in East Africa and broadly across Africa, women, compared with men, are worse off in terms of access to resources such as land and capital, and benefits owing to certain social, economic and economic factors

Among the challenges women face in making socioeconomic development and progress is the COVID-19 pandemic which adds another level of stress for women farmers in Africa. As the impacts of COVID-19 continue to be experienced all over the world, one of the groups most affected by the crisis is women who are a historically disadvantaged group in society (Alvi & Barooah, 2021). As governments increased preventive measures such as lockdowns, social distance and restrictions in terms of movement, in order to combat the spread of the novel virus (Asongu, Diop & Nnanna, 2020), most households suffered income losses (Alvi & Barooah, 2021). In Ghana particularly, a study by Alvi, Shweta and Barooah (2021) in the northern parts found that rural farmers experienced income losses due to the pandemic and they were not able to sell the produce in the urban markets because those markets were closed. Across the African continent, a number of scholars have reviewed or investigated the socioeconomic effects of the COVID-19 pandemic. For instance, the COVID-19 pandemic and the new poor in Africa: the straw that broke the camel's back (Diop & Asongu, 2021); the geography of the effectiveness and consequences of COVID-19 measures: global evidence (Asongu et al., 2020); COVID-19 economic vulnerability and resilience indexes: global evidence (Asongu, Diop & Nnanna, 2020); a brief policy and scholarly review of the economic implications of the COVID-19 pandemic in Africa (Ataguba, 2020); socioeconomic effects, opportunities and policy responses associated with the COVID-19 pandemic on Africa (Ozili, 2020); the incidence of the COVID-19 pandemic on remittances in Africa (Bisong, Ahairwe & Njoroge, 2020); and nexuses between COVID-19, inequality and social stratification (Obeng-Odoom, 2020) are some evidence of impacts of COVID-19 on the continent.

Although the challenges women face in the practice of agroforestry may differ in Jaman South even during the COVID-19 pandemic due to time, spatial and cultural setting disparities, the gap is that there is no empirical data on the factors suppressing or promoting women's participation in agroforestry practice in the Municipality. This study therefore examined the influence of socio-cultural and economic factors on women's participation in the practice of agroforestry in Jaman South Municipality. Largely, social, cultural, norms, customs and taboos determine the respective roles of women and men within society, community or the household (Kiptot & Franzel, 2011). Also, the lack of economic and financial resources therefore limits women's meaningful participation in productive systems such as agroforestry (Gebru, Wang, Kim & Lee, 2019). The examination of the factors influencing women's involvement in agroforestry practice is necessary to provide policy makers with information to develop appropriate policies to harness their capacities for improved production.

This chapter is divided into four sections. Following the introductory section are the materials and methods in section two which the study area and the research approach. The third section of this chapter covers the results and discussion. The fourth and last section presents the conclusion and recommendations of the chapter.

Materials and Methods

Study Area

The study was carried out in the Jaman South Municipality in the Bono Region of Ghana. The Municipality has a total land area of about 755.37290 square kilometres (km^2). It is located between latitudes 7°35′N and 7°58′N and longitudes 2°47′W and 2°78′W (Ghana Statistical Service, GSS, 2014). It shares borders with the Jaman North District in the North, Berekum Municipal in the South-East, Dormaa Municipal in the South-West and La Côte d'Ivoire in the West (Ghana Statistical Service, 2014) (Figure 1.1). Agroforestry is widely practised in the Municipality with both men and women being involved. In a study by Diawuo et al. (2019), most of the women involved in cashew agroforestry did so alongside their husbands, although some single women were also involved. What is not clear is whether women's involvement was due to their husbands' influence (in access to land for farming) or they could access land and other necessary resources on their own for agroforestry practice without any socio-cultural setbacks. It is for this reason that this chapter assesses the influence of social, cultural and economic factors on women's participation in the adoption and practice of agroforestry in the Jaman South Municipality.

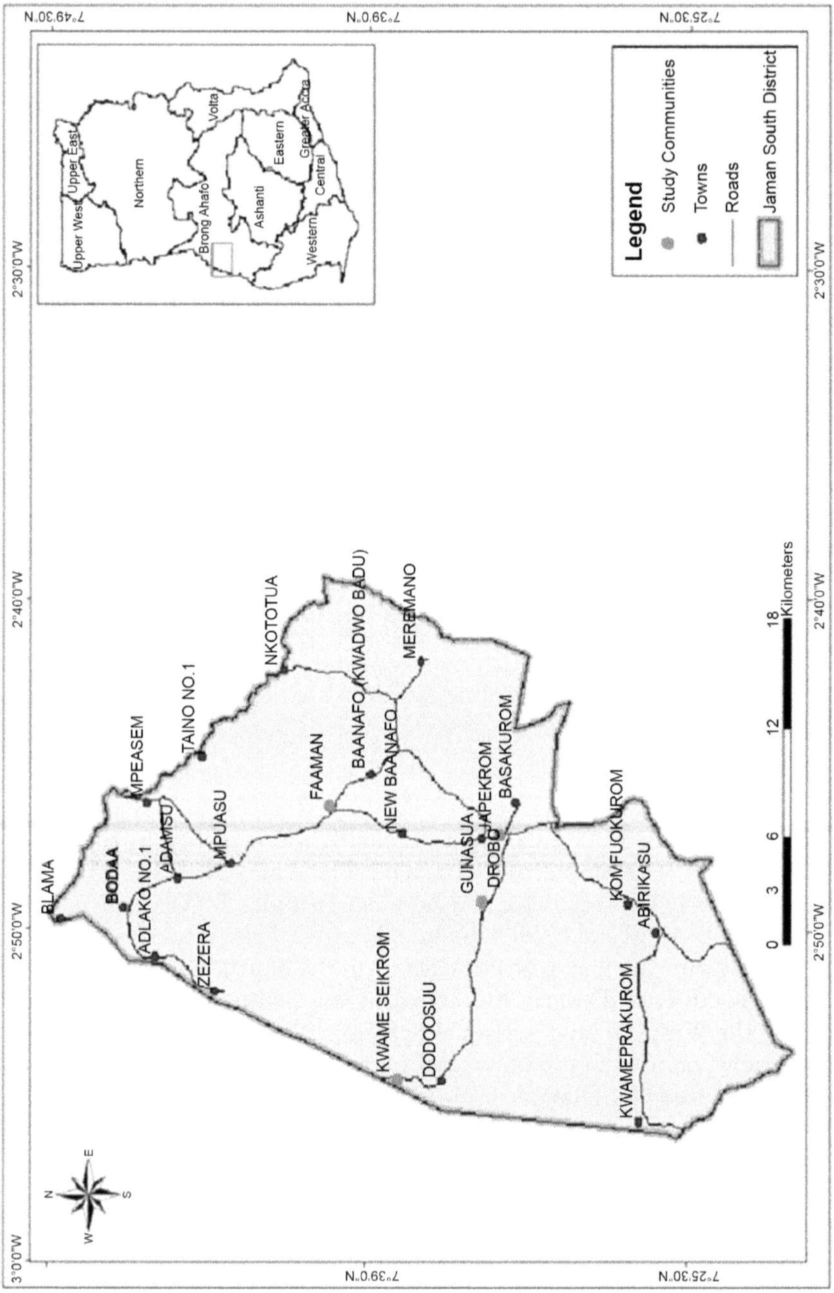

Figure 1.1 Map of the study area

Methodology

The study employed the mixed method design, using the interpretivist perspective (Gentle, Thwaites & Kim, 2014; Diawuo et al., 2019). This design was adopted due to its ability to use both qualitative and quantitative approaches in gathering, analysing and presenting data. A multi-stage random sampling method was used for selecting the respondents. The municipality was first grouped into two, urban and rural areas using the population composition of the towns. According to the Ghana Statistical Service [GSS], (2014), towns/communities with a population of more than 5000 are considered urban while those with less than 5000 population are rural areas.

Two communities were selected randomly from each status using the random number generation. The selected communities were Japekrom and Gonasua, and Faaman and Kwamesikrom for the urban and rural statuses, respectively. Each selected community was further grouped into sections using road demarcations to ensure even household selection; Japekrom ten sections, Gonasua eight sections, Faaman four sections and Kwameseikrom four sections (see Diawuo et al., 2019). Using these sections, households were randomly selected to constitute the study population. A household survey was therefore employed. Yamane (1967) sample size determination formula $\left(n = \dfrac{N}{1 + N * (\alpha)^2}\right)$ was used to arrive at 204 as the sample size.

Structured questionnaires were administered to selected households for the survey. In a house of two or more households, only one was randomly selected for the interview (Diawuo et al., 2019). Key informant interviews and focus group discussions (FGDs) (n=4 events, one FGD in each community with 12 participants each) were also used to collect data from the respondents. Key informants were purposely selected from among the chiefs and elders in the study communities, officials from the Ministry of Food and Agriculture and the Drobo Community Bank.

The quantitative data were transferred into the SPSS version 20 to conduct a multinomial logistic regression to estimate the extent of influence of social, cultural and economic factors on women's participation in agroforestry. This was measured based on an ordinal categorical nature of dependent variables derived through a five-point Likert rating scale; Strongly Disagree =1, Disagree =2, Neither Agree nor Disagree = 3, Agree= 4 and Strongly Agree= 5.

This model was adopted due to the nature of dependent variables being discrete in nature. The model is useful for situations where subjects are classified based on values of asset or predictor variables. This model is similar to logistic regression, but it is more general because a dependent variable is not restricted to two categories. The probability of a given household being in one of the levels of adoption given an asset of explanatory variables is given by the following expression:

$$Y = f(X) \tag{1}$$

where *Y* is the practice of agroforestry and *X* represents the socio-cultural and economic factors. Expanding the equation gives us

$$Y = f(\text{access to capital, land tenure system, taboos, extension services}) \quad (2)$$

The empirical model can be estimated from equations (1) and (2) as:

$$Y = \beta_o + \beta_1 X_1 + \beta_2 X_2 + \beta_n X_n + \varepsilon \quad (3)$$

where ε = error term, β_0 = intercept or constant term, β_1 to β_{10} = the slope of coefficients of the regressors or multipliers that describe the size of the effect the independent variables have on the dependent variable.

The qualitative data were classified, coded and patterns developed for analysis. This was done by reading through all the field notes and interviews and the transcription of audio recordings from the local dialect, *Twi* to English. The data were then presented in the form of narrations and descriptions to support analysis of quantitative data.

Results

Agroforestry Practice and Women's Tree Preference

The practice of agroforestry is not a new phenomenon in the area and women have been active participants in it. The study revealed that more than two-thirds (85%) of the respondents were active in the adoption and practice of agroforestry, while 15% were not practising agroforestry. The practice of agroforestry was highest in Kwameseikrom where at least one household in every house practised agroforestry, mainly cashew agroforestry. Responses from interviews indicated that the nearness of the community to the Ivorian border and ready market for cashew products in both Ghana and Cote D' Ivoire were noted to have boosted the production and marketing of cashew in the community and Municipality as a whole. Hence, the community is described by many as the 'hub of cashew production' in the municipality.

Interviews revealed that the high level of participation in agroforestry across the communities was because sale of crops (especially the tree crops) contributed to household income. Aside from cashew, the women had interest in trees of commercial and subsistence values. Common tree species they planted include *Theobroma cacao* (cocoa), *Anarcadium occidentale* (cashew), *Mangifera indica* (mango), *Persea americana* (avocado pear) and *Citrus sinensis* (orange). Multiple responses gathered on women's tree preference revealed that cashew was the most preferred tree women plant in agroforestry with 147 responses, followed by cocoa (85), orange (39) and 'others' (e.g., kola and teak as reported in Table 1.1).

The study noted that a key unfavourable development regarding mass farming of cashew is the disappearance of fertile lands for crop production. The findings point to one thing – food production and security will be a major problem soon.

Table 1.1 Multiple Response of Tree Species Preference

Common Name of Tree	*Frequency*
Cocoa	85
Cashew	147
Orange	39
Mango	20
Others	29

Source: The authors

NB: Multiple responses

The study learned that some households have already exhausted all their farmlands to cashew farming. A 46-year-old woman in Kwameseikrom in an interview hinted that she has no more land for food crop farming.

> *It was a family land that belonged to my father. I was the only child and since his death I have used everything for cashew. As of now, I do not have land to farm food crops for household consumption. I depend on other people for that access. That is, those who have the land and are now beginning planting. We go into agreement where I plant food crops for myself and the cashew for the owner of the land. In such instances I have no right over the cashew. That is how we have been surviving for the past two years.*
>
> (HI 1: Excerpts from Household Interview, December, 2018)

In some instances, access to land for cashew farming had resulted in quarrels among family members. In an interview with a stakeholder from the traditional council in Gonasua, he mentioned that the use of land for cashew agroforestry is 'sending people to their early graves'.

> *A lot of cases on farming lands come to our attention and most of them are about cashew farming. It is either someone has sold a family land to another or confrontation and quarrels among families over access and use of family lands, mainly for cashew agroforestry. In fact, these misunderstandings have sent some people to their early graves.*
>
> (KII 1: Excerpts from Key Informant Interview, December, 2018)

The findings presuppose that the excessive use of fertile lands solely for cashew farming can affect the availability of arable lands for other agricultural activities in the near future. This is supported by the GSS (2014) report that increasing use of land for cashew plantations may deprive food crop farmers of access to land for cultivation which will consequently affect household food security and eventually lead to hunger and poverty of the rural households.

Factors Influencing Women's Participation in Agroforestry

Three factors – social (with variable: labour, extension, and information services), cultural (with variables: land, taboos, household decision making) and economic (with variables: limited access to credit and capital) – were analysed to determine their likelihood of influence on women's participation in agroforestry using the multinomial logistic regression model. The likelihood ratio test of the model was used to show the distribution of each variable. The study showed that variables with significant likelihood influence on the model ($P < 0.05$) were lack of capital or credit, and extension services and information. The chi-square statistic is the difference in −2 log-likelihoods between the final model and a reduced model. The reduced model is formed by omitting an effect from the final model. The null hypothesis is that all parameters of that effect are 0. It therefore follows that access to land and land tenure (with $P > 0.05$ at = 0.117), taboos (at $P = 0.886$ more than $P < 0.05$), labour (at $P = 0.155$ more than $P < 0.05$) and household decision making and activities (at $P = 0.216$, more than $P < 0.05$) do not influence women's participation in the practice of agroforestry (see Table 1.2).

In essence, only two factors – lack of capital or access to credit, and extension service and information – greatly influenced women's participation in agroforestry in the area. This implies that though across Africa there may be similar factors influencing women's participation in agroforestry, the degree of influence of the factors varies across time and space. The cultural, economic and social factors are explained herein.

Cultural Factors

Cultural factors identified and discussed by the study are access to land and land tenure, taboos and household decision making. Majority (88.7%) of women practising agroforestry were found to own the land on which they were farming, with only 11.3% indicating they were farming on the land on a concessional basis

Table 1.2 Factors Influencing Agroforestry Practice

Effect	*−2 Log-Likelihood of Reduced Model*	*Chi-Square*	*df*	*Sig*
Intercept	121.090[a]	0.000	0	
Access to land and land tenure	128.474	7.384	4	0.117
Taboos	122.242	1.152	4	0.886
Lack of capital or access to credit	133.177	12.087	4	0.017*
Extension services and information	131.069	9.979	3	0.019*
Labour	127.746	6.656	4	0.155
Household decision making and activities	126.872	5.782	4	0.216

Source: The authors

*Significant at 0.05

Figure 1.2 Ownership and source of ownership of land

(see Figure 1.2). This explains why access to land was not significant at affecting women's practice of agroforestry ($P < 0.05$; $P = 0.117$).

Majority of the women that owned land acquired them through inheritance or ties with family (88.2%) or purchased (11.8%) (Figure 1.1). The study revealed that women were not discriminated against or restricted in accessing land based on gender or any other purpose. Like the men, women can access land for agriculture or housing purposes. This is, however, not a new phenomenon since, according to Kpieta and Bonye (2012b), land ownership in most parts of Ghana is either family ownership (e.g. acquired through allocation and inheritance) or individual ownership (e.g. through purchase and gifts).

The land tenure system in the area follows the matrilineal society style where inheritance is through the mother's line. Although women were not 'traditionally' expected to inherit land, the study found that with the modern state of affairs, the land tenure system has been more flexible, allowing women to have access to land and even own them. Arguably, the style of property rights is changing with land renting gaining roots, and more women taking control of land and landed resources. Like any other Akan societies, the Jaman South Municipality falls within the customary tenure system where families acquire land through their ancestry. In effect, a family land belongs to all the members of the family. As family size increases, a household's share of the land gets smaller since they have to pass on their portion to coming generations. This has led to the division of land into small portions which are hardly enough for household food production. Discussions with key informants revealed that family lands are vested in the *abusuapanin* (family head) who appropriates land to other members of the family.

A key informant at Drobo revealed that both women and men have access to family lands to plant crops to enable them to feed their families. However, it is a different story altogether when cash crops (which are seen as property) are planted. If a male member of the family plants cash or tree crops like cashew or cocoa on a family land, the crop is considered a family property. He further stated:

> *Everyone has rights to the family land, but when a male plants cashew the farm may be considered a family property. It is so because he did not own the land and therefore cannot give it to his children as inheritance.*
>
> (KII 2: Excerpts from Key Informant Interview, December, 2018)

Thus, after the demise of the farmer, the property would not be given to his children as inheritance in full. Usually, the farm is categorised as sharecropping called *abunu*, where the farm is divided into two halves; a half is given to the farmer's children as inheritance and half to the extended family.

However, in case a female member of the family (married or not) uses the land to cultivate economic or cash crops, she would have full access to the crops and all its returns. Even after her demise, the whole farm will be given to her children as inheritance. This is because per tradition, everything a woman has is retained in the family, unlike a man whose children would later trace their lineage through the mother's line. This aspect of tradition and land ownership has propelled many of the women to use the family lands for the practice of cashew agroforestry.

The discussions with respondents reflected a common knowledge among the matrilineal societies of the middle, southern and western Ghana where land is transferred from a deceased man to his brother or nephew in accordance with traditions. In such instances, women do not possess the inheritance rights to land. This is contrary to patrilineal societies such as in Northern Ghana, where a woman's right and access to land is through her husband. In the Upper East Region, for instance, women have limited access to and control over land. Also, widows tend to lose access to land unless they have male children, while unmarried women rarely have access to family land (Kpieta & Bonye, 2012a).

In the study area, women, be they married, unmarried or widowed, all have access to family lands and can even own and control land through purchase. This means that women have equal access to family land as do men. Interestingly, because men are the household heads, they are considered the ones with the title deeds to family lands. This means men make most of the important decisions on the usage and disposal of land, although the women's opinions are highly valued (Diawuo et al., 2019). This supports the claim by FAO (2010) and Kiptot and Franzel (2012) that men usually have the authority as pertains to tree products that are considered to have high returns. It should be noted that to a large extent, access to land and farm products in the study area greatly favours women than men. This is because when a woman farms on a family land that piece of farm can be transferred to her children as inheritance but the same cannot be said of a man.

Moreover, the study did not find any taboo or traditional norm that restricts women's participation in agriculture/agroforestry. Taboos are the inhibitions or bans resulting from social custom or emotional aversion, which are declared as sacred and forbidden by people (Diawuo & Issifu, 2015). In the municipality, nothing prohibits women to plant certain trees or concede ownership of certain trees to men. This explains why taboos are not significant at influencing women's participation in agroforestry practice ($P < 0.05$), $P = 0.886$ (see Table 1.3). Interviews and discussions with respondents revealed that the only taboo observed by the people is the *foda/nkyida*. On *foda/nkyida*, people are tabooed to visit their farms as it is a belief that the gods rest on this day. Failure to do so is believed to bring curse and sometimes death to those that disregard it. In strong terms, respondents revealed that *foda/nkyida* does not in any way obstruct their practice of agroforestry. Some even indicated that such days are necessary for resting.

In her opinion, a 28-year-old participant in an FGD in Faaman insisted that the revered days are necessary. '*It is a day for resting. I think one needs to rest after 6 days of farm work. The day also has a spiritual implication since our forefathers were those that instituted it*' (FGD 1: Excerpts from Focus Group Discussion, December 2018).

During the FGD in Japekrom, some respondents, however, were against that idea of *Nkyida*. They claimed because they do other businesses and also because they are not residents of communities in which they farm, the prohibited days affect their farm work. In an interview with a 37-year-old woman (food vendor) at Drobo, she indicated:

> *I don't always get time to go to the farm. It is usually annoying to learn that it is Foda when you are preparing to go to the farm. This happens because my farm is far from here [she farms in another community] as a result I go to farm only once a week.*
> (HI 2: Excerpts from Household Interview, December, 2018).

These respondents tend to hire labour for most of their farm management activities.

Furthermore, household decision making as a socio-cultural factor was not found to significantly influence women's participation in agroforestry practice ($P = 0.216$) (see Table 1.2). Interviews and focused group discussions with the women revealed they fully participated in farm management decision making, especially on issues related to agroforestry. For this reason, they disagreed that household decision making is an obstacle to farming. It was noted that in male-headed households, men are the major decision makers. However, the women (wives) see nothing wrong with that. According to a 63-year-old respondent, women are supposed to support their husbands, as long as husbands respect their wives. She maintained:

> *Even the Bible says women should help their husbands as much as husbands love their wives. Besides, husbands are the heads of the house, and we support them in*

> *what they do. My husband doesn't prevent me from making decisions that are good for the family, so no; it* (household farm decision making) *is not a problem at all.*
> (HI 3: Excerpts from Household Interview, December 2018)

Economic Factors

The study found that women's practice of agroforestry to a large extent was influenced by economic resources such as capital and credit facilities. The major economic factors identified by the study to have influence on women's participation in the agroforestry system was limited access to capital and credit facilities (P = 0.017, less than 0.05). Results of the study showed that all respondents (100%) perceived lack of capital and access to credit facilities as major limitations to the practice of agroforestry. It is evidenced in the literature that capital is considered a major factor affecting the participation of women in agroforestry (Kiptot & Franzel, 2011, 2012). The women further revealed that they are not able to access loans since financial institutions are not willing to give loans to smallholder farmers. In an FGD in Gonasua, the women revealed that traders and subscribers of micro enterprises get more loans than smallholder farmers. A 26-year-old female discussant disclosed:

> *The banks won't give us loans because we don't save with them; they prefer to give loans to traders who bank with them through mobile banking* (called Susu).
> (FGD 2: Excerpts from Focus Group Discussion, December 2018)

However, in a key informant interview at Drobo with the Head of Credit at the Drobo Community Bank Limited (DCBL), it was revealed that loans are given to everybody.

> *Loans are given to qualified persons, whether a trader or a farmer and it is normally dependent on the ability of the person to repay.*
> (KII 3: Excerpts from Key Informant Interview, Drobo, December 2018)

Notwithstanding this fact, investment in agroforestry activities is often limited by lack of capital, especially for women. Discussions held with the women revealed that some households borrow money from friends and relatives to hire labour which they pay back after harvesting. The women indicated, however, that they get financial assistance to supplement farming activities through sales of farm produce, remittances, petty trading, and others. Analysis of multiple response questions on income sources revealed that 198 respondents primarily derive most of their household income from selling of farm produce (see Table 1.3).

Farm products sold include products of tree crops such as cocoa and cashew, and other intercrops such as plantain, yam, maize, cassava, cocoyam and pepper

Table 1.3 Multiple Response of Source of Income

Source of Income	*Frequency*
Sales from farm produce	198
Petty trading	87
Remittances	71
Others	52

Source: The authors

(which are mostly farmed by women in Faaman). Petty trading received 87 responses. Activities traded include selling second-hand clothes, operation of provision stores and drinking spots, food vending, and buying and selling of food crops (e.g., pepper). Remittances constituted the third most dominant source of household income with 71 responses from all the communities (see Table 1.3). Some household respondents revealed they have their relatives (sons, daughters, brothers, sisters and husbands) living abroad that bring in money to supplement their household income. In an FGD at Faaman, there were unanimous conclusions from the women that they rely heavily on remittance to get money to hire farm labour. A discussant at an FGD indicated:

> *We use the money they send us to take care of ourselves and more importantly hire labour for farm activities. The money is also used to buy farm inputs such as seeds, cutlasses, and hoes.*
>
> (FGD 3: Excerpts from Focus Group Discussion, December 2018)

The last category described as 'others' also includes women working in private and public institutions as teachers, nurses, bankers, civil servants, hairdressers, and tailors/dressmakers. The study revealed that women in this category consider farming a secondary occupation. They are mainly involved in the farming of food crops for household consumption but because of their 'access to financial resources', they also embark on farming large acres of tree crops, mainly cashew and cocoa. Respondents here do not usually sell their food crops or go to farm, unlike those (respondents) having farming as their main occupation and a major source of household income.

Social Factors

The social factors identified by the study are extension and information services and labour. Majority of respondents (73.0%) agreed that lack of access to extension and information services affect their practice of agroforestry ($P = 0.019$, less than 0.05) with only 1.5% of respondents disagreeing. In addition, only 3% admitted they get extension service visits yearly (see Figure 1.3).

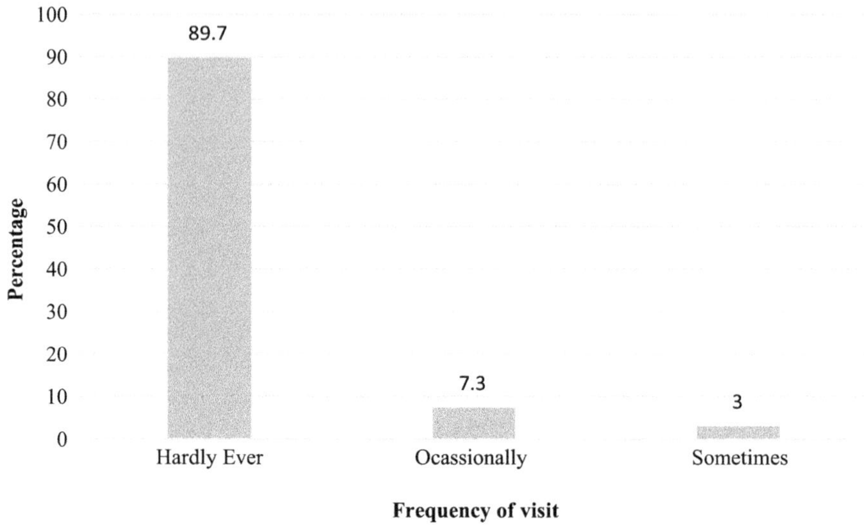

Figure 1.3 Frequency of extension visit

The findings on extension service provision indicate inadequate access to information on farming activities and extension supervision is common among women in rural areas, and a great impediment to women's participation in agricultural and development-related activities. This finding is akin to that of Karakara and Osabuohien (2019a, 2019b) where it was noted that household access to information and resources are crucial to their welfare outcomes. Even though women and farmers in general did not get visits from extension officers, their practice of agroforestry was because of the need to be self-sufficient in tree farming and their products.

Another important social factor that determines women's right in agroforestry is labour. The study revealed that some farm activities like land clearing and preparations require more than their strength could afford. These activities, according to responses by the women, were the only thing that men seemed to be doing better than them. Hence, women in male-headed households unlike those in female-headed households were able to offset that problem because of the availability of abled men. Labour is therefore not a factor that influences women's practice of agroforestry since many of the responses were married. The main source of labour for farming activities is family labour, revealed by 97% of respondents, while only 3% revealed their main source of labour is hired labour. Meanwhile, some respondents hire labour to supplement the household labour. Activities undertaken by hired labour include spraying, weeding, pruning, harvesting and transportation of produce.

Conclusion and Recommendations

The study assessed women's agroforestry systems and the extent of influence of social, cultural and economic factors on their active participation. Majority of women in the study were actively involved in agroforestry practice as men. They were active in cashew and cocoa agroforestry. The increasing use of agricultural land for cashew agroforestry was noted to likely affect access to fertile land for crop farming. This situation if not checked could affect food production in the Municipality in the near future. Among the identified socio-cultural and economic factors, lack of capital and credit and access to information and extension services negatively influenced the practice of agroforestry among women. Since they are smallholder farmers, the women hardly accessed financial credit to support their farming activities. They hardly also received agricultural extension visits and education, a situation that greatly militate against agroforestry practice and calls for pragmatic programmes and actions to motivate women in agroforestry.

Other socio-cultural factors such as labour, taboos and household decision making do not hinder women's active involvement in agroforestry. Land is noted across Africa to be a major constraint to women's practice of agriculture; however, women in the Jaman South Municipality face no such challenge. In fact, women in the study area had greater access to land, provided their family-owned land. Indeed, the matrilineal system of inheritance enhances women's access to land for farming and allows them to even own land as do their male counterparts either through inheritance or purchase.

To improve women's involvement in agroforestry, it is recommended that government and relevant institutions such as the Ministry of Food and Agriculture (MoFA) should intervene to encourage the development of rural microcredit institutions with regulations friendly to women so that they can have access to financial credit. Also, women farmers should form farmer groups and also strengthen existing ones to boost their accessibility to financial credit. When women are in groups, they could reach extension officers faster than individuals. The MoFA should also train volunteer extension officers, the majority of whom should be women, so that women can access extension services in a friendly manner.

It is important to say that data for this chapter were collected before the COVID-19 pandemic went viral therefore questions and findings do not reflect women's agroforestry experiences amidst the pandemic. Therefore, future studies can leverage on the COVID-19 pandemic impacts and how they relate to women's farming practices in the Jaman South District. Also, there is rare literature on the economic importance of agroforestry practice in the area. A study on the socioeconomic impacts of agroforestry, especially cashew agroforestry, will provide critical data for decision making and policy directions of the local government and contribute to empirical knowledge of the discipline in the area.

References

Aguilara, A., Carranza, E., Goldstein, M., Kilic, T. and Oseni, G. (2015). Decomposition of gender differentials in agricultural productivity in Ethiopia. *Agricultural Economics*, 46, 311–334.

Alvi, M. F. and Barooah, P. (2021). Food security and women's wellbeing: Insights from Rural Nepal. In *Agriculture, Gender, and COVID-19: Impact and Recovery*. All India Disaster Mitigation Institute, Issue No. 195, September, 2021.

Alvi, M. F., Gupta, S. and Barooah, P. (2021). Assessing the impact of COVID-19 on rural women and men in northern Ghana. *GCAN COVID-19 Impact Fact Sheet 1*. Washington, DC: International Food Policy Research Institute (IFPRI). https://doi.org/10.2499/p15738coll2.134446

Asongu, S. A., Diop, S. and Nnanna, J. (2020). The geography of the effectiveness and consequences of COVID-19 measures: Global evidence. *Journal of Public Affairs*, 21, e2483. https://doi.org/10.1002/pa.2483

Ataguba, J. E. (2020). COVID-19 pandemic, a war to be won: Understanding its economic implications for Africa. *Applied Health Economics and Health Policy*, 18(3), 325–328. https://doi.org/10. 1007/s40258-020-00580-x

Bisong, A., Ahairwe, P. and Njoroge, E. (2020). *The Impact of COVID-19 on Remittances for Development in Africa*. ECDPM Discussion Paper No. 269. May. https://ecdpm.org/publications/impact-covid-19-remittances-development-africa/. Accessed on 20/08/2020.

Degrande, A. and Arinloye, D. D. A. (2014). Gender in agroforestry: Implications for Action Research. *Nature and Fauna*, 29(1), 6–11.

Diawuo, F. and Issifu, K. A. (2015). Exploring the African traditional belief systems in natural resource conservation and management in Ghana. *The Journal of Pan African Studies*, 8(9), 115–131.

Diawuo, F., Kosoe, E. A. and Doke, D. A. (2019). Participation of women farmers in agroforestry practice in the Jaman South Municipality, Ghana. *Ghana Journal of Development Studies*, 16(2), 267–289.

Diop, S., & Asongu, S. A. (2021). The Covid-19 pandemic and the new poor in Africa: The straw that broke the camel's back. *The Forum for Social Economics*, 1–13. https://doi.org/10.1080/07360932.2021.1884583

FAO (2010). *"Climate-Smart" Agriculture: Policies, Practices and Financing for Food Security, Adaptation and Mitigation*, FAO, Rome.

FAO (2011). The role of women in agriculture. *Background Research in Support of the Preparation of FAO's The State of Food and Agriculture 2010–11: Women in Agriculture: Closing the Gender Gap for Development*. www.fao.org/publications/sofa/en/. Accessed on 02/06/2016.

FAO (2013). Forests, food security and gender: Linkages, disparities and priorities for action. *Background Paper for the International Conference on Forests for Food Security and Nutrition*, FAO, Rome, 13–15 May 2013. www.fao.org/forestry/37071-07fcc88f7f1162db37cfea44e99b9f1c4.pdf

Gebru, B. M., Wang, S. W., Kim, S. J. and Lee, W. K. (2019). Socio-ecological niche and factors affecting agroforestry practice adoption in different agroecologies of southern Tigray, Ethiopia. *Sustainability (Switzerland)*, 11(13), 1–19. https://doi.org/10.3390/su11133729

Gentle, P., Thwaites, R. and Kim, A. (2014). Differential impacts of climate change on communities in the middle hills' region of Nepal. *Natural Hazards*, 74, 815–836.

Ghana Statistical Service (GSS) (2014). 2010 population and housing census. *District Analytical Report*, Jaman South District.

IPCC (2012). Glossary of terms. In *A Special Report of Working Groups I and II of the Intergovernmental Panel on Climate Change (IPCC): Managing the Risks of Extreme Events and Disasters to Advance Climate Change Adaptation*, C. B. Field, V. Barros, T. F. Stocker, D. Qin, D. J. Dokken, K. L. Ebi, M. D. Mastrandrea, K. J. Mach, G.-K. Plattner, S. K. Allen, M. Tignor and P. M. Midgley, Eds. Cambridge: Cambridge University Press, 555–564.

Kalovoto, D.M., Kimiti, J.M., and Manono B.O. (2020). Influence of women empowerment on adoption of agroforestry technologies to counter climate change and variability in semi-arid Makueni County, Kenya. *International Journal of Environmental Sciences & Natural Resources*, 24(2). https://doi.org/10.19080/ijesnr.2020.24.556133

Karakara, A. A. and Osabuohien, E. (2019a). Households' ICT access and educational vulnerability of children in Ghana. *Cogent Social Sciences*, 5(1). http://doi.org/10.1080/23311886.2019.1701877

Karakara, A. A. and Osabuohien, E. (2019b). Households' ICT access and bank patronage in West Africa: Empirical insights from Burkina Faso and Ghana. *Technology in Society*, 56, 116–125. https://doi.org/10.1016/j.techsoc.2018.09.010

Kiptot, E. and Franzel, S. (2011). *Gender and agroforestry in Africa: are women participating?* ICRAF Occasional Paper No. 13. Nairobi: World Agroforestry Centre. http://apps.worldagroforestry.org/downloads/Publications/PDFS/OP16988.pdf. Accessed on 23/11/2016.

Kiptot, E. and Franzel, S. (2012). Gender and agroforestry in Africa: A review of women's participation. *Agroforestry System*, 84, 35–58.

Kiptot, E., Franzel, S. and Degrande, A. (2014). Gender, agroforestry and food security in Africa. *Current Opinion in Environmental Sustainability*, 6, 104–109. http://doi.org/10.1016/j.cosust.2013.10.019

Kpieta, B. A. and Bonye, S. Z. (2012a). Land as a "god": The gender dimensions of its wealth creation among the Dagaabas in North Western Ghana. *European Scientific Journal*, 8(14), 109–131.

Kpieta, B. A. and Bonye, S. Z. (2012b). Women, ownership and access to land in the Upper East Region of Ghana. *International Journal of Humanities and Social Science*, 2(9), 66–74.

Obeng-Odoom, F. (2020). COVID-19, inequality, and social stratification in Africa. *African Review of Economics and Finance*, 12(1), 3–37.

Osabohien, R., Adeleye, N., & De Alwis, T. (2020). Agro-financing and food production in Nigeria. Heliyon, 6(5), e04001.

Ozili, P. K. (2020). COVID-19 in Africa: Socioeconomic impact, policy response and opportunities. *International Journal of Sociology and Social Policy*, 42(3/4), 177–200.

Parwada, C., Gadzirayi, C. T., Muriritirwa, W. T. and Mwenye, D. (2010). Adoption of agro forestry technologies among smallholder farmers: A case of Zimbabwe. *Journal of Development and Agricultural Economics*, 2(10), 351–358.

Peterman, A., Behrman, J. and Quisumbing, A. (2010). *A review of empirical evidence on gender differences in non-land agricultural inputs, technology and services in developing countries*. IFPRI Discussion Paper 00975. Washington, DC: International Food Policy Research Institute. https://ebrary.ifpri.org/utils/getfile/collection/p15738coll2/id/1464/filename/1465.pdf. Accessed on 23/11/2016.

Shiva, A. and Aalok, A. (2014). *Role of Women in Agroforestry*. Proceedings of International Workshop on Women in Agroforestry 28–29 November 2013.

Yamane, T. (1967). *Statistics. An Introductory Analysis*, 2nd edition, New York: Harper and Row.

List of Household Interviews (HI)/ Key Informant Interviews (KII) / Focus Group Discussions (FGD)

KII 1: Excerpts from Key Informant Interview, December, 2018 2018 by a male stakeholder from the traditional council in Gonasua

HI 1: Excerpts from Household Interview, December, 2018 by a 46-year-old female household respondent in Kwameseikrom.

HI 2: Excerpts from Household Interview, December, 2018 by a 37-year-old female food vendor at Drobo

HI 3: Excerpts from Household Interview, December 2018 by a 63-year-old household respondent in Kwameseikrom.

KII 2: Excerpts from Key Informant Interview, December, 2018 by a male key informant at Drobo

KII 3: Excerpts from Key Informant Interview, December 2018 by the Head of Credit at Drobo Community Bank Limited (DCBL)

FGD 1: Excerpts from Focus Group Discussion, December 2018 by a 28-year-old female participant in an FGD in Faaman

FGD 2: Excerpts from Focus Group Discussion, December 2018 by a 26-year-old female participant in an FGD in Gonasua

FGD 3: Excerpts from Focus Group Discussion, December 2018 by a female participant in an FGD in Faaman

2 How Coffee Price Shock Transmits into the Economy?

Empirical Evidence from Ethiopia

Naser Yenus Nuru and Hayelom Yrgaw Gereziher

1. Introduction

Coffee is a beverage obtained from cherry which is a coffee plant's fruit and the coffee plant is a tree in the genus madder family. The tree is in fact a tropical evergreen shrub that has the possibility to grow around 100 feet tall. The two most frequently produced species of coffee plant that have paramount economic significance are *Coffea arabica and Coffea robusta*. While 70 per cent of the world's coffee production comes from the species of *arabica*, the rest 30 per cent are from *robusta* (USDA, 2012).

Tropical places with abundant precipitation and continual warm temperatures with no frost are conducive conditions for coffee trees to grow well in these regions. A mean temperature between 17°C and 23°C with plenty of rainfall and good soil conditions is required for good growth of coffee tree. The coffee plant stays fruitful for around 15 years once it gives its initial full crop of beans at around 5 years old (Oxfam, 2002),

Many developing countries, including Ethiopia, generate significant export revenue from commodities that they export and coffee, the underlying asset for the largest future markets in soft commodities is one of these (John and Baoying, 2011). Ethiopia, essentially, is a monoculture export economy. Arabica coffee is, by far, the country's major export. In Ethiopia, 35 per cent of the total exports of the country comes from coffee and it also sustains the livelihood of around 16 million people in its sector (growers, processors and marketing) (IMF, 2007). Ethiopia was positioned first from Africa, followed by the Ivory Coast and Uganda, and fifth in the world after Brazil, Vietnam, Indonesia, Colombia and India in terms of its production potential (USDA, 2012). Djimmah (kaffa), Limu, Lekempti, Teppi, Illubabor, Bebeka, Yirgacheffie, Sidamo and Harrar are some of the coffee varieties in Ethiopia and Yirgacheffie is the finest of all these coffee varieties.

Coffee also contributes for around 5 per cent of gross domestic product and 10 per cent of total agricultural production in the past few decades in Ethiopia. Taxes levied on the crop are also essential sources of government revenue (CTA, 2002). Ethiopia, nonetheless, accounts for only 4.4 per cent of the world's coffee production (Statista, 2019). The country thus exerts virtually no influence on international coffee prices; the price of coffee is set, not by any particular country but by

DOI: 10.4324/9781003208358-4

independent international commodity markets that are subject to a high degree of price volatility. Shocks to international coffee prices, such as the 26 per cent drop in the price of coffee on world markets in 2012, can have profound consequences for the Ethiopia's economy (International Coffee Organization, 2019).

In very small plots of land, around one million small-scale farmers produce over 95 per cent of Ethiopia's coffee. Coffee income is the main source of livelihood for farmers in coffee-producing areas. As significant proportion of coffee-producing farmers are food deficit and rely on purchased food grains for family consumption. During slack times when farmers lack cash income, coffee trees serve as collateral to get credit from informal moneylenders. In periods with good prices, farmers are able to buy sufficient food for family consumption, pay their agricultural credit and government taxes, and fulfil other duties from coffee sales. While good prices may have positive spill-over effects in terms of input use, consumption of manufactured goods and access to education and healthcare, a drop in coffee income may lead farmers to sell off their assets, such as oxen, land, or property, or leave their homes in search of work in other places (Oxfam, 2002), which, in turn, exacerbates household food security status.

There is, however, no empirical study that explicitly shows the impact of coffee price shock on the Ethiopian economy. While Asfaw (2017) examined the effect of coffee price shock on the school dropout status of children in rural Ethiopia using microdata, others (Gemech and Struthers, 2007; Mohan *et al.*, 2016) studied the impact of market reform programmes on the volatility of coffee prices in Ethiopia and the welfare impacts for Ethiopian coffee producers from eliminating volatility in coffee price, respectively. This chapter, therefore, examines the effects of shocks to the coffee price which is the only variety that Ethiopia exports on various macroeconomic fundamentals of the economy. This research could be crucial for policymakers in developing appropriate response strategies when an economy's primary export commodity prices fluctuate due to economic shocks, for example, the COVID-19 shock.

The chapter is structured as follows. A review of related literature is presented in Section 2. Data type and source as well as the econometric strategy are presented in Section 3. In Section 4, results are presented and discussed. Robustness checks and conclusion are presented in Sections 5 and 6, respectively.

2. Literature Review

Commodity prices, including coffee prices, are volatile and this becomes almost a stylized fact in the contemporary world economy. This is especially true for countries with commodity production as these economies are largely affected by the movements in international prices. Ethiopia is among those countries that are highly exposed to external shocks in international prices or coffee prices, being a price-taker in the international commodity market. The country will persist to be more prone to the natural cycles that are common in the production of such primary commodities as coffee (Gemech and Struthers, 2007). The reliance of developing countries on primary commodities to attain economic growth and sound macroeconomic performance while the prices of these commodities are volatile in the international commodity market appears as a great concern of these countries (Amu *et al.*, 2021).

Bangara and Dunne (2018), for instance, investigated the effect of an increase in tobacco price for the Malawian economy over the period of 1980Q1 up to 2012Q4. The findings, based on structural vector autoregressive (VAR) model, indicate that output responds positively and significantly while consumer price index (CPI) responds negatively to tobacco price shock. An increase in tobacco price has also an appreciation effect on exchange rate in Malawi. Pedersen (2019), using structural VAR model, also examined the effect of copper price shock on the Chile economy and documented that exchange rate appreciates in response to the copper price shock.

Addison and Ghoshray (2013), employing VAR model, examined the impact of agricultural commodity price innovation on economic growth in sub-Saharan African countries and exhibited that the impact of commodity price shock on economic growth of these countries is asymmetric. Noha *et al.* (2015), using Arellano Bond "Difference GMM", also assessed the effect of commodity terms of trade (CTOT) index on the real gross domestic product (GDP) per capita growth in 43 developing countries. The findings revealed that real GDP per capita growth responds positively and significantly in response to a positive change in commodity term of trade index. Additionally, the paper indicated for better management in the natural resources of developing economies, that is improved management is required in the energy sector to respond to the resource curse of economies with a low score on the governance index. This is related to the submission of Osabohien *et al.* (2020) regarding the interaction between governance and food security using the Nigerian case based on an autoregressive distributed lag (ARDL) model.

McGregor (2017), using panel VAR model, examined the effect of global commodity price shock in developing countries and found that per capita income increases by about 0.26 per cent in response to one standard deviation shock in commodity price in these countries. Government spending and investment also increases by about 4.4 per cent and 12.4 per cent, respectively. The effect is found to be stronger in less developed countries, those heavily dependent on commodity exports and economies with fixed exchange rate regimes.

Medina (2016) also assessed the responses of fiscal revenue and spending in response to commodity price shock in Latin American countries and found that commodity price shock has a positive effect on commodity price in these countries, though there are some differences across these countries. In a similar fashion, Vallejo (2017), employing panel VAR model, examined the responses of fiscal outcomes to commodity price shock in eight Latin American countries. The commodity price shock is identified using Cholesky identification scheme and a specific commodity index is generated based on Medina (2010) methodology. The result revealed that the movements in commodity price result in economic movements in Latin American countries and the size of the impact is larger in Latin American countries than the high-income commodity countries.

Roch (2019), using heterogeneous panel structural VAR model, studied the effects of commodity price shocks for a panel of 22 commodity exporting countries and found that commodity term of trade shock is an essential driver of business cycle movements, that is 30 per cent movement in output is explained by commodity term of trade shock. In addition to this, the study exhibited inflation targeting regimes, exchange rate flexibility, and fiscal rules which insulate the economy from commodity price fluctuations.

Gelos and Ustyugova (2017), employing several methods, examined the effect of commodity price shock on inflation across countries to a broad range of structural features and policy frameworks over the sample period 2001–2010. The result from the study showed that countries with larger food shares in CPI baskets, fuel intensities and pre-existing inflation levels are highly vulnerable to encounter continued inflationary impacts from commodity price shocks but this is not the case for economies with more independent central banks and higher governance scores. During the 2008 food price shock, the impact of the presence of inflation targeting regimes, however, appears modest and not evident. The paper also documented that the effect of commodity price shock on domestic inflation does not get significantly affected by trade openness, financial development, dollarization and the labour market flexibility. Atsushi and Takayuki (2017) also studied the response of headline inflation to commodity price shock with a cross-country panel and revealed that the response of inflation to commodity price shock almost tapers off within about one year after the shock.

Grimes and Hyland (2013) studied the effect of commodity price shock on rural and urban community outcomes for a panel of New Zealand districts employing VAR model. The study showed that commodity price shock has a positive effect on housing price (proxy for economic outcomes) and housing investment (proxy for population outcomes) across the country. Compared to the rural communities, urban communities are more influenced by the commodity price shock.

Asfaw (2017), using data collected before and after the 2008 global financial crisis and difference in difference estimation technique, examined the effect of exogenous coffee price shock caused by the crisis on the school dropout status of children by comparing the school dropout status of children in coffee-producing and non – coffee-producing villages in rural Ethiopia. The result showed that the decrease in the world price of coffee during the global financial crisis enlarged school dropout rates among children aged 15–18 years in coffee-producing villages. This effect is even larger among female children in this age group.

Gemech and Struthers (2007), employing Generalized Autoregressive Conditional Heteroskedasticity (GARCH) techniques, presented the impact of market reform programmes on the volatility of coffee prices in Ethiopia over the sample period 1982–2001 despite its main focus is after the beginning of the reforms in 1992. They found that volatility in coffee price significantly increases after the introduction of market-oriented reform programmes. Mohan *et al.* (2016) estimated the welfare impacts for Ethiopian coffee producers from eliminating volatility in coffee price over the sample period 1976–2012 and found that the welfare gain from eliminating volatility in coffee price is small, that is the gain per producer is only around US$0.76 in a year.

Nuru and Gereziher (2020) investigated the impact of commodity price shock on the Ethiopian economy and revealed that a shock to the commodity price positively and significantly affects output. Worako *et al.* (2008), using Cointegration and Error-Correction Model (ECM), analysed price transmission from the world coffee market to local markets, auction to producers, and from the world to auction markets in a deregulated economy and found that the short-run transmission of price signals from world to domestic markets has improved after a liberalization reform, but has remained weak in both auction-to-world and producer-to-auction markets. Andersson *et al.* (2016) studied whether regional warehouses that are connected to a national commodity exchange reduce transaction costs and price dispersion between regions and documented that the average price spread between market pairs is diminished by 0.86–1.775 Ethiopian Birr when both markets have an operating warehouse.

From the foregoing empirical review, we can figure out the following three points. First, the literature is mainly built on aggregate commodity price shock rather than a specific commodity. Second, the studies also give much emphasis on the cross-country study of developing countries. Last but most importantly, there is no a single research paper that examines the effect of coffee price shock on a given economy in single country case. Hence, this chapter fills this important knowledge gap in the literature by examining the effect of coffee price shock which is the only variety that Ethiopia exports on various macroeconomic fundamentals of the economy.

3. Data and Methodology

3.1. *Data Type and Source*

We use quarterly data in our estimation from 2001 first quarter (Q_1) to 2018 fourth quarter (Q_4). Seven variables are included in our model, namely coffee price, gross domestic product, inflation, money supply, real effective exchange rate, government spending and government revenue. Inflation rate is obtained as the first difference of the logarithm of the CPI. In a high frequency data such as our quarterly data, variables are less likely to respond to an exogenous shock within a quarter than in annual data (Blanchard and Perotti, 2002). The use of quarterly data also helps us to enlarge our degrees of freedom in estimation which is otherwise problematic in a small sample size. The variables are seasonally adjusted using census-X13. While the coffee price data is sourced from international coffee organisation, the data for the other variables is obtained from the National Bank of Ethiopia and Ministry of Finance and Economic Development.

All the variables are applied in their logarithm transformation, and augmented Dickey–Fuller and Phillips–Perron tests are used to check the stationarity properties of the variables. Using Schwarz information criterion (SIC), number of augmentation lags is determined to account for serial correlation in the Dickey-Fuller

Table 2.1 Unit Root Tests

	ADF			Phillips–Perron	
	Lags (SIC)	t-statistic	p-value	t-statistic	p-value
Coffee price	4	−2.070129	0.2572	−1.337620	0.6065
Real GDP	1	−0.624243	0.9737	−0.965445	0.9408
Inflation	0	−3.183396	0.0260	−3.110907	0.0311
Money supply	4	3.302014	1.0000	5.509446	1.0000
Real effective exchange rate	0	1.586983	0.9994	1.043079	0.9966
Government spending	2	0.431468	0.9988	−0.034918	0.9949
Government revenue	4	2.191025	1.0000	−0.844331	0.9552

Source: Authors' own calculation

H_0: Series has a unit root

regressions. Table 2.1 exhibits the results for the stationarity properties of the variables or the unit root tests. We see that all the variables are non-stationary at their level except inflation. After first difference, however, the non-stationary variables become stationary.

3.2. *Econometric Strategy*

To study the effect of coffee price shock in a small open economy, namely Ethiopia, in this study, we set up a seven-variable VAR model.

The structural-form equation or the SVAR is given in equation 2.1 as:

$$Ay_t = \beta + \varphi t + B_1 y_{t-1} + B_2 y_{t-2} + \cdots\cdots\cdots\cdots + B_p y_{t-p} + Be_t, \tag{2.1}$$

where y_t is an $n \times 1$ vector of variables at time t; β is an $n \times 1$ vector of constants; φt is an $n \times 1$ vector of time trends; A and B_l are each an $n \times n$ matrix of parameters for l = 1, . . ., p; e_t is an $n \times 1$ vector of structural/exogenous shocks with $e_{t\sim}$ $N(0, BE(e_t e_t')B')$. Starting from the structural-form equation, we can obtain the reduced form of VAR in the following way:

$$y_t = A^{-1}\beta + A^{-1}\varphi t + A^{-1}B_1 y_{t-1} + A^{-1}B_2 y_{t-2} + \cdots\cdots\cdots + A^{-1}B_p y_{t-p} + A^{-1}Be_t$$

or, equivalently,

$$y_t = \alpha + \gamma t + A_1 y_{t-1} + A_2 y_{t-2} + \cdots\cdots\cdots + A_p y_{t-p} + u_t \tag{2.2}$$

with $A_l = A^{-1}B_l, u_t = A^{-1}Be_t$ and $E(u_t u_t') = A^{-1}BE(e_t e_t')B' A'^{-1}$.

As it can be seen from equation (2.2), reduced form innovations are linear combinations of structural shocks and have only little economic significance.

The structural shocks are identified using Cholesky decomposition scheme which restricts B to a k-dimensional identity matrix and A to a lower triangular matrix based on the causal ordering of the model variables. Under the recursive approach, the most exogenous variable is ordered first while the less exogenous one is ordered last (Christiano *et al.*, 2005; Fatas and Mihov, 2001). Hence, the most exogenous variable (coffee price) is ordered first followed by real GDP, inflation, money supply, real effective exchange rate, government spending and government revenue, respectively. Relying on this causal ordering of the variables, the following contemporaneous zero-value restrictions are considered for $Au_t = Be_t$:

$$\begin{bmatrix} -\alpha_{cofp,\,cofp} & 0 & 0 & 0 & 0 & 0 & 0 \\ -\alpha_{GDP,cofp} & -\alpha_{GDP,GDP} & 0 & 0 & 0 & 0 & 0 \\ -\alpha_{\pi,cofp} & -\alpha_{\pi,GDP} & -\alpha_{\pi,\pi} & 0 & 0 & 0 & 0 \\ -\alpha_{m2,cofp} & -\alpha_{m2,GDP} & -\alpha_{m2,\pi} & -\alpha_{m2,m2} & 0 & 0 & 0 \\ -\alpha_{exc,cofp} & -\alpha_{exc,GDP} & -\alpha_{exc,\pi} & -\alpha_{exc,m2} & -\alpha_{exc,exc} & 0 & 0 \\ -\alpha_{govs,cofp} & -\alpha_{govs,GDP} & -\alpha_{govs,\pi} & -\alpha_{govs,m2} & -\alpha_{govs,exc} & -\alpha_{govs,govs} & 0 \\ -\alpha_{govr,,cofp} & -\alpha_{govr,GDP} & -\alpha_{govr,\pi} & -\alpha_{govr,m2} & -\alpha_{govr,exc} & -\alpha_{govr,govs} & -\alpha_{govr,govr} \end{bmatrix} \begin{bmatrix} u_t^{cofp} \\ u_t^{GDP} \\ u_t^{\pi} \\ u_t^{m2} \\ u_t^{exc} \\ u_t^{govs} \\ u_t^{govr} \end{bmatrix} =$$

$$\begin{bmatrix} 1 & 0 & 0 & 0 & 0 & 0 & 0 \\ 0 & 1 & 0 & 0 & 0 & 0 & 0 \\ 0 & 0 & 1 & 0 & 0 & 0 & 0 \\ 0 & 0 & 0 & 1 & 0 & 0 & 0 \\ 0 & 0 & 0 & 0 & 1 & 0 & 0 \\ 0 & 0 & 0 & 0 & 0 & 1 & 0 \\ 0 & 0 & 0 & 0 & 0 & 0 & 1 \end{bmatrix} \begin{bmatrix} e_t^{cofp} \\ e_t^{GDP} \\ e_t^{\pi} \\ e_t^{m2} \\ e_t^{exc} \\ e_t^{govs} \\ e_t^{govr} \end{bmatrix}$$

This specific ordering of the model variables has the following essential connotations: (i) coffee price does not respond instantaneously to shocks to other variables; (ii) output responds contemporaneously to coffee price shock, but it does not react instantaneously to inflation, money supply, exchange rate, government spending and government revenue shocks; (iii) inflation reacts instantaneously to coffee price and output shocks, but it is not affected contemporaneously by money supply, exchange rate, government spending and government revenue shocks; (iv) money supply responds contemporaneously to coffee price, output and inflation shocks, but it does not respond instantaneously to exchange rate, government spending and government revenue shocks; (v) exchange rate responds contemporaneously to coffee price, output, inflation and money supply shocks, but it does not respond instantaneously to government spending and government revenue shocks; (vi) government spending responds instantaneously to all shocks in the system except government revenue shock; and (vii) government revenue reacts instantaneously to all shocks in the model variables. All the variables, however, react freely after the initial period. For example, shocks in output, inflation, money supply, exchange rate, government spending and government revenue can affect coffee price in all periods after the initial period in which the shock arrived.

4. Results and Discussion

Structural shocks are identified in a VAR model and impulses responses are computed over ten horizons to examine the responses of the endogenous variables to coffee price shock for the Ethiopian economy.[1] The confidence bands in Figure 2.1 are 95 per cent wide and each shock is one standard deviation size. The point estimates of the mean of the impulse response are represented by the thick straight line while the 5th and 95th percentiles from Monte Carlo simulations based on 1,000 replications are depicted by the broken lines. The impulse response horizons are shown in the horizontal axis and changes in the response variable to shocks are indicated in the vertical axis. For the sake of brevity, we report only the responses of the endogenous variables to coffee price shock.

Coffee price shock is not persistent and dies out after the first sixth quarters. Output responds positively and significantly from the second quarter up to the ninth quarter in response to coffee price shock. One standard deviation positive shock in coffee price causes about 0.4 per cent increase in output. This finding is consistent with the result of McGregor (2017), Noha *et al.* (2015), and Bangara and Dunne (2018). This could be attributed to the increment of export volumes so as to reap the benefits of increased export prices in the international markets by the export producing economic agents. As the economic agents get encouraged, they sell their products at a higher price and bring foreign exchange reserves that could potentially assist the government as well as themselves to expand substantial development projects. Hence, a positive shock to commodity prices shifts the aggregate supply to the right and brings about an additional output (Bjornland, 2000).

Elaborating the effect of commodity price shock on inflation, inflation also rises insignificantly in response to the coffee price shock. In line with our findings, Arango *et al.* (2014) found a positive effect of commodity price shock on inflation, a bit smaller though. Hence, the reason behind the positive association between commodity price shock and inflation, in countries where the commodities are the core of economic activity, could be the transmission of fluctuations of commodity export prices towards the aggregate national income.

Money supply and exchange rate increases on impact before it declines in response to the coffee price shock. These findings support the results of Bangara and Dunne (2018). Since the positive commodity price shock increases the aggregate supply (output), money demand increases as the purchasing power of individuals rises as a result of increased output level. An encouraged export sector boosts the foreign exchange reserve of a given country making the domestic

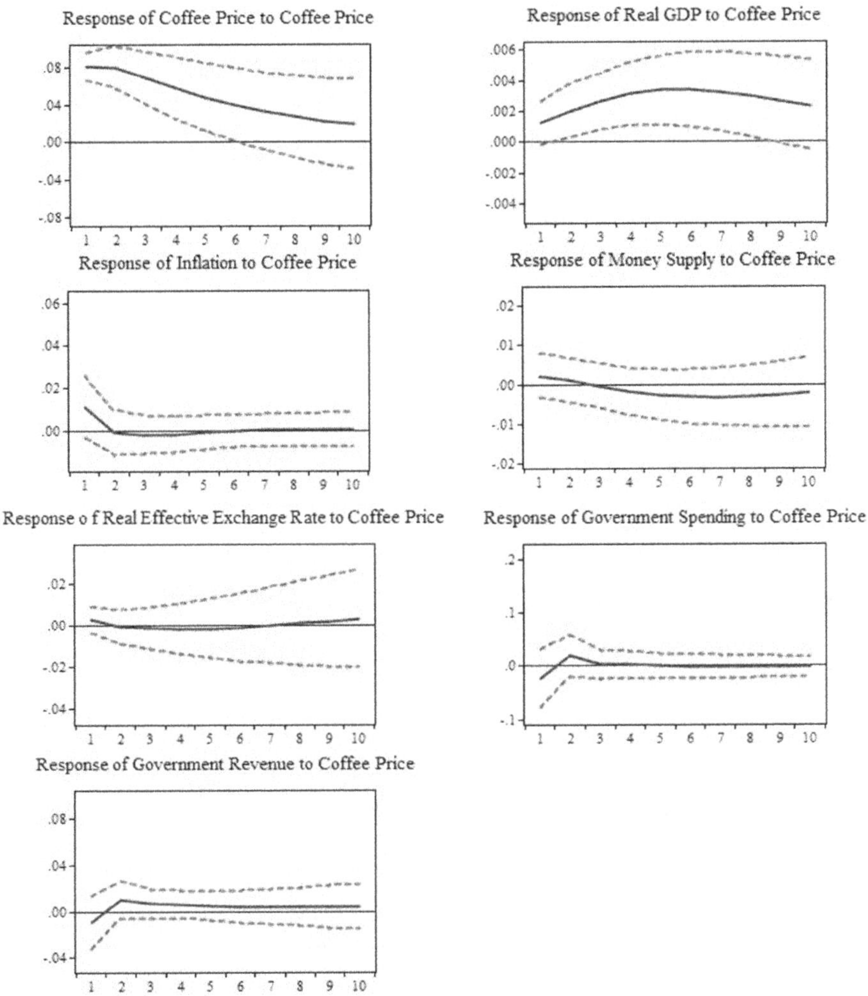

Figure 2.1 Impulse response functions to one standard deviation coffee price shocks

currency to appreciate substantially. Finally, coffee price shock also leads to an increment on government spending and government revenue, insignificant though, after the second quarter which is in conformity with the results of Medina (2016) and McGregor (2017).

5. Robustness Checks

VAR is a stochastic process which is mainly dependent of (and estimated as a function of) the true distribution of every dependent variable in the system.

While estimating VAR for mostly endogenous variables such as Ethiopian GDP and fully exogenous variables like the coffee price, the estimation may get overly biased, meaning it may not use the full information, especially, available for the exogenous variable. Hence, in this robustness checks section, we re-estimate our baseline model with a Bayesian VAR methodology. As it can be seen easily from Figure 2.2, the results are found to be almost the same with those estimated from the VAR methodology.

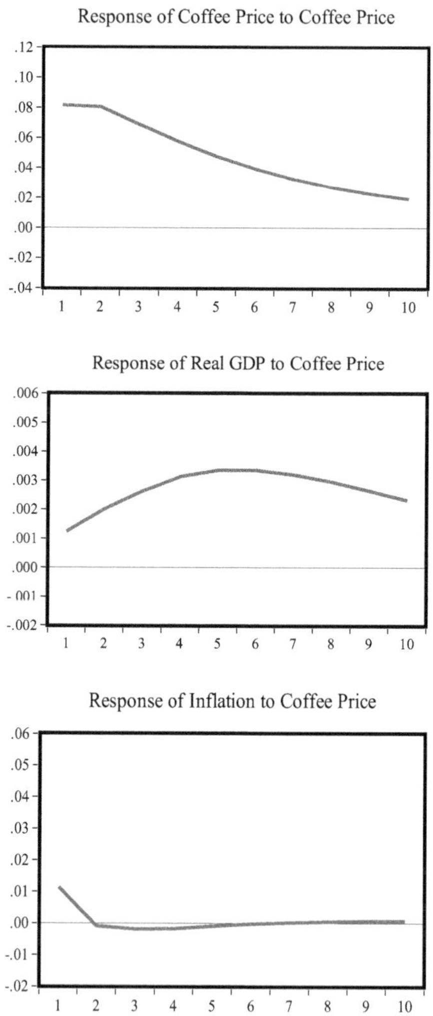

Figure 2.2 Impulse response functions to one standard deviation coffee price shocks using Bayesian VAR

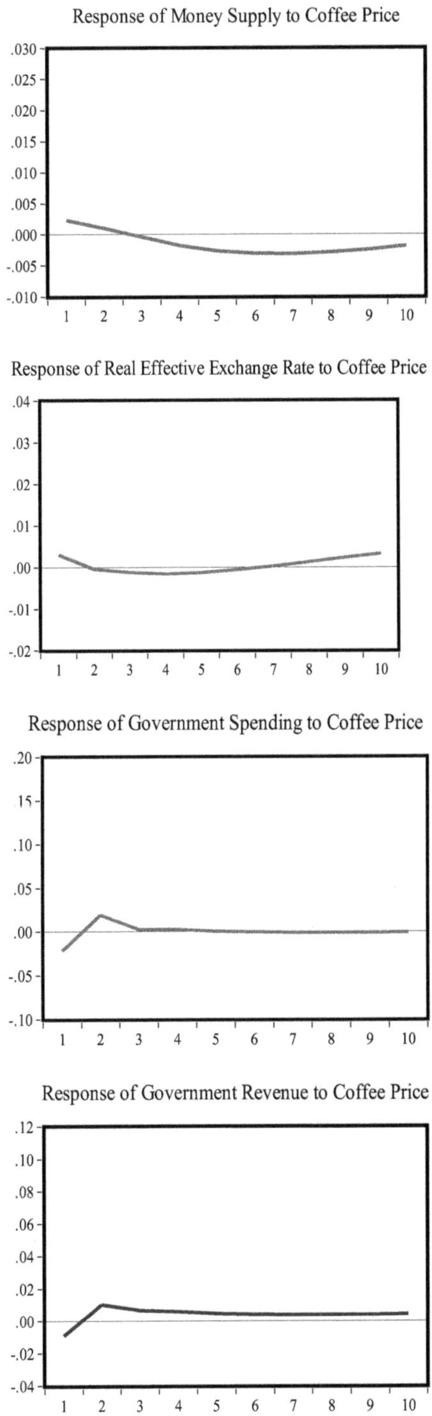

Figure 2.2 (Continued)

6. Conclusion

This study investigates the effect of coffee price shock in a small open economy, namely Ethiopia over the sample period 2001Q1–2018Q4. To address this objective, Cholesky identification scheme is employed in a VAR model.

The results exhibit that coffee price shock is not persistent and tapers off after the first sixth quarters. Output responds positively and significantly from the second quarter up to the ninth quarter in response to coffee price shock. One standard deviation shock in coffee price causes about 0.4 per cent increase in output. Inflation also rises insignificantly in response to the coffee price shock. Money supply and exchange rate increases on impact before it decreases in response to the coffee price shock. Coffee price shock also leads to an insignificant rise on government spending and government revenue after the second quarter.

These results can be justified standing from the economic theories. To begin with, a positive shock to commodity price shock boosts exports and raises the currency reserves which can play a pivotal role in expanding the production of goods and services (Bjornland, 2000). In return in an economy which heavily relays on exportable commodities, a positive shock to commodity price results in an increase in inflation (Arango *et al.*, 2014). As a result of increased level of output, the individual's purchasing power increases, demanding goods and services, this leads domestic currency to be dearer relative to foreign currency. This, in turn, causes the domestic currency to appreciate (Bangara and Dunne, 2018). Due to an increased production, the government revenue, as well as government expenditure, increases substantially even if the positive commodity price shock doesn't persist Boccara, 1994).

This study can have paramount importance for policy makers in designing appropriate response strategies when an economy faces volatility in price of its major export commodity in times of economic shocks. Since data is only available for a relatively short sample period, which is one of the limitations of our study. Therefore, we did not examine the effects of positive and negative coffee price shocks, because it would have vanished the degrees of freedom in our estimation. As more data become available over time, however, asymmetric transmission of coffee price shocks will be examined in our future research effort.

Note

1 Eviews 10 statistical software is used to obtain the results.

References

Addison, T., and Ghoshray, A. (2013). Agricultural commodity price shocks and their effect on growth in Sub-Saharan Africa (WIDER Working Paper No. 098). Retrieved from www.wider.unu.edu/publication/agricultural-commodity-price-shocks-and-their-effect-growth-sub-saharan-africa

Amu, B., Osabuohien, E., Alege, P., and Ejemeyovwi, J. O. (2021). Impact of real shocks on business cycles in selected sub-Saharan African countries. *Cogent Business and Management*, 8(1), 1875548. http://doi.org/10.1080/23311975.2021.1875548

Andersson, C., Bezabih, M., and Mannberg, A. (2016). The Ethiopian commodity exchange and spatial price dispersion. *Environment for Development, Discussion Paper Series*, EfD DP 16–02, January, 34p. https://media.rff.org/documents/EfD-DP-16-02.pdf

Arango, L. E., Chavarro, X., and González, E. (2014). Commodity price shocks and inflation within optimal monetary policy framework: The case of Colombia (Banco de la República). Retrieved from www.cemla.org/red/cbrn-xix-papers/cbrn-xix-papers-00016.pdf

Asfaw, A. A. (2017). The effect of coffee price shock on school dropout: New evidence from the 2008 global financial crisis. *Applied Economic Letters*, 25(7), 482–486.

Atsushi, S., and Takayuki, T. (2017). Effects of commodity price shocks on inflation: A cross-country analysis (CAMA Working Papers No. 2017–45). Retrieved from https://cama.crawford.anu.edu.au/sites/default/files/publication/cama_crawford_anu_edu_au/2017-07/45_2017_sekine_tsuruga.pdf

Bangara, B. C., and Dunne, P. J. (2018). Macroeconomic effects of commodity price shocks in a low-income economy: The case of tobacco in Malawi. *South African Journal of Economics*, 86(1), 53–75.

Bjornland, H. C. (2000). The dynamic effects of aggregate demand, supply and oil price shocks: A comparative study. *The Manchester School*, 68(5), 578–607.

Blanchard, O., and Perotti, R. (2002). An empirical characterization of the dynamic effects of changes in government spending and taxes on output. *The Quarterly Journal of Economics*, 117(4), 1329–1368.

Boccara, B. (1994). Why higher fiscal spending persists when a boom in primary commodities ends (Policy Research Working Paper No. 1295). Retrieved from https://ideas.repec.org/p/wbk/wbrwps/1295.html

Christiano, L. J., Eichenbaum, M., and Evans, C. I. (2005). Nominal rigidities and the dynamic effects of a shock to monetary policy. *Journal of Political Economy*, 113(1), 1–45.

CTA (Coffee and Tea Authority) (2002). *Annual Report: Planning and Programming Department.* CTA, Addis Ababa.

Fatas, A., and Mihov, I. (2001). The effects of fiscal policy on consumption and employment: Theory and evidence (Discussion Paper 2760). CEPR, London.

Gelos, G., and Ustyugova, Y. (2017). Inflation responses to commodity price shocks – How and why do countries differ? *Journal of International Money and Finance*, 72(C), 28–47.

Gemech, F., and Struthers, J. (2007). Coffee price volatility in Ethiopia: Effects of market reform programmes. *Journal of International Development*, 19(8), 1131–1142.

Grimes, A., and Hyland, S. (2013). Passing the buck: Impacts of commodity price shocks on local outcomes (Motu Working Paper No. 13–10). Retrieved from https://motu.nz/our-work/wellbeing-and-macroeconomics/economic-performance/passing-the-buck-impacts-of-commodity-price-shocks-on-local-outcomes/

IMF (2007). *World Economic Outlook*. International Monetary Fund, Washington, DC.

International Coffee Organization (2019). International Coffee Organization, London.

John, M. F., and Baoying, L. (2011). The interdependence of coffee spot and futures markets (INFER Working Papers No. 2011:1). Retrieved from https://ideas.repec.org/p/inf/wpaper/2011.1.html

McGregor, T. (2017). Commodity price shocks, growth and structural transformation in low-income countries. *The Quarterly Review of Economics and Finance*, 65, 285–303.

Medina, L. (2010). The dynamic effects of commodity prices on fiscal performance in Latin America (IMF Working Paper No. 10/192). Retrieved from www.imf.org/en/Publications/WP/Issues/2016/12/31/The-Dynamic-Effects-of-Commodity-Prices-on-Fiscal-Performance-in-Latin-America-24159

Medina, L. (2016). The effects of commodity price shocks on fiscal aggregates in Latin America. *IMF Economic Review*, 64(3), 502–525.

Mohan, S., Gemech, F., Reeves, A., and Struthers, F. (2016). The welfare effects of coffee price volatility for Ethiopian coffee producers. *Qualitative Research in Financial Markets*, 8(4), 288–304.

Noha, E., Amon, S., and Tricia, J. (2015). Commodity price changes and economic growth in developing countries (MPRA Paper No. 68678). Retrieved from https://mpra.ub.uni-muenchen.de/68678/1/MPRA_paper_68678.pdf

Nuru, N.Y., and Gereziher, H.Y. (2020). The effect of commodity price shock on the Ethiopian economy. *Journal of Economic and Administrative Sciences*, ahead-of-print (ahead-of-print). https://doi.org/10.1108/JEAS-06-2020-0087

Osabohien, R., Ufua, D., Moses, C. L., and Osabuohien, E. (2020). Accountability in agricultural governance and food security in Nigeria. *Brazilian Journal of Food Technology*, 23, e2019054. https://doi.org/10.1590/1981-6723.08919

Oxfam (2002). *Mugged: Poverty in Your Coffee Cup*. Boston, MA: Oxfam International.

Pedersen, M. (2019). The impact of commodity price shocks in a copper-rich economy: The case of Chile. *Empirical Economics*, 57, 1291–1318.

Roch, F. (2019). The adjustment to commodity price shocks. *Journal of Applied Economics*, 22(1), 437–467.

Statista (2019). *The Statistics Portal for Market Data, Market Research and Market Studies*, Hamburg. https://www.statista.com/

USDA (2012). *Coffee: World Market and Trade*. Foreign agricultural service/USDA office of global analysis, circular series.

Vallejo, P. L. (2017). Assessing the effect of commodity price shocks in the macroeconomic performance and fiscal outcomes in Latin America countries. *Cuestiones Económicas*, 27(2:2), 143–170.

Worako, T. K., van Schalkwyk, H. D., Alemu, Z. G., and Ayele, G. (2008). Producer price and price transmission in a deregulated Ethiopian coffee market. *Agrekon*, 47(4), 492–508.

3 Exchange Rate Variability and Palm Oil Export in West Africa

Evidence from Nigeria

Olanrewaju Omosehin and Evans Osabuohien

Introduction

Nigeria produces more palm oil than any other African countries, but still is the sixth-largest exporter in Africa (PwC Analysis-USDA, 2019). According to Tokgoz *et al.* (2020), Nigeria post-independence agricultural yield losses is on the increase and as a result of this, losses incurred by Nigeria yearly on international trade can be estimated at US$10 billion from cash crops, including palm oil. Exchange rate has been defined as the developmental strategy whereby a country's legal tender is trade-offs with another country's legal tender. There exist notions that exchange rate leverage on import and export impact on products traded cannot be over-emphasized (Lee & Masih, 2018). Glut in the world palm oil market as a result of adequate climatic conditions and improved seed, variety has further led to decline in palm oil export (PwC-USDA analysis, 2019). The effect of variation in exchange rate as against export in palm oil cannot be shed off. Prior to the early discovery of "black Gold" called crude oil, the agricultural sector was the main determinant of the nation's economy. The main crops exported include palm oil, cocoa, groundnut, cotton and rubber (Manasseh *et al.*, 2019)

Devaluating Naira (Nigeria domestic currency) as a means of attracting more incentives to agricultural trade flows in Nigeria has not had significant effect on exchange rate and export in agriculture (Etta *et al.*, 2011). Volatility in exchange rate has significant effect through probability costs and non-significant effect on the end-point and aggregate output (Cote, 1994). Exchange rate is an aggregate variable/elastic that is prone to fluctuations and spikes whose variation affect the outcome or result of the other total output of the economy (Hashim & Zarma, 1996). Pilbeam (2005) posit real exchange rate is a germane factor that takes an integral part in ensuring the free flow of the long-run success of export trade earnings to any nation

Adubi and Okunmadewa (1999) posit that unforeseen or inevitable occurrence associated with international trade tends to negatively affect export in Nigeria. Decision makers and academics has hammered more on vital sector called "export sector" of the economy acting a push to ensuring development of an economy and economic growth. This is true for emerging market and developing economy

DOI: 10.4324/9781003208358-5

(Kazeem & Ibrahim, 2015). Indication flow from macroeconomic variables can define decision making policies geared towards promotion of non-export sector (Onwe, 2015). Nigeria policy changes on Structural Adjustment Programme (SAP) has plunged the nations' exchange rate (ER) into incessant denigrate both in the past and present (Osabuohien, 2016). Moreover, instability in exchange rate demoralises production in agriculture and its exports thus leading to spikes in input and export income (Cho *et al.*, 2002; Tiku & Bullem, 2015). It is on this note that the study seeks to investigate the causal relationship between exchange rate variability and palm oil export having in mind this research question: how does exchange rate variability affect palm oil export in Nigeria? Several empirical studies have been carried out by researchers which centred on exchange rate variability/volatility and trades, exchange rate and non-oil export products such as palm oil (Bahmani-Oskooee & Kovyryalova, 2008; Zakaria, 2013; Shin *et al.*, 2014; Lawrence & Mohammed, 2015; Oluyemi & Isaac, 2017; Uremadu *et al.*, 2017; Bostan & Firtescu, 2018; Mordecki & Miranda, 2018; Uduakobong & Williams, 2018).

Furthermore, effect of real exchange rate wield on export in agriculture is overwhelming and therefore points that exchange rate volatility influence on Nigeria trade is negative (Kyle & Swinnen, 1994; Riedel & Donges, 1977; Kwanshie, 1997; Adubi & Okunmadewa, 2000). It is, however, similar and different from the work of Lee and Masih (2018) who collected their evidence from Malaysia, using the Autoregressive Distributed Lag Model (ARDL) and Non-autoregressive Distributed Lag Model (NARDL) as against this study, and this study critically examines impact of exchange rate variations on palm oil export in Nigeria, adopting Johansen Cointegration Model Approach.

Methodology

Theoretical explanation backing of this study can be traced to Marshall-Lener Theory (MLT) and the J-curve effect (JC), respectively. MLT and JC may help in concluding the long-term and short-term impacts of the denigrate of a country's legal tender and this also helps in looking up the effect of countries' exchange rate variability on terms of trade (Lee & Masih, 2019).

Sources of Data

Annual time series data spanning from 1980 to 2018 on exchange rate (ER) and palm oil export (POE), welfare (WELF), palm oil price (POP) and inflation (INF) for this study were sourced from Central Bank of Nigeria (CBN) Statistical Bulletin Various Issues (2019), United State Department of Agriculture (USDA, 2019)

Analytical Procedure and Model Specification

Augmented Dickey–Fuller and Cointegration Technique

Johansen Cointegration model approach was used for this study. Cointegration analysis provides a framework that permits the application of non-stationary data in such a way that the spurious regression phenomenon is circumvented. Two or more variables are cointegrated if there is presence of long-run equilibrium relationship(s) between each other. First, to justify the appropriateness of the model, a unit root test was carried out using augmented Dickey–Fuller test statistics which operates on the basis of assumption of first order $I(1)$ stationarity for the variables (Etta *et al.*, 2011; Omosehin *et al.*, 2022).

The ADF procedure was expressed as:

$$\Delta Yt = \beta 1 + \beta 2t + \delta Yt - 1 + \mu t \tag{3.1}$$

where

$\beta 1$ = Constant
$\beta 2t$ = Estimate on time trend
μt = White noise error
$Yt - 1$ = Lag order of autoregressive process
t = Normal "t" test.

The null hypothesis $\delta = 0$, was carried out in the unit root test against alternate hypothesis $\delta \neq 0$.

T-statistics was compared to the relevant critical value for the augmented Dickey–Fuller test. If the absolute test statistic (ADF) is less than the (larger negative) critical value at 5% significant level, then the null hypothesis of $\delta = 0$ is accepted and no unit root is present, but if higher, we reject the null hypothesis $\delta \neq 0$ (Phillips & Perron, 1988; Osabuohien *et al.*, 2018).

Johansen Cointegration Approach

This was used in investigating long run relationship between exchange rate and palm oil export. Following the work of Gujarati and Porter (2009), Bobola *et al.* (2015) and Omosehin *et al.* (2021), the Johansen model was generally expressed as:

$$X = \mu + a1Xt - 1 + a2Xt - 2 + \cdots\cdots\cdots\cdots apXt - p + Et$$

$$= \mu + \sum p\, i = 1 + aiXt - 1 + Et \tag{3.2}$$

where

X = px1 vector of prices
$Xt - 1$ = px1 vector of the ith lagged values of xi
μ = px1 vector of constraints
p = lag length
Et = px1 vector of identically and independently distributed error terms with zero mean and contemporaneous covariance matrix, $E(Et\,Et) = \Omega$.

Error Correction Model

The error correction model (ECM) was used to investigate the short-run dynamics with the long-run equilibrium without losing long-run information (Pesaran *et al.*, 2001), and also to check whether there is transmission of shock between the two series (ER and POE).

The general representation of ECM can be expressed as:

$$\Delta yt = \beta 0 + \beta 1 \Delta xt + \gamma \left(xt - 1 - yt - 1 \right) + \mu t \tag{3.3}$$

where

Δyt: First difference of $Y\left(yt - yt - 1\right)$
Δxt: First difference of $X\left(xt - xt1\right)$
yt: Endogenous variable
xt: Exogenous variable
μt: Error term.

Variance Decomposition and Impulse Response Function Analysis

Variance decomposition approach and impulse response function (IRF) were both employed in ascertaining the variations that existed in the short run, medium term and long run, respectively, between exchange rate and palm oil export.

Pairwise Granger Causality

Granger causality test was used to verify the causality effect, direction of exchange rate on palm oil export and vice versa since evidence of series causation and exogeneity was observed. Pairwise Granger causality test examines the hypothesis of casual effect of X (ER) on Y (POE). Following Bobola *et al.* (2015), and incorporating it into ER and POE, the representation goes thus:

$$\Delta Yt = \beta 0 + \beta 1 Y(t-1) + \beta 2 Y(t-1) + \Sigma\_(k=1)\wedge m$$
$$\delta\, k \Delta X(t-k) + \Sigma\_(k=1)\wedge n\alpha\, h \Delta Y(t-h) + \mu t \tag{3.4}$$

where:

X represent Exchange rate (ER)
Y represents Palm oil export (POE)
m and n represent the number of lags determined by Akaike Information Criterion.

Rejection of the null hypothesis (by a suitable F-test) that $\alpha_h = 0$ for $h = 1, 2, \ldots n$ and $\beta = 0$ indicated that POE is Granger-caused by ER.

Results and Discussion

Unit Root Test Estimation

The result of the unit root test on the variables in question is shown in Table 3.1

Based on the ADF test statistics, it was observed that all variables were not stationary at level *I*[0] except INF which was stationary at 5% significant level. But when the variables were subjected into first difference *I*[1], all the variables become stationary. Since Johansen approach was stated for ER and POE, it showed that the model is appropriate because Johansen approach operates when all the variables were integrated of the same order.

Results of Johansen Cointegration Estimation

Table 3.2 shows the result of Johansen cointegration test for exchange rate (ER) and palm oil export (POE), with both variables stationary at first difference, *I*(1). The standard test for interpretations is trace statistics. Decision rule is to reject the null hypothesis of no cointegration if the value of the test statistics is greater than the critical value estimate at least 5% level of significance. Here, the results showed at least *I*(1) cointegration equation. It can therefore be deduced that exchange rate and Palm oil export were strongly linked together in the long run. The deduction from this was that both variables have mutual predictors, *all things being equal.* Factors that might be responsible for this are poor infrastructure, outdated technology, inefficient government policies on agriculture products and even the menace of the novel coronavirus (COVID-19) which plunged the nation's economy to a standstill like border closure, restriction to import and export (Asongu *et al.*, 2021) which therefore leads to palm oil price becoming expensive for importers, making palm oil export to become less competitive. The economic implication is that this changes after palm oil producers in terms of investment, price fluctuations, welfare and forcing them to concentrate on the local markets. This assertion is supported by the findings by Lee and Masih (2018).

Table 3.1 Results of Unit Root Test-Based Approach

Variable	*Level I[0]*			*First Difference I[1]*		
	t-statistics	*Prob.*	*Remark*	*t-statistics*	*Prob.*	*Remark*
ER	−1.9703	0.2981	NS	−5.1464	0.0001	S
POE	−2.1323	0.2337	NS	−7.3634	0.0000	S
WELF	0.6450	0.9891	NS	−8.0949	0.0000	S
POP	−0.9337	0.7664	NS	−5.5099	0.0001	S
INF	−3.1285	0.0328	S	−6.3376	0.0000	S

Analysis of Error Correction Model

The error correction model (ECM) was conducted after confirming the presence of long-run relationship in the variable (ER and POE) series. The result of ECM means whether there is transmission of shocks between the two series. From Table 3.3, it was shown that there was one cointegrating equation. In the CointEq1, the coefficients of error correction model, ECM (−1) had a value of −0.00570 and significant at 5% level, indicating the existence of a long-run casual association in the model. This implies that previous years' shocks in the ER are transmitted to POE at slow adjustment rate of about 5.7%, *ceteris paribus*. These findings are consistent with those reported by Prasetyo and Marwanti (2017).

Impulse Response Functions

Figure 3.1 shows response of the series to one standard deviation shock. It revealed the response of ER to shocks over a ten years period. ER decreases sharply between period 1 and period 3 when shocks are applied to itself, but later increase between period 6 and period 8. Again, the response of ER to innovations

Table 3.2 The Summary of the Cointegration Test of Trace for ER and POE Series

Hypothesized No. of Cointegrating Equation	*Eigen Value*	*Trace Statistics*	*0.05 Critical Value*	*P -Value*
None*	0.390413	18.00971	15.49471	0.0205
At most 1	0.065581	2.170562	3.841466	0.1407

Source: The authors'

Note: Trace test indicate 1 cointegrating equation at the 0.05 level.

*Denote rejection of the hypothesis at the 0.05 level

Table 3.3 Results of Error Correction Model Standard Errors in ( ) and t-Statistics in [ ]

Series	*Cointegrating Equation 1*
ER(−1)	1.000000
POE (−1)	−2.886264 (2.51116) [−1.14937]
Constant	4.366950
Error Correction Model:	**D(ER) D(POE)**
CointEq1	−0.057046** 0.013976 (0.02398) (0.02116) [−2.37857] [0.066045]

Source: The authors'

Note: Level of significance is at ** 5%

or shocks in POE revealed a negative decrease between the period 1 and period 8, and later goes upward with positive between period 8 and period 10. This suggests that an increase in exchange rate (ER) will affect palm oil export (POE) adversely, thereby affecting Palm oil producers. This result is in line with the findings of Carmen and Nicolae (2011) in their study on the effect of exchange rate on export in Romania (2003Q3–2011Q1) period that the impulse-response function analysis revealed exchange rate shock has significant effect on export. They attributed it to higher price competitiveness of Romanian products. Also, Ogbonna (2012) on Structural Adjustment Programme (SAP) in Nigeria: An Empirical Assessment opined that effect of an exchange rate shock on trade balance (palm oil inclusive) is inverse and inconsequential. Oluyemi and Isaac (2017) in their study asserted that exchange rate responds positively to import but negatively to exports. This result is also similar to the findings of Lee and Masih (2018) who stated that a shock in exchange rate will yield a higher impact to other variables in the system like Palm oil export.

Analysis of Variance Decomposition

Table 3.4 depicts the vector autoregression's variance decomposition of the variables employed in the study. In the case of variance decomposition on ER period, ER accounts for about 100%, 96% and 78% of the variation in itself in the short run, medium term and long run, respectively. POE explains about 4% variation in ER in the medium term and 22% in the long run. Similarly, the responses of POE to the variation of ER in the medium and long run were nearly 20% and 18%, respectively. POE accounts for about 99%, 80% and 82% of the variation in itself in the short run, medium term and long run, respectively. A relatively significant proportion of the variation in ER is being accounted for by POE in the periods of decomposition, but a smaller proportion of variation was accounted for by POE to ER. This implies that exchange rate plays a significant role in determining the export of palm oil. The result from this study disagrees with the findings of Ogbonna (2012) who asserted that trade balance positions play a significant role in determining exchange rate dynamics. This also strengthens the error correction model for this study that shocks in exchange rate is transmitted to palm oil export at an adjustment rate of about 5.7% of *ceteris paribus*.

Pairwise Granger Causality Test (ER and POE)

According to Table 3.5, the causal relationship between ER and POE was depicted using pairwise Granger causality test. In this study, the evidence of series causation and exogeneity was observed, in which only one pair link displayed unidirectional Granger causality. The series link is: ER → POE. This implied that ER Granger-caused POE at 5% significant level (0.0205). One can deduce that ER has strong influence on POE, and as well determine the behaviour of POE over the years. This could be as a results of inefficient government regularization policies throughout the periods beneath study and furthermore, spikes evolving from

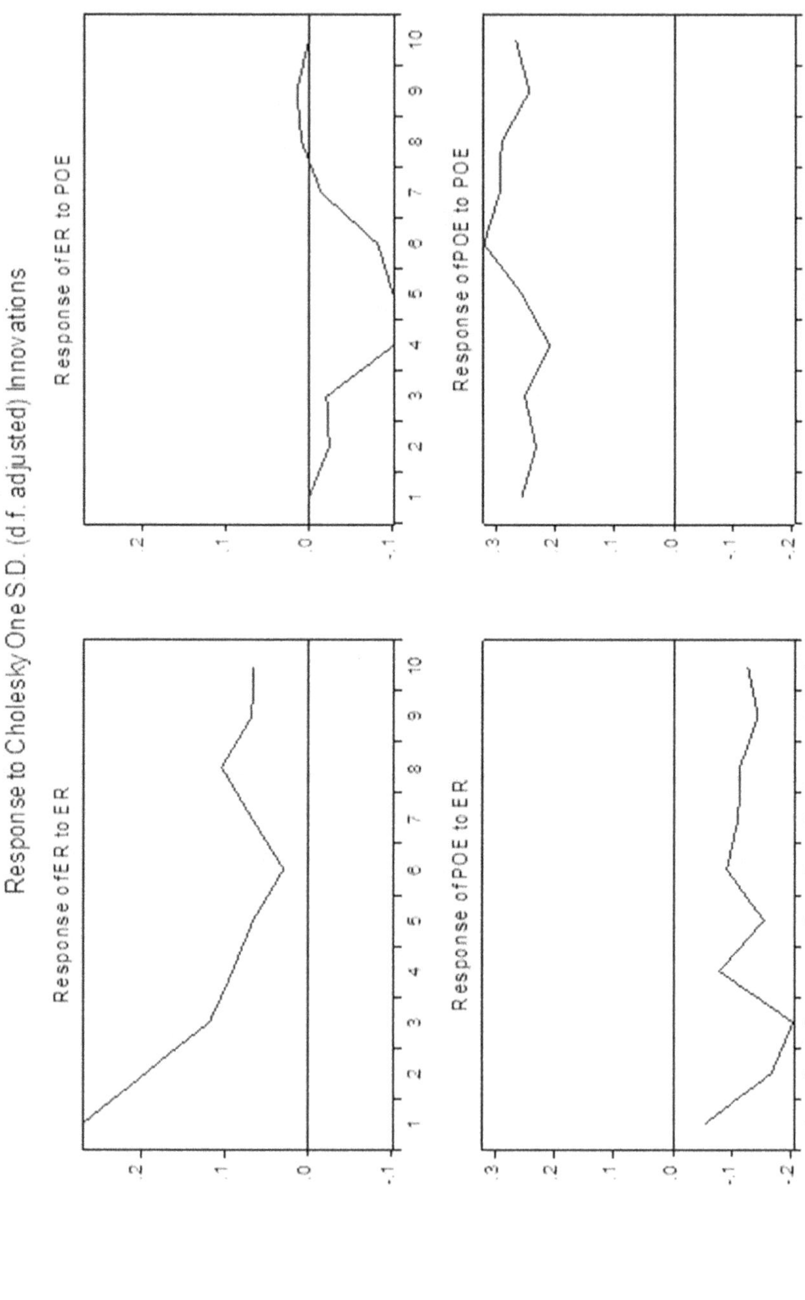

Figure 3.1 Results of impulse response factors of ER and POE

Table 3.4 Results of Variance Decomposition

VD on ER:			
Period	*S.E.*	*ER*	*POE*
1	0.293314	100.0000	0.000000
2	0.414242	99.94787	0.052133
3	0.474868	99.65327	0.346734
4	0.520875	98.33856	1.661440
5	0.558729	96.18200	3.818001
6	0.589764	93.26673	6.733265
7	0.617446	89.77426	10.22574
8	0.643670	85.91778	14.08222
9	0.669062	81.91747	18.08253
10	0.693969	77.92693	22.07307
V.D. of POE:			
Period	*S.E.*	*ER*	*POE*
1	0.258792	0.000343	99.99966
2	0.324348	8.715997	91.28400
3	0.404449	17.96248	82.03752
4	0.449889	19.56535	80.43465
5	0.482907	19.85020	80.14980
6	0.505746	19.78195	80.21805
7	0.522717	19.41138	80.58862
8	0.535403	18.92245	81.07755
9	0.545434	18.42292	81.57708
10	0.553654	17.95246	82.04754
Cholesky Ordering: ER POE			

Source: The authors'

Table 3.5 Results of Pairwise Granger Causality Test

Null Hypothesis	*Observation*	*F-Statistics*	*P-Value*
POE does not Granger-cause ER	32	0.81160	0.5899
ER Granger-cause POE	32	3.31545	0.0205**

Source: The authors'

** indicates significance at 5%

fastened charge per unit regime to a pegged regime and eventually to numerous variants of floating regime, with the introduction of the Structural Adjustment Programme (SAP), second-tier interchange market that was expected to introduce a mechanism for exchange rate determination and allocation so as to confirm short-run stability and semi-permanent balance of payments equilibrium in costs of marketable merchandise like palm oil.

Conclusion

The study was designed to investigate causal relationship between exchange rate variability and palm oil export in Nigeria from 1980 to 2018. Secondary data on palm oil export, exchange rate, inflation rate and gross domestic product, from 1980 to 2018, were obtained from databases of U.S. Department of Agriculture (USDA) and Central Bank of Nigeria Annual Statement (Various Issues), and analysed using Johansen Cointegration Approach. The results of Johansen cointegration test revealed that exchange rate and palm oil export were strongly linked together in the long run therefore indicating long-run relationship between ER and POE. The error correction model reveals that shock in ER was transmitted to POE at a slow adjustment rate of about 5.7% of *ceteris paribus*. The variance decomposition and impulse response function analysis on exchange rate and palm oil export revealed that exchange rate have significant effect on palm oil export thereby affecting producer's price. The result of Granger causality test implies that an increase in ER forces decrease in POP.

From the foregoing, the followings recommendations were made; government at state and federal levels should take into consideration Africa Continental Free Trade Agreement (AfCFTA) and ECOWAS Trade Liberalisation Scheme (ETLS) in order to serve as alternative pathway channel for palm oil export from Nigeria to other African countries' market so as to curb influence of exchange rate on palm oil export since those channels are devoid of exchange rate. Also, government can also strengthen the palm oil industry by embarking on large plantation and installation of extraction machines and mills to boost production of palm oil to promote export. Exchange rate can be stabilised to favour producer's price by giving export subsidies on inputs such as palm kernel seedlings, fertilizers to palm oil producers in order to aid speedy cultivation, harvesting and appreciable exports since there are so general demand for the product, and also as feedstock in bio-fuels.

Future research can look at the government policies causing strong influence of exchange rate (ER) on palm oil export (POE) and also which variety(s) of palm oil is creating the gap that ER has on POE. Furthermore, the aspect of asymmetric price spillovers which are more likely to occur for palm oil traded in different spatial markets can still be worked on while still making reference to this study.

References

Adubi, A. A., & Okumadewa, F. (1999). Price. Exchange Rate Volatility and Nigeria's Agricultural Trade Flows: A Dynamic Analysis, *African Economic Research Consortium Research Paper*, (87).

Adubi, A. A. & Okunmadewa, F. (2000). The Impact of exchange rate volatility on export growth: Some theoretical consideration and empirical results. *Journal of Policy Modeling*, 9, 205–210.

Asongu, S. A., Diop, S. & Nnanna, J. (2021). The geography of the effectiveness and consequences of COVID-19 measures: Global evidence. *Journal of Public Affairs*, 21, e2483. https://doi.org/10.1002/pa.2483

Bahmani-Oskooee, M. & Kovyryalova, M. (2008). Impact of exchange rate uncertainty on trade flows: Evidence from community trade between the United States and the US. *World Economy*, 31(8), 1097–1128.

Bobola, O. M., Mafimisebi, T. E. & Ikuemonisan, E. S. (2015). Price fluctuations, linkages and causality in the Nigerian beef market. *Journal of Fisheries and Livestock Production*, 3(2), 1–9. http://doi.org/10.4172/2332-2608.1000135

Bostan, I. & Firtescu, B. N. (2018). Exchange rate effects on international commercial trade competitiveness. *Journal of Risk and Financial Management*, 11(2), 19–28.

Carmen, S. & Nicolae, G. (2011). The relationship between exchange rate and exports in Romania using a vector autoregressive model. *Annales Universitatis Apulensis Series Oeconomica, Faculty of Sciences*, "1 Decembrie 1918" University, Alba Iulia, 2(13), 1–29. https://ideas.repec.org/a/alu/journl/v2y2011i13p29.html

Cho, G., Sheldon, I. M. & McCorriston, S. (2002). Exchange rate uncertainty and agricultural trade. *American Journal of Agricultural Economics*, 84(4), 931–942.

Cote, A. (1994). Exchange rate volatility and trade – A survey (No.1994-5). Bank of Canada, Working Paper No. 94–95.

Etta, B. E., Akpan, O. D. & Etim, R. S. (2011). Effect of price and exchange rate fluctuations on Agricultural exports in Nigeria. *International Journal of Economic Development Research and Investment*, 2(1), 1–10.

Gujarati, D. N. & Porter, D. C. (2009). *Basic econometrics*, 5th ed. New York: McGraw hill/ Irwin.

Hashim, I. A. & Zarma, A. B. (1996). The impact of parallel market on the stability of exchange rate: Evidence from Nigeria. *NDIC Quarterly*, 7(2).

Kazeem, I. O. & Ibrahim, R. D. (2015, December). Assessing the impact of exchange rate volatility on the Nigerian non-oil export performance. *Journal Asian Development Studies*, 4(4).

Kwanshie, M. (1997). *The Nigerian economy: Response of agriculture to adjustment policies*. Research Report African Economic Research Consortium, Nairobi Kenya.

Kyle, N. & Swinnen, T. (1994). The theory of contested markets and the degree of tradeness of agricultural commodities: An empirical test in Zaire. *Journal of African Economics*, 3(1), 93–113.

Lawrence, E. I. & Mohammed, I. (2015). Macroeconomic determinants of economic growth in Nigeria: A co-integration approach. *International Journal of Academic Research in Economics and Management Sciences*, 4(1). http://doi.org/10.6007/IJAREMS/V4-I1/1485

Lee, K. W. & Masih, M. (2018). Investigating the causal relationship between exchange rate variability and palm oil export: Evidence from Malaysia based on ARDL and Nonlinear ARDL approaches. *MPRA Paper No. 91801*, posted 2 February 2019 21:03 UTC. [Online]. Available at https://mpra.ub.uni-muenchen.de/91801/

Manasseh, O. C., Abada, F. C., Ogbuabor, J. E., Okoro, O. E. U., Egele, A. E. & Ozuzu, K. C. (2019). Oil price fluctuation, oil revenue and well-being in Nigeria. *International Journal of Energy Economics and Policy*, 9(1), 346–355. ISSN: 2146–4553. http://doi.org/10.32479/ijeep.5943 [online]. Available at www.econjournals.com

Mordecki, G. & Miranda, R. (2018). Real exchange rate volatility and exports: A study for four selected commodity exporting countries. *Panoeconomicus*, 66(4), 1–28.

Obadan, M. I. (2006). Overview of exchange rate management in Nigeria from 1986 to date. *CBN Bullion*, 30(3), 1–8.

Ogbonna, C. B. (2012). Structural Adjustment Program (SAP) in Nigeria: An empirical assessment. *Journal of Banking*, 6(1), 19–40. ISSN 1597–2569

Oluyemi, O. & Isaac, E. D. (2017). The effect of exchange rate on imports and exports in Nigeria from January 1996 to June 2015. *International Journal of Economics and Business Management*, 3(3), 23–35. Available at https://mpra.ub.uni-muenchen.de/id/eprint/91801

Omosehin, O., Ekundayo, B., Aturamu, O., & Olutumise, A. (2021). Price variation and transmission in beans consuming market of Southwest, Nigeria. *Jurnal Perspektif Pembiayaan dan Pembangunan Daerah*, 8(6), 609-618.

Omosehin, O., Oseni, J., Olutumise, A. & Osabuohien, E. (2022). Palm oil price fluctuations and welfare in Nigeria. In Osabuohien, E., Odularu, G., Ufua, D. and Osabohien, R. (Eds.) *COVID-19 in the African Continent*. Bingley: Emerald Publishing Limited, pp. 169–182. https://doi.org/10.1108/978-1-80117-686-620221014

Onwe, B. U. (2015). Implications of exchange rate variability on oil exports trade performance in Nigeria. *Global Advanced Research Journal of Management and Business Studies*, 4(11), 461–468. ISSN: 2315–5086. Available at http://garj.org/garjmbs/index.html

Osabuohien, E. (2016, June 20). Economy without buffer must experience shocks. *Daily Times*, p. B8.

Osabuohien, E., Obiekwe, E., Urhie, E. & Osabohien, R. (2018). Inflation rate, exchange rate volatility and exchange rate pass through interactions: The Nigerian experience. *Journal of Applied Economic Sciences, Volume XIII, and Spring*, 2(56), 574–585.

Pesaran, M. H., Shin, Y. & Smith, R. J. (2001). Bounds testing approaches to the analysis of level relationships. *Journal of Applied Econometrics*, 16(3), 289–326.

Phillips, P. C., & Perron, P. (1988). Testing for a unit root in time series regression. *Biometrika*, 75(2), 335–346.

Pilbeam, K. (2005). Theories of exchange rate determination. In *Finance and Financial Markets*. London: Palgrave, pp. 300–333.

Prasetyo, A., & Marwanti, S. (2017). The influence of exchange rate on CPO exports of Indonesia. *Jurnal Ekonomi Pembangunan: Kajian Masalah Ekonomi dan Pembangunan*, 18(2), 159–174.

PwC Analysis USDA. (2019). *X-raying the Nigerian Palm Oil Sector*. Available at www.pwc.com/ng

Riedel, J. & Donges, C (1977). The Expansion of Manufactured Exports in Developing Countries: An Empirical Assessment of Supply and Demand Issues. *WeltwirtschaftlichesArchir*.

Shin, Y., Yu, B., & Greenwood-Nimmo, M. (2014). Modelling asymmetric cointegration and dynamic multipliers in a nonlinear ARDL framework. In *Festschrift in Honor of Peter Schmidt*. New York: Springer, pp. 281–314.

Tiku, N. E., & Bullem, F. A. (2015). Oil palm marketing, Nigeria-lessons to learn from Malaysia experience, opportunities and foreign direct investment in Cross River State. *Journal of Development and Agricultural Economics*, 7(7), 243–252.

Tokgoz, S., Allen, S., Majeed, F., Paris, B., Adeola, O. & Osabuohien, E. (2020). Distortions to agricultural incentives: Evidence from Nigerian value chains. *Review of Development Economics*, 1–19. https://doi.org/10.1111/rode.12664

Uduakobong, S. I., & Williams, A. O. (2018). Non-oil exports, exchange rate volatility and co-integration: Evidence from Nigeria. *International Journal of Economics, Commerce and Management*, 6(6), 567–586.

Uremadu, S. O., Odili, O. & Ariwa, O. F. (2017). The effects of exchange rate variability on trade flows in Nigeria: A cointegration analysis. *Quarterly Journal of Econometrics Research*, 3(2), 12–51. http://doi.org/10.18488/journal.88.2017.32.12.51

Zakaria, Z. (2013). The relationship between export and exchange rate volatility: Empirical evidence based on the trade between Malaysia and its major trading partners. *Journal of Emerging Issues in Economics, Finance and Banking*, 2(2), 668–684.

Section 2

Resilience, Business and Value Chain Development

4 Climatic Shocks, Agricultural Income and Household Expenditure in Uganda

Nicholas Kilimani, John Bosco Nnyanzi and John Bosco Oryema

Introduction and Motivation

Adverse climatic shocks present several welfare impacts especially on households that live off smallholder rain-fed agriculture (Nguyen et al., 2020). Shocks can be idiosyncratic or covariate with the former, affecting individuals or households, for example, illness, injury or unemployment, and the latter correlated across households within a community, for example, floods, droughts, epidemics and pandemics (Doyle, 2020; Günther & Harttgen, 2009; Osabohien et al., 2020). For instance, the COVID-19 pandemic resulted adverse effects on the social welfare of households in many aspects. For example, schools were closed which could potentially exacerbate the pre-existing inequalities in educational outcomes. In terms of employment, the pandemic had a considerable impact on the country's labour force participation. Individuals in households in urban areas and those living in households in the top 40 per cent of the pre-pandemic per capita consumption distribution were the most affected with respect to the job interruptions (UBOS [Uganda Bureau of Statistics], 2021).

In developing economies, where credit markets and safety nets are nearly absent, the effects of covariate shocks can be more severe (Nguyen et al., 2020; Dabla-Norris and Gündüz, 2014). Consequently, households are often compelled to limit their expenditure on only key consumption items. In extreme circumstances, even such critical expenditure is either postponed or suspended (Genoni, 2012). Evidence of the impact of the COVID-19 pandemic on household food consumption shows that 8 per cent and 42 per cent of households, respectively, experienced severe and moderate food insecurity. It is important to note that there were no statistically significant differences in consumption across households in both urban and rural areas. However, households from the bottom 40 per cent of the consumption quintiles experienced moderate to severe food insecurity (UBOS [Uganda Bureau of Statistics], 2021). The literature shows heterogeneity in the types of goods that households must cut back their expenditure on to cope with shocks (Nguyen et al., 2020). Whereas Browning and Crossley (2009) and Hamermesh (1982) argued that luxury goods are often affected, Parker (1999) argued that households might cut back less on goods that have high utility costs of fluctuation. Data on changes in income sources since March 2020 shows that both

DOI: 10.4324/9781003208358-7

households involved in farm and non-farm family activities suffered income losses (i.e. less or no earnings) ranging from 60 per cent to 90 per cent following the COVID-19 outbreak (UBOS [Uganda Bureau of Statistics], 2021).

Studies on the welfare impacts of shocks tend to use data on total household consumption (Dercon et al., 2004; Gerry and Li, 2010; Kurosaki, 2015). However, Cameron and Worswick (2001) argue that using such data to analyse the effect of shocks may suffer from bias in consumption data aggregation due to the different consumption categories involved. It is therefore critical to disaggregate the effects on specific categories of household consumption. This chapter focuses on expenditure on food and education because these are pivotal in determining both short-term and long-term household welfare. Food accounts for a large proportion of total household expenditure especially in the low-income countries (Zezza et al., 2017). Furthermore, limited access to food presents adverse effects on health, wellbeing and labour productivity of households, the effects of which can be inter-generational.

Similarly, any reduction in household expenditure on education has consequences of an intergenerational nature (Kornrich & Furstenberg, 2013). Given the role of human capital in economic development, a lot of public policy focus and has been on investment in education with the view to improve national labour productivity. Households' expenditure on education is key in meeting the educational expenses of their school-going members. The focus of this chapter is vital for identifying some of the key factors in socioeconomic transformation since approximately 80 per cent of the total population lives in rural areas and derives its livelihood from agriculture (GoU [Government of Uganda], 2020).

The chapter contributes to the development economics literature on the impacts of covariate shocks and provides input for public policy not only in Uganda, but other agro-based developing economies. This chapter is among the limited few that provide a linkage between covariate shocks, agricultural income, household food consumption and expenditure on education using a nationally representative dataset. It thus provides insight into the impact of such shocks on key components of household welfare. Second, it analyses the effects of climate induced shocks on household food consumption from an objective standpoint. Third, while many previous studies separately investigate the impact of a single type of shock on household consumption, this chapter quantifies the impact of covariates shocks and identifies whether the existence of non-agricultural livelihood sources can act as a safety net. Forth, it highlights the welfare impacts of the COVID-19 pandemic based on current empirical evidence. This approach provides a basis for creating household resilience against covariate shocks.

Analytical Approach

Impact of Shocks on Agricultural Income

Given the role of agricultural income in determining several welfare indicators, this chapter examines the drivers of agricultural income and expenditure growth in Uganda. In the process, we identify points of policy relevancy by examining the correlation especially between crop income growth and changes in the internal production environment. To capture the impact of changes in the internal production environment on agricultural income growth, data on the area and ownership of the plot being harvested; the use of fertilizer, improved seeds and pesticides and household labour inputs (both hired labour and family labour) are used. Data on changes in market access and extension services is also considered.

Climatic shocks can impact agricultural income directly or indirectly through the way that households produce. For example, a positive climatic shock has a direct impact on crop income by determining production quantities, but it can also impact crop income indirectly through the household's decision to apply inputs as a response to a shock. As a result, when variables that reflect the internal production environment are included in the regression along with those that reflect the external environment, they are likely to capture some of the impact of the external environment on incomes. In this regard, we estimate two models. The first model includes variables on internal production environment, market access, extension services and the external environment.

Note that panel data analysis allows for the inclusion of household fixed effects to control for time-invariancy. However, omitted time-invariant characteristics can potentially influence both the internal production environment and agriculture income. If it occurs, the coefficients of the model's variables cannot be causal due to potential endogeneity. The results of the model provide a correlation between changes in income and changes in the internal production environment. In the second model, only those external environment variables are considered along with household fixed effects. Formally:

$$\ln(y_{it}) = \alpha_0 + \alpha_1 f_{it} + \alpha_2 c_{it} + \alpha_3 s_{it} + u_i + \varepsilon_{it} \quad (1)$$

$$\ln(y_{it}) = \alpha_0 + \alpha_1 s_{it} + u_i + \varepsilon_{it} \quad (2)$$

where $\ln(y_{it})$ is the log of the real value of per capita crop income of household i at time t.f_{it} is a set of variables representing internal production environment such as the average plot area harvested by household i at time t, dummy variables for inputs such as fertilizer, pesticide, seeds/seedlings and hired labour, and the amount of family labour spent on the farm. c_{it} includes community characteristics such as the distance in kilometres of household i to the nearest agro-inputs market at time t and whether extension services were provided to any household in the community. s_{it} is a set of variables capturing the external environment such as the climatic variables (rainfall and temperature) experienced by household i at time t, while household fixed effects are denoted by u_i.

Impact of Climatic Shocks on Household Consumption

The impact of shocks on household food consumption and education expenditure is investigated using three indicators: total household consumption expenditure per capita, household food consumption expenditure per capita and household education expenditure. Since data on total consumption and food consumption are generally available for each household, the ordinary least squares (OLS) method was employed in the estimation. The specifications for total consumption and food consumption are as follows:

$$\Delta \ln\left(E_{it}\right) = \alpha_1 + \beta_1 \Delta y_{it} + \tau_1 c_{it-1} + \pi_1 s_{it} + \eta_1 x_{it-1} + \theta_1 \Delta x_{it} + \Delta \varepsilon_{it} \tag{3}$$

where $\Delta \ln\left(E_{it}\right)$ denotes either the change in the natural logarithm of total consumption per capita or the change in the natural logarithm of food consumption per capita of household i between 2010 and 2012. s_{it} is the vector of climatic shocks as earlier on defined. Δx_{it} is the vector representing changes in household characteristics. x_{it-1} and c_{it-1} denote household characteristics and community characteristics in 2010, respectively.

As a robustness check, we also apply fixed-effects and random-effects models to investigate the impact of climatic shocks on total consumption per capita and food consumption per capita. The Heckman two-step model was also used to investigate the impact of shocks on household education expenditure. In the first step, the likelihood of whether a household spends on education is estimated using a probit model:

$$\begin{aligned} \text{prob}\left(de_{it} = 1\right) = \Phi\big(&\alpha_2 + \beta_2 \Delta y_{it} + \tau_2 c_{it-1} + \pi_2 s_{it} + \eta_2 x_{it-1} \\ &+ \theta_2 \Delta x_{it} + \psi_2 z_{it-1}\big) \end{aligned} \tag{4}$$

where $\Phi(.)$ is the standard normal cumulative distribution function, and de_{it} denotes whether household i spends on education in both years ($de_{it} = 1$, and 0 otherwise). z_i is a vector of selection instrument variables, which are assumed to significantly affect whether the household spends on education but do not affect much the household spends on education. It includes the following variables: dummy variables whether a household has a child of age <15, whether schools are available in the village, and share of old members.

In the second step, the OLS model is applied to estimate the change in the logarithm of education expenditure for the households that spend on education ($de_{it} = 1$). The estimation is:

$$\begin{aligned} \Delta \ln\left(educ\_exp_{it}\right) = \alpha_3 &+ \beta_3 \Delta y_{it} + \tau_3 c_{it-1} + \pi_3 s_{it} + \eta_3 x_{it-1} \\ &+ \theta_3 \Delta x_{it} + \varphi_2 \lambda_i + \Delta \varepsilon_{it}. \end{aligned} \tag{5}$$

where $\Delta \ln\left(educ\_exp_{it}\right)$ denotes the change in the natural logarithm of the education expenditure of household i between 2010 and 2012. The education expenditure includes expenditures on books, school materials, uniforms, school fees, tuition fees, rental fees, school bus and other costs related to schooling. λ is the inverse Mills' ratio.

Data

The main analysis is based on two waves of the Uganda National Panel Survey (UNPS) for 2009/10 and 2011/12, while evidence on the impact of the COVID-19 pandemic draws from the Uganda High-Frequency Phone Survey (HFPS) on COVID-19 by the Uganda Bureau of Statistics. Data on temperature and rainfall were derived from the Climate Research Unit (CRU) of the University of East Anglia (Harris et al., 2014). CRU provides monthly gridded mean temperature and precipitation data with a resolution of 0.5° latitude by 0.5° longitude. This climate dataset was generated by interpolating weather station data from over 4000 stations throughout the world, making it a reliable source of climate data for Sub-Saharan Africa (Zhang et al., 2013). Precipitation and temperature data were linked to the survey data at the village level using global positioning system coordinates collected as part of the UNPS data set containing the rest of the variables. These data were then used to generate measures of temperature and rainfall variability at the village level. The main variables of climate shocks are temperature (°C) and rainfall (mm/month) relative to a 1980–2012 reference period for the two main seasons: March–April–May (MAM) and September–October–November (SON), which coincide with the seasonal migration of the Intertropical Convergence Zone (ITCZ). To generate these variables, mean values for each season across years were taken. These mean values were then transformed into z-scores relative to all other consecutive periods from the same season of the same duration from 1980 to 2012. Here we constructed a negative rainfall dummy=1 when rainfall in the previous season is 1 standard deviation below the long-term average, while a temperature shock was assigned a dummy=1 when the temperature is 2 standard deviations above the long-term average.

Results and Discussion

Summary Statistics

As Table 4.1 provides summary statistics of some of the key variables, it can be seen that on average, there was little change in the use of agricultural inputs. This demonstrates the huge task which any agricultural transformation drive must find ways to address. Evidence already documents the problem of low input use in Uganda in comparison to other countries in the region with data collected using a similar survey instrument (Hill & Mejia-Mantilla, 2017; Sheahan & Barrett, 2017; Binswanger et al., 2014). From a policy perspective, this is one concern that must be addressed if the agricultural sector is to play a vital role of contributing to the economy and overall household welfare.

Impact of Shocks on Crop Income

The results from the empirical estimation of equation 1 are presented in Table 4.1. As expected, per capita crop income is higher among those that utilise their farms

Table 4.1 Key Summary Statistics by Wave

Variable	*2009/10*		*2011/12*	
	Mean	*Std Dev*	*Mean*	*Std Dev*
Weather				
Annual rainfall (mm)	1239.43	181.85	1236.90	182.37
Annual temperature (°C)	21.9	14.8	21.66	14.8
Internal production environment				
Received any visits by extension services past 12 months (1=yes)	0.16	0.37	0.08	0.27
Proportion of planted area harvested (Ha)	0.792	0.871	0.665	0.733
Renter (land)	0.14		0.19	
Use of fertilizer (1=yes)	0.22		0.22	
Use of pesticides (1=yes)	0.16		0.14	
Use of improved seeds (1=yes)	0.80		0.69	
Hired labour used (1=yes)	0.57		0.52	
Household characteristics				
Age of household head	47.62	14.90	48.17	14.90
Sex of HH head (1=male)	0.72	0.45	0.69	0.46
Education of HH head (years)	5.7	4.2	8.67	3.12
Has Non-farm employment (1=yes)	0.03	0.17	0.05	0.21
HH size	5.95	2.85	5.93	2.88
Male adult share	0.42	0.26	0.41	0.27
Dependency ratio	1.86	1.38	1.82	1.48
Community characteristics				
Distance to agricultural market	6.99	8.43	6.92	9.19

Source: Own computations from UNPS 2010/2012

represented by the proportion of planted area, apply more labour, and engage in the use of agricultural productivity enhancing technologies (the use of pesticides, improved seeds). While still limited in use, households that have adopted modern farming practices have had their crop incomes rise than their non-adopting counterparts. Hill and Mejia-Mantilla (2017) in a related study show that the correlation between the use of such modern farm practices and crop income was higher for the households that were in the bottom 40 per cent of the income distribution. Underscoring the role of agricultural transformation as a panacea for both poverty and resilience against the adverse shocks, they show that for poorer households, crop incomes were 22 per cent higher for those that used fertilizer and 14 per cent higher for those that used pesticides.

Households that farmed more land received higher per capita crop income. However, there was a reduction in the proportion of area of land cultivated during the two waves (see Table 4.1). It is important to note that empirical evidence on area of land cultivated in other Africa countries shows that relying on self-reported responses on issues concerning land area results in considerable (and systematic) measurement errors (Hill and Mejia-Mantilla, 2017; Kilic et al., 2014; Carletto et al., 2015). Indeed, there is a reduction in reported area of land cultivated between the two waves perhaps more than the true area of land cultivated. Households that employ more labour (both family and hired labour) also had higher crop incomes, as expected. An increase in the number of days of family labour provided by the household is correlated with higher crop income. Evidence indicates that the amount of household labour reportedly spent on agricultural production has been on the increased substantially since the inception of the survey in 2006. The results indicate that households that utilized hired labour have higher incomes much as the use of hired labour fell between the two waves.

The roles of extension services access and the distance between households and their agricultural input market do not significantly drive income. Overall, while the use of modern agricultural technologies is seen to play a critical role in driving crop incomes in Uganda, evidence suggests limited uptake in the use of the same (Kilimani et al., 2020). Indeed, as Hill and Mejia-Mantilla (2017) in their study spanning six waves of survey found, households that did change production practices had large changes in income. Unfortunately, very few households changed production practices over the study period. The little change in production practices among farmers could be attributed to potentially several factors that trap majority farming households into subsistence agriculture. Several works in the literature on the limited use of modern agricultural technologies despite their benefits point to several factors. For instance, farmers in some cases have found low actual returns to modern technologies (Bold et al., 2015), difficulties in accessing and proper utilization of inputs (the lack of knowledge due to the limited extension services (Kilimani et al., 2020) or the financing needed to make input purchases (Bandiera et al., 2015). More analysis on the limited use of modern production technologies is needed to better understand input adoption and utilization. This is vital as it represents the core of socioeconomic transformation of especially the agro-based developing economies.

The results further highlight the role of the external environment in influencing crop income growth in Uganda. The estimates show that negative rainfall and temperature shocks adversely affect crop income. The results underscore the role of adverse climatic shocks on impacting the overall welfare of farming households given that their livelihoods are more dependent on favourable climate. This is because agriculture sector is rainfed and subsistent in nature. From the findings, income and overall welfare improvement of farming households require concerted efforts geared towards radical transformation of the agricultural sector through the use productivity enhancing technologies, that is, grand scale use of improved seeds, fertilizer, pesticides and irrigation – and diversification and the sector acts as a linkage with other forms of employment. An analysis of data before and during the COVID-19 pandemic shows that the share of farming households increased from 72 per cent in 2019 to 78 per cent in 2020. This underlines the importance of agriculture as a source of livelihoods for a large percentage of the population.

Table 4.2 Drivers of Crop Income in Uganda: Fixed Effects Model

Variables	
internal production environment	
Proportion of planted area harvested (Ha)	0.00734**
	(0.00313)
Land ownership (dummy=1)	0.0682
	(0.126)
Fertiliser use	0.0846
	(0.0523)
Pesticides use	0.148*
	(0.077)
Improved seeds	0.0138*
	(0.0074)
Hired labour	0.248**
Log of days of family labour (weekly)	0.173***
	(0.0343)
community characteristics	
Distance to agricultural inputs market	−0.00613
	(0.0194)
Agricultural extension services use (past 12 months)	0.0600
	(0.0457)
external environment	
Rainfall	−0.007***
	(0.002)
Temperature	−0.046***
	(0.006)
Constant	−2.048
	(1.521)
Observations	2,143
Wald Chi^2 (12)	68.91
Prob. >Chi^2	0.000

Source: Own computations using UNPS 2010/2012

Notes: Dependent variables is log of real per capita crop income. Robust standard errors in parentheses.

*$p < 0.1$
**$p < 0.05$, $p < 0.01$.

The increase in the incidence of farming was most pronounced among those in the top 20 per cent of the pre-COVID-19 house-hold per capita consumption distribution (UBOS, 2021).

Table 4.3 presents results that test the internal and external environmental factors driving crop income that include year fixed effects. The climate variables are robust to this addition and the magnitude of the coefficients remains unchanged.

Table 4.3 Drivers of Agricultural Income (Robustness Checks with Year Fixed Effects)

Variables	
Distance to agricultural market	−0.0251
	(0.0268)
Agricultural extension services use (past 12 months)	0.0188***
	(0.0053)
external environment	
Rainfall	−2.210***
	(0.558)
Temperature	−0.012*
	(0.0068)
Constant	−5.717
	(4.209)
Observations	2,825
Wald Chi^2 (12)	113.84
Prob. > Chi^2	0.000

Source: Own computations using UNPS 2010/2012

Notes: Dependent variables is log of real per capita crop income. Robust standard errors in parentheses.

*p < 0.1
**p < 0.05
***p < 0.01.

The results from Table 4.4 show that climatic shocks have an adverse impact on households' total income (see column 1, row 2 of Table 4.4). Basically, a negative rainfall results in a reduction in total income, with the effect being more pronounced on agricultural income. In column B, a negative rainfall on average lowers agricultural income by close to 10 per cent. A somewhat lesser, but nonetheless similar impact is observed for temperature shocks, except for the non-farm wage. The results suggest that households shift towards engagement in more wage-earning activities, both agricultural and non-farm work, to mitigate negative rainfall shocks. The resulting surge in labour supply has the effect of depressing both the agricultural and non-farm wage. Technically, this implies that the labour participation is accompanied by larger the wage adjustment effect. Chuang (2018) finds a different market adjustment process for the case of India.

Impact of Climatic Shocks on Household Consumption

In Table 4.5, we present results from the estimation of the effects of climatic shocks on total household consumption and food consumption in column 1 and 2, respectively. Total consumption and food consumption are both negatively affected by rainfall shocks, while temperature shocks do not seem to significantly

Table 4.4 Impact of Climatic Shocks on Income

Variables	*Total Income (A)*	*Agricultural Income (B)*	*Agricultural Wage (C)*	*Non-farm Wage (D)*
Rainfall	−0.685***	−0.954**	−0.102**	−0.402***
	(0.059)	(0.386)	(0.050)	(0.099)
Temperature	−0.124*	−0.135*	−0.103***	−0.401
	(0.065)	(0.071)	(0.023)	(0.371)
Constant	−6.619***	36.68***	−4.628*	8.217***
	(2.010)	(5.804)	(2.418)	(0.897)
Observations	2781	2497	2,825	2397
R^2	0.230	0.206	0.196	0.098
Household fixed effects	Yes	Yes	Yes	Yes

Source: Own computations using UNPS 2010/2012

Notes: all monetary units are in logs of Uganda shillings. Coefficients are estimated using seemingly unrelated regressions as dependent variables are correlated. The control variables included are as per the results in Table 4.2. All coefficients are based on weighted analysis using the original sampling weight. Household fixed effects estimation with robust standard errors in parentheses.

*p < 0.1
**p < 0.05
***p < 0.01.

Table 4.5 Effect of Shocks on Total Household Consumption (OLS)

Variables	*Δlog of Total Consumption Per Capita*	*Δlog of Food Consumption Per Capita*
Age of HH head	0.0013	0.0010
	(0.0014)	(0.0016)
HH head education (years)	−0.0500	0.0018
	(0.0368)	(0.0526)
Nonfarm employment	0.0202**	0.0236**
	(0.008)	(0.009)
Household size	−0.0068	−0.0032
	(0.0110)	(0.0135)
ΔHousehold size	−0.1667***	−0.1657***
	(0.0215)	(0.0263)
Male adult share	0.1626	0.1498
	(0.1718)	(0.2000)
ΔMale adult share	0.0411	0.0346
	(0.2510)	(0.2885)
Dependency ratio	0.0511	−0.0286
	(0.2510)	(0.1424)
ΔDependency ratio	−0.1351**	−0.1114
	(0.046)	(0.2224)

Variables	*Δlog of Total Consumption Per Capita*	*Δlog of Food Consumption Per Capita*
Average plot area harvested (Ha)	0.4288	−0.0024
	(0.3350)	(0.0019)
Land ownership (renter=1)	−0.0548	−0.2216
	(0.0713)	(0.4024)
Fertiliser use	0.0563	0.2170**
	(0.0791)	(0.0904)
Pesticide use	−0.0350	0.147**
	(0.0811)	(0.0695)
Improved seeds	0.1051	0.0161
	(0.1019)	(0.1062)
Hired labour	−0.0010	0.209***
	(0.0398)	(0.0653)
Log of days of family labour (weekly)	−0.0455	0.231***
	(0.0476)	(0.0476)
Community characteristics		
Distance to agricultural market	−0.0456	−0.0251
	(0.0340)	(0.0268)
Agricultural extension services use (past 12 months)	0.0615	0.188***
	(0.0658)	(0.0572)
external environment		
Rainfall	−0.195***	−0.00974***
	(0.057)	(0.00277)
Temperature	−0.0354***	0.00161
	(0.007)	(0.000995)
Constant	−6.619***	0.1465
	(2.010)	(0.2818)
Observations	2,143	
Wald Chi^2 (21)	188.04	113.84
Prob. > Chi^2	0.0000	0.0000

Source: Own computations using UNPS 2010/2012

Notes: Dependent variables is log of real per capita crop income. Robust standard errors in parentheses.

*p < 0.1
**p < 0.05
***p < 0.01.

affect food consumption. Rainfall shocks tend to affect large parts of communities, making the effectiveness of community mitigation strategies limited to protect household consumption against the shock. This finding serves to underscore the impact of rainfall shocks in a rain-fed agricultural country. The influence of rainfall shocks in affecting household consumption is also seen in Karim (2018) and Nguyen et al. (2020) where a rainfall shock that presented in the form of floods presented significant effects on household agricultural income and expenditure. In order to underscore the extent of the impact which rainfall shocks present in farming developing economies, Kurosaki (2015) shows that rainfall shocks in the form of floods have significant and negative impacts on consumption, while other climate induced impacts tend to be negligible.

Effect of Shocks on Household Education Expenditure

The results from the estimation of the effects of shocks on education expenditure are presented in Table 4.6. Column 1 presents results of the effects of shocks and other covariates on the likelihood that a household spends on education. Column 2 presents the effects of shocks on the change in education expenditure.

Table 4.6 Effect of Shocks on Household Education Expenditure (Heckman Two-Step Model)

Variables	*Education Expenditure (Yes=1)*	*Change in log of Education Expenditure*
Age of HH head	0.0090	0.0128*
	(0.0062)	(0.0072)
HH head education (years)	0.2265	−0.2017
	(0.1399)	(0.1289)
Nonfarm employment	0.0915	0.1065**
	(0.1574)	(0.045)
Household size	0.2685***	−0.1233**
	(0.0550)	(0.0535)
ΔHousehold size	0.0410	−0.0724
	(0.0791)	(0.0604)
Male adult share	−0.9592	0.4258
	(0.6730)	(0.4381)
Δmale adult share	0.5512	−0.9874
	(1.0001)	(0.6270)
Dependency ratio	1.0869	0.7704
	(0.6938)	(0.4975)
Δdependency ratio	−1.5711*	0.4225
	(0.8918)	0.4225
Average plot area harvested (Ha)	0.063***	0.039**
	(0.024)	(0.020)
Land ownership (renter=1)	0.018	0.044
	(0.014)	(0.126)
Fertiliser use	0.057**	0.102***
	(0.022)	(0.036)
Pesticide use	0.059	0.059
	(0.037)	(0.037)

Variables	*Education Expenditure (Yes=1)*	*Change in log of Education Expenditure*
Improved seeds	0.009	0.304***
	(0.025)	(0.046)
Hired labour	0.012	−0.018
	(0.029)	(0.012)
Log of days of family labour (weekly)	−0.031	−0.047***
	(0.022)	(0.014)
Community characteristics		
Distance to agricultural market	−0.0003	−0.072***
	(0.0044)	(0.019)
Agric. Extension use (past 12 months)	0.101**	0.008
	(0.051)	(0.019)
	(0.2484)	(0.1522)
external environment		
Rainfall	−0.0231**	−0.232*
	(0.0098)	(0.027)
Temperature	−0.035	−0.012
	(0.132)	(0.038)
Constant	−2.8403***	0.8565
	(0.8432)	(0.9555)
Selection instruments	Yes	
Inverse Mills' ratio		−0.6407*
No. of observations	2143	
Wald Chi^2 (21)	109.53	
Prob. > Chi^2	0.0000	

Source: Own computations using UNPS 2010/2012

Notes: Selection instruments include whether households have a child of age < 15, whether schools are available in the village, and the share of old members. Robust standard errors in parentheses.

*p < 0.1, **p < 0.05, ***p < 0.01.*** p<0.01, ** p<0.05, * p<0.1

The decision of whether a household spends on education is strongly affected by the rainfall shock. Furthermore, changes in household education expenditure are affected by rainfall shocks. This finding is in line with Escobal et al. (2005) who report a significant effect of shocks on household education expenditure. Column 2 shows no effect of temperature shocks on household education expenditure.

Our results are in line with Nguyen et al. (2020), Kim and Prskawetz (2010) and Garbero and Muttarak (2013) who also show that weather shocks affect household education expenditure. Evidence on the coping strategies following the COVID-19 pandemic shows that the most common strategy was a reduction in expenditure on food. Ferreira and Schady (2009) note that covariate shocks can induce income and substitution effects on household education expenditure.

A positive substitution effect resulting from a reduction in opportunity costs of schooling has the potential to increase household expenditure on education (Nguyen et al., 2020; Ferreira and Schady, 2009; Lundberg and Wuermli, 2012). In our case, the rainfall shock triggered an income effect, resulting in a reduction in educational expenditure. As climatic shocks affect many household earning activities, the resulting loss of earning opportunities increases the opportunity cost of schooling as households attempt to limit their expenditure. Many of the out of school children tend to engage in child labour in order to bolster their faltering household income. This induces a negative effect on household education expenditure. It is important to note that a definite determination of the intervening factors that drive the observed reduction in education expenditure in the wake of shock is outside the scope of our current investigation. What is key is that climatic shocks present negative impact on education as demonstrated in the decrease in household education expenditure resulting from the rainfall shock.

Conclusion and Emerging Issues

Households, in low-income agrarian economies, face increasing exposure to several covariate shocks. Given the near absence of social safety nets, shocks present serious consequences for their welfare as households nearly have no recourse, but to reduce their expenditure on key welfare indicators. Furthermore, households may respond to shocks by liquidating vital assets or withdrawing children from school, decisions that have adverse consequences that are of an intergenerational nature. Evidence from the COVID-19 pandemic shows that the effects of covariate shocks are particularly severe for households within the lower income quintiles (UBOS [Uganda Bureau of Statistics], 2021; Doyle, 2020).

The findings bear important lessons for building socioeconomic resilience against covariate shocks. This is key since evidence from the COVID-19 pandemic shows that a sector such as agriculture can act as a safety net against covariate shocks in terms of income, employment and food security. In this chapter, it was established that on the one hand, non-farm employment is a key mitigating factor against climate related shocks. On the other hand, agriculture was found to act as a safety net against covariate shocks that mainly originate outside of it such as the COVID-19 pandemic. However, the absence of formal social safety nets to cushion vulnerable households against the adverse effects of covariate shocks often results in households undertaking drastic measures to cope with shocks. Yet, reliance on such informal coping mechanisms has negative long-term effects in addition to keeping households in perpetual vulnerability.

The study is relevant for policy with respect to the role of alternative livelihood strategies in mitigating the adverse impact of climatic shocks on households. This would help in informing policy regarding how to shape interventions that are essential for building household resilience against covariate shocks. The findings are also expected into inform interventions in the realm of agricultural investment. This is based on evidence that while agriculture is a vital livelihood source, its transformation with respect to production technology has been rather slow.

The analysis made in this chapter is without limitations. First, the evidence on the impact of COVID-19 was based on current data. However, the pandemic continues to evolve at an unpredictable pace. Consequently, the evidence on the impacts is bound to also change unexpectedly. To this end, the evidence only provides a perspective of the recent developments that can be used by public policy to identify interventions to mitigate the adverse effects of the shock. Second, correlations do not themselves establish a causal relationship between the onset of the pandemic and the outcomes of interest. For example, many households were food insecure before the pandemic. Future research should use the pre-COVID-19 data in order to establish a pre- and post-pandemic panel.

References

Anttila-Hughes, J. K., & Hsiang, S. M. (2013). *Destruction, disinvestment, and death: Economic and human losses following environmental disaster.* Available at: http://dx.doi.org/10.2139/ssrn.2220501

Bandiera, O., Burgess, R., Deserranno, E., Morel, R., Rasul, I., & Sulaiman, M. (2015). *Key findings from randomized evaluation of microcredit and agriculture services in Uganda.* Research Preview 2, BRAC October 2015. Available at: https://www.atai-research.org/wp-content/uploads/2016/06/Research-Preview-2-20151105.pdf

Binswanger-Mkhize, Hans P. & Savastano, Sara, (2014). Agricultural intensification: the status in six African countries, Policy Research Working Paper Series 7116, The World Bank. Available at: http://hdl.handle.net/10986/20649

Bold, T., Kaizzi, K. C., Svensson, J., & Yanagizawa-Drott, D. (2015). *Low quality, low returns, low adoption: Evidence from the market for fertilizer and hybrid seed in Uganda.* International Growth Center Working Paper F-43805-UGA-1, June 2015. Available at: https://ideas.repec.org/p/cpr/ceprdp/10743.html

Browning, M., & Crossley, T. F. (2009). Shocks, stocks, and socks: Smoothing consumption over a temporary income loss. *J. Eur. Econ. Assoc.*, 7 (6), 1169–1192.

Cameron, L. A., & Worswick, C. (2001). Education expenditure responses to crop loss in Indonesia: A gender bias. *Econ. Dev. Cult. Change*, 49 (2), 351–363.

Carletto, G., Ruel, M., Winters, P., & Zezza, A. (2015). Farm-level pathways to improved nutritional status: Introduction to the Special Issue. The Journal of Development Studies, 554 51(8), 945-957.

Chuang, Y. (2018). Climate variability, rainfall shocks, and farmers' income diversification in India. *Econ. Lett* 174, 55–61. https://doi.org/10.1016/j.econlet.2018.10.015

Dabla-Norris, E., & Gündüz, Y. B. (2014). Exogenous shocks and growth crises in low-income countries: A vulnerability index. *World Dev.*, 59, 360–378.

Dercon, S. (2004). Growth and shocks: Evidence from rural Ethiopia. *J. Dev. Econ.*, 74 (2), 309–329.

Dercon, S., Hoddinott, J., & Woldehanna, T. (2005). Shocks and consumption in 15 Ethiopian villages, 1999–2004, special issue on risk, poverty and vulnerability in Africa. *J. Afr. Econ.*, 14 (4), 559–585.

Doyle, O. (2020). COVID-19: Exacerbating educational inequalities. *Public Policy*, 1–10.

Escobal, J., Jaime, S., & Pablo, S. (2005). *Economic shocks and changes in school attendance levels and education expenditure in Peru.* Young Lives Working Paper, Vol. 13. Young Lives, Oxford.

Ferreira, F. H., & Schady, N. (2009). Aggregate economic shocks, child schooling, and child health. *World Bank Res. Obs.*, 24 (2), 147–181.

Garbero, A., & Muttarak, R. (2013). Impacts of the 2010 droughts and floods on community welfare in rural Thailand: Differential effects of village educational attainment. *Ecol. Soc.*, 18 (4), 27.

Genoni, M. E. (2012). Health shocks and consumption smoothing: Evidence from Indonesia. *Econ. Dev. Cult. Chang.*, 60 (3), 475–506.

Gerry, C. J., & Li, C. A. (2010). Consumption smoothing and vulnerability in Russia. *Appl. Econ.*, 42 (16), 1995–2007.

Government of Uganda. (2020). *Background to the budget fiscal year 2020/21: Stimulating the economy to safeguard livelihoods, jobs, businesses and industrial recovery*. Government of Uganda, Ministry of Finance, Planning and Economic Development.

Günther, I., & Harttgen, K. (2009). Estimating household's vulnerability to idiosyncratic and covariate shocks: A novel method applied in Madagascar. *World Dev.*, 37 (7), 1222–1234.

Hamermesh, D. (1982). Social insurance and consumption: An empirical inquiry. *Am. Econ. Rev.*, 72 (1), 101–113.

Harris, I., Jones, P. D., Osborn, T. J., & Lister, D. H. (2014). Updated high-resolution grids of monthly climatic observations – The CRU TS3.10 dataset. *International Journal of Climatology*, 34 (3), 623–642. http://doi.org/10.1002/joc.3711

Hill, R., & Mejia-Mantilla, C. (2017). *With a little help. Shocks agricultural income, and welfare in Uganda.* World Bank Policy Research Working Paper 7935. Available from: https://doi.org/10.1596/1813-9450-7935

Karim, A. (2018). The household response to persistent natural disasters: Evidence from Bangladesh. *World Dev.*, 103, 40–59.

Kilic, T., Zezza, A., Carletto, C., & Savastano, S. (2014). *Missing(ness) in action: Selectivity bias in GPS based land area measurements*. Policy Research Working Paper 6490, World Bank, Washington, DC.

Kilimani, N., Nnyanzi, J.B., Bbaale, E., & Okumu, I.M. (2020). Agricultural Productivity and Household Welfare in Uganda: Examining the Relevance of Agricultural Improvement Interventions in E. S. Osabuohien (ed.), The Palgrave Handbook of Agricultural and Rural Development in Africa, https://doi.org/10.1007/978-3-030-41513-6_8.

Kim, J., & Prskawetz, A. (2010). External shocks, household consumption and fertility in Indonesia. *Popul. Res. Policy Rev.*, 29(4), 503–526.

Kornrich, S., & Furstenberg, F. (2013). Investing in children: Changes in parental spending on children, 1972–2007. *Demography*, 50 (1), 1–23.

Kurosaki, T. (2015). Vulnerability of household consumption to floods and droughts in developing countries: Evidence from Pakistan. *Environ. Dev. Econ.*, 20 (2), 209–235.

Lundberg, M., & Wuermli, A. (2012). *Children and youth in crisis: Protecting and promoting human development in times of economic shocks*. World Bank, Washington, DC.

Nguyen, T.-T., Nguyen, T. T., & Grote, U. (2020). Multiple shocks and households' choice of coping strategies in rural Cambodia. *Ecol. Econ.*, 167, 106442.

Osabohien, R., Matthew, O., Ohalete, P., & Osabuohien, E. (2020). Population – poverty – inequality nexus and social protection in Africa. *Soc. Indic. Res.*, 151, 575–598.

Parker, J. A. (1999). The reaction of household consumption to predictable changes in social security taxes. *Am. Econ. Rev.*, 89 (4), 959–973.

Sheahan, M., & Barrett, C. B. (2017). Ten striking facts about agricultural input use in Sub-Saharan Africa. Food Policy, 67, 12–25. https://doi.org/10.1016/j.foodpol.2016.09.010.

UBOS. (2021). *COVID-19 impact monitoring: Uganda High-Frequency Phone Survey (HFPS) on COVID-19 is implemented by the Uganda Bureau of Statistics (UBOS) during the period of June 2020-May 2021*. Available from: www.worldbank.org/en/programs/lsms/brief/lsms-launches-high-frequency-phone-surveys-on-covid-19

Zezza, A., Carletto, C., Fiedler, J. L., Gennari, P., & Jolliffe, D. (2017). Food counts. Measuring food consumption and expenditures in household consumption and expenditure surveys (HCES). Introduction to the special issue. *Food Policy*, 72, 1–6.

Zhang, Q., Körnich, H., & Holmgren, K. (2013). How well do reanalyses represent the southern African precipitation. *Clim. Dyn.*, 40, 951–962.

5 Coronavirus (COVID-19) Pandemic and Food Price Increase in Nigeria

Examining the Role of ICT

Onyinye Ochuba, Nora Francis Inyang, and Romanus Osabohien

The Coronavirus Pandemic; Economic Outlooks, and Food Security in Nigeria

Coronavirus outbreak watered down global economic projections, as virtually all sectors and nations of the globe were negatively impacted. Countries had to cut down budgets; corporations laid-off staff and adopted many other viable alternatives to remain in business. The International Monetary Fund (IMF) had to reduce the global economic growth projections due to doubts arising from the pandemic. Currently, Nigeria has recorded over 200,000 cases of Coronavirus, with more than 3,000 deaths (Worldometer, 2022). This is due to the fact that Africa is seen as the poorest, and most vulnerable continent to infectious diseases (Lone & Ahmad, 2020). However, a recent report by allAfrica indicates that over 11 million people have been infected by the virus in 55 African countries, with over 300 million people vaccinated (allAfrica, 2022).

In Nigeria, both the federal and state governments were not spared the adverse effect of the pandemic arising from the drop in revenue occasioned by poor international demand for oil due to lack of activities in various trading modes among countries as a result of imposed movement restrictions. The fall in oil demand and subsequent price crash negatively affected all sectors of the economy which forced the nation to review its budget downwards (Osabuohien, Gershon, Oye, & Efobi, 2020). In terms of trade, businesses witnessed weak projections due to border closure, uncertainties regarding sales and profitability as well as market failures. These factors resulted in alteration of the conventional way of doing things. There was a massive drift towards adoption of information technology in virtually all facets of human activities ranging from virtual meetings to virtual learning and e-commerce, to mitigate the impact of COVID-19. Businesses made proactive move towards technology by advising staff to work from home and moving most of their sales online (Deloitte, 2020). But this prompt switch to virtual transactions was not so visible in the agricultural output sector given the importance of food to livelihood (Deloitte, 2020).

Also, as part of containment measures in Nigeria, food markets were not completely closed down; rather, the number of days the markets opened were reduced at

DOI: 10.4324/9781003208358-8

the inception of the lockdown. Given the peculiar characteristics of an average Nigerian who believes in being physically present in the market and the fact that most buyers do not have access to online payment system, still the market places could be seen heavily congested and transactions mostly done by cash. These negate the tenets of social distancing which is critical for the containment of the virus. Only a small portion of the consumers who understand the place of social distancing in reducing the spread of the virus and who can afford to pay extra for shipment patronised online shopping which was facilitated by social media outfits (Adegboye, 2020).

Despite these initiatives, available statistics indicates that proportion of Nigerian population experiencing severe food insecurity rose to 30.3% in June 2020 as compared to 11.8% in 2018 and 5.9% in 2019, respectively. Those witnessing moderate food insecurity grew to 76.8% in June 2020 compared to 53.8% in 2018 and 37.0% in 2019 (National Bureau of Statistics, 2020). This is not unconnected with the deferment in one of the major cardinals of food security; accessibility as depicted by the spike in the prices of essential food items in the country during this period. The price hike reduced household's purchasing parity and access to food. Data from NBS covering the periods January 2017 to June 2020 shows that food prices exhibited the highest steepness from January to June 2020 as compared to the preceding years. This reflects sudden increment in the price of essential food items in Nigeria in COVID-19 period (National Bureau of Statistics, 2020). This emerging trend is dealing very heavy blow on the nation's ability to attain the global Sustainable Development Goals (SDGs) which has as one of its focal points as 'the eradication of hunger'(United Nations, 2015).

Food Production and Distribution in Nigeria

Food production and distribution in Nigeria has largely been undertaken by the informal sector. Food distribution is mostly done in the open-air market. Due to the huge consumer population potentials of the country, certain big names such as UAC, Shoprite, and Nestle have pitched their tents in Nigeria (Researchandmarkets, 2020). But the harsh economic realities, poor state of the nation's infrastructure, and certain government policies have adversely affected their performance. Other discouraging factors include: environmental concerns, insecurity, technology, poor state of research and development, innovation, and skilled labour availability, to mention a few. These have resulted in decline in investments in formal food distribution in Nigeria (Researchandmarkets, 2020). In August 2020, Shoprite, one of the major food distribution giants in Nigeria, announced voluntary closure of business in the country. Part of the reasons for its decision is the harsh economic environment occasioned by the pandemic outbreak and the fluctuation in the nation's currency among other reasons (Olawoyin, 2020).

Various governments in Nigeria oversee the distribution of farm inputs such as seedlings and fertilizers to farmers. Recently, in a bid to forestall food shortage in the country as a result of the pandemic, the Federal Ministry of Agriculture flagged off the distribution of inputs to farmers (Falaju, 2020). This is expected to avert food crisis in the coming year. But this initiative has been bedevilled by late or

Table 5.1 Nigeria's Top-10 Agricultural Produce with Their Global Ranking as at 2018

S/N	*Crop*	*Annual Output (Millions of Tons)*	*Global Ranking*
1	Cassava	59.4	Largest Producer
2	Yam	47.5	Largest Producer
3	Mazie	10.1	14th largest Producer
4	Palm Oil	7.8	4th Largest Producer
5	Sorghum	6.8	2nd largest Producer
6	Rice	6.8	14th largest Producer
7	Sweet Potatoes	4	3rd largest Producer
8	Tomatoes	3.9	11th Largest Producer
9	Taro	3.3	Largest Producer
10	Plantain	3	5th Largest Producer

Source: Adapted from Food and Agricultural Organisation (2020)

non-delivery of inputs, exclusion of rightful beneficiaries and supply of substandard inputs (Federal Ministry of Agriculture and Rural Development, 2016). This prompted the Federal Ministry of Agriculture to launch the Agricultural Promotion Policy which is aimed at ensuring timely, price competitive and high-quality agricultural inputs are made available to the right beneficiaries. To achieve this, the ministry is encouraging domestic production of high-quality inputs, rechannelling subsidy programmes to ensure probity and accountability, enhancing access to innovation and market information, encouraging the amendment of the current land use act, ensuring the development of processing and storage facilities, and facilitating the passage of fertilizer and seedlings bills before the National Assembly (Federal Ministry of Agriculture and Rural Development, 2016).

Food production in Nigeria is largely done by small holding farmers, with regional disparity in quantity supplied (see Table 5.1). The disparity is as a result of available cultivable land to various parts of the country. The North is the highest food producer with available cultivable land space of 79.1%, followed by the West with 12.4% and the East at 8.5% of cultivable land (Okolo, 2006). The variation in the arable land and the subsequent output gives rise to regular internal food movement in the country mostly from the North to other part of the country to make up for food production shortfalls. Despite these internal food transfers, the country is still not meeting up to the required nutritional requirements which increase the nation's vulnerability to food insecurity (Okolo, 2006).

Food Price Analysis in Nigeria

Food prices in Nigeria have been on a steady increase since the food crisis of 2008. But the trend assumed an astronomical dimension following the outbreak of the pandemic and the subsequent movement restrictions. Food price in the country currently stands at 16.66% inflation rate (Oyekanmi, 2020). Table 5.2 illustrates the price differentials of various staple foods in the country from 2017 to second quarter of 2020 with the differential in prices for the period under review.

Table 5.2 Percentage Price Differential of Selected Food Items for 2017 to Second Quarter 2020

S/N	*Selected Food Items*	*2017 % Diff.*	*2018 % Diff*	*2019 % Diff.*	*2020 % Diff.*
1	Agric eggs medium size	0.99	10.58	2.40	3.55
2	Agric eggs (medium size price of one)	2.22	3.35	−1.79	4.34
3	Beans brown, sold loose	5.11	4.57	−3.89	1.77
4	Beans: white, black eye. Sold loose	6.65	3.99	−3.48	−0.61
5	Beef Bone in	9.34	−1.99	3.28	2.52
6	Beef, boneless	7.72	−0.80	−0.05	2.23
7	Bread sliced 500 g	2.75	−1.39	−1.31	4.56
8	Bread unsliced 500 g	6.18	−1.51	0.03	3.36
9	Broken Rice (Ofada)	14.02	−0.65	−1.57	2.47
10	Catfish (obokun) fresh	1.31	0.29	−1.10	2.49
11	Catfish: dried	1.74	−3.63	−2.75	0.21
12	Catfish Smoked	2.21	−8.04	1.87	1.73
13	Chicken Feet	−1.53	−3.14	−1.88	3.07
14	Chicken Wings	−3.46	−1.20	−1.20	2.21
15	Dried Fish Sardine	3.52	−2.83	2.90	0.47
16	Evaporated tinned milk carnation 170 g	12.33	−1.12	−1.22	5.20
17	Evaporated tinned milk (peak), 170 g	17.83	−0.78	−0.56	3.50
18	Frozen chicken	10.30	−0.64	−0.42	−0.33
19	Gari white, sold loose	18.94	−1.18	−5.18	24.31
20	Gari yellow, sold loose	24.00	−0.33	−8.41	20.45
21	Groundnut oil: 1 bottle, specify bottle	2.94	6.74	−2.54	5.50
22	Iced Sardine	1.16	4.80	1.48	3.59
23	Irish potato	3.69	18.00	−0.14	8.14
24	Mackerel: frozen	2.60	0.96	0.93	2.95
25	Maize grain white sold loose	9.37	−11.47	−4.40	13.82
26	Maize grain yellow sold loose	8.67	1.81	−3.40	14.58
27	Mudfish (aro) fresh	1.79	−2.94	−0.91	0.76
28	Mudfish: dried	21.74	−5.91	−1.19	−0.14
29	Onion bulb	−16.51	−3.76	−8.82	−1.67
30	Palm oil: One 150 cl bottle	6.51	−0.10	−1.48	2.57
31	Plantain (ripe)	3.79	2.68	−0.52	11.63
32	Plantain (unripe)	5.01	1.09	−0.44	11.45
33	Rice Agric sold loose	−1.51	0.96	0.63	4.24
34	Rice local sold loose	5.24	1.67	−1.35	4.99
35	Rice Medium Grained	−1.09	3.36	−0.46	5.78
36	Rice, imported high quality sold loose	−1.34	2.58	−1.88	5.90
37	Sweet potato	2.28	17.98	1.41	11.21
38	Tilapia fish (epiya) fresh	1.60	4.29	−1.47	0.62
39	Titus: frozen	4.48	2.52	1.36	4.83
40	Tomato	32.89	13.41	−3.86	15.71
41	Vegetable oil: One 150 cl bottle	5.32	1.89	−2.57	6.89
42	Wheat flour: prepacked (golden penny 2 kg)	1.85	0.55	0.91	4.14
43	Yam tuber	20.46	20.36	0.32	21.91

Source: Authors' computation

Factors Responsible for the Price Hike during the Coronavirus Period in Nigeria

Close look at the table indicates that food price hike was highest in 2020. Using a structured questionnaire that was electronically distributed to respondents across the nation, the respondents attributed the increase in food prices to a host of factors ranging from hike in transportation cost, hoarding, scarcity psychology, inaccessibility of raw materials, and lastly poor agricultural output. Figure 5.1 provides a pictorial representation of the responses.

Hike in transportation cost across the nation was confirmed by data which was made available by NBS. It revealed that commuter bus journey increased by 25.76% year on years, intra-city journey fare increased by 13.49%, while water transport fare increased by 14.18% during the period (National Bureau of Statistics, 2020). This was attributed largely to movement restrictions across the nation. As a result of this, there was reduced access to the farms for harvesting and onward distribution of the proceeds especially to urban centres. This resulted in a spike in the nation's population that are experiencing food insecurity. Consequently also, food vendors that had supply employed the tool of hoarding as uncertainty looms as regards the world at large. With hoarding came the drop in supply relative to demand. The reduction in supply resulted in the hike that the country experienced.

Again, with the dawning reality of insufficiency already prevalent, the scarcity psychology set in. Consumers as well as producers just feel the air of lack and inadequacy. Holding back and miserly attitude became the order of the day. Inaccessibility of raw materials was also a result of movement restriction and border closure for imported ones. Most factories across the globe especially China who are the major trading patterns of Nigeria were under total lockdown for a period of time. This gave rise to scarcity of raw material and consequently the unavailability of certain essential commodities.

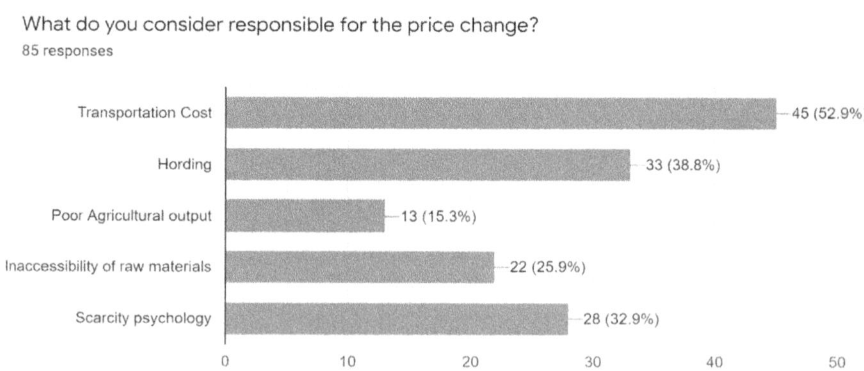

Figure 5.1 Causes of Food Price changes

Source: The authors

Poor agricultural output during this period was a result of poor farm maintenance. Since there were restrictions of movement, the farmers could not assess their fragmented farmlands which are mostly away from home settlement to weed. The infestation of these farmlands with weeds resulted in loss of soil nutrients to weeds rather than the crop and also increased pest infestation on farmers' farmland hence reduction in quality or marketable outputs. There was no access to agricultural loans and credit guarantee scheme so most farmers operated more on subsistence farming (where production is for individual families with no surplus for trade) hence no room for expansion to accommodate demand. There was absence of inflow of fertilizers since vehicular movements were for only food stuffs. Most agricultural commodities are perishable in nature and since farmers could not store them for long periods to be sold out on a later date, there were post–harvest losses. The pandemic took a toll on the nation during the peak of farming season. This disrupted cultivation with resultant low output. Figure 5.1 is how our respondents reacted to factors responsible for price hike in the country.

Information and Communication Technology and Agriculture in Nigeria

Information and communication technology (ICT) has been around in Nigeria dating back to 1950. The trend was, however, revolutionised in 1996 with the introduction of internet in the country. Full internet access was gotten in 1998 and by 2001, over 150 internet service providers (ISPs) were already licensed nationwide, currently, Nigeria has over 108 million internet users (Adomi, 2005). Ever since, ICT has played very vital roles in all facets of human endeavour reducing the universe to a global village.

Agriculture in Nigeria has had a face lift from ICT. ICT has seen the deployment if geographical information system (GIS) in agriculture. This has greatly facilitated the maximal utilisation of arable land, estimation of environmental impacts resulting from natural and manmade hazards, and comparison of different agricultural scenarios (Nnadi, Atoma, Egwuonwu, & Echetama, 2012). It has equally advanced the cause of research and extension services in Agriculture by providing better data base and web publishing of learning materials. This has greatly assisted in rural as well as agricultural education by bringing knowledge closer to the people. Worthy of mention is advancement in molecular biology which has facilitated provision of improved seedlings and other agricultural inputs. For instance, genome editing, biological-based crop protection, and precision agriculture and technologies that facilitate traceability from farm to fork are some ICT innovations which has enhanced food system efficiency and climate change resilient outputs (World Bank, 2019).

Genome editing or gene-editing is that technology that allows the alteration of the DNA of an organism either by adding or removing or modifying the genetic materials artificially (Medline Plus, 2012). Such modification is necessary for the production of crops and animals with inbuilt capabilities to withstand adverse climatic condition and disease outbreak. Biological-based crop protection involves the introduction of natural enemies that are found to be harmful to pests and diseases which attack crops and animals (Royal Brinkman, 2020). These natural enemies help to keep pests and diseases under control and enhance productivity. ICT aids monitoring to observe infiltration of pests and diseases and also the introduction of the natural enemies.

Precision agriculture on the other hand involves the use of information technology in ensuring that soil, crops and animals receive what is essential for its optimal health, development, and productivity (Wigmore, 2016). This solution ensures environmental protection, sustainability of species, and ultimate profitability for agro investors. It relies heavily on real-time data and specialised equipment and software to access the condition of the soil, crop as well as other necessary conditions for optimal productivity. Most important is the role ICT has played and is still playing in the development of agribusiness (marketing) for farmers and investors in agriculture. This it has achieved with the aid of mobile phones, computers, and other electronic devices by providing links to both credit and market for players in agriculture. This enables easy linking of sellers of agricultural products (farmers) and buyers (consumers) thereby reducing existing inequalities in accessing information, technology, knowledge, and the market. In Nigeria, the federal government in conjunction with Cellulant, an ICT company, provided e-wallets for verified farmers for the delivery of fertilizers (Akinboro, 2014). Other information gotten through these e-wallets include weather and crop advisory, updates on government programmes for farmers, and pricing both for inputs and outputs. Information on pricing is particularly important because it increases farmers' bargaining power and income by giving them better chances of competitive bargain (USAID, 2013).

Apart from enhancing farmers' income, it is very vital for the attainment of Farm to Fork in Nigeria. Farm to Fork is a concept that encourages traceability of products, especially agricultural produce from the point of production (Farm) to the consumer's table. When the farmers display their produce via internet, potential buyers who most times are the final consumers can easily reach them and conclude the transaction. This reduces food distribution chain and ensures value for money by giving both the farmer and the consumer the best possible price for the best quality of product. It also enhances the reduction in post-harvest losses arising from information gap between the producers and the consumers. This culminates in improved public service and smarter farms through well informed producers (farmers) and buyers (consumers). Aside pricing benefits, it helps in reducing physical contacts which is the hallmark of open-air markets that are the predominate distribution channel for agricultural produce. Following the outbreak of coronavirus pandemic, the need to ensure social distancing was made dominate as it is seen as one of the best possible means of containing the spread of the virus. ICT made this possible although the potential for this remains largely underutilised. Our proposed roadmap to ensure full utilisation of ICT in this regard include: proper tracing and identification of produce from farm to fork, decentralisation of agricultural output distribution using information technology, and effective agricultural data gathering and dissemination which will enhance decision making for farmers, agro investors, and consumers.

This fact is, however, being challenged by a number of factors such as unstable and very erratic power supply in Nigeria, high cost of ICT support infrastructures and facilities, and high level of illiteracy especially computer illiteracy among the farmers coupled with high poverty rate (Nnadi, Atoma, Egwuonwu, & Echetama, 2012). The identified challenges can, however, be addressed if governments and international bodies can subsidise massive deployment of ICT infrastructures to all parts of the country especially in rural/ farm settlements. This will encourage cyber extension and there should also be extensive content monitoring to ensure safety of the cyber space. Massive awareness creation should also be done to intimate all agricultural stakeholders on the importance and use of ICT.

Policy Implications in Nigeria

This work will be relevant to stakeholders in various sectors of the Nigerian economy ranging from agricultural investors and other key players in the sector, information technology and communication sector, transportation and logistics as well as the financial sector. Also, it will form a blueprint to policy makers towards formulating policies that will facilitate the investment in ICT in general and agricultural facilitation ICT solutions. The Federal Ministry of Agriculture and Rural Development (FMARD) will strategise their policy towards improving agricultural value chain to reduce wastage and increase food sufficiency, thus reducing food insecurity.

References

Adegboye, F. (2020). *COVID-19, Social Distancing and Food Prices in Nigeria*. Ontario: Eat Local: Taste Global EVC.

Adomi, E. (2005). Internet Development and Connectivity in Nigeria. *Program: Electronic Library and Information System*, 39(3), 257–268. www.researchgate.net/deref/http%3A%2F%2Fdx.doi.org%2F10.1108%2F00330330510610591

Akinboro, B. (2014, June 24). *Bringing Mobile Wallets to Nigerian Farmers*. CGAP. www.cgap.org/blog/bringing-mobile-wallets-nigerian-farmers

allAfrica. (2022, July 4). *Africa: Nearly 256,000 Covid-19 Deaths Confirmed Across Continent*. Retrieved from allafrica.com/stories/202207040377: https://allafrica.com/stories/202207040377.html

Deloitte. (2020). *Addressing Financial Impact of COVID-19 in Nigeria*. London: Deloitte Touche Tohmatsu.

Falaju, J. (2020, June 11). Federal Government Flags off Distribution of Agric Inputs to Avert Food Crisis. *The Guardian*. https://guardian.ng/business-services/federal-government-flags-off-distribution-of-agric-inputs-to-avert-food-crisis/

Federal Ministry of Agriculture and Rural Development. (2016). *Agriculture Promotion Policy 2016–2020*. Abuja: Federal Ministry of Agriculture and Rural Development.

Food and Agricultural Organisation. (2020). *Nigeria at a Glance*. Roma: FAO.

Lone, S., & Ahmad, A. (2020). COVID-19 Pandemic - An African Perspective. *Emerging Microbes and Infections* 9(1), 1300–1308. https://doi.org/10.1080/22221751.2020.1775132

Mawi, P. (2020, October 30). Coronavirus: What is Happening to the Numbers in Africa. *BBC News*. www.bbc.com/news/world-africa-53181555

Medline Plus. (2012). *What Are Genome Editing and CRISPR-cas9?* Chicago: U.S. National Library of Medicine.

National Bureau of Statistics. (2020). *COVID-19 Impact Monitoring Round 2 June 2020*. Abuja: NBS.

Nnadi, F., Atoma, C., Egwuonwu, H., & Echetama, J. (2012). ICT for Agriculture Knowledge Management in Nigeria. Lessons and Strategies for Improvement. *Science Journal of Agriculture Research and Management*. Vol 2012, Pg 1 - 8

Okolo, D. (2006). *Agricultural Development and Food Security in Sub-Saharan Africa (SSA). Building a Case for More Public Support. The Case of Nigeria*. Roma: FAO.

Olawoyin, O. (2020, August 4). EXPLAINER: Five Reasons Shoprite is Leaving Nigeria. *Premium Times*. www.premiumtimesng.com/news/top-news/406768

Osabuohien, E., Gershon, O., Oye, Q., & Efobi, U. (2020, April 1). Addressing Budget and Debt Vulnerability Amidst COVID-19, Policy Pathway for Nigeria. *CEPDeR Policy Brief*.

Oyekanmi, S. (2020, October 15). Nigeria's Inflation Rate Hits 13.71% as Food Prices Soar. *Nairametrics*. https://nairametrics.com/2020/10/15/breaking-nigerias-inflation-rate-hits-13-71-as-food-prices-soar/

Researchandmarkets. (2020). *Wholesale and Retail of Food in Nigeria, 2019 Report*. Dublin: Global Newswire.

Royal Brinkman. (2020). *Biological Crop Protection*. London: Royal Brinkman.

United Nations. (2015, August 11). *17 Goals to Transform the World for Persons with Disability*. Retrieved from Envision 2030. www.un.org/development/desa/disabilities/envision2030.html

USAID. (2013). *Using ICT to Enhance Marketing for Small Agricultural Producers (Briefing Paper)*. Accra: Agrilink.org.

Wigmore, I. (2016). *Precision Agriculture*. Newton: TechTarget Network.

World Bank. (2019). *Future of Food: Harnessing Digital Technologies to Improve Food System Outcome*. New York: World Bank.

Worldometer. (2022, July 06). Nigerian Coronavirus Cases. Retrieved from https://www.worldometers.info/coronavirus/country/nigeria/: https://www.worldometers.info/coronavirus/country/nigeria/

6 Building Economic Resilience in COVID-19 Africa

What Role for Digital Transformation?

Arthur Minsat and Elisa Saint Martin

Introduction

How has the COVID-19 crisis affected Africa's digital revolution? Africa is the developing region that has been most affected by the COVID-19 crisis. Nevertheless, the crisis has also boosted Africa's digitalisation, revealing that Africa's digitalisation revolution is both profound and transformative. This chapter contributes to the literature by providing an up-to-date summary of economic, digital, infrastructure and legal developments that took place before 2020 and after the COVID-19 crisis struck the continent until the time of writing in 2021. The existing academic literature has not yet assessed how the COVID-19 crisis impacted Africa's ongoing digitalisation.

Digitalisation means the increased use of digital technologies and data in economic transactions and daily life. It includes the interconnection leading to new activities or changes to existing activities. Digital technologies comprise mobile data networks (4G and 5G, for example), mobile payment and financial products, the internet of things (IoT), blockchain, artificial intelligence (AI), big data analytics and cloud computing. Digital transformation points to the changes that digitalisation is making to the economy and society. These changes affect virtually all sectors. They have impacts on the inputs, functions and economic models of less digital-intensive sectors such as agriculture, construction and trade. For these sectors, the use of digital technologies contributes to lowering transaction costs and addressing information asymmetries associated with certain activities like access to finance.

At the same time, digital transformation reshapes the distribution of production, value addition and economic rents across workers, firms and spaces according to the ability of workers and firms to control, own and access these new modes of production. For example, digitally intermediated data services and algorithms are increasingly underpinning decision making and production processes and have become an important source of value. A countrywide digital transformation strategy aimed at creating jobs, therefore, needs to extend beyond the information and communication technology (ICT) activities to embrace all economic sectors in order to benefit from jobs indirectly created by digitalisation (AUC/OECD, 2021).

DOI: 10.4324/9781003208358-9

How Digital Transformation Can Help Achieve Greater 'Resilience' to Shocks

Digital Transformation in Africa: Review of the Existing Literature

The literature argues that digitalisation can help strengthen the resilience of African economies through several channels, including greater financial inclusion, lower production and distribution costs, and enhanced transparency and efficiency of commercial transactions.

First, digitalisation enables populations excluded from traditional banking to gain access to financial services, for instance, through mobile banking (Njuguna Ndung'u, 2018). Africa's mobile phone adoption is a well-known example of leapfrogging: mobile technology has now replaced fixed-line phones. Suri and Jack (2016) highlight the positive impact of increased access to mobile money services on households and businesses in Kenya. Between 2008 and 2014, it helped raise at least 194,000 households out of extreme poverty and enabled 185,000 women to switch their main occupations from subsistence agriculture to small businesses or retail.

Second, digitalisation gives African firms better access to inputs for their production. It enhances marketing and sales opportunities at local, regional and global levels. Recent empirical studies provide evidence on the positive outcomes of digitalisation in terms of employment and firms' productivity. Hjort and Poulsen (2019) show that for 12 African countries, high-speed internet positively increases the employment rate for workers with both high and low education. Other papers have shown an even higher impact of digitalisation on the performance of firms (productivity, sales and new export opportunities), and on their access to longer-term financing. Data on more than 30,000 firms from 38 developing countries – including 9 African countries – show that a 10% increase in e-mail use by firms raises their total annual sales by 37%–38%, sales per worker by 22%–23% and the number of full-time workers by 12%–14% (Cariolle et al., 2019). These opportunities lower the cost of accessing global services and markets. It generates economies of scale at lower levels of capital investment.

Finally, digitalisation enhances the transparency and efficiency of commercial transactions. Distributed ledger technologies, such as digital and blockchain applications, offer solutions for real-time tracking and tracing the origins of products at lower cost (GSMA, 2017). Applying paperless procedures and adopting smart clearance technology can increase the transparency, predictability and efficiency of custom control at borders

However, digitalisation also brings risks for African economies. Existing literature highlights heightened competition from global digital players, automation of low-skilled jobs and the lack of adequate social protection for gig workers, and threats to cyber security and to privacy of personal data and increasing levels of inequality between those who have access to digital tools and the others as major challenges for policymakers (Bukht and Heeks, 2017; Gillwald and Mothobi, 2019). For instance, Serianu (2017) estimates that the cost of cybercrime in

Africa was about US$3.5 billion in 2017. The fast-development of technologies, their global reach and their cross-border nature calls for governments to respond with 'fit-for-purpose' regulatory frameworks and enforcement mechanisms (OECD, 2019).

Since 2020, access to digitalisation enabled firms and households to stay connected despite social distancing implemented during the ongoing COVID-19 pandemic. A binding constraint for developing economies is that realising these economies of scale requires higher human capital, an endowment that usually correlates with countries' per capita income (Banga et al., 2018; Foster and Azmeh, 2019).

Contribution and Research Objectives

A contribution of this chapter consists in bringing an up-to-date and comprehensive analysis of how the COVID-19 crisis affects Africa's digital transformation by the time of writing in September 2021. A comprehensive overview to date is the report by the African Union and OECD Development Centre, *Africa's Development Dynamics 2021: Digital Transformation for Quality Jobs*, which is co-authored by the authors of this chapter. However, this report published in January 2021 did not assess the impact of the COVID-19 crisis on Africa's digital transformation, since the research could not substantially include developments between 2020 and 2021. To fill this gap, this chapter will analyse the state of Africa's digital transformation before 2020 when the COVID-19 crisis hit the world economy, compared to latest developments since 2020. It will review the latest developments across different channels for transformation, including infrastructure development, investment dynamics in the ICT sector, internet usage, innovations by African entrepreneurs and public policies formulated to benefit from the opportunities of digitalisation and mitigate the crisis' impact. A second contribution consists in analysing how African strategies for digitalisation can increase Africa's resilience to large shocks like COVID-19. The chapter will draw policy recommendations to increase resilience, and reflect on how African strategies for digitalisation can help increase resilience.

To achieve these research objectives, the chapter will first explain how the COVID-19's socioeconomic shock spurred Africa's digital transformation. Second, it will bring up-to-date knowledge of Africa's digital transformation, examining comprehensive data sources on infrastructure development, Africa's mobile money revolution, start-up development and the digitalisation of African economies. It will highlight the limited spread of digitalisation in certain parts of societies, in particular among small- and middle-sized enterprises, and in the informal sector. It will analyse the boost given to the use of digital innovation since 2020, using the latest data and own calculations. It will focus on increased usage of mobile communication accounts, higher investment in ICT infrastructure and the acceleration of digital innovation notably in financial services, healthcare, and education. Third, the chapter concludes by arguing that the main binding constraints to Africa's digital transformation are inequalities in access to digital solutions by households and firms, particularly informal firms as well as micro-, small- and middle-sized Enterprises (MSMEs). To tackle these obstacles, the chapter recommends implementing key policies that will promote the diffusion of digital technologies and innovations beyond Africa's large urban centres and empower African entrepreneurs and start-ups in the digital era.

Methodological Strategies

The chapter relies on literature review, data analysis and field interviews to examine trends of the ongoing digital transformation in Africa. This literature review draws on the latest academic research, and on regional analysis conducted by international and regional organisations. These reports have the advantage of delivering a broad but nuanced continental outlook on trends at continental, regional and country levels, while taking stock of the relevant literature. Additionally, analysis of new and updated databases will show the latest trends in specific areas relevant to Africa's ongoing digitalisation. This data analysis is complemented by surveys conducted for the *Africa's Development Dynamics* report series and by qualitative interviews with policy makers at continental, regional and national levels, as well as with telecommunication operators on the continent and civil society representatives. Where appropriate, country-level evidence will bring more accurate case studies. These concrete examples will show how digitalisation can improve African societies' resilience, notably by explaining how digital innovations were developed, and how African countries implemented digitalisation policies. These will guide policy recommendations and digitalisation strategies tailored to the African context.

The COVID-19 Pandemic Hit African Economies Hard

The COVID-19 pandemic triggered Africa's first recession in the past 25 years. The global economy contracted by at least 3% in 2020. Africa's growth contracted by 1.6% in 2020 according to our aggregation of IMF estimates from April 2022. Overall, 36 of African 54 countries entered into a recession in 2020 (IMF, 2022). By comparison, only 11 countries went into recession when the global financial crisis hit the continent in 2009 (AUC/OECD, 2021). The COVID-19 pandemic heightened African vulnerabilities and increased the need for long-term structural changes to the economy required to achieve productive transformation. Productive transformation will increase Africa's resilience to shocks by increasing productivity across sectors, diversifying its productive structure and broadening the fiscal base (AUC/OECD, 2019).

The pandemic is disrupting Africa's progress and could erase years of development gains. Employment fell by about 8% in 2020, throwing millions of people into poverty – with an estimated 28 million people below US$1.90 per day thresholds and 26 million below US$3.2 per day poverty threshold in Africa (Diop and Asongu, 2021). Disruptions to education have jeopardised employment prospects for millions of youth. Income inequality is increasing, as lockdowns disproportionally affected informal sector workers who represent about 86% of Africa's workforce and social protection generally excludes them.

The adverse effects of COVID-19 on productive capacities could last more than a decade, further reducing Africa's resilience to future shocks. Simulations by Djiofack et al. (2020) found that Africa's capital accumulation and productivity could remain below their pre-COVID-19 trajectories until 2030. The most consequential disruptions in national economies could be productivity decline, reduced capital utilisation and increased trade costs (OECD, 2020).

Africa's Digital Transformation Is Part of the Solution for a Sustainable Recovery

Prior to 2020, Africa's digital transformation was already well underway and accelerating. It is most visible through the rapid expansion of communications infrastructure, Africa's mobile money revolution and start-up development. However, digitalisation also heightens pre-existing socioeconomic inequalities between countries, socioeconomic groups, and firms in different sectors, particularly informal versus formal firms, and between firms of different sizes. The key challenge remains the diffusion of digital technology to the non-digital sectors, in order to benefit all.

Africa's Digital Transformation Prior to 2020

Africa's Rapid Expansion of Communications Infrastructure

Over the past decade, most African countries have actively developed their communications infrastructure networks, favoured by government policies and investment by the private sector. By 2018, 45 African countries had an active digital broadband infrastructure development strategy in 2018, compared to only 16 in 2011 (ITU, 2018). Rapid communication infrastructure development was possible thanks to significant investment from the private sector. In 2018, communications infrastructure financing stood at US$7 billion, with 68% of this amount coming from private sector investments (Figure 6.1). This contrasts with other infrastructure sectors like energy or transports where private sector financing accounted for only 14% and 1%, respectively, in 2018.

Different stages of infrastructure development can be defined by distinguishing between *first-mile*, *middle-mile* and *last-mile* communication infrastructure. The first mile refers to the points where the internet enters a country. The middle mile refers to national backbone network and the associated elements such as data centres and internet exchanges. The last mile refers to local access networks that connect the end users.

Telecom companies and global tech actors have spearheaded the development of *first-mile* communications infrastructure – submarine cable systems and landing stations – connecting African countries to the global internet. The continent's

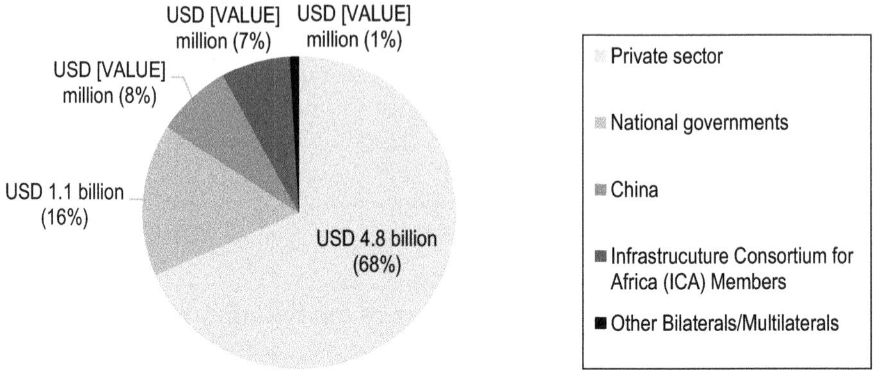

Figure 6.1 Financing of communications infrastructure by source, 2018
Source: ICA (2018), *Infrastructure Financing Trends in Africa: 2018*[1]

total inbound international internet bandwidth reached 10.962 terabytes per second by December 2018. In May 2020, Facebook and a group of telecom companies – including China Mobile International, MTN GlobalConnect, Orange and Vodafone – began collaborating to deploy 37,000 km of subsea cables by 2024 to connect Africa's internet broadband network to Europe and the Middle East. This new broadband network, called 2Africa, should deliver more than the total combined internet traffic capacity of all 26 subsea cables serving Africa today (2AfricaCable, 2020).

Since 2014, Africa doubled its *middle-mile* internet infrastructure. Africa's operational fibre-optic network reached 1.02 million km in June 2019, compared to 564 091 km in 2014 (Hamilton Research, 2020). As the majority of African users access the internet through mobile devices, the development of fourth generation (4G) systems made a greater usage possible. By 2020, the share of Africa's population covered by 4G mobile networks was almost 60%, compared to 86.5% in Latin America and the Caribbean (LAC) and 88% in developing Asia (Figure 6.2). Although Africa's communications infrastructure coverage is yet not as high as in other world regions, the continent is developing its infrastructure at lower levels of income, showing much potential for faster development and digital innovation. In 2019, Africa's GDP per capita stood at US$5196 – compared to Developing Asia and LAC, at 11,145 and 17,556, respectively.

Despite the progress, *last-mile* infrastructure connecting the internet to end-users remains insufficient. Currently, nearly 300 million Africans still live more than 50 km away from a fibre or cable broadband connection. Complementary solutions to improve the transmission network such as internet exchange points (IXPs), data servers and satellite transmission systems remain underdeveloped. Almost half (42%) of African countries still do not have IXPs. Their domestic internet traffic must be routed abroad to reach its destination (ITU/UNESCO, 2019).

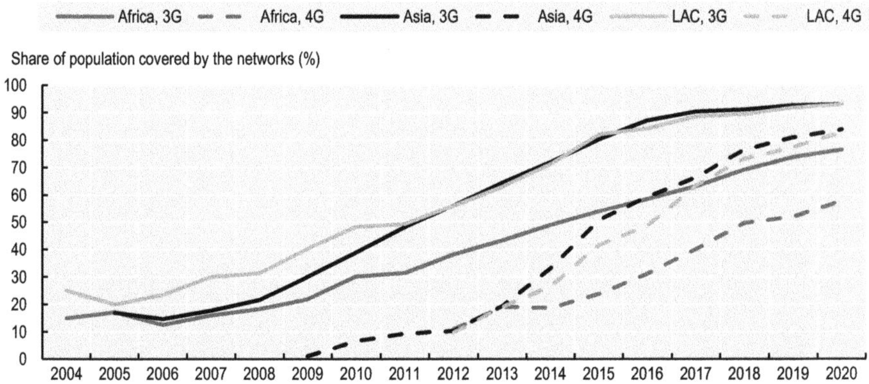

Figure 6.2 Share of the population covered by the 3G and 4G networks in Africa, Asia and LAC, 2004–2020

Source: Authors' calculations based on GSMA (2020a), GSMA Intelligence (database)

Africa's Mobile Money Revolution

Africa's mobile money revolution is hallmarked by the introduction of mobile money services through M-Pesa in Kenya, launched in 2007 by Vodafone Group plc and Safaricom. By 2019, Africa registered over 450 million mobile money accounts, more than any other regions in the world. More than 500 companies now provide technology-enabled innovation in financial services (*fintech*). Mobile money services enabled previously unbanked population to access financial services for the first time. In 2017, about 41% of Africa's population had a bank account, with almost 10% relying exclusively on mobile money services (author's calculations based on Demirgüç-Kunt et al., 2018). Beyond financial inclusion, access to mobile money services triggered positive spill over effects on households and businesses. In Kenya, it helped raise at least 194,000 households out of extreme poverty between 2008 and 2014. It also enabled 185 000 women to switch their main occupations from subsistence agriculture to small businesses or retail over the same period (Suri and Jack, 2016). In 2019, Interswitch (specialised in fintech solutions) became Africa's first start-up company valued at more than a billion dollars.

Digitalisation Fuels the Development of African Start-Ups

Digital development led to flourishing innovation hubs and incubators in several African countries. By 2019, 643 tech hubs were active across Africa, up from 314 in 2016, and only a handful in 2010 (AFRILABS and Briter Bridges, 2019). Nonetheless, the number of tech hubs remains low by global standards, being comparable to the number of tech hubs in Bavaria, Germany.

Among the top 10 most attractive activities of African start-ups, eight depend on the digital economy (Figure 6.3). The top three activities by start-ups relate to

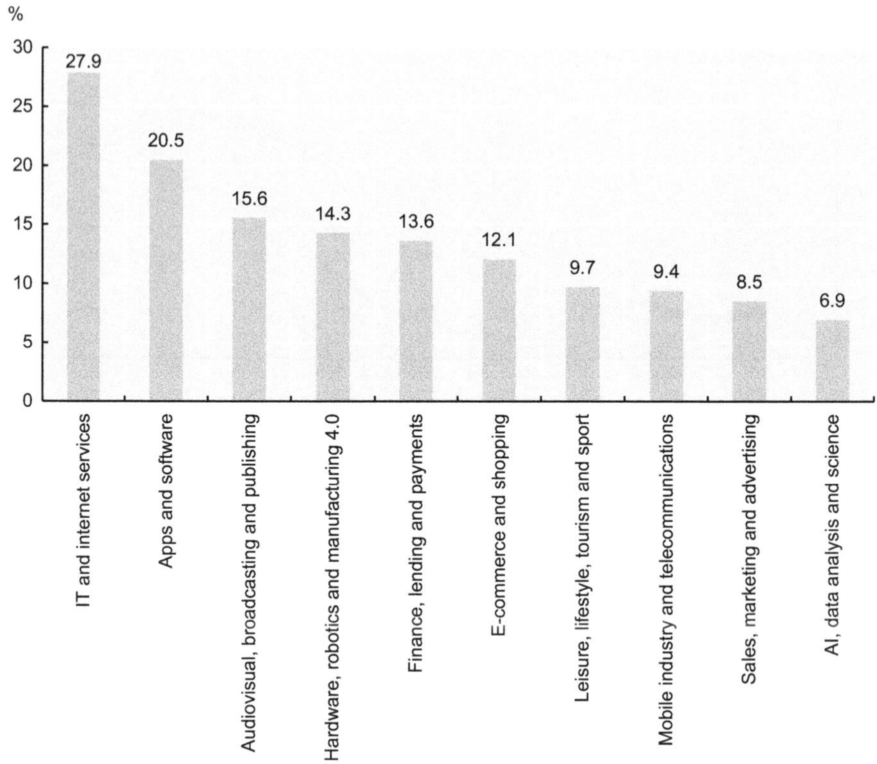

Figure 6.3 The most attractive activities of African start-ups: eight out of ten rely on the digital economy

Source: Authors' calculations based on *Crunchbase (2020)*, Crunchbase Pro (database)

the digital economy. E-commerce comes 6th (12%). The majority of start-ups run more than one activity (56%). Indeed, 29% run two categories of activities and 27% run three or more. Venture capital (VC) funding for start-ups grew sevenfold between 2015 and 2019. Tech start-ups raised a total of US$2.02 billion in VC funding in 2019, a 74% increase compared to US$1.16 billion in 2018 (Partech, 2020). Most (55%) VC funding went to the fintech and financial sectors.

How COVID-19 Accelerated Africa's Digitalisation Since 2020

Increased Use

The COVID-19 crisis led to a big push in internet use. Digital technologies enabled connectivity despite social distancing, limiting the spread of COVID-19, and enabled some individuals to work remotely or bank online, reducing the

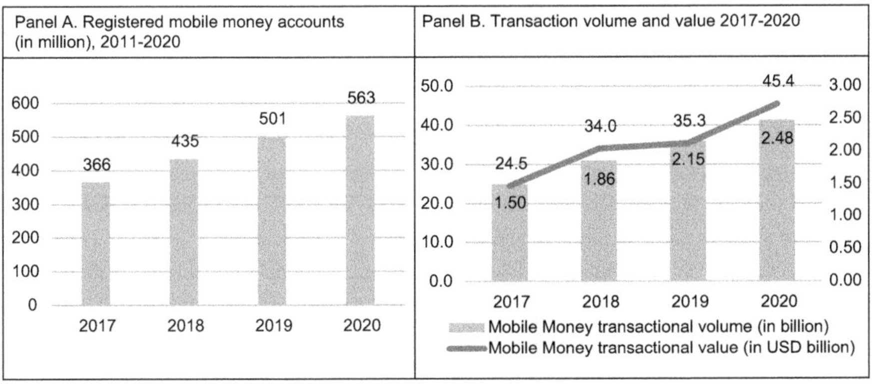

Figure 6.4 Growth in mobile money use in Africa in 2020

Source: GSMA (2021), *Mobile money metrics* (database)

economic costs of lockdowns (Ufua et al., 2021). Between 2017 and 2019, cross-border internet traffic in Africa grew at a compound annual rate of 43%, in parallel to the fast expansion of international internet bandwidth from 5,972 Gigabits per second (Gbps) to 12,212 Gbps – the world's most rapid growth. In 2020, this trend accelerated: among the top 100 bilateral internet connections involving an African country, 42 routes saw peak traffic increasing by 50% or more (authors' calculations, based on Telegeography, 2020). Increased demand and supply in digital payments solutions was also observed. Figure 6.4 shows registered mobile money accounts reaching 563 million accounts up from 501 million in 2019 (+15%), accompanied by increases in mobile money transactions' volume (+15%) and value (+23%) compared to 2019 (GSMA, 2021).

Surge in Foreign Direct Investment in ICT

The 2020 economic shock led to a contraction of foreign direct investment (FDI) in all sectors, except in the ICT industry. The ICT industry attracted US$8.4 billion in FDI in 2020, marking a jump in FDI of 285% from 2016 to 2019, hitting the highest recorded level since 2003. This surge in FDI is likely caused by markets' expectations that Africa's internet economy will continue to grow strongly. According to recent estimates, Africa's internet economy accounted for 4.5% of Africa's GDP in 2020 and could reach US$180 billion (5.2% of GDP) by 2025. With supportive policies, the potential contribution of the internet economy could amount US$712 billion or 8.5% of the continent's GDP by 2050 (Google Analytics/IFC, 2020).

Funding for African start-ups continued to increase in 2020. The number of technology start-ups securing funding in Africa increased 44% from 2019, riding five-year growth at a rate six times greater than that globally (BCG, 2021). By

August of 2021, funding for African start-ups had already increased 69% from the previous year's total inflows (Disrupt Africa, 2021).

Changes in Government Regulations Favoured Digital Innovations

Encouraged by changes in government regulations, Africa's private sector implemented a host of digital solutions to increase effectiveness of public policies in different sectors such as healthcare, education and finance.

Governments encouraged the use of mobile money and digital payments to support social distancing and limit the spread of the virus. African governments implemented policies to facilitate digital payments including fee waivers, increased transactions and balance limits or flexible on-boarding requirements (GSMA, 2020b). In Rwanda, the Central bank registered large increase in mobile payment transactions (+85%) and value (+206%) on a year-on-year basis (MFW4A, 2020).

Many businesses strived to adapt to the "new normal" by accelerating their adoption of technologies. More than one in five firms surveyed in the World Bank report *Africa's Pulse* started or expanded their use of digital technology in response to the COVID-19 shock. The percentage of Kenyan firms adopting digital technologies in response to the pandemic rose from 47% in June–August 2020 to 71% in September–October 2020 (World Bank, 2021). According to a Dell Technologies study, 79% of South African organisations fast tracked their digital transformation programmes, which is on par with the 80% reported globally (Banda, 2021).

Providing reliable payment systems can unlock Africa's digital trade potential and increase its resilience to shocks, notably through easier cross-border digital payments. The African Union Digital Transformation Strategy (2020–2030) recognises the need to tackle barriers to e-payment within the African Continental Free Trade Area (AfCFTA) to facilitate greater intra-African trade. It estimates that the Digital Free Trade Area (DFTA) could save US$450 million by reducing administrative requirements of cross-border trade, when fully implemented by 2030. In March 2021, the first blockchain-based intra-African commercial transaction was executed by OCP from Morocco to Ethiopia. Its value was US$400 million (OCP, 2021).

So far, only 28% of e-commerce marketplaces operating in Africa offer integrated payment solutions. Most rely on cash-on-delivery payments options (ITC, 2020). Surveyed firms in Kenya, Rwanda and Nigeria rank the lack of online payment solutions, insecure payments, costly payment services and poor interoperability among the top-three obstacles hindering cross-border e-commerce (Banga et al., 2021).

Innovation accelerated in healthcare. The COVID-19 pandemic exposed Africa's high reliance on global markets to procure pharmaceuticals, medical supplies and equipment. To respond to this challenge, the Africa Centres for Disease Control and Prevention – in collaboration with 20 international partners and foundations – launched a not-for-profit continental e-platform to help African government procure diagnostic tests and medical equipment from certified suppliers. The private sector developed multiple tools: Solar Wash is a sun-powered, touch-free water dispenser in Ghana; WhatsApp Chatbots, developed in South Africa, is now used by 50 million globally to simulate human communications through artificial intelligence; self-diagnostic tools in Angola, or DiagnoseMe, a remote mobile app in Burkina Faso; contact-tracing apps in Ghana; and mobile health information tools and COVID-19 triage tools in Nigeria. According to a survey across 18 economies, more than 50% of the digital technology innovations in health were ICT-based applications (58%), 25% involved 3D printing and about 10% were robotics (World Bank, 2021).

In education, more than 40 African countries offered teleclasses to students via e-learning platforms, TV or radio channels to respond to schools' closure (UNESCO, 2020). African ministries of education built on collaborations with mobile operators to increase access to digital learning tools (e.g., zero-rating, lifting data caps, tapping into Universal Service Funds, SMS learning system and free SIM cards).

Accelerated Technology Adoption Heightens Entrenched Inequalities

While the response to COVID-19 heavily relied on digital technologies, persistent digital divides constrain Africa's capacity to fully benefit from new technologies and use them to recover from the pandemic. In Ghana, for instance, a survey on the impact of COVID-19 across 4311 firms reported that only a tenth of firms (9%) were able to start or increase their use of internet to do business (GSS/UNDP/World Bank, 2020). Regarding education, while 73% of African governments set up distance learning mechanisms, only 24% implemented measures to ensure the inclusion of students living in remote areas. This policy implementation gap magnifies already-high inequalities in learning (UNESCO, 2021).

Similarly, about 95% of African Technical and Vocational Education and Training (TVET) providers closed schools and training centres during COVID-19, and over 50% reported that no online or offline distance learning alternatives have been provided (ILO, 2021). This accelerating digitalisation shows the need for concerted efforts in many African countries in taking advantage of the opportunities that digital transformation provides (Karakara and Osabuohien, 2019, 2020; Ejemeyovwi and Osabuohien, 2020; Ejemeyovwi et al., 2021).

Policy Priorities to Accelerate Africa's Digital Transformation

Africa's digital transformation can be achieved if digital technologies are widespread and help many companies become more productive. Policy makers will need to address remaining divides to ensure that Africa's digital transformation works for all, by prioritising two pillars: (i) diffusing digital technologies, especially among the most vulnerable population groups; and (ii) bridging the competitiveness gap, which hinders the growth of start-ups and SMEs.

Inequality in Access to Digital Solutions Remains the Largest Policy Challenge

More than 75% of Africa's youth owns a mobile phone (Figure 6.5). However, the share of people regularly using the internet widely varies across gender groups (30% of women and 44% of men), education levels (8% of those with less than a primary education and 77% of those with an upper secondary or higher education) and employment status (16% of those self-employed and 58% of those with waged jobs). These inequalities are acute for vulnerable groups (e.g. uneducated young women) living in rural areas. Rural dwellers are less likely to connect to the internet than urban inhabitants. Only 22% of rural inhabitants regularly use the internet, compared to 53% of urban inhabitants. Reducing spatial inequalities in internet usage can tackle several overlapping inequalities across gender, education levels, employment status and space.

The digital economy concentrates in major urban areas. Five cities host 49% of the 7,000 African start-ups identified by Crunchbase in 2019: Cape Town (12.5%), Lagos (10.3%), Johannesburg (10.1%), Nairobi (8.8%) and Cairo (6.9%). They account for 53 million inhabitants, less than 4% of the total African population, but offer strong digital ecosystems (AUC/OECD, 2019). In contrast, the majority of Africa's intermediary cities remains underserved. Across the continent, only 35% of intermediary cities are within 10 km from a high-speed terrestrial fibre-optic network, compared to 68% for big cities.

Map 1 shows that most Africa's intermediary cities are located far from a high-speed terrestrial fibre-optic network. In Central Africa, only 5% of the intermediary cities are within 10 km of the backbone network, compared to 36% of the big cities. In Southern and East Africa, on the other hand, the backbone network has expanded further across the urban networks, with 71% and 51%, respectively, of the intermediary cities connected to the terrestrial fibre-optic broadband network. Overall, only 35% of intermediary cities are close to a high-speed terrestrial fibre-optic network, despite representing 70% of Africa's urban population.

Strengthening communications infrastructure in intermediary cities and rural areas could yield high returns, as 73% of Africans will continue to live there by 2040. Intermediary cities can act as transmission hubs that serve the rural hinterland, strengthen rural-urban linkages and drive rural transformation. Increasing productive activities – such as food processing, agricultural inputs supply services, logistics or warehousing – in intermediary cities will better connect Africa's rural-urban supply chains (Traoré and Saint-Martin, 2020; Minsat, 2018). This will help local SMEs meet regional demand. Firm-level data on Côte d'Ivoire shows that when the concentration of firms increases by 10% in intermediary cities like Daloa or in Odienne, firms operating there increase their sales by 15%–17% (Fall and Coulibaly, 2016).

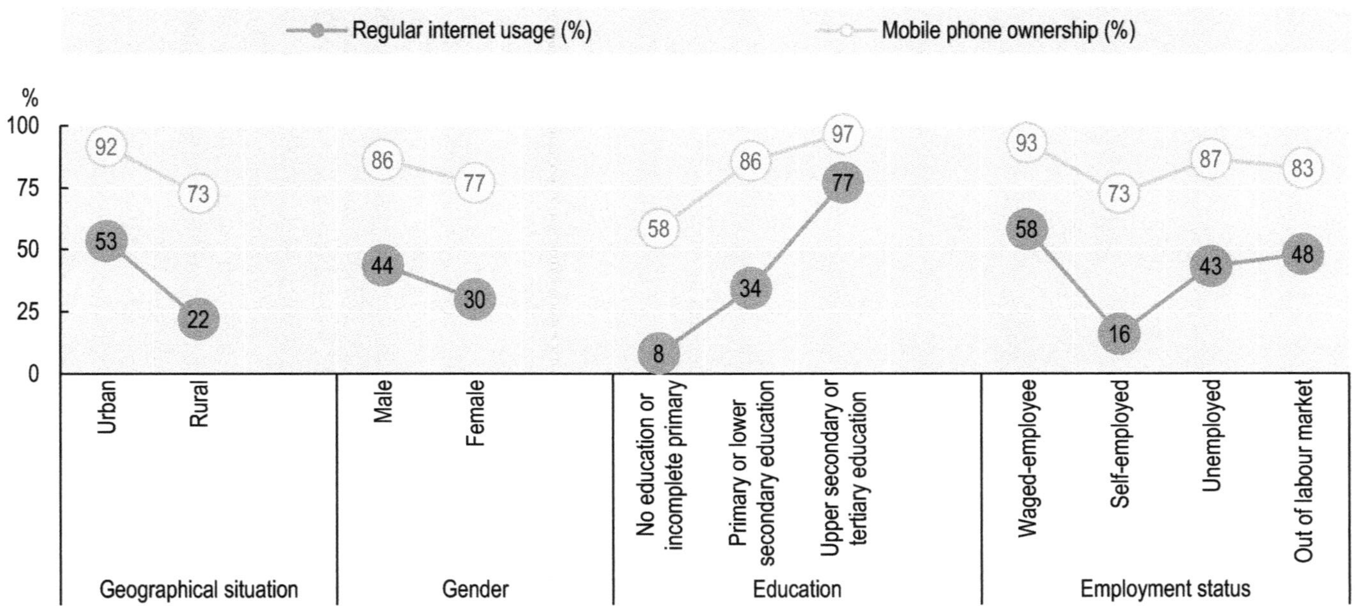

Figure 6.5 Mobile phone and Internet usage among Africa's youth (2015–2018)

Source: Authors' calculations based on Afrobarometer (2019), *Afrobarometer* (database)[2]

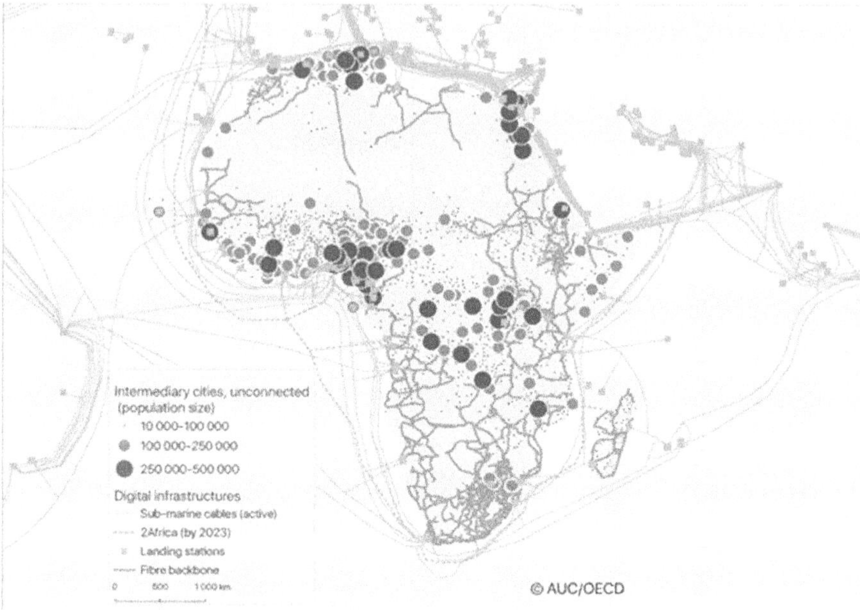

Figure 6.6 Digital infrastructure and unconnected intermediary cities by population size
Source: AUC/OECD, 2021; realised by the authors and the OECD Development Centre's Africa team

Diffusing Digital Innovations Beyond Large Urban Centres Will Reduce Much Inequality in Accessing Digitalisation

To bridge the digital divide, governments need to promote *last-mile access* to the internet. Nearly six in ten (57%) of African cities that are not connected to the network lie within only 50 km of it. In 2015, these cities accounted for a population of 146 million (AUC/OECD, 2021). Achieving universal access to broadband connectivity by 2030 would require laying out at least 250 000 km of fibre across the region, costing approximately US$100 billion in total or USD 9 billion a year (ITU/UNESCO, 2019). Attracting private investments for broadband connectivity for small towns and intermediary cities will enable resource-constrained governments to generate multiplier effects, through greater jobs creation, companies' growth and tax collection.

Expanding infrastructure is not a sufficient condition, however. Governments must also improve the affordability of internet services. According to our estimates, only 17% of Africa's population can afford one gigabyte of data, compared to 37% in LAC and 47% in Asia. Governments can make prices affordable through policies that (i) create new public-private alliances for rural connectivity, (ii) improve the use of Universal Service and Access Funds (USAFs) and

(iii) ensure fair competition among telecommunication providers. Already 37 African countries have created USAFs – special programmes with funding schemes for universal internet access and services. However, a recent review found that US$408 million, or 46% of funds collected, was still unspent by end of 2016 (Thakur and Potter, 2018). In countries like Algeria, Ghana, Kenya and Nigeria, the public sector successfully partnered with mobile telecom companies and with telecommunications equipment providers to bring cost-effective mobile broadband services to their rural populations.

Africa's Entrepreneurs Must Improve Their Capacity to Compete in the Digital Era

Africa benefits from a strong entrepreneurial spirit, which is fuelling this "bottom-up digital revolution" on the continent. Africa boasts the world's highest rate of entrepreneurship at about 22% of the labour force (AfDB/OECD/UNDP, 2017). Data from the Global Entrepreneurship Monitor surveys conducted between 2013 and 2019 show that Africa scores higher than Asian and LAC countries in both entrepreneurial intention and total early-stage entrepreneurial activity (GEM, 2020). In addition, the highest total entrepreneurial activity rates for women are found in Sub-Saharan Africa (21.8% to 25.0%), followed by LAC (17.3%). The global average rate is 10.2%. In Nigeria, for instance, nearly four in every ten working-age women are engaged in early-stage entrepreneurial activity (40.7%). Digital transformation can unlock many opportunities for this large entrepreneurial workforce.

Digital connectivity can enable Africa's entrepreneurs to enter new niches. To be reachable online, SMEs can opt for developing their own website or for using social media or specialised trade platforms (e.g. Jumia). For example, a number of small tourism companies in East Africa served new niche activities within wildlife tourism and eco-tourism and for tourists from emerging markets (Foster et al., 2017). Results from an econometric analysis of 27,000 manufacturing SMEs in 116 developing countries (including 31 African countries)[3] confirm that SMEs which adopt digital technologies are more likely to engage in international trade. Having a website is positively associated with a 4.6 percentage point increase in the share of imports among firm inputs and a 5.5 percentage point increase in the share of direct exports in firms' sales (AUC/OECD, 2021).

Entrepreneurs can produce digitally delivered services and avoid weak transport and logistics infrastructure. Since 2015, electronic transmission has become the dominant mode for Africa's trade in professional services (e.g. finance, insurance ICT and technical support). It accounted for US$18.8 billion, or 57% of Africa's export in professional services in 2017, up from US$8 million in 2005.

Forecasts say the gaming industry will surpass US$200 billion of revenue globally by 2023, up from an estimated US$145.7 billion in 2019 (Newzoo, 2019). In 2016, Kiro'o Games released Aurion, an African-themed video game, to the global market via the Steam platform. This small company of 20 employees, based in Cameroon, raised US$57,000 in April 2016 to develop games from

1310 backers through Kickstarter, an online crowdfunding platform (Kickstarter, 2019). It joins a recent wave of African video game makers from Egypt, Nigeria and South Africa that focus on producing unique, local narratives for the continental market (Dahir, 2017).

However, most start-ups and SMEs still face difficulties in scaling up and innovating. Currently, only 17% of Africa's early-stage entrepreneurs expect to create at least six jobs, the lowest percentage globally. In spite of having promising business ideas, many early-stage entrepreneurs face obstacles in obtaining loans from local banking systems. Only 5.4% of the total funds raised go to start-ups younger than five years old. The gender gap is wide: women-led start-ups only receive 2% of funding. Lockdowns and the potential of long-term economic fallout due to the COVID-19 pandemic further challenge the growth of these small enterprises (Ufua et al., 2021).

Increasing resilience will require stronger digital adoption, especially among MSMEs. Among firms from the World Bank Enterprise Surveys, 59% of all African firms use the internet to interact with clients and suppliers, and only 50% of small African firms. The share of firms having their own website is even lower, at 31% among all African firms and 23% among small ones (Figure 6.6). Barriers to digital adoption for MSMEs range from structural factors such as infrastructure to firm-specific factors such as financial and organisation capability. The continent's consumer e-commerce market is still in its infancy: it was estimated at US$5.7 billion in 2017, which is less than 0.5% of its combined GDP, compared to a global average of 4%.

Continental agencies play a leading role in accelerating continental cooperation on roaming services, data regulation and digital security to achieve a Digital

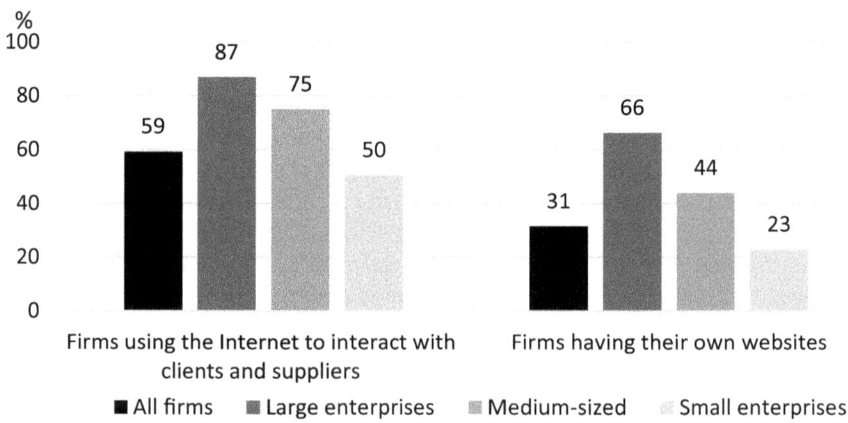

Figure 6.7 Formal manufacturing and service firms in Africa that use the internet and have websites

Source: Authors' calculations based on World Bank (2020), *World Bank Enterprise Surveys* (database), www.enterprisesurveys.org/en/data, using the latest data available for each country

Single Market and increase intra-African trade and productive integration. Reducing high roaming costs can be an operational objective for African policy makers. High roaming costs and related barriers to the use of data can severely reduce the benefits of the digital economy and slow the implementation of a regional digital single market (Bourassa et al., 2016; Cullen International, 2016, Cullen international, 2019). African countries must make more progress for affordable or free intra-African roaming services, notably to ensure an effective AfCFTA. Only three of Africa's eight Regional Economic Communities – the Economic Community of West African States (ECOWAS), EAC and SADC – are planning to reduce roaming costs (AUC/OECD, 2021: 59).

Finally, multilateral development cooperation can support Africa's digital transformation even further. Strategic partnerships can help in building capacity while financing Africa's development agenda. For instance, in December 2020, the European Commission and the African Union launched the Digital4Development (D4D) Hub. The platform gathers key stakeholders in order to scale up investments in Africa's digital transformation, promote knowledge sharing, and identify and implement strategic policies within inclusive national digital transformation plans. Many lessons can be learned by sharing experiences from different countries and world regions. The report *Africa's Development Dynamics 2021: Digital transformation and quality jobs*, prepared jointly by the African Union and the OECD Development Centre, with the support of other institutions like the European Union, BMZ/GIZ or the African Capacity Building Foundation, promotes evidence-based policy dialogue between African policy makers, entrepreneurs, academic communities and the civil society.

Conclusion

This chapter feeds on the growing literature on Africa's digital transformation and its potential to increase resilience to external shocks such as the COVID-19 pandemic. The pandemic significantly boosted the use of digital technologies as seen with the host of digital solutions implemented at local, national, regional and continental levels to mitigate the impact of COVID-19. Several African governments such as South Africa, Cameroon, Egypt, Ghana or Kenya already defined digital transformation as a priority sector in their recovery plans. However, addressing inequality in digital access and use will be crucial to enable digital diffusion – key to jobs creation and productivity gains – and support a sustainable recovery.

In order to reap the benefits of fast-paced digitalisation trends and overcome remaining challenges, this chapter highlighted selected policy implications. First, diffusing digital innovations beyond large urban centres to bridge the persistent digital divide by prioritising the development of broadband infrastructure in intermediary cities or improving the affordability of data services. Second, supporting Africa's dynamic start-ups and entrepreneurs to compete and innovate in the digital era by facilitating intellectual property registration or developing mechanisms to finance start-ups. Finally, accelerating continental and regional coordination will be essential to complement national strategies, harmonise existing standards and protocols, and support digital transformation throughout the continent.

Notes

1 ICA members include all G8 countries (Canada, France, Germany, Italy, Japan, the United Kingdom, the United States and Russia), two G20 countries (Spain and South Africa). African Institutions: The African Union Commission (AUC), the African Union Development Agency the (AUDA-NEPAD); the United Nations Economic Commission for Africa (UNECA), the African Development Bank (AfDB), the AfreximBank, the European Investment Bank (EIB), the International Finance Corporation (IFC), the Islamic Development Bank (IsDB), the Africa Finance Corporation (AFC), and the World Bank. Regional Development Finance Institutions and Bilaterals: The French Development Agency (AFD), the West African Development Bank (BOAD) and the Development Bank of Southern Africa (DBSA).

2 The results are based on survey data from 34 African countries. Primary education: Completed elementary education or less (up to 8 years of basic education); Secondary: Completed some secondary education and up to 3 years tertiary education (9 to 15 years of education); Tertiary: Completed 4 years of education beyond high school or received a 4-year college degree.

3 The sample includes more than 27,000 SMEs from the World Bank Enterprise Survey. The regressions control for a number of firm characteristics such as ownership status (foreign versus domestic owner), the experience of the manager, capital intensity and the capital utilisation rate. Using the Generalised Linear Model estimator, the regression also includes fixed effects for each country, sector (ISIC 3 digit level) and year.

References

2AfricaCable (2020), "2Africa: A transformative subsea cable for future internet connectivity in Africa announced by global and African partners", *Press Release*, 14 May 2020, www.2africacable.com/.

AfDB/OECD/UNDP (2017), *African Economic Outlook 2017: Entrepreneurship and Industrialisation*, OECD Publishing, Paris, https://doi.org/10.1787/aeo-2017-en.

AFRILABS and Briter Bridges (2019), *Building a Conducive Setting for Innovators to Thrive: A Qualitative and Quantitative Study of a Hundred Hubs Across Africa*, www.afrilabs.com/wp-content/uploads/2019/11/AfriLabs-Innovation-Ecosystem-Report.pdf.

Afrobarometer (2019), *Afrobarometer* (database), https://afrobarometer.org/fr.

AUC/OCDE (2021), *Africa's Development Dynamics 2021: Digital Transformation for Quality Jobs*, CUA, Addis Ababa/Éditions OCDE, Paris, https://doi.org/10.1787/0a5c9314-en.

AUC/OECD (2019), *Africa's Development Dynamics 2019: Achieving Productive Transformation*, OECD Publishing, Paris/African Union Commission, Addis Ababa, https://doi.org/10.1787/c1cd7de0-en.

Banda, M. (2021). "Global pandemic accelerates Digital transformation in South Africa", *Intelligent CIO. 12*, www.intelligentcio.com/africa/2021/03/12/global-pandemic-accelerates-digital-transformation-in-south-africa/.

Banga, K. and D.W te Welde. (2018), "Digitalisation and the future of African manufacturing", *Briefing Paper*, Supporting Economic Transformation, Overseas Development Institute, https://set.odi.org/wp-content/uploads/2018/03/SET_Future-of-manufacturing_Brief_Final.pdf.

Banga, K., et al. (2021), "E-commerce in preferential trade agreements: Implications for African firms and the AfCFTA", *Overseas Development Institute*, African Trade Policy Centre, UNECA, https://cdn.odi.org/media/documents/e-commerce_in_preferential_trade_agreements_report.pdf.

BCG (2021), *Overcoming Africa's Tech Startup Obstacles*, www.bcg.com/publications/2021/new-strategies-needed-to-help-tech-startups-in-africa.

Bourassa, F., et al. (2016), "Developments in international mobile roaming", *OECD Digital Economy Papers, No. 249*, OECD Publishing, Paris, https://doi.org/10.1787/5jm0lsq78vmx-en.

Bukht, R. and R. Heeks (2017), "Defining, conceptualising and measuring the digital economy", *Development Informatics Working Paper No. 68*, Centre for Development Informatics, Global Development Institute, University of Manchester, https://diodeweb.files.wordpress.com/2017/08/diwkppr68-diode.pdf.

Cariolle, J., M. Le Goff and O. Santoni (2019), "Digital vulnerability and performance of firms in developing countries", *Working Papers, No. 709*, Banque de France, www.banque-france.fr/sites/default/files/medias/documents/wp_709.pdf.

Crunchbase (2020), *Crunchbase Pro* (database), www.crunchbase.com/search-home.

Cullen International (2016), *Building a Digital Single Market Strategy for Latin America*, CAF, Buenos Aires, https://scioteca.caf.com/handle/123456789/980.

Cullen International (2019), *Regional and Sub-Regional Approaches to the Digital Economy: Lessons from Asia Pacific and Latin America*, CAF, Caracas, https://scioteca.caf.com/handle/123456789/1381.

Dahir, A. L. (2017), "African video game makers are breaking into the global industry with their own stories", *Quartz Africa*, https://qz.com/africa/974439/african-video-game-makers-are-breaking-into-the-global-industry-with-their-own-stories/.

Demirgüç-Kunt, A., et al. (2018), *The Global Findex Database 2017: Measuring Financial Inclusion and the Fintech Revolution*, https://globalfindex.worldbank.org/.

Disrupt Africa (2021), *More Than 300 African Tech Startups Have Raised Over $1.1bn So Far in 2021*, https://disrupt-africa.com/2021/08/12/more-than-300-african-tech-startups-have-raised-over-1-1bn-so-far-in-2021/.

Djiofack, C. Z., H. Dudu and A. G. Zeufack (2020), "Assessing COVID-19's economic impact in sub-Saharan Africa: Insights from a CGE model", in *COVID-19 in Developing Economies*, VoxEU, CEPR Press, London, pp. 53–68, https://voxeu.org/content/covid-19-developing-economies.

Ejemeyovwi, J. O. and E. S. Osabuohien (2020), "Investigating the Relevance of Mobile Technology Adoption on Inclusive Growth in West Africa", *Contemporary Social Science*, 15(1), 48–61.

Ejemeyovwi, J. O., E. S. Osabuohien and E. I. K. Bowale (2021), "ICT Adoption, Innovation and Financial Development in a Digital World; Empirical Analysis from Africa", *Transnational Corporations Review*, 13(1), 16–31.

Fall, M. and S. Coulibaly (2016), "Diversified Urbanization: The Case of Côte d'Ivoire", *Directions in Development: Countries and Regions*, The World Bank Group, Washington, DC, https://doi.org/10.1596/978-1-4648-0808-1.

Foster, C., & S. Azmeh (2019), "Latecomer Economies and National Digital Policy: An Industrial Policy Perspective", *Journal of Development Studies*, 56(7), 1247–1262. https://doi.org/10.1080/00220388.2019.1677886

Foster, C., et al. (2017), "Digital control in value chains: Challenges of connectivity for East African firms", *Economic Geography*, 94(1/2018), Informa UK Limited, https://doi.org/10.1080/00130095.2017.1350104.

GEM (2020), “Entrepreneurial Behaviour and Attitudes: the Adult Population Survey (APS)”, *Global Entrepreneurship Monitor (database)*, https://www.gemconsortium.org/data/key-aps.

Gillwald, A. and O. Mothobi (2019), “After access 2018: A demand-side view of mobile internet from 10 African countries”, *Policy Paper Series No. 5 After Access: Paper No. 7*, Research ICT Africa, Cape Town, https://researchictafrica.net/2019_after-access_africa-comparative-report/.

Google Analytics/IFC (2020), *e-Conomy Africa 2020: Africa’s $180 Billion Internet Economy Future*, www.ifc.org/wps/wcm/connect/publications_ext_content/ifc_external_publication_site/publications_listing_page/google-e-conomy.

GSMA (2017), *Blockchain for Development: Emerging Opportunities for Mobile, Identity and Aid*, www.gsma.com/mobilefordevelopment/wp-content/uploads/2017/12/Blockchain-for-Development.pdf.

GSMA (2020a), *GSMA Intelligence* (database), www.gsmaintelligence.com/data/ (accessed 28 June 2020).

GSMA (2020b), *Tracking Mobile Money Regulatory Responses to COVID-19*, www.gsma.com/mobilefordevelopment/programme/mobile-money/gsma-mobile-money-regulatory-response-to-covid-19-tracker-and-analysis/.

GSMA (2021), *Mobile Money Metrics* (database), www.gsma.com/mobilemoneymetrics.

GSS/UNDP/World Bank (2020), “How COVID-19 is affecting firms in Ghana: Results from the Business Tracker Survey”, *Ghana Statistical Service*, https://statsghana.gov.gh/covidtracker/Business%20Tracker%20Brief%20Report_GSS_web.pdf.

Hamilton Research (2020), “Africa: Africa’s operational fibre optic network reaches 1 million route kilometres”, *Africa Bandwidth Maps*, www.africabandwidthmaps.com/?p=6158.

Hjort, J. and J. Poulsen (2019), “The arrival of fast internet and employment in Africa”, *American Economic Review*, 109(3), 1032–1079, https://doi.org/10.1257/aer.20161385.

ICA (2018), *Infrastructure Financing Trends in Africa: 2018*, Infrastructure Consortium for Africa, Abidjan, Côte d’Ivoire, www.icafrica.org/fileadmin/documents/IFT_2018/ICA_Infrastructure_Financing_Trends_in_Africa_-_2018_Final_En.pdf.

ILO (2021), *Skills Development in the Time of COVID-19: Taking Stock of the Initial Responses in Technical and Vocational Education and Training*, www.ilo.org/skills/areas/skills-training-for-poverty-reduction/WCMS_766557/lang-en/index.htm.

IMF (2022), *World Economic Outlook, April 2022* (database), International Monetary Fund, Washington, DC, https://www.imf.org/en/Publications/WEO/weo-database/2022/April.

ITU (2018), *The State of Broadband 2018: Broadband Catalysing Sustainable Development*, Broadband Reports, International Telecommunication Union, Geneva, www.itu-ilibrary.org/science-and-technology/the-state-of-broadband-2018_pub/810d0472-en.

ITU/UNESCO (2019), *Connecting Africa through Broadband: A Strategy for Doubling Connectivity by 2021 and Reaching Universal Access by 2030*, International Telecommunication Union, Geneva/United Nations Educational, Scientific and Cultural Organization, Paris, www.broadbandcommission.org/Documents/workinggroups/DigitalMoonshotforAfrica_Report.pdf.

Karakara, A. A. and E. S. Osabuohien (2019), “Households’ ICT access and bank patronage in West Africa: Empirical insights from Burkina Faso and Ghana”, *Technology in Society*, 56, 116–125.

Karakara, A. A. and E. S. Osabuohien (2020), “ICT adoption, competition and innovation of informal firms in West Africa: Comparative study of Ghana and Nigeria”, *Journal of Enterprising Communities*, 14(3), 397–414.

Kickstarter (2019), "Aurion: Legacy of the Kori-Odan", *Yaoundé*, www.kickstarter.com/projects/plugindigitallabel/aurion-legacy-of-the-kori-odan.

MFW4A (2020), *Rwanda: Mobile Payment Transactions Grow by 206%*, https://www.mfw4a.org/news/rwanda-mobile-payment-transactions-grow-206.

Minsat, A. (2018, August), "Small and intermediary cities will make or break the sustainable development goals in Africa", *Urban Planning International*, 33(5), http://doi.org/10.22217/upi.2018.328.

Ndung'u, N. S. (2018), "Next steps for the digital revolution in Africa: Inclusive growth and job creation lessons from Kenya", *Working Paper*, Africa Growth Initiative, Brookings, https://media.africaportal.org/documents/Digital-Revolution-in-Africa_Brookings_AGI_20181022.pdf.

Newzoo (2019), *Newzoo Global Games Market Report 2019: Light Version*, https://newzoo.com/insights/trend-reports/newzoo-global-games-market-report-2019-light-version/.

OCP (2021), *La trade and development bank, le groupe OCP, et DLTledgers propulsent le commerce intra-africain d'engrais grâce à la blockchain en pleine pandémie de covid-19*, https://ocpsiteprodsa.blob.core.windows.net/media/2021-03/CP%20OCP_OCP-TDB-DLT_29032021_vFR.pdf.

OECD (2019), *Regulatory Effectiveness in the Era of Digitalisation*, www.oecd.org/gov/regulatory-policy/Regulatory-effectiveness-in-the-era-of-digitalisation.pdf.

OECD (2020), *OECD Policy Responses to Coronavirus (COVID-19), COVID-19 and Africa: Socio-economic Implications and Policy Responses*, OECD Publishing, Paris, www.oecd.org/coronavirus/policy-responses/covid-19-and-africa-socio-economic-implications-and-policy-responses-96e1b282/#biblio-d1e2476.

Partech (2020), *African Tech Start-ups Reach a New Symbolic Milestone with US$ 2.02 Billion Raised in Equity Funding, Representing 74% YoY Growth*, https://partechpartners.com/press-room/partech-africa-publishes-its-annual-report-african-tech-start-ups-reach-new-symbolic-milestone-us-202-billion-raised-equity-funding-representing-74-yoy-growth/.

Serianu (2017), *Africa Cyber Security Report 2017: Demystifying Africa's Cyber Security Poverty Line*, Nairobi, www.serianu.com/downloads/AfricaCyberSecurityReport2017.pdf.

Suri, T. and W. Jack (2016), "The long-run poverty and gender impacts of mobile money", *Science*, 354/6317, 1288–1292, https://science.sciencemag.org/content/354/6317/1288.

TeleGeography (2020), *TeleGeography Global Internet Research Service*, www2.telegeography.com/hubfs/assets/product-tear-sheets/product-page-content-samples/global-internet-geography/telegeography-global-internet-geography-executive-summary.pdf.

Thakur, D. and L. Potter (2018), *Universal Service and Access Funds: An Untapped Resource to Close the Gender Digital Divide*, World Wide Web Foundation, Washington, DC, http://webfoundation.org/docs/2018/03/Using-USAFs-to-Close-the-Gender-Digital-Divide-in-Africa.pdf.

Traoré, B. and E. Saint-Martin (2020), "Energising Africa's productive transformation: How intermediary cities can be a game changer", *OECD Development Matters Blog*, 6 March 2020, https://oecd-development-matters.org/2020/03/06/energising-africas-productive-transformation-how-intermediary-cities-can-be-a-game-changer/.

Ufua, D. E., E. Osabuohien, M. E. Ogbari, H. O. Falola, E. E. Okoh and A. Lakhani (2021), "Re-strategising government palliative support systems in tackling the challenges of COVID-19 lockdown in Lagos State, Nigeria", *Global Journal of Flexible Systems Management*, 1–14, https://doi.org/10.1007/s40171-021-00263-z.

UNESCO (2020), *COVID-19 Response* (database), https://en.unesco.org/covid19.

UNESCO (2021), *A Snapshot of Educational Challenges and Opportunities for Recovery in Africa*, https://unesdoc.unesco.org/ark:/48223/pf0000377513.

World Bank (2020), *World Bank Enterprise Surveys* (database), www.enterprisesurveys.org/en/data.

World Bank (2021), *Africa's Pulse, No. 23, April 2021: An Analysis of Issues Shaping Africa's Economic Future*, World Bank, Washington, DC, https://openknowledge.worldbank.org/handle/10986/35342.

7 Addressing Non-health Effects of COVID-19 Pandemic and Development of Future Resilience in Nigeria

A Systemic Intervention

Daniel Ufua, Olusola Joshua Olujobi, Romanus Osabohien, Evans Osabuohien, and Gbadebo Odularu

Introduction

More often than not, policymakers seem to have a proper perspective about the world, where formulating the appropriate plans concerning policies aims to put the economy on the path to address identified socioeconomic shocks (Organisation for Economic Cooperation and Development [OECD], 2020). Presently, governments across countries are striving to curtail the impact of socioeconomic shocks occasioned by the global pandemic, called the coronavirus, otherwise known as the COVID-19 pandemic (Djalantea, Shaw, & DeWit, 2020). The emergence of the COVID-19 pandemic has created a series of adverse effects on man across different parts of the world (see Figure 7.1). This has resulted in major economic shock and imbalances both in developed and developing countries, which has also had obvious negative impacts on these nations' economic growth and development (Barua, 2020). Among the broad effects of the COVID-19 pandemic is an uncontrollable disruption for world health and development societies at large (Igoe & Chadwick, April 13, 2020a). These effects have been felt by the individuals, organisations, states, regions, and countries in different parts of the world (IMF Annual Report, 2020). While the challenges of COVID-19 pandemic have spread across limits and bounds, man has been left with the problem to develop an effective response towards addressing the profane issues resulting from the outbreak of the COVID-19 pandemic (Amoo et al., 2020; Rajan et al., 2020).

The primary effect of the pandemic was traced to its devastating challenge to human health; however, its non-health effects have constituted critical worldwide issues of concern that seem to have no limitations. Social and economic boundaries across the globe have been adversely affected resulting from various reactive steps taken by (e.g. national government), to address the messy nature of the COVID-19 pandemic (Osabuohien, Gershon, Oye, & Efobi, 2020). For instance, many supply and value chain activities were brought to an abrupt halt and human

DOI: 10.4324/9781003208358-10

movement being restricted to total lockdown, initiated by the government authorities across the globe due to the primary danger of COVID-19 pandemic to human health (Heymann & Shindo, 2020). Similarly, various actions by government authorities such as total lock down and restriction of movement have equally dashed the hope of man, further resulting in the disruption of socioeconomic activities in the various sectors (Lexology Report, April 6, 2020). These have led to adverse non-health effects of COVID-19 pandemic, in broad forms such as economic recession and stagnation, astronomical increments in national debt, other social, economic, political and contractual breaches across sectors of the world economy (Olujobi, 2021; Bedford et al., 2020).

In Figure 7.1, panel A means: worst-case scenario (uncontrolled) – no intervention; panel B means: controlling with the moderate social distancing approach – maximum result when the epidemic is controlled via interventions to prevent contacts in general public, including social distancing (more than 40% rate of decline in contacts). Panel C means: controlling using a heavy social distancing mechanism (1.6) – the introduction of a severe social distancing approach which will minimise the percentage of people in public places by more than 60% once the 1.6 deaths per 100,000 per week trigger is achieved. Panel D means: suppression with heavy social distancing (0.2) – the introduction of a serious social distancing approach which minimises the proportion of contact in public places by about 6% once the 0.2 demises per 100,000 per week trigger is achieved (United Nations Economic Commission for Africa-UNECA, 2020).

Similarly, the low-income families (i.e. those on less than one dollar/per day), on average, already spend about 36% of their income on expenses related to health issues. Other issues include access to health care provisions that may become seemingly unaffordable in the wake of COVID-19 pandemic. This leads

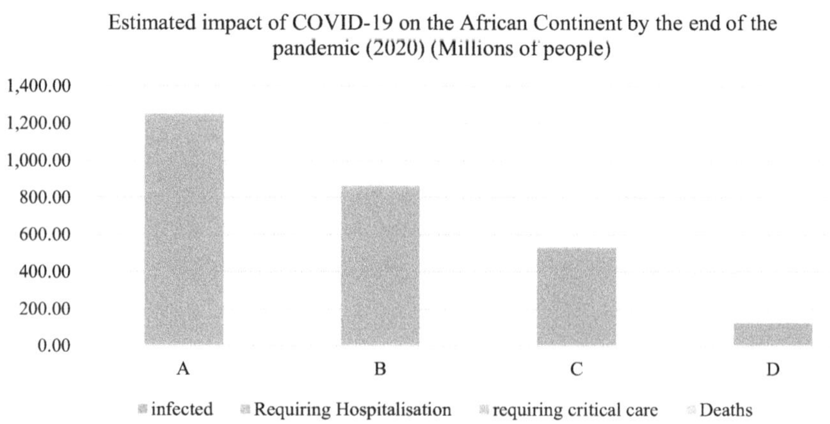

Figure 7.1 Effect of COVID-19 pandemic (estimated) on Africa by the end of the pandemic (2020)

Source: United Nations Economic Commission for Africa, UNECA (April, 2020)

to an increase in the number of people falling below the poverty line (UNECA, 2020; Osabohien, Matthew, Ohalete, & Osabuohien, 2020). Thus, this research aims at making valuable contributions towards addressing these effects, which tend to increase in proportions. Many decisions, such as budgets for palliative material distribution and actions, have been initiated and taken by several stakeholders in their response to the pandemic outbreak. For instance, for the national governments in various parts of the world, the current study is set to propose an approach that could be useful to strive to address the non-health effects of the COVID-19 pandemic, especially in the African continent (Hopman, Allegranzi, & Mehtar, 2020). The focus on Africa and indeed Nigeria in this research is due to the apparent reason, being a continent that has the ready challenge of fewer resources required and poor access to certain privileges such as funding for critical continental issues such as COVID-19 pandemic (Gilbert et al., 2020).

Materials and Methods

The current study emphasises the engagement of key stakeholders in developing a critical understanding of the depth and prospects of the effects of non-health challenges, posed by the emergence of the COVID-19 pandemic. The research explores the complex realities of the non-health effects of the COVID-19 pandemic, based on the current context and from the perspectives of the affected stakeholders (Queirós, Faria, & Almeida, 2017). The research relies on extant literature to develop a conceptual review of the topic. It also reflects on current realities of non-health effects of COVID-19 pandemic in Nigeria. Data were sourced primarily from published Reports about the non-health effects of COVID-19 pandemic, by reputable development agencies such as the United Nations, Google Scholar database and the authors' institutional and personal libraries (Onu, Kessler, & Smith, 2016). A content review of literature was applied to ascertain the depth of non-health effects of COVID-19 pandemic in Nigeria. The intention is also to explore the topic from diverse perspectives and views of researchers, institutional and practitioners (Carr, 2009).

The research aims to contribute to the debate on advancing learning from the experience of the COVID-19 pandemic, and project reliance for the future. The study suggests the adoption of systemic intervention as an effective plan that can provide pragmatic solutions to the focused challenges in the current research (Ufua, Olujobi, Tahir et al., 2022). Systemic intervention embraces an inclusive approach to the development of suitable policies and procedures by the key stakeholders, through a joint development process to develop and implement solutions to the critical issues of non-health effects of COVID-19 pandemic (Pyka, Kudic, & Müller, 2019; Sánchez-Lara & Flores-Choperena, 2021).

The next section provides a conceptual discussion on the usefulness of systemic intervention to the proposed approach to address the non-health effects of COVID-19 pandemic.

Results

The Usefulness of Systemic Intervention in the Quest to address the Non-health Effects of the COVID-19 Pandemic

Many researchers have adopted the use of systems theories to solve complex organisational issues. Systemic intervention is a subset of systems thinking (Simonovic, 2010; Cabrera, Colosi, & Lobdell, 2008). It is a methodology applied by researchers in an intervention. Midgley (2000) defines intervention as a purposeful action by the agent(s) to create a change. Therefore, the utmost aim for the application of systemic intervention is to develop a departure from the identified current state to the desired state (Ufua, Papadopoulos, & Midgley, 2018). It embraces the use of different methods, ideas, techniques and concepts from soft systems thinking to develop a methodological approach that suits the identified issues and context, based on the intentions of the interveners (Ufua, Salau, Ikpefan, Dirisu, & Okoh, 2020).

The non-health effects of the COVID-19 pandemic is a non-linear issue that covers different sectors and across several boundary demarcations. Therefore, the use of systemic intervention can provide a platform to identify, engage, and involve the key stakeholders effectively. These are either affected or concerned with the non-health effects of the COVID-19 pandemic. This also poses a complicated situation that may need a depth of rational thinking and actions by human agents (herein referred to as stakeholders, interveners or agents).

Systemic intervention adopts a collaborative approach, involving participating stakeholders who are either involved or affected by a phenomenon of interest. These are productively engaged in a process of interactions and innovation to develop a working approach to address identified issues of interest (Midgley & Lindhult, 2021). Systemic intervention process requires the application of more than one approach to effectively address (Stacey, Griffin, & Shaw, 2000). It also entails the involvement of human elements at different levels and interactions with environmental structures such as government policies, which creates the need for the interveners' critical thinking while engaging these factors in addressing the non-health effects of COVID-19 pandemic (Checkland, 1981; Jackson, 2003).

The complexity associated with the COVID-19 pandemic requires boundary judgement that may involve the inter-subjectivity that may affect productive debate among the interveners included in the systemic intervention (see Ufua, 2020). The focus on the set boundary will help the stakeholders focus on the structure of the identified critical issues, based on their agreed value judgement and perception about the effects of the COVID-19 pandemic (Smith & Shaw, 2019). The entire ambience of the non-health effects of COVID-19 pandemic tends to show different characteristics covering critical environmental issues such as unemployment, insecurity, low government revenues, failure of businesses, and criminalities, among others (Ufua & Adebayo, 2019). It is arguably useful to adopt an approach that can embrace incremental advancement of solutions that aim to provide the means to address the identified issues from the perspective of the different stakeholders who are either affected or involved with the challenging effects of the COVID-19 pandemic (Midgley & Rajagopalan, 2019).

According to Midgley and Pinzón (2011), effective systemic intervention provides a platform for critical group dynamics issues such as diversities and conflict of interest in an intervention process. They suggest the need for the participants to be supported through dialogue focusing on values. The aim is to enact a fair process for making decisions. They also suggest the reflections on moral frameworks and boundary concerns that suits an intervention (Kaiser, Fahrenbach, Kragulj, & Grisold, 2018; Ufua et al., 2021). The stake of the current research is based on the potency of the interveners who should voluntarily involve in COVID-19 pandemic intervention process to develop a creative medium to engage the process. The effort will be premised on the detailed understanding and structure of the current state of non-health effects of the pandemic and engage a joint operation to develop the means to address them effectively. It also requires a process of due recognition of the diversity of the worldviews and expectations and addressing same via interactive actions among participants in the systemic intervention process (Midgley et al., 2013; Cunha & Morais, 2019).

The justification for the choice of systemic intervention as a suitable methodology to address the complex non-health effects of the COVID-19 pandemic is underpinned by the fact that while the challenges seem to be numerous, it is arguable to state that the application of a transdisciplinary approach can be suitable. The researchers also observe from extant literature on the implementation of systems thinking, especially in the practical use of systemic intervention, which fits well with the non-health effects of the COVID-19 pandemic (Nembhard, Burns, & Shortell, 2020). This can encourage participative planning and purposeful deliberations to develop improved approaches towards addressing the effects of COVID-19 pandemic (White, Burger, & Yearworth, 2016). Likewise, systemic intervention, being adopted as a methodological approach, can reduce incidences of policy resistance via the involvement of the affected stakeholders as participants in systems thinking, which embrace detailed analysis of the context and the various non-health challenges related to the COVID-19 pandemic, and also draw on ideas advanced from different stakeholders' perspectives (Atun, & Menabde, 2008; Ufua, Salau, Dada, & Adeyeye, 2020). Other characteristics justifying the adoption of systemic interventions are discussed in the next section.

The Relevance of Stakeholders' Engagement in Addressing the Non-health Effects of the COVID-19 Pandemic

The consultation of key stakeholders has remained a hallmark of the application of systemic intervention in addressing complex issues of concern. The engagement of relevant stakeholders provides the leverage to resolve identified issues. While the non-health effects of COVID-19 pandemic readily projects complex problems to a society, it is bound to involve the diverse thoughts and perspectives of the stakeholders in the process of exploration and the development of a solution to address its effects (Alford & Head, 2017; Igoe & Chadwick, May 23, 2020b). It would also require a joint effort from these stakeholders to adequately and satisfactorily address in the long run, instead, the conventional top-down leadership thinking. This is because such may be obsessed with an inadequate understanding of the different stakeholder perspectives of the identified complex situation, such as the non-health effects of the COVID-19 pandemic, focused in this research (Ufua et al., 2021).

Moreover, active stakeholders' engagement can provide the necessary emancipatory means for the policymakers to avoid making unrealistic policies that do not reflect the perspectives of the affected stakeholders while striving to address the complex effects of the COVID-19 pandemic. In other words, stakeholder engagement practice can result to learning and the development of suitable ideas and approaches that can lead to more awareness and build the confidence of the affected stakeholders on the process of systemic intervention based on the current context (Dentoni, Bitzer, & Schouten, 2018; Ufua et al., 2022). It is, therefore, argued in this research that policymakers tend to face challenges of making policy decisions that are truly reflective of the depth of the situation and the stakeholders' interest (Peters, 2017; IMF Press Release, April 8, 2020). The stance of the current research is that only a joint approach, such as the adoption of systemic intervention, can sufficiently provide a meeting point between the inherent complexity and the diverse interest of the affected stakeholders.

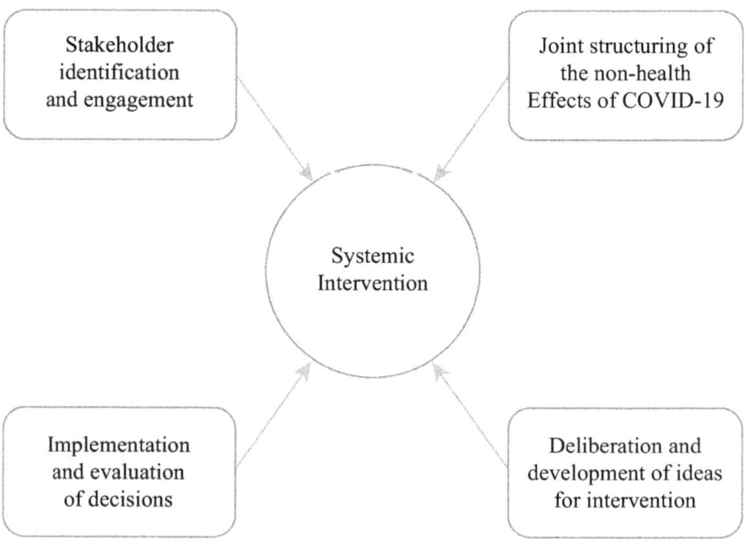

Figure 7.2 Proposed systemic intervention model for addressing non-health effects of COVID-19 pandemic

Source: The authors compilation

Further Discussion on Systemic Intervention in Addressing the Non-health Effects of the COVID-19 Pandemic

The application of systemic intervention in addressing the non-health effects of the COVID-19 pandemic, as a suitable approach, demands the skills and expertise of the stakeholders involved. First, systemic intervention requires a concerted development of connected thinking via a process of interactions and deliberations among participants, aimed at appreciating the depth of the non-health effects of COVID-19 pandemic, either on a systematic or a systemic that can inform the right actions to effectively address (Boyd, Brown, & Midgley, 2004). Connected thinking, being an engaging practice among participants in an intervention, will result to learning and improvement of ideas and thoughts among participants via a process of continuous innovation at various levels, with the aim to achieving the set objective (Olokundun, Ogbari, Obi, & Ufua, 2019).

Implementing systemic intervention can become an efficient means of addressing complex issues. This is because the systemic intervention provides a piece of machinery for exhaustive consideration of various options in a collaborative decision process (Arnold & Wade, 2015). Ufua, Papadopoulos, and Midgley (2018) note that decisions can be slow-paced in a systemic intervention process. Nevertheless, a considerable advantage from its process is the endpoint joint decisions that can enhance acceptability and more comfortable evaluation for improvement. It is, therefore, suitable for addressing multiple complex situations such as the non-health effects of the COVID-19 pandemic. The joint approach embedded in the systemic intervention also supports clear accountability in its process (Ufua, Salau, et al., 2022). While this can result in effectiveness in joint development of solution to identified issues, it is arguable to note that it can become a more efficient means to identify complex issues of interest in the long run. This is because multiple problems are addressed in an intervention process (Ison, 2017). Similarly, due to the overriding principles of stakeholders' engagement, there seem to be minimal chances for actions that are misleading (Holmes et al., 2020).

Having understood the structure of the complex issues, however, the application of systemic intervention requires setting boundaries based on a unified approach by the participants in a systemic intervention. A boundary is a set of issues identified in an intervention to be addressed at a given point in a systemic intervention process (Foote et al., 2007). It guides the interveners in setting the necessary priorities on what issues to address in an intervention. Boundary setting is based on the concerns and interests of the stakeholders and other environmental factors that may affect the intervention process (Yolles, 2001). The concept of boundary critiques is relevant to the current research. It can provide the needed guidance in identifying and choosing options, sourcing and deploying scarce resources to address identified non-health effects of the COVID-19 pandemic (see Ulrich, 2003; Odiboh, George, Salau, Ekanem, Yartey, & Banda, 2020). While Ufua (2020) reckons that boundaries can be set and re-adjusted at any point in an intervention, it is argued in the current research that the affected stakeholders are most suitable to set acceptable boundaries that can reflect the actual state of their varied perspectives. This is because the set boundaries are made flexible, depending on the context to reabsorb further emergence of issues that may require boundary adjustment to keep the intervention in focus with the set objectives. The involvement of participants in boundary-setting can make the intervention become void of an 'expert-driven or dictated solutions that could be rigid, misleading or unacceptable to participants in the intervention process' (Midgley, 2000; Narwankar, Elatlassi, & Wang, 2016).

Benefits of Systemic Intervention in Addressing Non-health Effects of the COVID-19 Pandemic

As suggested in this research, the basic principles underpinning the application of systemic intervention can result in benefits in the address. First, systemic intervention stands in a position to enhance creativity among participants in an intervention. It is, therefore, argued in this research that the complexity posed by the non-health effects of the COVID-19 pandemic fits well with the need for creativity in the application of the systemic intervention. The adoption of systemic intervention will align with the strive to address the emergent non-health effects of COVID-19 pandemic, with critical effects on the development of agreeable solutions that can address identified issues. This will point to the obvious need for re-started economic growth and development (see, World Bank Group, June 2019; Ufua, Olujobi, Osabohien, Odularu,& Osabuohien, 2022).

Furthermore, systemic intervention provides awareness among stakeholders in an intervention to develop a proactive apparatus for addressing the re-emerging situation of concerns in an intervention (Ufua, Olonade, et al. 2022). This is important to the strive to address the COVID-19 pandemic, as there tend to be further issues that may require the attention of the interveners, which may not have been envisaged at the inception of the intervention (Ufua, 2020; Rajan et al., 2020).

Critical Issues of Caution in the Application of Systemic Intervention in Addressing the COVID-19 Pandemic

Effective implementation of systemic intervention requires the representation of stakeholders' interests. While this requirement tends to make it a painstaking process aimed to address complexities, extant literature suggests the need for the intervener to consider the core value of fairness in the process of its implementation (Ulrich, 2000; Díaz et al., 2020).

The non-health effects of the COVID-19 pandemic pose a wide range of challenges on the public and private sectors (the government authorities, indigenes, private organisations, and the healthcare system). It is suggested that a fair approach be enacted in the process. This arguably necessitates the departure from political 'oppositionalism' to effective 'collaborativism' among stakeholders in the application of systemic intervention that can effectively direct stakeholders' interests towards the achievement of set objectives, especially the non-health effects of the COVID-19 pandemic. This can project a means to minimise conflict in the systemic intervention process and create a fair and unified platform that aims to address the complexities identified (Sturm & Gadlin, 2007; Ropers, 2008).

The timing of systemic intervention should be set and agreed upon among stakeholders as a critical guide that can moderate actions and interactions within an intervention process. This can also serve the interveners to measure performance and the prompting for adjustment to meet set objectives effectively in an intervention (Cao, Clarke, & Lehaney, 2004; Seiffert & Loch, 2005; Olonade et al., 2021). However, Ufua, Papadopoulos, and Midgley (2018) observe that systemic intervention takes more time in response. Nevertheless, they also found that the effects in terms of decisions based on the agreement reached projects actions that are both sustainable and acceptable to the participants in an intervention (Olujobi, 2020; Ufua et al., 2021). The stake of the current research is the adoption of systemic intervention in addressing a complicated critical situation such as the non-effects of COVID-19 pandemic, which should include a framework for intermittent evaluation and improvement to emancipate the affected stakeholders in the process.

Policy Implications of Systemic Intervention in Addressing Non-Health Effects of the COVID-19 Pandemic

Systemic intervention as an approach to address the identified non-health challenges of COVID-19 pandemic, given its flexibility, is expected, *ceteris paribus*, to rapidly restore the economy from the current health shocks. It has also led to the economy of the world and Nigeria in particular, falling into a recession from the effects of the pandemic which started in the fourth quarter of 2019 into the third quarter of 2020 at the time of this study. The GDP growth rate of Nigeria is closely correlated with crude oil prices (Statistica Report, 6th June, 2020). The COVID-19 pandemic has led to the collapse of oil prices in the international market and an abrupt halt in Nigeria's already fragile economic recovery. Oil price fall in March 2020 has impacted the economy and led to a downgrade to annual growth outlook between 5% and 10% (World Bank, 2020).

The process of systemic intervention can project effective innovation among policymakers and stakeholders that can result in acceptable policy changes via the engagement of relevant stakeholder group representatives who are either affected or involved in the intervention to recover the economy. It would also offer them the opportunity to critically evaluate the effects of their chosen approach in a systemic intervention, and positions them to develop improvement models (Ufua et al., 2021; Foote et al., 2021). This can also ensure critical focus on emerging issues such as the marginalisation of certain minority stakeholder groups. It would help policymakers at different levels in the Nigerian state create an idea to use powers and positional privileges to productively address human and economic challenges posed by the COVID-19 pandemic (see Ufua, 2020; Ufua, Papadopoulos, & Midgley, 2018).

Conclusion

In this study, we focused on the non-health effects of the COVID-19 pandemic by exploring the health challenges posed by the emergence of the pandemic and underscoring the non-health issues traceable to the spread of COVID-19 pandemic. The adoption of systemic intervention was suggested as a flexible approach in addressing the identified non-health challenges of the COVID-19 pandemic. The research also emphasised the identification and engagement of the affected stakeholders in the intervention process to address the non-health effects of COVID-19 pandemic.

The adoption of systemic intervention can support prompt and accountable use of available resources and a periodic evaluation of the intervention by the stakeholders, particularly those who are affected. This would support economic growth and development and a concerted commitment of these stakeholders to the process. While the economy is faced with obvious challenges, especially during and after COVID-19 pandemic, it is fundamental for the policymakers to adopt a systemic approach that strives to take full account of all policy implementation processes and ensure a process improvement measure. This can project long-run economic emancipation and productivity across various sectors of the economy. This can create a positive boost on the confidence of all supportive stakeholders, such as the external creditors. They provide credit funding to some of the critical projects in the economy and foreign investors in various sector of the economy. Thus, for the policymakers, systemic intervention is fundamental for the engagement of the right stakeholders on the right project and the time with the broad aim to address the non-health effects of COVID-19 pandemic in Nigeria.

This study, however, could adopt an empirical approach that could have engaged other data collection approaches such as interviews, questionnaires, and observation. This was a result of the prolonged lockdown and restrictions to the movement of goods and persons experienced in all the states of Nigeria to slow down and curb the spread of the COVID-19 pandemic virus, as well as the seeming lack of reliable secondary data directly relating to the non-health effects of COVID-19 pandemic, focused in the current study. It is, therefore, recommended that further research should focus on these approaches to generate more learning on the subject of non-health effects on the COVID-19 pandemic.

References

Alford, J., & Head, B. W. (2017). Wicked and less wicked problems: A typology and a contingency framework. *Policy and Society*, *36*(3), 397–413.

Amoo, E. O., Adekeye, O., Olawole-Isaac, A., Fasina, F., Adekola, P. O., Samuel, G. W., . . . & Azuh, D. E. (2020). Nigeria and Italy divergences in coronavirus experience: Impact of population density. *The Scientific World Journal*. https://doi.org/10.1155/2020/8923036 https://www.hindawi.com/journals/tswj/2020/8923036/ Accessed on June 30, 2022.

Arnold, R. D., & Wade, J. P. (2015). A definition of systems thinking: A systems approach. *Procedia Computer Science*, *44*(2015), 669–678.

Atun, R., & Menabde, N. (2008). Health systems and systems thinking. In *Health systems and the challenge of communicable diseases: Experiences from Europe and Latin America* (pp. 121–140). Berkshire: Open University Press, McGraw Hill Education.

Barua, S. (2020). *Understanding coronanomics: The economic implications of the coronavirus (COVID-19) pandemic*. Available at SSRN: https://ssrn.com/abstract=3566477 or http://doi.org/10.2139/ssrn.3566477. Accessed on March 25, 2021.

Barura, A. (2020). The impact of COVID-19 pandemic: Education sector of Bangladesh, BIPSS Commentary. *Bangladesh Institute of Peace and Security Studies. bipss. org. bd/pdf/The% 20impact% 20of% 20COVID-19% 20Pandemic-Education% 20sector% 20of% 20Bangladesh. pdf.*

Bedford, J., Enria, D., Giesecke, J., Heymann, D. L., Ihekweazu, C., Kobinger, G., . . . & Ungchusak, K. (2020). COVID-19: Towards controlling of a pandemic. *The Lancet*, *395*(10229), 1015–1018.

Boyd, A., Brown, M., & Midgley, G. (2004). Systemic intervention for community OR: Developing services with young people (under 16) living on the streets. In *Community operational research* (pp. 203–252). Boston, MA: Springer.

Cabrera, D., Colosi, L., & Lobdell, C. (2008). Systems thinking. *Evaluation and Program Planning*, *31*(3), 299–310.

Cao, G., Clarke, S., & Lehaney, B. (2004). The need for a systemic approach to change management – A case study. *Systemic Practice and Action Research*, *17*(2), 103–126.

Carr, A. (2009). The effectiveness of family therapy and systemic interventions for adult-focused problems. *Journal of Family Therapy*, *31*(1), 46–74.

Checkland, P. (1981). *Systems thinking, systems practice*. Chichester: Wiley & Sons.

Cunha, A., & Morais, D. (2019). Problem structuring methods in group decision making: A comparative study of their application. *Operational Research*, *19*(4), 1081–1100.

Dentoni, D., Bitzer, V., & Schouten, G. (2018). Harnessing wicked problems in multi-stakeholder partnerships. *Journal of Business Ethics*, *150*(2), 333–356.

Díaz, S., Settele, J., Brondízio, E., Ngo, H., Guèze, M., Agard, J., . . . & Chan, K. (2020). Summary for policymakers of the global assessment report on biodiversity and ecosystem services of the *Intergovernmental Science-Policy Platform on Biodiversity and Ecosystem Services*, *34*(3), 62.

Djalantea, R., Shaw, R., & DeWit, A. (2020). Building resilience against biological hazards and pandemics: COVID-19 and its implications for the Sendai Framework. *Progress in Disaster Science*, 6, 100080. https://doi.org/10.1016/j.pdisas.2020.100080

Foote, J. L., Gregor, J. E., Hepi, M. C., Baker, V. E., Houston, D. J., & Midgley, G. (2007). Systemic problem structuring applied to community involvement in water conservation. *Journal of the Operational Research Society*, 58(5), 645–654.

Foote, J. L., Midgley, G., Ahuriri-Driscoll, A., Hepi, M., & Earl-Goulet, J. (2021). Systemic evaluation of community environmental management programmes. *European Journal of Operational Research*, 288(1), 207–224.

Gilbert, M., Pullano, G., Pinotti, F., Valdano, E., Poletto, C., Boelle, P., . . . & Colizza, V. (2020). Preparedness and vulnerability of African countries against importations of COVID-19: A modelling study. *The Lancet*, 395(10227), 871–877.

Heymann, D. L., & Shindo, N. (2020). COVID-19: What is next for public health? *The Lancet*, 395(10224), 542–545.

Holmes, E. A., O'Connor, R. C., Perry, V. H., Tracey, I., Wessely, S., Arseneault, L., . . . & Ford, T. (2020). Multidisciplinary research priorities for the COVID-19 pandemic: A call for action for mental health science. *The Lancet Psychiatry*, *7*(6), 547–560.

Hopman, J., Allegranzi, B., & Mehtar, S. (2020). Managing COVID-19 in low-and middle-income countries. *Jama, 323*(16), 1549–1550.

Igoe, M., & Chadwick, V. (2020a, April 13). After the pandemic: How will COVID-19 transform global health and development? Retrieved April 17, 2020, from Devex: https://www.devex.com/news/after-the-pandemichow-will-covid-19-transform-global-health-and-development-96936. Accessed on March 30, 2022.

Igoe M & Chadwick, V. (2020b, May 23). *After the pandemic: How will COVID-19 transform global health and development?* Retrieved from devex.com/news/after-the-pandemic-how-will-covid-19-transform-global-health-and-development-96936. Accessed on June 30, 2022.

IMF Annual Report. (2020). *A crisis like no other*. Available at www.imf.org/external/pubs/ft/ar/2020/eng/spotlight/covid-19/. Assessed on March 22, 2021.

IMF Press Release. (2020, April 8). *IMF Executive Board approves US$ 3.4 billion in emergency support to Nigeria to address the COVID-19 pandemic*. Available at www.imf.org/en/News/Articles/2020/04/28/pr20191-nigeria-imf-executive-board-approves-emergency-support-to-address-covid-19. Assessed on April 19, 2020.

Ison, R. (2017). Systemic intervention. In *Systems practice: How to act* (pp. 293–312). London: Springer.

Jackson, M. C. (2003). *Systems thinking: Creative holism for managers*. Chichester: Wiley.

Kaiser, A., Fahrenbach, F., Kragulj, F., & Grisold, T. (2018). *Towards a prioritisation of needs to support decision making in organisational change processes*. Available at https://scholarspace.manoa.hawaii.edu/handle/10125/50442. Assessed on March 25, 2021.

Lexology Report. (2020, April 6). *Policy & regulatory measures against the coronavirus pandemic in Nigeria*. Available at www.lexology.com/library/detail.aspx?g=6eb5782c-0929-4906-9f47-f33b295a5e8a. Assessed on August 19, 2020.

Midgley, G. (2000). *Systemic intervention: Philosophy, methodology and practice*. London: Kluwer Academic/Plenum Publishers.

Midgley, G., & Lindhult, E. (2021). A systems perspective on systemic innovation. *Systems Research and Behavioral Science*, *38*(5), 635–670.

Midgley, G., Cavana, R. Y., Brocklesby, J., Foote, J. L., Wood, D. R., & Ahuriri-Driscoll, A. (2013). Towards a new framework for evaluating systemic problem structuring methods. *European Journal of Operational Research*, *229*(1), 143–154.

Midgley, G., & Pinzón, L. A. (2011). Boundary critique and its implications for conflict prevention. *Journal of the Operational Research Society*, *62*(8), 1543–1554.

Midgley, G., & Rajagopalan, R. (2019). Critical systems thinking, systemic intervention and beyond. In *The handbook of systems science*. New York: Springer.

Narwankar, C. S., Elatlassi, R., & Wang, S. (2016). Increasing competency in human activity systems using boundary critique. In *Proceedings of the international annual conference of the American society for engineering management* (pp. 1–10). American Society for Engineering Management (ASEM). https://www.proquest.com/openview/a6e9964bbf71950a273aaf571ca99294/1?pq-origsite=gscholar&cbl=2037614 Accessed on June 30, 2022

Nembhard, I. M., Burns, L. R., & Shortell, S. M. (2020). Responding to COVID-19: Lessons from management research. *NEJM Catalyst Innovations in Care Delivery*, *1*(2).

Odiboh, O., George, T., Salau, O., Ekanem, T., Yartey, D., & Banda, M. (2020). The Public and Public Relations: Examining their nexus in environmental pollution, laws, and policies of government. In *E3S Web of Conferences* (211)02023. EDP Sciences.

OECD Economic Outlook (December, 2020). Turning hope into reality. https://www.oecd.org/economic-outlook/december-2020/ Accessed June 28, 2022.

Olokundun, A. M., Ogbari, M. E., Obi, J. N., & Ufua, D. E. (2019). Business incubation and student idea validation: A focus on Nigerian universities. *Journal of Entrepreneurship Education*, *22*(1), 1–6.

Olonade, O. Y., Busari, D. A., Imhonopi, D., Akinsanya, A. O., George, T. O., Femi, A. F., & Adetunde, C. O. (2021). Megamalls and lifestyles of urban dwellers in selected cities in southwest, Nigeria. *African Journal of Reproductive Health*, *25*(5s), 55–67.

Olujobi, O. J. (2020). The legal sustainability of energy substitution in Nigeria's electric power sector: Renewable energy as alternative. *Protection and Control of Modern Power Systems*, *5*(32), 1–12.

Olujobi, O. J. (2021). Combating insolvency and business recovery problems in the oil industry: Proposal for improvement in Nigeria's insolvency and bankruptcy legal framework. *Heliyon*, *7*(2021), e06123.

Onu, D., Kessler, T., & Smith, J. R. (2016). Admiration: A conceptual review. *Emotion Review*, *8*(3), 218–230.

Osabohien, R., Matthew, O., Ohalete, P., & Osabuohien, E. (2020). Population-poverty-inequality nexus and social protection in Africa. *Social Indicators Research*, 151, 575–598. https://doi.org/10.1007/s11205-020-02381-0

Osabuohien, E., Gershon, O., Oye, Q., & Efobi, U. (2020, April). Addressing budget and debt vulnerability amidst COVID-19: Policy pathways for Nigeria. *CEPDeR Policy Brief*, 2020/01. https://doi.org/10.13140/RG.2.2.18998.04160

Peters, B. G. (2017). What is so wicked about wicked problems? A conceptual analysis and a research program. *Policy and Society*, *36*(3), 385–396.

Pyka, A., Kudic, M., & Müller, M. (2019). Systemic interventions in regional innovation systems: Entrepreneurship, knowledge accumulation and regional innovation. *Regional Studies*, *53*(9), 1321–1332.

Queirós, A., Faria, D., & Almeida, F. (2017). Strengths and limitations of qualitative and quantitative research methods. *European Journal of Education Studies*, *3*(9). http://dx.doi.org/10.46827/ejes.v0i0.1017

Rajan, D., Koch, K., Rohrer, K., Bajnoczki, C., Socha, A., Voss, M., . . . & Koonin, J. (2020). Governance of the COVID-19 response: A call for more inclusive and transparent decision-making. *BMJ Global Health*, *5*(5), e002655.

Ropers, N. (2008). Systemic conflict transformation: reflections on the conflict and peace process in Sri Lanka. In *A systemic approach to conflict transformation: Exploring strengths and weaknesses* (pp. 11–41). Berlin: Berghof Handbook Dialogue Series

Sánchez-Lara, B., & Flores-Choperena, O. E. (2021). Consulting as a systemic intervention process. In: Balderas-Cañas, P.E., Sánchez-Guerrero, G.D.L.N. (Eds.) *Problem Solving in Operation Management*. Cham: Springer. https://doi.org/10.1007/978-3-030-50089-4_3

Seiffert, M. E. B., & Loch, C. (2005). Systemic thinking in environmental management: Support for sustainable development. *Journal of Cleaner Production*, *13*(12), 1197–1202.

Simonovic, S. P. (2010). *Systems approach to management of disasters: Methods and applications*. New Jersey: John Wiley & Sons.

Smith, C. M., & Shaw, D. (2019). The characteristics of problem structuring methods: A literature review. *European Journal of Operational Research*, *274*(2), 403–416.

Stacey, R. D., Griffin, D., & Shaw, P. (2000). *Complexity and management: Fad or radical challenge to systems thinking*? London and New York: Psychology Press.

Statistica Report. (2020, June 6). *Impact of coronavirus (COVID-19) on price of oil in Nigeria in 2020 (in U.S. dollar per barrel)*. Available at www.statista.com/statistics/1122723/impact-of-coronavirus-on-oil-price-in-nigeria/. Assessed on August 19, 2020.

Sturm, S., & Gadlin, H. (2007). Conflict resolution and systemic change. *Journal of Dispute Resolution, 1*.

Ufua, D. E. (2020). Exploring the effectiveness of boundary critique in an intervention: A case in the Niger Delta Region, Nigeria. *Systemic Practice and Action Research*, *33*(5), 485–499.

Ufua, D., Olujobi, O. J., Osabohien, R., Odularu, G., & Osabuohien, E. (2022). Household conflict and COVID-19 Lockdown: Conceptual Reflection from Nigeria. In *COVID-19 in the African Continent* (pp. 235–246). Bingley: Emerald Publishing Limited.

Ufua, D. E., Ibidunni, A. S., Papadopoulos, T., Matthew, O. A., Khatoon, R., & Agboola, M. G. (2021). Implementing just-in-time inventory management to address contextual operational issues: A case study of a commercial livestock farm in southern Nigeria. *The TQM Journal*. https://doi.org/10.1108/TQM-09-2021-0268

Ufua, D. E., Olonade, O. Y., Yaseen, M., Dada, J. A., Olujobi, O. J., & Osabuohien, E. (2022). Intrinsic conflict among Nigerian public security forces: A systems model for compliant security service delivery in Nigeria. *Systemic Practice and Action Research*, 1–19. https://doi.org/10.1007/s11213-022-09593-0

Ufua, D. E., Osabuohien, E., Ogbari, M. E., Falola, H. O., Okoh, E. E., & Lakhani, A. (2021). Re-strategising government palliative support systems in tackling the challenges of COVID-19 lockdown in Lagos State, Nigeria. *Global Journal of Flexible Systems Management*, 1–14.

Ufua, D. E., Papadopoulos, T., & Midgley, G. (2018). Systemic lean intervention: Enhancing lean with community operational research. *European Journal of Operational Research*, *268*(3), 1134–1148.

Ufua, D. E., Salau, O. P., Dada, J. A., & Adeyeye, M. O. (2020). Application of systems approach to achieving cleaner and sustainable environment: A study of waste dumping issue on Idiroko Road, Ota, Ogun State, Nigeria. *International Journal of Environmental Science and Technology*, 1–10.

Ufua, D. E., Salau, O. P., Ikpefan, O., Dirisu, J. I., & Okoh, E. E. (2020). Addressing operational complexities through re-inventing leadership style: A systemic leadership intervention. *Heliyon*, 6(7), e04270.

Ufua, D. E., Olonade, O. Y., Yaseen, M., Dada, J. A., Olujobi, O. J., & Osabuohien, E. (2022). Intrinsic conflict among Nigerian public security forces: A Systems model for compliant security service delivery in Nigeria. *Systemic Practice and Action Research*, 1-–19.

Ufua, D. E., Emielu, E. T., Olujobi, O. J., Lakhani, F., Borishade, T. T., Ibidunni, A. S., & Osabuohien, E. S. (2021). Digital transformation: a conceptual framing for attaining Sustainable Development Goals 4 and 9 in Nigeria. *Journal of Management & Organization*, *27*(5), 836–849.

Ufua, D. E., Olujobi, O. J., Tahir, H., Okafor, V., Imhonopi, D., & Osabuohien, E. (2022). Social services provision and stakeholder engagement in the Nigerian informal sector: A systemic concept for transformation and business sustainability. *Business and Society Review*, 127(2), 403–421.

Ufua, D. E., & Adebayo, A. O. (2019). Exploring the potency of rich pictures in a systemic lean intervention process. *Systemic Practice and Action Research*, *32*(6), 615–627.

Ufua, D. E., Salau, O. P., Saleem, O., Ogbari, M. E., Osibanjo, A. O., Osabuohien, E., & Adeniji, A. A. (2022). Systems approach to address human resource issues: A case in a commercial livestock farm in Southern Nigeria. *SAGE Open*, *12*(2), 21582440221093370.

Ulrich, W. (2000). Reflective practice in the civil society: The contribution of critically systemic thinking. *Reflective Practice*, *1*(2), 247–268.

Ulrich, W. (2003). Beyond methodology choice: Critical systems thinking as critically systemic discourse. *Journal of the Operational Research Society*, 54(4), 325–342.

United Nations Economic Commission for Africa -UNECA. (2020, April). *COVID-19 in Africa protecting lives and economies*. Available athttps://repository.uneca.org/handle/10855/43756on March 25, 2021.

White, L., Burger, K., & Yearworth, M. (2016). Understanding behaviour in problem structuring methods interventions with activity theory. *European Journal of Operational Research*, 249(3), 983–1004.

World Bank. (2020, June). *Nigeria in times of COVID-19: Laying foundations for a strong recovery*. Available at https://openknowledge.worldbank.org/handle/10986/34046. Assessed on March 25, 2021.

World Bank Group. (2019, June). *Nigeria on the move: A journey to inclusive growth*. Available at http://documents1.worldbank.org/curated/en/891271581349536392/pdf/Nigeria-on-the-Move-A-Journey-to-Inclusive-Growth-Moving-Toward-a-Middle-Class-Society.pdf. Assessed on August 10, 2020.

Yolles, M. (2001). Viable boundary critique. *Journal of the Operational Research Society*, 52(1), 35–47.

Section 3

Institutional Framework and Human Capital Development

8 Employment and Productivity of Uganda's SMEs in the Face of COVID-19

A Gender Perspective

Sserunjogi Brian, Nathan Sunday, Paul Lakuma and Rehema Kahunde

Introduction

Small- and medium-sized enterprises (SMEs) are the engines of economic growth, given their role in job creation, innovation and entrepreneurship, wealth and income generation and promotion of equitable development (Jiang et al., 2019). Despite their enormous contribution, the business environment in which they operate remains unconducive. In Uganda, challenges such as inadequate collateral to secure loans, poor infrastructure, lack of information and sensitisation, low levels of technical and management skills and inability to afford long-term financing continue to affect SMEs (Turyahikayo, 2015).

The existing challenges in the SMEs business environment have been exacerbated by the emergency of the COVID-19 pandemic and the subsequent measures to contain its spread (Osabuohien et al., 2022). Most importantly, the impact has been much bigger on women, compared to the men. The World Bank's Gender Innovation Lab indicates that more women and girls have been adversely affected by the pandemic relative to their male counterparts, given their concentration in informal, low-paying jobs with no formal social protection to build their resilience against such shocks. More succinctly, the Economic Policy Research Centre (EPRC) predicted that in Uganda, 3.8 million workers would lose their jobs temporarily while 0.6 million would lose their employment permanently if COVID-19 persists for six months, with over 75% of the permanent job losses coming from the services sector.

Employment is a very important issue for policy attention given Uganda's unemployment rate of 9.7% (UBOS, 2018). Women particularly suffer from slightly higher unemployment rate-estimated at 11.4% (*ibid*). These are expected to be hit hard by the economic slowdown due to the pandemic. Relatedly, the slowdown in economy threatens to reinforce youth unemployment and push young entrepreneurs in SMEs out of employment. Despite the impeding threat of COVID-19 on women, limited evidence exits about gender disaggregated impact of the COVID-19 pandemic on labour, employment and productivity of SMEs in Uganda. Existing evidence about gendered impact of COVID-19 remains largely anecdotal and as such cannot effectively inform policy to prevent the anticipated

DOI: 10.4324/9781003208358-12

negative impact on labour, employment and productivity. In this study, we use a firm-level survey to examine the impact of COVID-19 on employment, labour and productivity, taking into perspective the gender dimension. Additionally, we examine the response and the coping strategies that SMEs have adopted to reduce the impact of the pandemic on employment. Specifically, the chapter addresses the following objectives: assesses the impact of COVID-19 on the labour market, at firm level; and assesses the response, coping mechanisms that firms have adopted considering the COVID-19 pandemic.

Literature Review

COVID-19 and its containment measures have been very detrimental on businesses across the globe. This is attributed to the decline in demand for goods and services that resulted from movement restrictions, border closures and massive job losses (Ufua et al., 2021). Businesses in developing countries, especially those in Sub-Saharan African countries. UNECA (2020) revealed that four out of five businesses in Africa indicated having been severely affected by the pandemic.

The effect of COVID-19 was majorly felt by MSMEs relative to their larger counterparts. This has worsened the historical fragility of such businesses. According to the United Nations Capital Development Fund (UNCDF), COVID-19 and its containment measures such as the lockdown increased the financial distress of all businesses in Uganda as their revenues decreased. Additionally, the productivity of these enterprises reduced further and this was mainly attributed to the reduction in hours of operation. A rapid assessment conducted by the EPRC found a 35% decline in productivity of businesses as a result of the pandemic (Lakuma et al., 2020).

Worse still, the pandemic has had a disproportionate impact on the most vulnerable groups particularly, the women since majority of these enterprises are mainly female-owned (Akina Mama Wa Afrika, 2020). The closure of shopping malls, small shops, hair salons and other smaller businesses resulted into job losses, further removing the means of survival for the daily wage earners (ibid). Even upon reopening, these enterprises encountered severe financial challenges. A post-lockdown analysis conducted by the Economic Policy Research Centre further highlights the widened financial gap faced by female-owned enterprises as a result of COVID-19. This alludes to the cash flow constraints that were exhibited by such enterprises which are owned by women even before COVID-19 (EPRC, 2021).

The harsher impact of COVID-19 on female-owned enterprises could be attributed to the raise in the amount of unpaid care work during the lock down. This reduced the amount of time spent on their businesses. Gulesci et al. (2021) found that 75% of the female business owners increased the time spent caring for their household members relative to 68% for their male counterparts. They further found that more female-headed households suffered income losses compared to the male-headed households. This has implications on the household demand for goods and services.

Given the highlighted negative impact of the pandemic on businesses, firms employed various coping strategies as a way of cushioning themselves against the same. Notably, there were gender differences even in the mechanisms employed. For example, Gulesci et al. (2021) found that female business owners mainly relied on extended family members while male-owned enterprises reported either having borrowed money or looked for alternative sources of income.

Methodology

Theoretical Framework

Considering a gender perspective, the impact of COVID-19 on labour market outcomes follow two channels (Titan et al., 2020[1] and Malte et al., 2020).[2] The first channel points to societal norms and expectations that have shaped the gendered division of household labour and contribute to the gender pay gap (Vella, 1994;[3] Fortin, 2005).[4] In this respect, in many societies, women bear a large share of the childcare and home-schooling responsibilities. Besides child care responsibilities, in most low- and middle-income countries, women-owned businesses employ a major part of the workforce in the informal economy, characterised by low-paying informal jobs where there are few social protections, and they are not reached by government support measures (Enfield, 2021).[5]

The second important channel is the gendered difference based on sectors most affected by the COVID-19 pandemic (Titan et al., 2020). In other words, differences in sectoral composition between female-owned and male-owned businesses can determine how the pandemic affects employment and productivity based on gender. Coskun and Dalgic (2020),[6] reported sectoral differences based on gender in periods of extreme economic downturn (economic recession). Specifically, in the developed world, men-owned enterprises tend to be concentrated in sectors with a high cyclical exposure, whereas women are highly represented in sectors with relatively stable employment over the cycle. However, the reverse is true in low-income countries since most women enterprises are informal, capital constrained and small scale. Notwithstanding the aforementioned linkages, this study relies on the International Labour Organization (ILO) framework to demonstrate the linkages of COVID-19 and gender.

The Rapid Diagnostic Model

Based on the ILO's (2020) work,[7] the model presents the different pathways through which the COVID-19 pandemic could impact gender among small and medium enterprises. The model (see Figure 8.1) shows that the health crisis (COVID-19) impacts businesses and workers through both direct and indirect channels. Directly, the containment measures adopted to contain the spread of the virus as well as disruptions of global supply chains result into a decline of

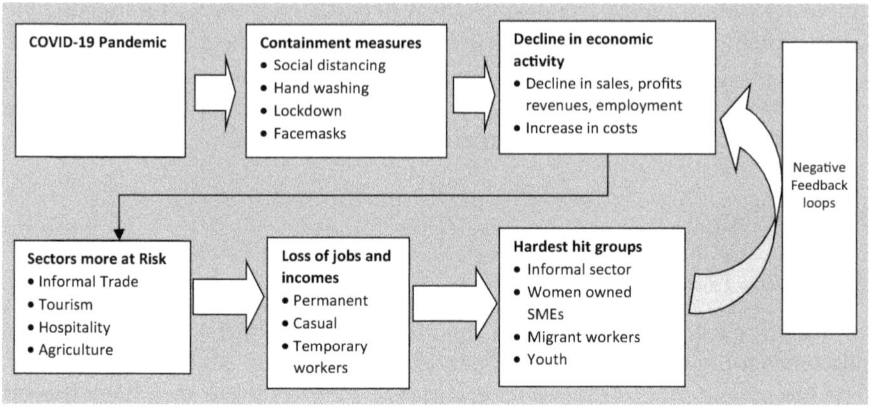

Figure 8.1 The diagnostic model of the impact of COVID-19
Source: Adapted from ILO (2020)

economic activity across various sectors of the economy. Nonetheless, the impact on the economic sectors varies across sectors. ILO (2020) reported that women are particularly vulnerable to this crisis due to their overrepresentation in the health care sector workforce, which is in the frontline of fighting the epidemic, and the higher demands on their care-work, given the closure of schools and care facilities. The disproportionate impact of the pandemic on various sectors leads to loss of work and income which affect various groups harder than others. The rapid diagnostic model is important for this study, since it allows us to study the impact of the pandemic not only between male- and female-owned enterprises but also at the employee level.

Data

The study employed mixed methods combining desk reviews and quantitative analysis of primary data supplemented by qualitative data from key informant interviews. Primary data was collected through a structured questionnaire administered to firms in EPRC's business climate index (BCI) sampling frame. Under the BCI frame, surveyed firms are a panel of businesses based on the Uganda Bureau of Statistics Census of Business Establishment 2011, first tracked by EPRC in 2012. This approach was undertaken using firm-level survey with two modules: (i) the business manager's module and (ii) employee module. The overall sample for the study was made up of two sub-samples.

The random sample for the study was drawn from the EPRC quarterly BCI sampling frame which follows a stratified random sampling with three levels of stratification (region, size and the activity sector). In the sampling frame, the country was divided into five regions: Kampala, Central, Eastern, Western and

Northern. In each of the regions (except Kampala), districts were selected using Probability Proportional to Size (PPS) leading to selection of districts with highest business concentration in the regions. Due to significant differences in business activities across regions, the number of districts selected varied by region, with the central and western having the highest number of districts (six each). The selected districts served as enumeration areas (EAs) for the study. In terms of size, businesses were categorised based on the number of employees, following the classification by Uganda's SME policy (<5 "Micro", 5–49 "Small", 50–100 "Medium", >100 "Large"). Stratification by sector was undertaken along agriculture, manufacturing, and services. Nonetheless, the subsectors[8] in each sector were analysed. The study targeted 177 businesses but managed to interview 174, indicating a response rate of 98%.

The gender disaggregate impact of COVID-19 on SMEs was studied by comparing male- and female-owned SMEs against several variables such as business performance, employment, remuneration and work-related entitlements and time spent at work. Finally, the different coping strategies adopted by female and male-owned SMEs were analysed. To account for size, sector and regional heterogeneity in terms of the impact of COVID-19, the study disaggregated SMEs by size, region and the sector of operation.

Results

Impact of COVID-19 on the Labour Demand, at Firm Level

Table 8.1 shows that there is a gender dimension as regards to the impact of COVID-19 on labour demand. Whereas a slightly higher percentage of female-managed firms reported to have reduced employees compared to

Table 8.1 Reduction in Employment Between Female- and Male-Owned Businesses

	Percentage of Firms That Reduced Workers	*Percentage Reduction in the Size of Workforce*	*Estimated Number of Workers Laid-Off*
Sector			
Agriculture	36.0	17.6	136,915
Manufacturing	48.9	17.8	305,699
Services	61.9	28.6	1,965,287
Size			
Small	57.1	24.8	1,714,162
Medium	63.2	35.1	693,740
Gender			
Female	68.8	25.5	581,362
Male	56.0	26.6	1,826,540
Total	**58.2**	**26.3**	2,407,902

Source: Authors' construction using EPRC rapid survey data 2020

male-managed, the percentage reduction in employment by male-managed firms was higher than that for female-managed firms by 5 percentage points. The evidence presented in Table 8.1 shows that a higher percentage of female-managed firms laid off more workers (68%) than male-owned firms (56%). However, in absolute terms, the number of workers laid off by male-owned firms were larger than those of female-owned firm. The relatively smaller proportion of firms managed by males suggest that those firms had more workers in comparison to their female-managed counterparts. Therefore, they could afford to reduce cost by cutting their workforce, while maintaining some level of operations. In a nutshell, the relatively high percentage of jobs lost among informal, micro and female-managed firms suggest limited flexibility in shifting the burden of the pandemic to workers as is the case with their formal, small and male-managed firms.

Impact of COVID-19 on Labour Productivity

Overall, the COVID-19 pandemic led to a 32-percentage decline in sales per worker. This is equivalent to an overall reduction in duration of work per worker by three hours (Table 8.2). Considering the gender, women's productivity reduced by as much as 38%, compared to 29% among males, while the number of hours spent at work reduced proportionately by three hours. This suggest that, unlike female-managed firms, male-managed firms can counter a decline in sales by adjusting workers, which prevents huge productivity losses. This further speaks to the constraints women face in generating growth of real incomes,

Table 8.2 How COVID-19 Has Affected Productivity of SMEs

	Productivity Before (UGX)	*Productivity After (UGX)*	*Percentage Reduction in Sales Per Worker*	*Reduction in Working Hours*
Sector				
Agriculture	4,433,006	1,567,493	66.8	1.6
Manufacturing	10,400,00	3,151,805	55.2	2.4
Services	5,497,844	3,565,468	25.1	2.7
Size				
Small	5,959,066	3,243,353	29.1	2.8
Medium	7,396,629	4,254,482	49.7	1.4
Gender				
Female	9,843,930	5,754,867	37.8	2.6
Male	4,322,985	2,205,444	29.0	2.6
Total	**6,153,545**	**3,382,407**	31.9	2.6

Source: Authors' construction using EPRC rapid survey data 2020

which have been worsened by the pandemic. This could exacerbate poverty and widen gender-based inequalities.

Impact of COVID-19 on the Labour Market, at Employee Level

Structuring remuneration and incentives to implement realistic performance goals during a period of extreme economic volatility and uncertainty is a timely issue for firms, especially MSMEs, in Uganda.

Overall, about 60% of all firms reduced salaries and or wages for their employees due to the COVID-19 pandemic (Table 8.3). The salary cuts were more pronounced in male-owned firms (65.7%) compared to female-headed SMEs (45%). A further sectoral disaggregation reveals that, male-owned firms in the agriculture and services sector reported a higher salary reduction as compared to the female-headed firms. These results are not surprising, given the downturn, the pandemic has had on both the services and agriculture sectors which are male-dominated but which employ majority of female workers. According to the Uganda National Household survey (2016/17), 3.3% of female working population aged 14 to 64 years is employed in hotels, restaurants and bars, in comparison to only 0.9% of their male counterparts. Considering business size, overall medium-sized firm registered a high salary cut compared to small-sized SMEs. However, there existed differences in salary cuts between male- and female-headed firms. In this respect, female-headed medium-sized SMEs registered higher reduction while for male-owned SMEs, small-sized firms registered higher salary cuts than their medium-sized counterparts. Indeed, while all categories of workers suffered a reduction in salary, the percentage reduction in the wage between female and male workers was about 33%.

Table 8.3 How COVID-19 Affected Wages Across Different Categories of Firms

	Percentage of Firms Reporting Decrease in Wages			*Percentage Reduction in the Wage*		
Sector/Size	*Female*	*Male*	*Total*	*Female*	*Male*	*Total*
Sector						
Agriculture	84.5	95.2	92.7	52.7	27.8	33.8
Manufacturing	71.4	42.2	47.4	26.0	34.0	32.8
Services	40.1	70.1	59.0	32.4	33.6	33.1
Size						
Small	43.6	66.4	58.4	32.0	33.6	33.0
Medium	66.5	61.9	62.6	50.2	30.7	34.1
Total	**45.0**	**65.7**	**59.9**	**33.0**	**33.2**	**33.1**

Source: Authors' construction using EPRC rapid survey data 2020

Impact of COVID-19 on Workplace Social Protection and Social Care

The COVID-19 crisis has exposed the volatility of social protection and social care in the face of harsh economic shocks in Uganda. Table 8.4 reveals that before the emergency of the pandemic, about 53% of the businesses were contributing to National Social Security Fund (NSSF) for their workers and only 35% had medical insurance cover for their employees. However, with the emergency of the pandemic, about 60% of firms halted NSSF benefits while more than half-cessed provision of accommodation allowance. In this regard, a higher percentage of female-owned SMEs stopped providing social protection and social care compared to their male-owned firms.

The results thus reveal the high disparities in the ability between female-managed firms and male-managed firms to provide social protection. Disproportionately fewer female-managed firms provide stable and reliable forms of social protection such as NSSF and medical insurance (Table 8.4).

Impact of COVID-19 on Business Recruitment Plans

Sector disaggregation (Table 8.5) reveals that COVID-19 disproportionately affected recruitment plans in sectors with a high concentration of women. More succinctly, the evidence in Table 8.5 reveals that a higher percentage of services sector firms (60%) halted recruitment compared to manufacturing (53%) and agriculture (25%). Furthermore, recruitment tended to increase in firm size. In this case, the smaller the firm, the higher the likelihood of halting recruitment.

COVID-19 has exacerbated the employment gap by severely disrupting recruitment plans of firms. Table 8.5 shows that more than half (58%) of the female-owned firms, halted recruitment of employees. This is partly due to diminished resources to hire candidates driven by lowered demand and increased

Table 8.4 Changes in Employment-Related Entitlements Before COVID-19

	Percentage of Firms That Had the Entitlement Before COVID-19			*Percentage of Firm That Halted the Entitlements due to COVID-19*[9]		
Entitlements	*Female*	*Male*	*Total*	*Female*	*Male*	*Total*
NSSF	56.2	51.4	52.9	66.5	56.3	59.8
Medical insurance	35.1	35.6	35.4	62.5	60.8	61.2
Accommodation allowance	11.9	31.8	25.7	90.7	70.7	76.0
Transport allowance	59.7	48.3	51.8	52.4	56.1	54.8

Source: Authors' construction using EPRC rapid survey data 2020

Table 8.5 COVID-19 Impact on Recruitment Plans Between Male- and Female-Owned Businesses (% of Firms)

	Halt Recruitment	*No Impact*	*Plan to Downsize the Workforce*	*Plan to Hire More Workers*
Sector				
Agriculture	25.0	7.3	66.2	1.5
Manufacturing	52.5	20.5	17.5	9.5
Services	60.0	15.4	19.8	4.8
Size				
Small	56.7	11.9	24.4	7.1
Medium	54.4	19.2	24.3	2.1
Gender				
Female	57.7	22.6	16.7	3.1
Male	54.9	13.3	24.9	6.9
Total	56.62	16.04	21.74	5.59

Source: Authors' construction using EPRC rapid survey data 2020

cost. In addition, the pandemic has increasingly made it risky to meet prospective candidates in person. Due to the pandemic, employers are increasingly scheduling job interviews through digital technology. This is a rapid change in recruitment procedures that firms, especially MSMEs, have struggled to keep pace with.

Response and Coping Mechanisms Adopted by Firms

In the absence of a cure for COVID-19 in the foreseeable future, the uncertainty among firms is profound. To cope with the crisis, enterprises have started looking for ways to reduce their business costs and increase their revenue. Overall, Figure 8.2 shows that about 47% of enterprises reported making of home deliveries to clients for increased safety during the pandemic. Another 37% of business embraced e-commerce, mainly online marketing. More so, about 30 were engaged in hawking while 26% changed line of business to cope with the pandemic.

The results further demonstrate the extent of the challenges to informal and female-managed firms with regard to coping during the pandemic. Figure 8.2 shows that female-owned firms were less likely to adopt to online marketing, home delivery of their products to clients and changing line of business when compared to male-owned firms. Instead, female-owned firms were more likely to hawk their goods as coping strategy. These results point to systemic challenges related to connectivity, financial inclusion, skills and trust in female-owned firms.

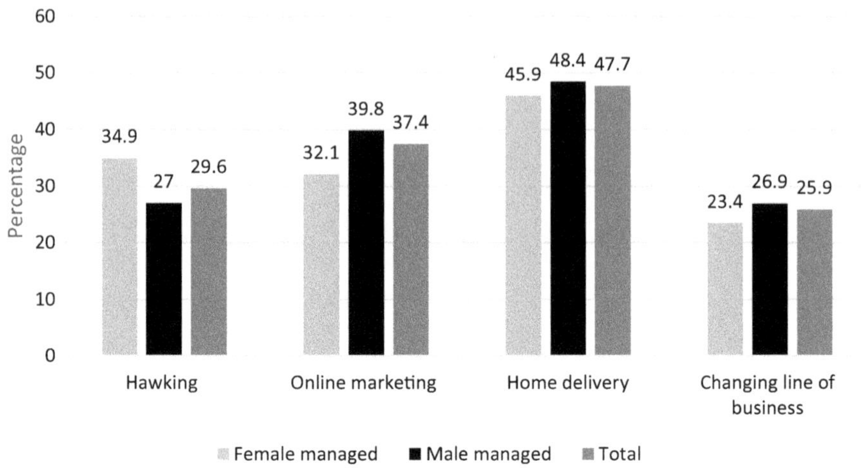

Figure 8.2 Coping strategies adopted by SMEs in response to COVID-19 (% of firms)
Source: Authors' construction using EPRC rapid survey data 2020

Conclusion and Policy Recommendations

The chapter has examined the impact of the COVID-19 pandemic on employment and productivity taking into consideration the gender perspective. The study finds that more than half of all firms registered a reduction in their wages. The drastic reduction in wages has serious implications not only on the stability of employee occupation but also on employee resilience to future shocks. This is because with lower incomes, workers are forced to seek alternative jobs to sustain their livelihoods. This can lead to a loss of workers with specialized skills to low paying most vulnerable sectors. In addition, less pay means that employees deplete their savings, sell assets and acquire more debt hence leaving them extremely vulnerable to future shocks (Wilkinson, 2020)

The pandemic has exacerbated the gaps in productivity between women- and male-owned firms. The results imply that COVID-19 worsened unpaid care work burden towards female-owned business. With the closure of schools, social distancing and restrictive movements, the increased demand on women to provide social care increased, reducing productivity in turn (Zeidy, 2020). Considering provision of workplace social protection, the findings reveal that social safety nets are highly vulnerable and volatile in the face of harsh economic shocks. With the emergency of the pandemic, disproportionately higher number of female-managed firms halted provision of social protection and social care to workers. The results point to a need to strengthen social protection policy for the most vulnerable informal sector workers, especially women. In this case, innovation informal sector saving schemes could be devised to delivery suitable social protection.

Remarkably, our analysis shows less women-headed firms are likely to adopt that e-commerce and home delivery as a coping mechanism against the effects of the pandemic. This implies that while e-commerce presents an avenue for building resilience of most vulnerable firms, female-headed SMEs are less likely to adopt it. Therefore, government needs to invest in digital infrastructure and awareness to close the digital divide between male- and female-owned businesses.

Notes

1 Titan, A., Doepke, M., Olmstead-Rumsey, J. and Michèle, T. (2020). Impact of COVID-19 on Gender Equality. *Working Paper 26947*. National Bureau of Economic Research. www.nber.org/system/files/working_papers/w26947/w26947.pdf

2 Malte, R., Kinga, M. and Anahit, S. (2020). *The Impact of COVID-19 on Gender Inequality in the Labor Market and Gender-role Attitudes*. European Societies, 23 (Sup1), S228-S245, https://doi.org/10.1080/14616696.2020.1823010

3 Vella, F. (1994). Gender Roles and Human Capital Investment: The Relationship Between Traditional Attitudes and Female Labour Market Performance. *Economica, New Series*, 61(242), 191–211.

4 Fortin, N.M. (2005). Gender Role Attitudes and the Labour-market Outcomes of Women Across OECD Countries. *Oxford Review of Economic Policy*, 21(3), 416–38.

5 Enfield, S. (2021). Covid-19 Impact on Employment and Skills for the Labour Market. *K4D Helpdesk Report*. Brighton: Institute of Development Studies. http://doi.org/10.19088/K4D.2021.081

6 Coskun, S. and Husnu, D. (2020). *The Emergence of Procyclical Fertility: The Role of Gender Differences in Employment Risk*. CEPR Discussion Paper No. DP17316, <https://ssrn.com/abstract=4121508>.

7 ILO. (2020). A Rapid Diagnostics for Assessing the Country-Level Impact of Covid-19 virus on the Economy and Labour Market. *Technical Report*, May (https://www.ilo.org/wcmsp5/groups/public/---ed_emp/documents/publication/wcms_743644.pdf)

8 Accommodation, food, recreation and tourism; agriculture and agro processing; banking, insurance, communication, IT and other professional services; industry and manufacturing; mechanical services; retail and wholesale trade; and social services (education, health, community services etc.)

9 This is a percentage of firms that had the entitlements before COVID-19.

References

Akina Mama Wa Afrika. (2020). Gendered Dimensions of the Economic Impact of COVID-19 in Uganda. *Technical Report*, July. https://www.akinamamawaafrika.org/wp-content/uploads/2020/10/Gendered-dimensions-of-the-economic-impacts-of-covid19.pdf

Coskun, S. and Husnu, D. (2020). *The Emergence of Procyclical Fertility: The Role of Gender Differences in Employment Risk*. CEPR Discussion Paper No. DP17316, https://ssrn.com/abstract=4121508

Enfield, S. (2021). Covid-19 Impact on Employment and Skills for the Labour Market. *K4D Helpdesk Report*. Brighton: Institute of Development Studies. http://doi.org/10.19088/K4D.2021.081

EPRC. (2021). *The Plight of Micro, Small and Medium Enterprises in Uganda: A Post Lockdown Analysis Based on Business Climate Survey*. Economic Policy Research Centre, Kampala, Uganda.

Fortin, N. M. (2005). Gender Role Attitudes and the Labour-market Outcomes of Women Across OECD Countries. *Oxford Review of Economic Policy*, 21(3), 416–438.

Gulesci, S., Loiacono, F., Madestem, A. and Stryjan, M. (2021). *COVID-19, SMEs and Workers: Findings from Uganda*. www.theigc.org/publication/covid-19-smes-and-workers-findings-from-uganda/gulesci-et-al-november-2020-final-report/

ILO. (2020). *A Rapid Diagnostics for Assessing the Country-Level Impact of Covid-19 Virus on the Economy and Labour Market*. Technical Report, May https://www.ilo.org/wcmsp5/groups/public/---ed_emp/documents/publication/wcms_743644.pdf

Jiang, L., Tong, A., Hu, Z. and Wang, Y. (2019). The Impact of the Inclusive Financial Development Index on Farmer Entrepreneurship. *PLoS One*, 14(5), https://doi.org/10.1371/journal.pone.0216466

Lakuma, C.P., Sunday, N., Sserunjogi, B., Kahunde, R. and Munyambonera, E. (2020). How Has the COVID-19 Pandemic Impacted Ugandan Businesses? Results from a Business Climate Survey. *EPRC BCI Special Issue No. 1*. https://eprcug.org/publication/652-how-has-the-covid-19-pandemic-impacted-ugandan-businesses-results-from-a-business-climate-survey/

Malte, R., Kinga, M. and Anahit, S. (2020). *The Impact of COVID-19 on Gender Inequality in the Labor Market and Gender-role Attitudes*. *European Societies*, 23(Sup1), S228–S245, https://doi.org/10.1080/14616696.2020.1823010

Osabuohien, E., Odularu, G., Ufua, D. and Osabohien, R. (2022). *COIVD-19 in the African Continent: Sustainable Development and Socioeconomic Shocks*. Bingley: Emerald Publishers Limited [ISBN: 978-180117687-3]. https://doi.org/10.1108/978-1-80117-686-620221002

Titan, A., Doepke, M., Olmstead-Rumsey, J. and Michèle, T. (2020). Impact of COVID-19 on Gender Equality. *Working Paper 26947*. National Bureau of Economic Research. www.nber.org/system/files/working_papers/w26947/w26947.pdf

Turyahikayo, E. (2015). Challenges Faced by Small and Medium Enterprises in Raising Finance in Uganda. *International Journal of Public Administration and Management Research*, 3(2), 21–33.

UBOS. (2018). The National Labour Force Survey 2016/17, *Main Report*, Uganda Bureau of Statistics, – Main Report, Kampala, Uganda.

Ufua, D., Osabuohien, E., Ogbari, M., Falola, H., Okoh, E. and Lakhani, A. (2021). Re-Strategising Government Palliative Support Systems in Tackling the Challenges of COVID-19 Lockdown in Lagos State, Nigeria. *Global Journal of Flexible Systems Management*, 22, 19–32. https://doi.org/10.1007/s40171-021-00263-z

UNCDF. (2020). *Impacts of COVID-19 on Ugandan MSMEs: Inputs to the United Nations Socio-Economic Impact Assessment of COVID-19 in Uganda*. United Nations Capital Development Fund.

Vella, F. (1994). Gender Roles and Human Capital Investment: The Relationship Between Traditional Attitudes and Female Labour Market Performance. *Economica, New Series*, 61(242), 191–211. [Crossref], [Web of Science ®], [Google Scholar].

Wilkinson, N. (2020). *Impact of COVID-19: Poverty and Livelihoods*. www.theigc.org/blog/impact-of-covid-19-poverty-and-livelihoods/

Zeidy, I. A. (2020). Economic Impact of COVID-19 on Micro, Small and Medium Enterprises (MSMES) in Africa and Policy Options for Mitigation. COMESA *Special Report*.

9 Creation of Knowledge Cities in Africa

A Case Study of Gqeberha Port Elizabeth City in South Africa

Roseline Tapuwa Karambakuwa and Ronney Ncwadi

Introduction

The development of African cities has been negatively affected by the coronavirus (COVID-19) pandemic. Some resources earmarked for development were diverted to mitigating the virus effects while some projects were put on hold (Odularu et al., 2022; Ufua et al., 2021). To worsen the situation, COVID-19 came at a time when the surge and concentration of human populations is already putting a strain on development of cities (Cizelj and Bostjan Sinkovec, 2012). The negative impact of COVID-19 is on health, jobs and incomes while existing inequalities are exacerbated (Organisation for Economic Cooperation and Development, 2020). This is worse for countries like South Africa that already experience high levels of inequalities. The COVID-19 pandemic has been the source of economic disruption at a scale and speed that is unprecedented with no doubt (Baldwin and di Mauro, 2020). Using economic vulnerability index and economic resilience index, Africa ranks as second on economic vulnerability to COVID-19 after the Asia-Pacific and the Middle East which rank as the most vulnerable regions (Diop et al., 2021). Further, the contraction in GDP growth brought by the pandemic could increase the international poverty lines in African countries (Diop and Asongu, 2021). Thus, it is imperative for Africa to create smart cities to overcome these challenges and come up with innovative ways that will ensure sustained development post COVID-19 given infrastructural and resource constraints One of the ways to create smart cities is to promote knowledge-based management (KBM), a situation value is created from assets that are intangible thereby defeating the resource constraint problem.

There are problems faced in sustaining the current industrial capitalist model of urban regional development such that as cities grow, they continue to demand more inputs and generate greater outputs while emitting more waste. The cities eventually risk surpassing the manageable limits for superimposed growth which leads to collapse environmentally, socially, economically and psychologically (Cigu, 2015). Overcrowding in cities tends to increase the incidence of violent activities, lack of social identity amongst the population, outbreaks of pandemics such as COVID-19 and the possibility of terrorism (Carrillo, 2004). Hence, the capitalist model of developing cities now faces functionality problems

DOI: 10.4324/9781003208358-13

(Carrillo, 2004). On the contrary, the development that is knowledge based is socially responsible and leads to equity economically, sustainability of the environment and considers needs, particularities, history and mentalities of a region (Cigu, 2015). The unique advantage of knowledge cities is that they are dynamic centres that are responsible for creating new knowledge and bringing it into use while it is leveraged Chatzkel (2004). It is estimated that urban dwellers will account for 86 per cent of the global population by 2050 in nations that are more developed while in nations that are less developed it will account for 67 per cent. This will increase concentration of human populations, threatening quality of life and straining further the ecosystem of the world (Cizelj and Bostjan Sinkovec, 2012).

The challenges facing modern societies call for development strategies that are knowledge-based (Cigu, 2015). When a society is knowledge-based, it prepares for a situation where future generations meet their needs while maintaining an environment that is productive biologically, healthy and physically attractive (Malone, 1995; Malone and Yohe, 2002). Knowledge city refers to all aspects pertaining the cultural, social and economic life of a city and it is important for cities to invent and implement approaches that are efficient and effective to manage the knowledge (Cigu, 2015). The emergence of knowledge societies has significantly increased the reliance on knowledge of productivity innovations and social transformations and to innovate capital in a knowledge-based economy, individuals and companies maintain and enhance their knowledge capital (Carrillo, 1999, 2002).

Laszlo and Laszlo (2002) point that the unaddressed challenges that are addressed by knowledge-based development policies include making development relevant to the local people while incorporating global developments, ensuring that a higher quality of life is promoted, ensuring that humans have a simple way of living meaningfully while being productive and supporting participatory democracy. A knowledge city addresses the aforementioned challenges in various ways. The city structure can be such that it enables democracy to function in a better way with support for online debates, allows knowledge-sharing among the people and allows for real-time access to information facilities that are consistent and up to date (Ergazakis et al., 2005); Montre´al Knowledge City Advisory Committee, 2003; Carrillo, 2004). Democracy entails creation, storing, sharing and using knowledge in a way that enables it to flow to all agents. Participatory democracy ensures involvement of all citizens while sharing responsibility for making appropriate decisions and choices that enables the wellbeing of society (Ergazakis et al., 2005).

Such an environment enables people to learn, understand and create meaning such that they are empowered to foster lifelong learning and sustainability in their lives (Carrillo, 2004). Citizens are offered the social context for cooperation, and they acquire competencies to change present conditions, to influence the future and to make informed life-changing choices. In a knowledge city, all citizens have right to education and training, the right to benefit from services available and the right to transparent public administration and this

Table 9.1 Features Necessary for Successful Knowledge Cities

Successful Knowledge Cities	
Design and Development Features	*Operational Features*
Political and societal features	Access to advanced communication networks at low cost.
Strategic vision and development plan	Research excellence
Financial support and strong investments	Existence of public libraries
Agencies to promote development of knowledge-based regions	
International, multi-ethnic character of the city	
Metropolitan website development	
Value creation to citizens	
Creation of urban innovation regions	
Assurance of knowledge society rights of citizens	

Source: Adapted from Ergazakis et al., (2005)

applies to all levels of decision making. (Montre´al Knowledge City Advisory Committee, 2003). Knowledge economy involves developing technical knowledge for the innovation of products and services including urban services, market knowledge for understanding changes in the economy, financial knowledge to measure the inputs and outputs of production and development processes, and human knowledge in the form of skills and creativity, within an economic model (Lever, 2002).

There are some significant features necessary in the process of design, development and operation of successful knowledge cities, as shown on Table 9.1.

Problem Statement and Objectives

The development of Gqeberha city has dramatically slowed or stopped because of two major challenges. Firstly, the fight against the COVID-19 pandemic depleted resources for development while some projects were halted by the city. Secondly, the human resources critical for city development either fell sick from the virus or stayed at home to avoid contracting COVID-19. Economic activity declined mainly because of many businesses that had to close, leading to reduction in incomes. The Government of South Africa increased disbursements of social grants to cushion the population from economic effects of the pandemic, but this becomes unsustainable due to limited funds. There has therefore been escalation of the problems of poverty, unemployment, crime and other social ills in Gqeberha.

Most importantly, the COVID-19 pandemic resulted in reduced revenue intake by the city as residents fail to pay municipal bills due to fall in income (Department of Planning Monitoring and Evaluation, 2020). Several municipalities, including Gqeberha, find it increasingly difficult to deliver water, sanitation and electricity to communities, compromising quality of life. COVID-19 led to higher levels of unemployment and lowered real disposable income, increasing indebtedness and defaulting on payments for municipal services. Gqeberha, like most South African cities, is developing based on the capitalist model, relying mostly on availability of funds from revenue and investment for development. It is therefore difficult to continue sustaining the present model of development given the socioeconomic shocks and economic effects of COVID-19.

The increase in population due to rural-urban migration coupled with limited resources has threatened livelihoods and growth of the city. This has resulted in high incidence of outbreaks such as COVID-19, high crime rate and poverty, and poor provision of public infrastructure such as schools, hospitals and housing for the poor. The impact of past segregation due to apartheid remains entrenched with high inequality, limited collaboration across spheres of society and low social capital. Major sections of society are excluded from the mainstream of the economy, for example, the city's youth, women and people who live in townships who do not have the means to enter and become productive within the economy of the city. Given this background, becomes necessary for cities such as Gqeberha to pursue development models that are knowledge based and sustainable. The cities need to work towards creation of knowledge cities where economic activities are driven by using brainpower, technology and research to create high-value-added products.

The main objective of the chapter is to determine how knowledge-based management can be implemented in African cities to ensure sustainable development, given limited tangible resources, with Gqeberha (Port Elizabeth) city in South Africa as a case study.

The sub-objectives include: to find out how urban development can be relevant to the local people while catering for global developments; determine how development can lead to a higher standard of life in African cities, using the knowledge-based management approach; and establish ways in which city inhabitants can achieve a simpler, more meaningful way of life, while achieving higher productivity and participation.

Methodology

The methodology involves a review of literature on knowledge-based management to address the objectives. Systematic literature review on knowledge-based management is utilised as it can enhance and promote evidence-informed policymaking (Mallett et al., 2012). Firstly, we utilise the development paradigm of Knowledge-Based Urban Development (KBUD) which is quickly gaining popularity in many parts of the world (Carrillo et al., 2014). The KBUD paradigm for developing creative urban regions involves knowledge production and its reflection on the urban form and functions (Chang et al., 2018). Secondly, we examine the global best practice experiences so that we determine how other cities globally are developing their creative urban regions. This establishes a base for knowledge city formation in cities as they recover from COVID-19 socioeconomic shocks and economic effects.

Knowledge-Based Urban Development Framework

KBUD is a new strategic development approach used to achieve sustainable urban development and economic prosperity. The aim of KBUD is to promote smart and sustainable cities through the implementation of a knowledge management integrated approach while meeting increasing global economic competition (Yigitcanlar and Lönnqvist, 2013. It pertains understanding and management of value dynamics, capital systems, governance of urban areas and development and planning (Chang et al., 2018). Practical examples of KBUD are development of human and social capital, better financial systems, infrastructural development and technological improvements, all aimed at improving the quality of life and creation of attractive living places in cities.

It is important to develop cities as they lead in economic growth with most innovations and entrepreneurship taking place in the cities (Pancholietal, 2014).

Many economies globally have considered KBUD as a strategy in policymaking to attain long-term competitiveness of cities (Yigitcanlar and Lönnqvist, 2013). With KBUD, the ideal climate can be created for both business and people and for governance and integration. The main advantage of the knowledge-based economy is that the intangible asset that is managed, knowledge, does not depreciate like material resources as they are used. Rather, the intangible asset gains more value through use (Laszlo and Laszlo, 2007). To achieve socio-cultural development, cities should develop the knowledge base and skills of residents who can then achieve individual and community development (Gonzalez et al., 2005). There is need for knowledge infrastructure for the cities to compete nationally and internationally, for example, technological development, connections to the global economy and universities and research and development institutes that create well-educated people (Chang et al., 2018).

Literature suggests that government commitment, large enterprises, small and start-up corporations, quality universities, public involvement and quality of life and place are all important in development and growth of knowledge cities (Landry, 2000). We apply the KBUD framework qualitatively to assess the different development approaches for creative urban regions in Gqeberha city. The KBUD framework has four areas of knowledge development, namely economic, socio-cultural, enviro-urban and institutional development (Yigitcanlar, 2014). KBUD was initially triggered by the success of Silicon Valley and Cambridge Science Park in the 1970s (Castells and Hall, 1994). The KBUD framework is illustrated in Figure 9.1.

In the KBUD framework illustrated in Figure 9.1, economic development, pertains the knowledge economy where knowledge is the key to production and hence prosperity of cities. The second area is socio-cultural development where educational and cultural strategies create opportunities for people to develop

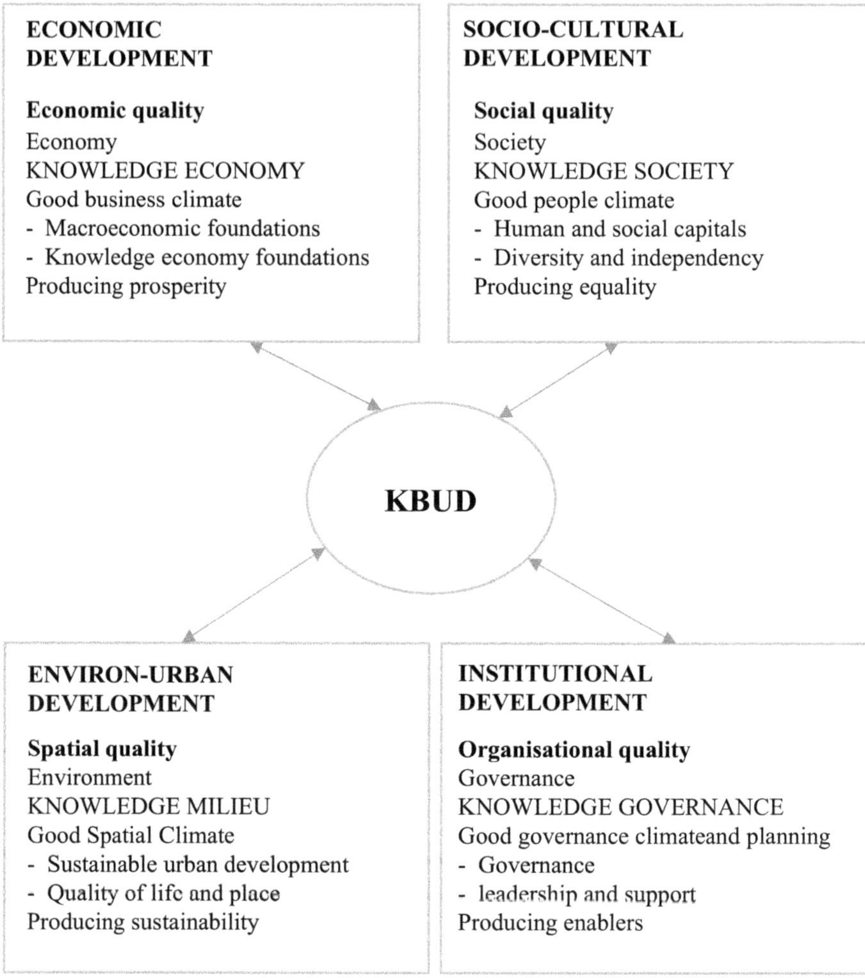

Figure 9.1 The KBUD framework
Source: Adapted from (Chang et al., 2018)

skills and attain equity. The generation, distribution, diffusion, use, integration and manipulation of knowledge and information all are significant economic, political and cultural activities in the society. To develop both natural and built environments, enviro-urban development is necessary for cities. Human needs are met while the environment is preserved to ensure that the needs are also met by future generations (Yigitcanlar, 2014). Hence, enviro-urban development produces sustainable urban development which leads to a better quality of life and spatial quality.

Institutional development enables the creation of a knowledge governance which, in turn, creates good governance, eventually generating good organisational quality. The aim is to ensure organisation, facilitation and strategic planning by all main actors which are requirements for knowledge-intensive activities (Yigitcanlar, 2014). Hence, to ensure institutional development, cities should observe the principles of institutional leadership, good governance, strategic planning, socioeconomic and socio-politic equality. They cities also need to ensure they brand the city by promising value to ensure that the city achieves its knowledge city status (Baum et al., 2009). The major international organizations, such as the World Bank, European Commission, United Nations and Organisation for Economic Cooperation and Development (OECD) have also adopted knowledge management frameworks as they chart their strategic directions regarding global development (Morgan, 2007; Cooke et al., 2006).

A knowledge-based economy creates, distributes and uses knowledge to generate value and gives rise to a network society. The economy creates high-value-added products using research, technology and brainpower. The socioeconomic position of individuals and firms is determined by the opportunity and their capability to access and join knowledge and learning intensive relations. Talent and innovation are also very necessary in generating knowledge (van Winden et al., 2007). Attracting and sustaining the knowledge worker should be one of the first development strategies for a city, region or country. Workers who are talented in addition to the knowledge and high-tech industries play critical roles in enabling and increasing urban economic growth (Florida, 2005). Even though creation of knowledge economies is one way to reduce the negative COVID-19 effects on cities, care should be taken to ensure that sectors that have been especially compromised by the pandemic are paid more attention to. For example, the education and health sector have been compromised due to lockdowns and influx of hospital admissions.

The rapid advances in information and communication technologies (ICTs) during the past two decades have established the necessary infrastructure for scaling up knowledge-based economy. Effective use of ICTs also enables improved governance within a knowledge-based economy as the use of ICT helps to reduce costs such as administration costs and the cost of providing services (Mansell, 2002a). Sustainable development can be ensured by ICTs in addition to creating opportunities for deepening democratic processes with support information sharing in the community (Cigu, 2015). With the COVID-19 pandemic and the need to practice social distance, business activities conducted using ICTs have sharply increased. However, the use of ICTs may be hindered by the problem of 'digital divide' where those without the capacities to access ICTs or to use them effectively are further marginalised. ICT policies and strategies by the government, the private sector and members of civil society, are necessary to eradicate this problem (Cigu, 2015).

City authorities, policymakers, private sector investors and social organisations need to be aware of the advantages of creative urban regions or knowledge cities at global, national, regional or local level. Thus, sound strategic visions are needed for success in all attempts to transform urban regions into creative urban regions and cities into knowledge cities. For the strategic visions to be sound, the authorities should incorporate KBUD policies to ensure they attract and retain knowledge workers and empower citizens and industries as knowledge creators and innovators. Government policies at the local level pay an important role in fostering the conditions and spatial relationships of urban development clusters

According to Yigitcanlar (2014), the common strategies for building successful creative urban regions and knowledge cities are political and societal will, good governance, strategic vision and agencies to promote KBUD. Strategies also include strong financial support, urban innovation, research excellence, e-governance and e-democracy, skills development, affordable housing and urban services and low-cost access to advanced communication networks. However, planning aforementioned strategies and policies requires a team with broad intellectual capacities. KBUD requires social and institutional strategies that provide a comprehensive approach to the economic and urban goals. When planning for KBUD, it is also important for regions or cities to understand the diverse spatial forms of creative urban regions and knowledge cities (Yigitcanlar, 2014). In some developing countries, it is difficult to produce scientific and technical knowledge, creating limitations on KBUD implementation. There is need for cities to be wary of ignoring other important technologies or occupations with regulations favouring certain knowledge fields, hampering development of other forms of new knowledge. The result would be a decline in knowledge attraction and worse still scientists may emigrate to other regions or cities.

Lessons from the International Best Practices

An increasing number of cities worldwide are benefitting from knowledge-based urban management in the transformation of their cities. In some African cities, knowledge-based urban planning is done but the problem comes with implementation, which is not done due to a myriad of challenges. Such non-implementation exacerbates the socioeconomic shocks caused by the COVID-19 pandemic. If African economies successfully implement the knowledge-based plans, they can be in a better position to mitigate the effects of the pandemic on citizens. To understand various ways of implementing such plans, there are global perspectives and lessons from the international best practices that are discussed in this section, from Austin, Barcelona, Helsinki, Melbourne and Singapore.

The city of Austin, Texas, was considered as the human capital and the music capital of the world. Led by business organisations, the city managed to attract large corporations by offering the relatively low cost of living and the quality of university graduates. The city of Austin developed a vision for its future and constantly updated its vision and strategic goals as changes occurred. This gave the city a competitive advantage in becoming a leader among the other cities that were aiming to attract and retain investment and talent. The success of the city was mainly driven by human centred strategic long-term planning that involved public-private-academia cooperation (Yigitcanlar, 2014). Austin's success factors included dynamic vision and sound strategic planning, strong knowledge-based economy, well-connected university, industry and government relations. Success factors also included significant investment in human capital, high quality of life and place, efficient urban and transport system, including affordable housing, watching its competitors closely, investing on research and development, and education and good governance (Chang et al., 2018).

During the late 1990s, the city of Barcelona in Spain undertook profound technological and cultural changes to position itself among the major cities of the global knowledge society. The city emphasised the necessity of the cultural sector to become the main driver of transformation and also the expansion of ICT and tourism industries (Bontje et al., 2011). The private sector enabled the development of infrastructures and knowledge businesses of the KBUD process. Barcelona's achievements included a new culture and knowledge-oriented economy, a rich variety of cultural institutions and a strong creative class of knowledge workers, quality public amenity and services, conserved heritage-built environments, conservation of natural surroundings and strong global ties for knowledge exchange. The success factors of the city included sound vision and planning, community involvement in urban transformation, full leadership of the local public initiatives, strategic urban marketing promotion and historical and cultural strengths of the city (Yigitcanlar, 2014).

In Finland, Helsinki's success mainly originated from early strategic actions taken at the national level. The city had very strong hold in ICT, had a safe and well-functioning living environment, was strong in terms of its share of high-skilled people, was also strong in research and development and had a high level of social equality, which helped to facilitate networking (Bontje et al., 2011). Helsinki had high level of educated population, high quality of life, high quality of place and high level of accessibility. The city had large investment in arts and culture, high level of social equity and regional focus on developing high-quality infrastructure and services. It was considered the telecommunication and technology capital of Europe with the presence of giant telecommunication company, Nokia. Its success factors included a sound vision and strategic planning mechanism, targeting a dynamic world-class centre for business and innovation and a strong, knowledge-based economy. However, the city's economic structure was affected by recent global competition on the mobile technology. This caused a serious risk as Nokia started to lose its leading ground against competitor companies such as Apple, Samsung and HTC (Bontje et al., 2011). It is therefore important to diversify the economy and continuously be innovative to avoid losing the competitive edge.

In Australia, Melbourne had a reputation of being the art and culture capital of the Asia-Pacific region and the ICT capital of Oceania. Its achievements included partnership between local government, private sector and community, skilled training programme for young people, youth employment scheme and community jobs programme. Melbourne's success factors included developing a gateway for biotechnology, developing affordable and high-quality housing and educational centres, attracting strategic knowledge based and innovative start-up businesses and developing a place of business culture. It also included promoting growth in tertiary education, developing diverse and highly skilled workforce and enhancing liveability and lifestyles (Yigitcanlar, 2014).

For Singapore, the biggest knowledge-based urban development project 'One-North knowledge community precinct' is a cutting-edge project that establishes the country's reputation as a knowledge economy and establishes it as a regional centre of research and development. Singapore's success is in its science and technology parks and knowledge precincts: for example, Singapore's Changi airport which is ranked among top international airports in the world. Singapore is also recognised as having top-quality eco-efficiency strategies in the world that made the city-state a leader in the sustainable development area (Yigitcanlar, 2014). Singapore's achievements include being an icon for the knowledge-based economy, a hub for knowledge and creative industries to merge and a comprehensive large-scale knowledge community precinct development. The success factors for Singapore were government commitment, quality universities, research and development institutions and international large private companies. Success factors also included small- and medium-sized companies, public enthusiasm, quality of life and place, attracting knowledge workers and becoming a city of constant change.

In the Netherlands, Brainport Eindhoven has successful creative urban region and knowledge city through offering a complete high-tech infrastructure on a very small scale. This includes a wide diversity in technologies, world-class (technical) universities, international knowledge institutes, researchers, high R&D expenditure, start-ups, student teams, shared R&D and advanced manufacturing facilities. There are also opportunities to commercialise knowledge where high-tech companies work closely together with high-tech suppliers and knowledge institutes and innovation and technology spotting is achieved.

For Montréal, Canada strategies included deliberate post-industrial transformation towards a knowledge economy and concentration of sector-specific expertise and capacity for innovation. The city became a leader in education and research, awarding the highest number of university degrees in Canada each year. Further, Montreal identified and developed metropolitan industrial 'clusters' to encourage interaction among firms and support each industry's capacity for innovation and regional competitiveness. The city developed a metropolitan plan for Economic Development 2015–2020 to further attract talent and drive the growth of its clusters of knowledge economy activities. Montreal is incentivizing the relocation of international organizations (both governmental and non-governmental) and business investment internationally and markets Montréal as a gateway to the Americas for European trade and business. Further, there is promotion of quality of life and cultural amenities (Moser et al., 2019).

Creation of a Knowledge City for Gqeberha (Port Elizabeth)

This section focuses on how Gqeberha can create a knowledge city, using findings from literature review and using lessons from various cities around the world. The city can promote the development of a knowledge economy where knowledge is taken as the key to production hence and prosperity. This will ensure that the city is in a better way to handle the short- and long-term impacts of COVID-19 and the shocks it has created. In Gqeberha, there are a number of universities and learning institutions, including Nelson Mandela University, UNISA and training (TVET) colleges. These universities can play a key role in promoting knowledge economy by developing diverse and highly skilled workforce. Promoting growth in the number of universities offering tertiary education and research and development institutions is key towards becoming a knowledge city. Authorities in Gqeberha can collaborate with these universities on research and development, to enhance the development of technical knowledge, market knowledge, financial knowledge and human knowledge. This will create the economy of a knowledge city which creates high–value-added products using research, technology and brainpower. As noted by Gonzalez et al. (2005), the city can achieve socio-cultural development, through increasing the skills and knowledge base of residents.

The city can expand its knowledge economy by positioning itself as a leader in education and research, ensuring research excellence while pursuing strategies to leverage its urban, demographic and industry-specific assets (Turkina, 2018). Existing of public libraries can be utilised for this purpose. Further, the city can focus on retaining higher numbers of university graduates and skilled workers, overcoming real and perceived language barriers while leveraging cultural assets, and attracting international organizations and outside investment. The promotion of quality of life and place and cultural amenities is very important for growth of knowledge city.

The city can focus on initiatives to increase prospects and incentives for international students to remain in the city after graduating (Serebrin, 2017b). The international, multi-ethnic character of the city can aid its development as a knowledge city. The city can further focus on attracting expertise to outcompete other cities in the region in specific areas of the knowledge economy, such as artificial intelligence. Gqeberha can market itself as a gateway to Southern African trade and business as it has a viable airport and seaports, in addition to a robust road and rail network. The city can conduct outbound 'investment missions' to foreign cities, provide regulatory and logistical support, implement strategic plans and actively negotiate agreements around investment and job creation. Initiatives also include providing support for start-up and entrepreneurial activities (Serebrin, 2017b). The city can make use of its existing efficient urban transport system and high-quality infrastructure to position itself as a knowledge city. In all this, community involvement in urban transformation is critical.

The development of metropolitan industrial 'clusters', that is, concentrations of interconnected companies and institutions in a particular field in order to encourage interaction among firms and support each industry's capacity for innovation and regional competitiveness, is also important. Using the case of Montreal, Gqeberha can form specialised research and industry clusters, for example, a focus on artificial intelligence and life sciences research. Several types of business clusters, based on different kinds of knowledge, can be formed in Gqeberha.

High-tech clusters are high technology-oriented, well-adapted to the knowledge economy, and typically have as a core renowned universities and research centres. Historic know-how-based clusters are based on more traditional economic activities that maintain their advantage in know-how over the years, and for some of them, over many centuries. They are often industry-specific. Factor endowment clusters are created because a comparative advantage they might have linked to a geographical position. Financial support and strong investments are also very important to ensure success of the clusters.

Knowledge services clusters and low-cost manufacturing clusters can be developed in industries, such as automotive production, electronics or textiles in the city. Multinational corporations can play important role in "customizing" business conditions in these clusters. One example for this is the establishment of collaborative linkages with local universities to secure the supply of qualified, yet lower-cost engineers. Diversification within the manufacturing sector, diversification of markets for manufactured products and services, investment in the intellectual capital and creativity can accelerate the production of all economic sectors. To ensure enviro-urban development, the city needs to consider meeting human needs while preserving the environment thereby ensuring sustainable urban development and a better quality of life and place ensuring achievement of spatial quality. Further, there is enormous potential for the ocean economy in the city, as well as mineral and energy resources. It is important for the city to strengthen (and monitor) participation in multi-party large-scale ocean economy development initiatives.

Low-cost access to advanced communication networks can help to ensure sustainable development, deepening of the democratic processes in the city ensure improved governance (Mansell, 2002a). However, the problem of 'digital divide' in the city needs to be eradicated through ICT policies and strategies (Ergazakis et al., 2005). Above all, institutions need to function efficiently for the effectiveness of all the initiatives to develop knowledge cities. To ensure the city's institutional development, there is need to observe principles of institutional leadership and good governance. The city needs to target socioeconomic and socio-politic equality, and brand itself as the city of value.

With prosperity from knowledge management, Gqeberha as well as other African cities can emerge from the negative COVID-19 impact.

Conclusion

The socioeconomic and economic shocks caused by the COVID-19 pandemic have negatively affected quality of life and development of African cities. To manage these effects, it is imperative for the African cities to come up with innovative development strategies. One approach is the KBM which is increasingly contributing to successful development of cities worldwide because of its numerous advantages over the industrial capitalist growth approach. The approach ensures that the basic human needs can be met by future generations while maintaining a healthy, physically attractive and biologically productive environment in the cities. KBM can be implemented by African cities to ensure sustainable development that is relevant to local economies while meeting global standards, while using limited tangible resources.

The city of Gqeberha can achieve sustainable growth and mitigate COVID-19 impact through developing diverse and highly skilled workforce, retaining university graduates, promoting research and development, ensuring advanced communication networks and attracting multinational companies. The city can market itself as gateway to regional trade and business and negotiate agreements around investment and job creation. The city can also utilise its existing infrastructure, create low-cost manufacturing clusters, knowledge services clusters, ensure diversification of the local economy and come up with viable strategic plans. As the city is closer to the sea, it can promote and benefit from the ocean economy.

If African countries develop knowledge cities, development can promote higher quality of life and place through creating high-value-added products using research, technology and brainpower. Important also is to ensure the preservation of the environment while developing the cities to ensure better spatial quality. The inhabitants of African cities can live simply, meaningfully, and yet productively and participle towards the development of their cities so that they overcome COVID-19 imposed challenges. Above all, observing principles of institutional leadership and good governance is imperative to achieve successful knowledge cities.

Future research could focus on how African cities can use the KBM approach to be ready to for disasters and pandemics, such that when they happen, the economic impact would be minimal. While adopting the lessons learnt from the international best practices, African countries need to take note of the limitations they face, for example, the digital divide in the use of information and technology.

References

Baldwin, R., and Di Mauro, B.W. (2020). *Mitigating the COVID Economic Crisis: Act Fast and Do Whatever It Takes*. CEPR Press. Available from: https://voxeu.org/content/mitigating-covid-economic-crisis-act-fast-and-do-whatever-it-takes

Baum, S., O'Connor, K., and Yigitcanlar, T. (2009). The implications of creative industries for regional outcomes. *International Journal of Foresight and Innovation Policy*, 5(1–3), 44–64.

Bontje, M., Musterd, S., and Pelzer, P. (2011). *Inventive City-regions: Path Dependence and Creative Knowledge Strategies*. Ashgate. United Kingdom

Carrillo, F.J. (1999). The knowledge management movement: Current drives and future scenarios. *Paper Presented at the 3rd International Conference on Technology, Policy and Innovation: Global Knowledge Partnerships – Creating Value for the 21st Century*, University of Texas, Austin, TX. Available from: www.knowledgesystems.org

Carrillo, F.J. (2002). Capital systems: Implications for a global knowledge agenda. *Journal of Knowledge Management*, 6(4), 379–399.

Carrillo, F.J. (2004). Capital cities: A taxonomy of capital accounts for knowledge cities. *Journal of Knowledge Management*, 8(5), 28–46.

Carrillo, F.J., Yigitcanlar, T., Garcia, B., and Lönnqvist, A. (2014). *Knowledge and the City: Concepts, Applications and Trends of Knowledge-based Urban Development*. New York: Routledge.
Chang, D.L., Sabatini-Marques, J., Moreira da Costa, E., Mauricio Selig, P., and Yigitcanlar, T. (2018). Knowledge-based, smart and sustainable cities: A provocation for a conceptual framework. *Journal of Open Innovation*, 4, 5. https://doi.org/10.1186/s40852-018-0087-2.
Chatzkel, J. (2004). Greater Phoenix as a knowledge capital. *Journal of Knowledge Management*, 8(5), 61–72.
Cigu, E. (2015). Emerging Markets Queries in Finance and Business: The Making of Knowledge Cities in Romania. *Procedia Economics and Finance*, 32, 534–541. Science Direct
Cizelj, B., and Sinkovec, N. (2012). Knowledge cities and Smart cities. *Knowledge Economy Network*, Brussels. Weekly Brief No. 20.
Cooke, Philip & Leydesdorff, Loet. (2006). Regional Development in the Knowledge-Based Economy: The Construction of Advantage. *The Journal of Technology Transfer*, 31, 5–15. http://doi.org/10.1007/s10961-005-5009-3.
Department of Planning Monitoring and Evaluation (2020) Annual Report 2020-2021. Republic of South Africa.
Diop, S., and Asongu, S.A. (2021). The COVID-19 pandemic and the New Poor in Africa: The straw that broke the Camel's back. *Forum for Social Economics*. http://doi.org/10.1080/07360932.2021.1884583
Diop, S., Asongu, S.A., and Nnanna, J. (2021). COVID-19 economic vulnerability and resilience indexes: Global evidence. *International Social Science Journal*, 71, 37–50. https://doi.org/10.1111/issj.12276
Ergazakis, K., Metaxiotis, K., and Psarras, J. (2005). An emerging pattern of successful knowledge cities' main features. In Carrillo, F.J. (Ed.), *Knowledge Cities: Approaches, Experiences and Perspectives*. New York: Butterworth-Heinemann.
Florida, R. (2005). The Flight of the Creative Class (London: Harper Collins)
Gonzalez, M., Alvarado, J., and Martinez, S. (2005). A compilation of resources on knowledge cities and knowledge-based development. *Journal of Knowledge Management*, 8(5), 107–127.
Landry, C. (2000). *The Creative City: A Tool Kit for Urban Innovators*. London: Earthscan.
Laszlo, K.C., and Laszlo, A. (2002). Evolving knowledge for development: The role of knowledge management in a changing world. *Journal of Knowledge Management*, 6(4), 400–412.
Laszlo, K.C., and Laszlo, A. (2007). Fostering a sustainable learning society through knowledge- based development. *Systems Research and Behavioral Science*, 24(1), 493–503. Latour.
Lever W.F. (2002). Correlating the knowledge-base of cities with economic growth. *Urban Studies*, 39(5–6), 859–870. http://doi.org/10.1080/00420980220128345.
Mallett, R., Hagen-Zanker, J., Slater, R., and Duvendack, M. (2012). The benefits and challenges of using systematic reviews in international development research. *Journal of Development Effectiveness*, 4(3), 445–455. http://doi.org/10.1080/19439342.2012.711342
Malone, T.F. (1995). Reflections on the human prospect. In Socolow, R.H. (Ed.), *Annual Review of Energy and the Environment*. Palo Alto, CA: Annual Reviews, pp. 1–19.
Malone, T.F., and Yohe, G.W. (2002). Knowledge partnerships for a sustainable, equitable and stable society. *Journal of Knowledge Management*, 6(4), 368–378.

Mansell, R. (2002a). Constructing the knowledge base for knowledge-driven development. *Journal of Knowledge Management*, 6(4), 317–329.

Montre´al Knowledge City Advisory Committee (2003), "Montre´al, knowledge city", report prepared by the Montre´al Knowledge City Advisory Committee, available at: www.montrealinternational.com/docs/MtlSavoir_En.pdf

Moser, S., Fauveaud, G., and Cutts, A. (2019). *Montréal: Towards a Post-industrial Reinvention*. Montréal: Towards a Post-industrial Reinvention. https://doi.org/10.1016/j.cities.2018.09.013

Odularu, G., Osabuohien, E., Ufua, D., and Osabohien, R. (2022). Conclusion: COVID-19 and pandemic preparedness in a digital age. In Osabuohien, E., Odularu, G., Ufua, D., and Osabohien, R. (Eds.), *COIVD-19 in the African Continent: Sustainable Development and Socioeconomic Shocks*. Bingley: Emerald Publishers Limited, pp. 351–356. http://doi.org/10.1108/978-1-80117-686-620221033

Organisation for Economic Cooperation and Development (2020). *Policy Responses to Coronavirus (COVID-19). Protecting People and Societies*. Available from: www.oecd.org/coronavirus/policy-responses/covid-19-protecting-people-and- societies-e5c9de1a/

Serebrin, J. (2017b). International students see more opportunity in Montreal, but most leave. *Montreal Gazette*, December 1, 2017. Available from: http://montrealgazette.com/business/ international- students-seeing-more-opportunity-in-montreal-but-most-still-leave

Turkina, E. (2018). The importance of networking to entrepreneurship: Montreal's artificial intelligence cluster and its born-global firm element AI. *Journal of Small Business & Entrepreneurship*, 30(1), 1–8. https://doi.org/10.1080/08276331.2017.1402154

Ufua, D., Osabuohien, E., Ogbari, M., Falola, H., Okoh, E., and Lakhani, A. (2021). Re-strategising government palliative support systems in tackling the challenges of COVID-19 lockdown in Lagos State, Nigeria. *Global Journal of Flexible Systems Management*, 22, 19–32. https://doi.org/10.1007/s40171-021-00263-z

Van Winden, W., van den Berg, L., and Pol, P. (2007). European Cities in the Knowledge Economy: Towards a Typology. *Urban Studies*, 44(3), 525–549, special theme: supertall living. Sage Publications, Inc.

Yigitcanlar, T. (2014). Innovating urban policymaking and planning mechanisms to deliver knowledge-based agendas: A methodological approach. *International Journal of Knowledge Based Development*, 5(3), 253–270.

Yigitcanlar, T., and Lönnqvist, A. (2013). Benchmarking knowledge-based urban development performance: Results from the international comparison of Helsinki. *Cities*, 31(1), 357–369.

10 Socio-economic Shocks of COVID-19 Pandemic: Evidence from Sub-Saharan Africa

Oluwayemisi Khadijat Adeleke and Omowumi Monisola Ajeigbe

Introduction

Overtime, human capital development has become very integral or important in any economy. This is because it has been observed that abundance of natural resources in any country does not automatically lead to increased growth or productivity, rather human capital development brings about increased productivity, creating wealth, improved welfare, growth and development in any country. Moreover, its contribution to economic advancement is seen in terms of quality of employment, increase in economic growth and productivity and sustainability in any economy. Preceding the COVID-19 pandemic, the African region lagged behind in terms of human capital development (Odularu et al., 2022). This can be seen with an index of 0.29 for Chad, while Kenya and Mauritius being exceptions, have the highest of 0.52 and 0.63, respectively, while other countries in Sub-Saharan Africa lagged between (World Bank, 2018). Also, the World Bank (2020) and IMF (2020) report has predicted a fall in growth rate and GDP growth rate in Sub-Saharan Africa to -1.6% and -5.1%, respectively. This is not surprising as socio-economic factors, such as employment, education and income in African countries cannot be compared to other developed regions.

Due to the pandemic, severe adverse socioeconomic consequence of the coronavirus was felt in all sectors of the African economy (e.g., aviation, financial markets, health sector, education, sports and; tourism), as most countries experienced, loss of jobs, reduced income and; increased corruption (Ufua et al., 2021). While, some countries used the opportunity to leverage on the gaps in the system as consumer price index increased. Imported goods became very expensive as most African countries who depends solely on China and other developed economy faced huge challenges (UNDP, 2020; Ozili, 2020; Buheli et al., 2020). All these socioeconomic shocks in the system automatically reduced the human capital index of most countries in the African continent, as they experienced paralysed domestic activity, disruptions in distribution channels, increased cost of trade and increase in death rate, thus, productivity declined (UNDP, 2020; Buheji et al., 2020).

Also, literature on socioeconomic impact of COVID-19 on human capital development in African countries remains unknown. This is because several

DOI: 10.4324/9781003208358-14

studies have focused on specific factors, such as mining, health care, economy, tourism, economic contraction and mortality in the past and policy responses (Laing, 2020: Ather et al., 2020; Haleem et al., 2020; Goossling et al., 2020; Chinazzi et al., 2020; Barro et al., 2020; Ozili, 2020). While other studies focused on the economic impact of the pandemic, its effectiveness and relevance of different measures used, as well as its economic outcomes, poverty and the construction of indexes that relates the pandemic to economic vulnerability and resilience using four case scenarios (Asongu, et al., 2020; Diop et al., 2021). Given the huge socioeconomic effect experienced by Africa because of the COVID-19 pandemic, which is buttressed by the UNDP report (2020), which believes that there would be a steep decline in human capital development, the question therefore is: "to what extent has socio economic shock affected human capital development during COVID-19 and in what way can the effect of the Pandemic be reduced in Sub-Saharan Africa?"

Therefore, this study sets out to determine the effect of socioeconomic shock on human capital development in Sub-Saharan Africa countries during the COVID-19 pandemic and whether the policy response by government have been able to reduce its effect. The chapter focuses on Sub- Saharan Africa country because Africa was worst hit by the pandemic in terms of lack of welfare package for its citizen to cushion the effect of the shock. The study is arranged in four sections. Introduction in section one, methodology in section two, while section three and four consists of empirical results and conclusion, respectively.

Methodology

Data Sources and Measurement

The data used for the study was sourced from the World Bank Development Indicator, World population review and the Trading Economics and Economic Forecast Outlook. The data was further disaggregated into monthly data from February to October 2020, using E-Views disaggregation technique. The study covered 46 Sub-Saharan African countries except for Eritrea and Somalia based on lack of sufficient data.

The Human capital development Indicator is captured using the human development index (HDI) because it captures long and healthy life, which is proxied with life expectancy at birth (life expectancy index), Knowledge, which is proxied with years expected for schooling and mean of years of schooling (education index) and a decent standard of living, which is proxied with Gross National Income per capita (GNI index). All these constitute the Human development Index.

The socio-economic variables that were captured because of the COVID-19 pandemic was adopted and modified from the study of (Stojkoski et al., 2020) and they are factors such as, Unemployment (captures loss of jobs), gross domestic product annual growth rate, inflation (reflects the stability of the macroeconomy) and government debt. In capturing the COVID-19 cases for Sub-Saharan Africa, daily cases were used and disaggregated into monthly data using E-Views to ensure uniformity with the other variables.

Cointegration Test

The cointegration test is performed only when we have integration of the same order of the variables used for a study. Thus, the cointegration equation allows that if on the long run, two or more series move in the same direction, the transformation between the series remains constant. It is assumed that the series possess a long run equilibrium relationship due to the stationarity between them (Hall and Henry, 1989). If the series are not cointegrating, then it suggests that the variables have no long-run relationship which implies that the variables are randomly broadening from one another (Dickey and Fuller, 1979). For this study, the Johansen Kao Residual Cointegration test would be employed. This can be expressed if the vector of *n* stochastic variable is denoted by Y_t based on the existence of a *p*-lag vector autoregression Gaussian errors. Therefore, the Johansen's methodology can take a point in the vector autoregression based on the order p which is given by equation (1).

$$Y_t = \pi + \Delta_i Y_{t-1} + \ldots \Delta_p Y_{t-p} + \varepsilon_t \tag{1}$$

where Y_t represents *nx1* based on integration of order of vector of variables which can be denoted by equation (1), ϵ_t represent *nx1* vector of innovations. Thus, the VAR equation can be expressed in equation (2) as:

$$\Delta Y_t = \pi + \delta Y_{t-1} \sum_{i=1}^{p-1} \tau_i \Delta Y_{t-1} + \epsilon_t \tag{2}$$

$$\Gamma = \sum_{i-1}^{p} M_{i-1} \qquad and\, \tau_i = -\sum_{j=i+1}^{p} M_j \tag{3}$$

To examine the number of cointegration vectors, two statistical tests were recommended by Johansen and Juselius (1990) and Johansen (1988, 1990). Initially, the study tests the null hypothesis based on the number of distinct cointegration vector which can either be less than or equal to *q* standing against the general unrestricted alternatives *q=r*. The test was estimated using the equation stated equation (4).

$$\lambda trace(r) = -\Pi \sum_{i=r+1} \ln[1 - \hat{\lambda}_t] \tag{4}$$

where Π stands as the number of observations to be used and the λs stands as the predictable Eigen value from matrix.

Secondly, the study tests the maximum Eigen value test ($\lambda\, max$) which is calculated based on the following equation:

$$\lambda \max\left(r, r+1\right) = -\Pi \ln(1 - \lambda r + 1) \quad (5)$$

The main concern of the test of Null hypothesis is to show that there is *r* of cointegrating vectors as against the alternative r+*1* cointegrating vector.

Panel Vector Autoregressive Model

To determine empirically, the effect of socioeconomic shock on human capital development with emphasis on Sub-Saharan Africa, this study made use of the Panel Vector Autoregressive (PVAR) model. The structure of the panel VAR is the same as the VAR model because all variables are assumed to be endogenous and interdependent. However, a cross sectional dimension is included in the PVAR model. Thus, a panel VAR model is specified:

$$y_{it} = A_{0i}\left(t\right) + A_i\left(\ell\right)Y_{t-1} + \mu_{it} \quad (6)$$

I i = 1, . . ., N; t = 1, . . .,T

where μ_{it} *is a Gx1 vector of random disturbances*

$A_{0i}\left(t\right)$ *and* A_i *depebends on the unit*

Considering a panel VARX, the model is specified as:

$$y_{it} = A_{0i}\left(t\right) + A_i\left(\ell\right)Y_{1t-1} + F_i\left(\ell\right)W_t + \mu_{1t} \quad (7)$$

where $\mu_t = \mu_{1t}, \mu_{2t}, \ldots, \mu_{Nt}{}^{1}_{\sim}$ iid (0, Σ)

F_{ij} *are GxM matrices for each lag* $j = 1, \ldots, q$

W_t *is a Mx1 vector of exogenous variables common to all units i.*

The panel VAR has some characteristics and the first one is that the lags of endogenous variables of all units are in the model for unit *I* and this is also known as dynamic interdependencies. Also, μ_{it} is correlated across *I*, which represents static interdependencies and lastly, the slope, variance and intercept of the shocks μ_{1it} could be unit specific, which is known as cross-sectional heterogeneity. Thus, the specification of our model in panel VARX model is

$$y_{1t} = A_{11}\left(\ell\right)Y_{1t-1} + A_{12}\left(\ell\right)Y_{2t-1} + A_{13}\left(\ell\right)Y_{3t-1} + F_1\left(\ell\right)W_t + \mu_{1t} \quad (8)$$

$$y_{2t} = A_{21}\left(\ell\right)Y_{1t-1} + A_{22}\left(\ell\right)Y_{2t-1} + A_{23}\left(\ell\right)Y_{3t-1} + F_2\left(\ell\right)W_t + \mu_{2t} \quad (9)$$

$$y_{3t} = A_{31}\left(\ell\right)Y_{1t-1} + A_{32}\left(\ell\right)Y_{2t-1} + A_{33}\left(\ell\right)Y_{3t-1} + F_3\left(\ell\right)W_t + \mu_{3t} \quad (10)$$

$$W_t = M\left(\ell\right)W_{t-1} + w_t$$

Furthermore, the Panel VAR technique is used to estimate the impulse response function and variance decomposition (VDCs), and this is gotten from the coefficient's estimation of the panel VAR. The impulse response function explains the endogenous variable response of endogenous variable over a period because of shock in another variable in the system. Also, variance decomposition explains the contribution of individual shock to the variance of individual endogenous variable at a given prediction limit. The Cholesky decomposition is used to compute the IRFs, and it assumes that series listed prior in the VAR order influence the other variables while series recorded later in the VAR order affect variables listed previously only with lag (Canova and Ciccarelli, 2013).

Model Specification

The study made use of the panel vector autoregressive (VAR) model and this is because all endogenous variables can be estimated simultaneously and enables interaction amongst the variables endogenously (Canova and Ciccarelli, 2013). The panel VAR has its benefits as it allows for the use of a large dataset. The study would test for order of integration and cointegration tests before the estimation of the panel VAR model. Thus, given our variables, the panel VAR for the study would be specified as follows:

$$\begin{aligned} HDI_{1t} = {} & A_{11}(\ell)COVID_{1t-1} + A_{12}(\ell)GDPGR_{2t-1} + A_{13}(\ell)INF_{3t-1} \\ & + A_{14}(\ell)UNEMP_{4t-1} + A_{15}(\ell)GVDBT_{1t-1} + +F_1(\ell)W_t + \mu_{1t} \end{aligned} \tag{11}$$

$$\begin{aligned} COVID_{2t} = {} & A_{21}(\ell)HDI_{1t-1} + A_{22}(\ell)GDPGR_{2t-1} + A_{23}(\ell)INF_{3t-1} \\ & + A_{24}(\ell)UNEMP_{4t-1} + A_{25}(\ell)GVDBT_{1t-1} \\ & + +F_2(\ell)W_t + \mu_{2t} \end{aligned} \tag{12}$$

$$\begin{aligned} GDPGR_{3t} = {} & A_{31}(\ell)COVID_{1t-1} + A_{32}(\ell)HDI_{2t-1} + A_{33}(\ell)INF_{3t-1} \\ & + A_{34}(\ell)UNEMP_{4t-1} + A_{35}(\ell)GVDBT_{1t-1} \\ & + +F_3(\ell)W_t + \mu_{3t} \end{aligned} \tag{13}$$

$$\begin{aligned} INF_{4t} = {} & A_{41}(\ell)COVID_{1t-1} + A_{42}(\ell)GDPGR_{2t-1} + A_{43}(\ell)HDI_{3t-1} \\ & + A_{44}(\ell)UNEMP_{4t-1} + A_{45}(\ell)GVDBT_{1t-1} \\ & + +F_4(\ell)W_t + \mu_{4t} \end{aligned} \tag{14}$$

$$\begin{aligned} UNEMP_{5t} = {} & A_{51}(\ell)COVID_{1t-1} + A_{52}(\ell)GDPGR_{2t-1} + A_{53}(\ell)INF_{3t-1} \\ & + A_{54}(\ell)HDI_{4t-1} + A_{55}(\ell)GVDBT_{1t-1} \\ & + +F_5(\ell)W_t + \mu_{5t} \end{aligned} \tag{15}$$

$$\begin{aligned} GVDBT_{6t} = {} & A_{61}(\ell)COVID_{1t-1} + A_{62}(\ell)GDPGR_{2t-1} + A_{63}(\ell)INF_{3t-1} \\ & + A_{64}(\ell)UNEMP_{4t-1} + A_{65}(\ell)GVDBT_{1t-1} \\ & + +F_6(\ell)W_t + \mu_{6t} \end{aligned} \tag{16}$$

where;

COVID-19 (Cases of infection in each country in SSA)
HDI (Human Development Index)
GDPGR (Gross Domestic Product Growth Rate)
INF (Inflation rate)
UNEMP (Unemployment rate)
GVDBT (Government Debt as a ratio of GDP).

However, the direction of effects cannot be ascertained, it is expected that socio-economic shocks on human capital development during the COVID-19 period to be negative. This will bring about several policy responses from government to reduce the negative effect on the economy as a whole and human development index specifically. This is because the COVID-19 period brought about total lock down in most economies globally which affected education, health and almost all the sectors. Thus, this has policy implication on human capital development of most countries in Sub-Saharan Africa, so that corrective measures will be taken against future outcome.

Result and Discussion

Descriptive Statistics

From **Table 10.1**, the average index for COVID-19 for the period of study is 9568 with maximum values of 693739.4. HDI has an average value of about 0.48 and at maximum 0.70. The GDP growth rate had mean value of -2.49 with a maximum value of 6.71, inflation and unemployment had average values of 25.41

Table 10.1 Descriptive Statistics

	COVID-19	*HDI*	*GDPGR*	*INF*	*UNEMP*	*GVDBT*
Mean	9568.647	0.487750	−2.490109	25.41873	11.93374	49.82618
Median	682.0651	0.501162	−0.6425	5.523333	10.27083	48.61667
Maximum	693739.4	0.706108	6.715000	662.4000	34.33750	124.9300
Minimum	0.000000	-0.017025	−32.49833	0.000000	0.404167	0.000000
Std. Dev.	57066.44	0.134975	9.315334	97.92371	8.929979	28.46450
Skewness	10.36309	-1.893643	−1.684497	6.028281	0.871594	0.672081
Kurtosis	114.3042	8.586765	5.572122	38.88600	2.790206	3.182779
Jarque-Bera	221114.1	785.8320	309.9122	24722.10	53.17691	31.74310
Probability	0.000000	0.000000	0.000000	0.000000	0.000000	0.000000
Sum	3961420.	201.9285	−1030.905	10523.36	4940.569	20628.04
Sum Sq. Dev.	1.34E+12	7.524104	35838.26	3960279.	32934.49	334624.0
Observations	414	414	414	414	414	414

Source: Authors' computation

and 11.93 with a maximum of 662.40 and 34.33, respectively, while government debt showed average value of 49.82 and maximum statistic of 124.93. In comparing the mean values of variables across the measures used reveals that the Sub-Saharan African region has much shortfall in the growth rate of GDP relative to other variables. Government debt appears to be more in proportion compared to the other socioeconomic variables employed in the study. The minimum value of the variables shows a high level of consistency as the mean and median values lies within the range of the minimum and maximum value.

The standard deviation measures the degree of dispersion or variation of each variable from its mean and from our findings, it shows that there are deviations in the actual data from the mean. This is not the same with the standard deviation of COVID-19, as it is very high which can be related to increase in infection rate of persons with COVID-19. Also, the result of skewness implies both positive and negative skewness of the variables, with all the variables being positively skewed except for HDI and GDP growth rate, which was negatively skewed. The result shows that most of the variables have coefficient of skewness moving towards zero, thus, implying that the data used for the study are normally distributed. The result of the kurtosis provides information about the peakness of distribution. The result shows that COVID-19 and inflation have platykurtic distribution, while the other variables have leptokurtic distribution. Lastly, the normality test is the Jarque-Bera statistics, and it reveals from the probability that the variables are normally distributed at the 1% level for all series.[1]

Kao Residual Cointegration Result

The Kao cointegration test in **Table 10.2** reveals the value of the probability which is more than 5%, given the implication that we cannot reject the null hypothesis, thus; the result shows that there exist no cointegration among the variables or non-existence of long-run relationship among the variables.

VAR Lag Criteria

The VAR lag length is necessary in selecting the model. This approach is used by fitting VAR models with orders $p = 0, 1, 2 \ldots p_{max}$ and then select the value of p which minimises the model selection criteria (Lebari, 2018; Lutkepohl, 2005).

Table 10.2 Kao Residual Cointegration Test

	t-Statistic	*Prob.*
ADF	-1.60567	0.0548
Residual variance	397147.76	
HAC variance	161836.75	

Source: Authors' computation

Table 10.3 VAR LAG Selection Criteria

Lag	*Log L*	*LR*	*FPE*	*AIC*	*SC*	*HQ*
0	-9566.324	NA	2.67E+18	59.45543	59.52576	59.48351
1	4638.759	27792.56	1.61E−20	-28.5513	-28.05897	-28.35475
2	24924.88	38934.22*	3.81E−75*	-154.3284*	-153.4141*	-153.9634*

Source: Authors' computation

* indicates lag order selected by the criterion
LR: sequential modified LR test statistic (each test at 5% level)
FPE: Final prediction error
AIC: Akaike information criterion
SC: Schwarz information criterion
HQ: Hannan-Quinn information criterion

The VAR lag criteria is important because the resultant effect of choosing few lags might result to logical deviation in the residuals and otherwise having several lags reduces the degrees of freedom. **Table 10.3** presents the result of the VAR lag criteria and all the criteria chose the same lag of 2.

Impulse Response Function

To examine the effects of socioeconomic shocks, as well as the model's response to shocks on human capital development during the COVID-19 pandemic, the impulse response function and the variance decomposition was employed based on the PVAR. The impulse response function is presented in a diagram showing the generalised impulses one standard deviation (SD) innovations which draw more meaningful interpretations for the long run and short run responses to shocks. Also, the results of the impulse response function traced the reaction of the dependent variables in the PVAR shocks to every single variable and it is a response to Cholesky one standard deviation innovations. The horizontal axis indicates the timing into the future, and we have ten months into the future. The zero-line separates the lower bound and upper bound as well as serves as the origin. The line that represents the reaction function is positive when it is above the zero line and negative when below the line.

Figure 10.1explains that a positive shock of one standard deviation to COVID-19 had a positive and increasing trend in the first four months, but after that, a downward trend was noticed and it became negative. The response of HDI to COVID-19 shows no effect in the first six months but had a negative effect from the seventh month to the tenth month. This implies that in the initial period of COVID-19 had no significant effect, but in the long run, because of COVID-19, HDI had a negative response implying an adverse effect on the welfare of people in the Sub-Saharan Region. Furthermore, no significant response was seen on the COVID-19 pandemic on inflation which shows the macroeconomic performance in SSA. Also, a positive shock of one standard deviation on

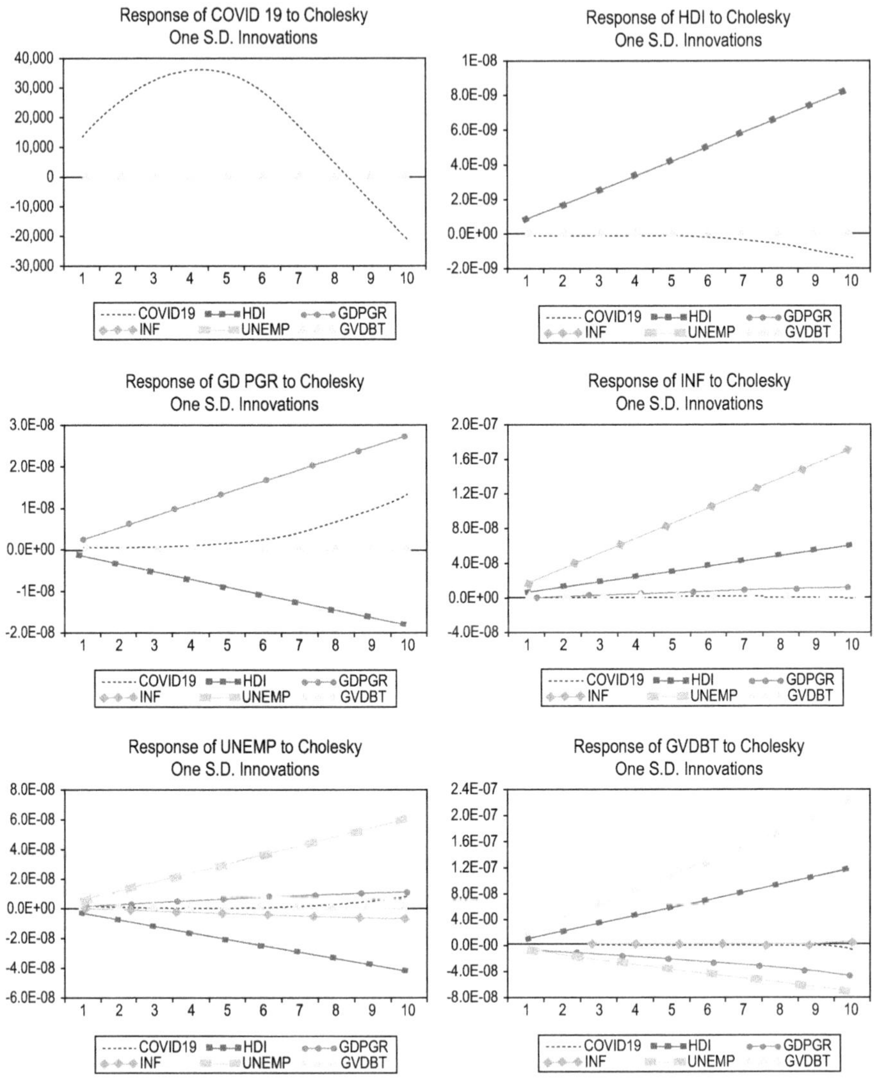

Figure 10.1 Monte Carlo response function of PVAR framework

unemployment had no significant effect for the first eight months but had a positive effect from the eight months till the tenth month, which is in line with the work of Gbemisola et al. (2020). This could be because of policy response of government to reduce the adverse effect of COVID-19. Lastly, no significant effect was seen in both periods for government debt because of COVID-19. Based on this, the effect of socioeconomic shocks to HDI, inflation and government debt had a positive and increasing effect on HDI, while GDP growth rate and unemployment had a negative and downward trend on HDI.

Variance Decomposition

The variance decomposition estimates determine a comparative effect of a variable on other variables in the model. The outcomes of the variance decomposition are revealed in Tables 10.4 to Tables 10.8. In Table 10.4, the short run explains that 99% of forecast error variance in HDI is described by the variable itself. This implies that other variables except for COVID-19 do not have strong influence on HDI. Thus, the variable shows strong exogeneity, which implies weak influence on HDI. In the long run, 98.7% forecast error variance of HDI is explained by itself with little influence from COVID-19. Therefore, implying that HDI exhibits a strong influence on itself both in the short-run and long-run period. Although other variables have risen, they do not have significant effect on HDI.

Table 10.5 revealed that, in the short run, 67% of forecast error variance in GDP growth rate is explained by the variable itself, showing strong endogeneity and it implies strong influence from the variable. The result also showed that other

Table 10.4 Variance Decomposition HDI

Period	*S.E.*	*COVID-19*	*HDI*	*GDPGR*	*INF*	*UNEMP*	*GVDBT*
1	8.39E−10	0.479111	99.52089	0.000000	0.000000	0.000000	0.000000
2	1.87E−09	0.202041	99.79796	1.90E−14	2.68E−13	1.99E−11	2.24E−16
3	3.13E−09	0.087450	99.91255	4.98E−14	8.86E−13	6.55E−11	1.04E−15
4	4.59E−09	0.043716	99.95628	8.25E−14	1.79E−12	1.32E−10	2.65E−15
5	6.21E−09	0.030756	99.96924	1.18E−13	2.99E−12	2.20E−10	5.09E−15
6	7.99E−09	0.052262	99.94774	1.64E−13	4.50E−12	3.31E−10	8.18E−15
7	9.91E−09	0.142987	99.85701	2.32E−13	6.39E−12	4.71E−10	1.16E−14
8	1.20E−08	0.348593	99.65141	3.44E−13	8.76E−12	6.46E−10	1.49E−14
9	1.42E−08	0.703734	99.29627	5.27E−13	1.17E−11	8.65E−10	1.77E−14
10	1.65E−08	1.215395	98.78461	8.18E−13	1.54E−11	1.14E−09	1.96E−14

Source: Authors' computation

Table 10.5 Variance Decomposition GDPGR

Period	*S.E.*	*COVID-19*	*HDI*	*GDPGR*	*INF*	*UNEMP*	*GVDBT*
1	3.40E−09	3.553294	28.45616	67.99055	0.000000	0.000000	0.000000
2	7.53E−09	2.018429	28.90907	69.07250	2.75E−12	2.31E−10	1.55E−14
3	1.26E−08	1.233929	29.14059	69.62548	9.46E−12	7.96E−10	5.23E−14
4	1.83E−08	0.885345	29.24350	69.87116	1.97E−11	1.66E−09	1.07E−13
5	2.48E−08	0.840230	29.25686	69.90291	3.34E−11	2.81E−09	1.80E−13
6	3.20E−08	1.119590	29.17449	69.70592	5.07E−11	4.27E−09	2.72E−13
7	3.98E−08	1.842340	28.96130	69.19636	7.17E−11	6.04E−09	3.85E−13
8	4.84E−08	3.136856	28.57941	68.28374	9.67E−11	8.15E−09	5.22E−13
9	5.78E−08	5.051356	28.01459	66.93405	1.26E−10	1.06E−08	6.84E−13
10	6.80E−08	7.502911	27.29132	65.20577	1.59E−10	1.33E−08	8.73E−13

Source: Authors' computation

variables accounted for insignificant effect on GDP growth rate, with the exception of HDI which has 28%, as they were strongly exogenous, which implies weak influence. In the long run, 65% of forecast error variance of GDP growth rate is explained by itself, while HDI had significant effects but other variables had no significant influence.

Table 10.6 shows that, in the short run, 88% of forecast error variance in inflation is explained by the variable itself, showing strong endogeneity which implies strong influence from the variable. The result also showed that other variables accounted for insignificant effect on GDP growth rate, with the exception of HDI which has 11%, as they were strongly exogenous, which implies weak influence. In the long run, the same result was noticed as 88% of forecast error variance of inflation is explained by itself, while HDI had significant effects but no other variables had any significant influence.

Table 10.7 indicates that 64% of variance of forecast error in unemployment is explained by the variable itself in the short run, showing strong endogeneity

Table 10.6 Variance Decomposition INF

Period	*S.E.*	*COVID-19*	*HDI*	*GDPGR*	*INF*	*UNEMP*	*GVDBT*
1	1.83E−08	0.002880	11.05367	0.441294	88.50216	0.000000	0.000000
2	4.10E−08	0.010070	11.05294	0.441257	88.49573	3.93E−10	4.25E−15
3	6.86E−08	0.017739	11.05217	0.441217	88.48888	1.40E−09	1.50E−14
4	1.00E−07	0.023614	11.05159	0.441185	88.48361	3.00E−09	3.19E−14
5	1.36E−07	0.026329	11.05136	0.441167	88.48115	5.18E−09	5.48E−14
6	1.75E−07	0.025608	11.05150	0.441164	88.48172	7.95E−09	8.38E−14
7	2.17E−07	0.022166	11.05195	0.441174	88.48471	1.13E−08	1.19E−13
8	2.62E−07	0.017359	11.05255	0.441189	88.48890	1.53E−08	1.60E−13
9	3.10E−07	0.012724	11.05313	0.441204	88.49294	1.98E−08	2.08E−13
10	3.60E−07	0.009530	11.05356	0.441212	88.49570	2.49E−08	2.63E−13

Source: Authors' computation

Table 10.7 Variance Decomposition UNEMP

Period	*S.E.*	*COVID-19*	*HDI*	*GDPGR*	*INF*	*UNEMP*	*GVDBT*
1	7.47E−09	0.548312	31.86877	2.653349	0.912379	64.01719	0.000000
2	1.67E−08	0.194641	31.98208	2.662769	0.915624	64.24488	2.99E−13
3	2.79E−08	0.069958	32.02202	2.666080	0.916768	64.32517	1.06E−12
4	4.08E−08	0.043954	32.03034	2.666759	0.917006	64.34194	2.25E−12
5	5.53E−08	0.038085	32.03220	2.666901	0.917060	64.34575	3.87E−12
6	7.11E−08	0.025193	32.03632	2.667230	0.917179	64.35408	5.92E−12
7	8.82E−08	0.023613	32.03681	2.667258	0.917193	64.35513	8.40E−12
8	1.06E−07	0.080142	32.01868	2.665735	0.916675	64.31877	1.13E−11
9	1.26E−07	0.246581	31.96533	2.661280	0.915148	64.21166	1.47E−11
10	1.47E−07	0.557110	31.86581	2.652981	0.912299	64.01180	1.84E−11

Source: Authors' computation

Table 10.8 Variance Decomposition GVDBT

Period	*S.E.*	*COVID-19*	*HDI*	*GDPGR*	*INF*	*UNEMP*	*GVDBT*
1	2.64E−08	0.019546	20.36886	2.906732	0.016019	7.747404	68.94144
2	5.91E−08	0.003914	20.37208	2.907194	0.016021	7.748657	68.95213
3	9.89E−08	0.007748	20.37134	2.907091	0.016021	7.748399	68.94940
4	1.45E−07	0.017169	20.36946	2.906824	0.016020	7.747707	68.94282
5	1.96E−07	0.023345	20.36824	2.906652	0.016019	7.747266	68.93848
6	2.52E−07	0.022859	20.36837	2.906674	0.016019	7.747341	68.93873
7	3.13E−07	0.017352	20.36953	2.906842	0.016021	7.747806	68.94245
8	3.78E−07	0.011938	20.37067	2.907007	0.016022	7.748263	68.94610
9	4.46E−07	0.012867	20.37052	2.906988	0.016022	7.748229	68.94538
10	5.19E−07	0.025177	20.36804	2.906637	0.016020	7.747313	68.93681

Source: Authors' computation

which implies strong influence from the variable. However, HDI had significant influence with a value of 31%, while GDP growth rate had little influence of 2%. However, other variables accounted for insignificant effect on unemployment, as they were strongly exogenous, which implies weak influence. The same result was noticed in the long run.

Table 10.8 shows that, in the short run, 68% of variance of forecast error in government debt is explained by the variable itself, showing strong endogeneity which implies strong influence from the variable. The result also showed that other variables accounted for insignificant effect on government debt, with the exception of HDI which has 20%, as they were strongly exogenous, which implies weak influence. In the long run, the same result was noticed as 68% of variance in forecast error of government debt is explained by itself, while HDI had significant effects but no other variables had any significant influence.

Conclusion

This study estimated the effect of socioeconomic shocks on human capital development during the COVID-19 pandemic in Sub-Saharan African countries using monthly data from February to October 2020. The panel VAR method which incorporates the impulse response and variance decomposition was employed to achieve the objective. The Kao residual Johansen cointegration reveals that there exists no relationship on the long run among the variables. The impulse response of the combined graph shows that HDI, GDP growth rate, unemployment and government debt shows a positive trend to a Cholesky one standard deviation while inflation was positive but had a minimal impact. Findings further revealed that HDI did not respond to COVID-19 in the short run but exhibited a negative effect on the long run. Inflation and government debt had no effect in both periods, while unemployment was insignificant in the short run but became positive and significant in the long run. The effect of socioeconomic shocks to HDI revealed that inflation and government debt had a positive and upward trend while GDP growth rate and unemployment had a negative and downward trend on HDI. Lastly, variance decomposition revealed that all socio-economic variables show strong exogeneity or weak influence on HDI in both periods, while COVID-19 has a positive but minimal effect.

Summarily, the findings point to the fact that socioeconomic variables except for inflation had a positive effect on HDI during the COVID-19 pandemic. Also, COVID-19 had no effect on HDI in the short run but had a negative and significant effect on HDI in the long run. Also, socioeconomic variables with the exception of unemployment had no significant effect in both periods. Lastly, socioeconomic variables in the variance decomposition shows weak influence on HDI during the COVID-19 pandemic. Therefore, the study recommends that government should put in place welfare policies that would reduce the negative effect of COVID-19 on human development index as it affects life expectancy, knowledge and standard of living. This supports the findings of OECD (2020), which advocates for policy measures to cushion the income and job losses on the socio-economy. Several immediate policy responses should be put in place to reduce the effect of the pandemic and make the economy in SSA more industrialised. Also, efforts should be made to reduce the transmission rate of COVID-19, so that the incidence of locking down the economy a second time would not occur, because of its adverse consequence on the income of the economy as well as eroding the income of individual household in the Sub-Saharan African region.

In respect to the caveats of the study, it is important to note that more variables can be used to capture the socioeconomic effects of OVID-19 that was not addressed in this study. They can be considered in future studies. Also, this research can be improved by undertaking country-specific effect and comparison between countries on how the measures put in place to reduce the pandemic shock was achieved and to what extent the macroeconomic goals of the country were achieved. Lastly, future studies can increase the data span to further establish its effects.

Note

1 Correlation test was conducted, and the result (not reported due to space) indicate that there exists no multicollinearity problem among the explained variables as the absolute values ranged from 0.0001 to 0.4014.

References

Asongu, S.A., Diop, S., & Nnanna, J. (2020). The geography of the effectiveness and consequences of COVID-19 measures: Global evidence. *Journal of Public Affairs*, 21(4), e2483. https://doi.org/10.1002/pa.2483

Ather, A., Patel, B., Ruparel, N.B., Diogenes, A., & Hargreaves, K.M. (2020). Coronavirus disease 19 (COVID-19): Implications for clinical dental care. *Journal of Endodontics*, 46(5), 584–595.

Barro, R.J., Ursúa, J.F., & Weng, J. (2020). The coronavirus and the great influenza pandemic: Lessons from the "Spanish flu" for the coronavirus's potential effects on mortality and economic activity (No. w26866). *National Bureau of Economic Research*. http://www.nber.org/papers/w26866.

Buheji, M., Costa Cunha, K., Beka, G., Mavrić, B., Carmo de Souza, Y.L., Costa Silva, S.S., Hanafi, M., & Yein, T.C. (2020). The extent of COVID-19 pandemic socio-economic impact on global poverty. A global integrative multidisciplinary review. *American Journal of Economics*, 10(4), 213–224. http://doi.org/10.5923/j.economics.20201004.02

Canova, F., & Ciccarelli, M. (2013). Panel vector autoregressive model: A survey. *European Central Bank* (ECB), Working Paper Series 1507. https://www.ecb.europa.eu/pub/pdf/scpwps/ecbwp1507.

Chinazzi, M., Davis, J. T., Ajelli, M., Gioannini, C., Litvinova, M., Merler, S., & Viboud, C. (2020). The effect of travel restrictions on the spread of the 2019 novel coronavirus (COVID-19) outbreak. *Science*, 368(6489), 395–400.

Dickey, D., & Fuller, W. (1979). Distribution of the estimators for autoregressive time series with a Unit Root. *Journal of the American Statistical Association*, 74(366), 427–431.

Diop, S., Asongu, S.A., & Nnanna, J. (2021). COVID-19 economic vulnerability and resilience indexes: Global evidence. *International Social Science Journal*, 76 (S1), 37–50. https://doi.org/10.1111/issj.12276.

Gbemisola, O., Amparo, PL., Kevin, M., and Akuffo, A. (2020). Tracking the socioeconomic impacts of the pandemic in Nigeria: Results from the first three rounds of the Nigeria COVID-19 National Longitudinal Phone Survey. https://blogs.worldbank.org/opendata/trackingsocioeconomic-impacts-pandemic-Nigeria-results-first-three-rounds-Nigeria-covid.

Gössling, S., Scott, D., & Hall, C.M. (2020). Pandemics, tourism, and global change: A rapid assessment of COVID-19. *Journal of Sustainable Tourism*, 19(1), 1–20. DOI: https://doi.org/10.1080/09669582.2020.1758708

Haleem, A., Javaid, M., & Vaishya, R. (2020). Effects of COVID 19 pandemic in daily life. *Current Medicine Research and Practice*, 10, 78–79.

Hall, S.G., & Henry, S.G.B. (1989). Macro economic modelling: Contributions to economic analysis. International Journal of Forecasting, 6(1), 140–141.

IMF. (2020). *Regional Economic Outlook for Sub-Saharan Africa*. https://www.imf.org/en/Publications/REO/SSA/Issues/2020/10/21/regional-economic-outlook-for-sub-saharan-africa-october-2020.

Johansen, S. (1988). Statistical analysis of cointegration vectors. *Journal of Economic Dynamics, and Control*, 12, 231–254.

Johansen, S. (1990). Estimation and hypothesis testing of cointegration vectors in gaussian vector autoregressive models, *Econometrica*, 59, 1551–1580.

Johansen, S., & Juselius, K. (1990). Maximum likelihood estimation and inference on cointegration with applications to the demand for money. *Bulletin of Economics and Statistics*, 52, 169–210.

Laing, T. (2020). The economic impact of the Coronavirus 2019 (COVID-2019): Implications for the mining industry. *The Extractive Industries and Society*, 7(2), 580-582.

Odularu, G., Osabuohien, E., Ufua, D, & Osabohien, R. (2022). Conclusion: COVID-19 and pandemic preparedness in a digital age. In Osabuohien, E., Odularu, G., Ufua, D., & Osabohien, R. (Eds.), *COIVD-19 in the African Continent: Sustainable Development and Socioeconomic Shocks* (pp. 351–356). Bingley: Emerald Publishers Limited. http://doi.org/10.1108/978-1-80117-686-620221033

OECD (2020). *COVID-19 and Africa: Socio-economic Implications and Policy Responses*. www.oecd.org/coronavirus/policyresponses/covid19

Oseni, G., Palacios-Lopez, A., McGee, K., & Amankwah, A. (2020). *Tracking the Socioeconomic Impacts of the Pandemic in Nigeria: Results from the First Three Rounds of the Nigerian COVID-19 National Longitudinal Phone Survey*. https://blogs.worldbank.org/opendata/tracking-socioeconomic-impacts-pandemic-nigeria-results-first-three-rounds-nigeria-covid.

Ozili, P. K. (2020). *Covid-19 Pandemic and Economic Crisis: The Nigerian Experience and Structural Causes*. Available at SSRN 3567419.

Stojkoski, V., Utkovcki, Z., Jolakoski, P., & Kocarev, L. (2020). *The Socio-Economic Determinants of the Coronavirus Disease (COVID-19) Pandemic*. www.researchgate.net/publication/340712025.

Ufua, D., Osabuohien, E., Ogbari, M., Falola, H., Okoh, E., & Lakhani, A. (2021). Re-Strategising Government Palliative Support Systems in Tackling the Challenges of COVID-19 Lockdown in Lagos State, Nigeria. *Global Journal of Flexible Systems Management*, 22, 19–32. https://doi.org/10.1007/s40171-021-00263-z

UNDP (2020). *COVID-19 and Human Development: Assessing the Crisis, Envisioning the Recovery*. https://www.undp.org/pacific/publications/covid-19-and-human-development-assessing-crisis-envisioning-recovery.

World Bank (2018). The human capital project. https://worldbank.org/curated/en/363661540826242921.

World Bank Report. (2020). *Global Economic Prospects*. https://doi.org/10.1596/978-1-4648-1553-9

11 Socioeconomic Shocks in the COVID-19 Era

Wyclife Ong'Eta

1. Introduction

According to the International Monetary Fund (IMF) report (2020), the COVID-19 pandemic has caused serious harm to lives and economies worldwide. Protecting lives and allowing health care systems to cope have required isolation, lockdowns and widespread closures to slow the spread of the virus. The health crisis is therefore having a severe impact on socioeconomic activities (Osabuohien et al., 2021; Ufua et al., 2021). As a result of the pandemic, the global economy is projected to contract sharply by 3% in 2020, much worse than during the 2008–2009 financial crises. The Global Preparedness Monitoring Board Report (GPMBR, 2020) has given the approximate cost of COVID-19 as over US$11 trillion plus the future loss of US$10 trillion in earnings. As such, the International Labour Organization (ILO) and United Nations Children's Fund (UNICEF) (2020) have reported that the pandemic has already increased economic and social insecurity, profoundly disrupted supply chains and halted manufacturing as tightening credit is constrains financial markets in many countries. The situation continued in 2021, when the world experienced increasing nationalism, geopolitical strains and skyrocketing inequality (GPMBR, 2021). In 2022, things are not expected to be any batter; World Bank (2022) and IMF (2022) projection shows deceleration of global economic growth over 1%. This is due to disruptions in the supply chain, high energy prices, increasing inflation and weak social protection policies. For emerging economies, the situation is likely to be worse in a row up to 2023 due to relaxed macroeconomic policies.

In Kenya, socioeconomic shock is deepened as the government is caught in between the need to suppress the virus and the need to arrest economic downturn. People living in informal settlements (IS) are the worst hit, as virus containment measures prevent them from eking their daily bread. A large majority of people living here, regardless of their community of origin, earn below a living income; thus, the health crisis is exacerbating their vulnerability and weakening their resilience (Trends and Insight for Africa (TIFA), 2020a; World Bank, 2020). In 2021, the situation became even dire due to disruption of the supply chain, deterioration in access to credit and discontinuation of some social protection schemes that have impacted more people living across IS (World

DOI: 10.4324/9781003208358-15

Bank, 2021). As the UNDP (2019) reports alludes, parents' incomes and circumstances affect their children's health, education and incomes. Children born to low-income families are more prone to poor health and lower education. Those with lower education are less likely to earn as much as others. In addition, when children grow up, if they partner with someone who has similar socioeconomic status, inequalities across generations persist. This is emblematic to lives across ISs, and it is what peace scholars are calling structural violence or the absence of positive peace.

The Institute for Economics and Peace report (2019) cites improvements in the well-functioning government, low levels of corruption, free flow of information and equitable distribution of resources as pillars of positive peace highly associated with economic output as well as government spending responsive to the equitable distribution of resources. Improvements in this pillar are associated with declines in income inequality and a reduction in the poverty gap. Therefore, positive peace is a condition where there is an equitable distribution of resources among the populace characterized by the presence of physical, health, education and economic infrastructure essential in advancing a prosperous society. In IS, as noted earlier, this kind of infrastructure is lacking. As such, in the case of socioeconomic shocks such as those caused by the COVID-19 pandemic, this is likely to render the slum population more vulnerable than the affluent population. Thus, against this backdrop, this chapter has analysed socioeconomic shocks in the COVID-19 era and its aftermath and implications for positive peace among vulnerable populations living in slums.

Consequently, the chapter has suggested appropriate normative and policy interventions, such as strengthening the institutions of governance to curb corruption, establishing a pro-poor subsidy programme, and lifting upgrade programmes to uplift the lives of people living in slums. The specific objectives of this chapter are to

- examine how income inequality has affected positive peace among people living across IS in Kenya;
- examine social safety nets and positive peace among people living across IS in Kenya; and,
- interrogate economic recovery initiatives to safeguard livelihood and positive peace among people living across IS in Kenya.

In summary, this chapter explores the interplay between socioeconomic shocks due to COVID-19 and structural violence among people living across the IS of Nairobi. After reviewing recent developments in the next section, I found that the impact of the pandemic on socioeconomic activities has been exacerbated by structural violence prevalent in our society, especially among vulnerable and poor groups. Addressing the question of how, the materials and methods Section 3 has followed. As a presentation and discussion of findings drawn from Kenya, COVID-19 surveys and reports are presented in Section 4. Then, Section 5 gives the concluding observations and some policy recommendations.

2. Literature Review

2.1 *What Is Structural Violence?*

Delving about structural violence, Galtung (1969) noted that this kind of violence is silent, it does not show it is essentially static, it is the tranquil waters. In a static society, personal violence will be registered, whereas structural violence may be seen as about as natural as the air around us. Conversely, in a highly dynamic society, personal violence may be seen as wrong and harmful but still somehow congruent with the order of things, whereas structural violence becomes apparent because it stands out as an enormous rock in a creek, impeding the free flow and creating all kinds of eddies and turbulences. In Kenya, this violence is commonplace in IS, and people here lack essential physical, health, education and economic infrastructure despite being committed taxpayers, contributing to the county's revenue stream. As Castro (2015) work shows, lack of development and unequal access to resources, between and among different ethnicities, races, religions and socioeconomic groupings, are behind violent conflicts occurring globally. As seen in the next sections, gender-based violence is on the rise in slums. The cause of this violence is said to have been rotating around livelihood, resource scarcity and an uninhabitable environment. These are some of the aspects that have to be approached in this context in a bid to boost the resilience of people in the midst of the pandemic and to create conditions to achieve their aspirations and shared prosperity.

Rowson (2012), however, has argued that most visions of development focus on the idea that development should alleviate conditions of structural violence, but the history of development shows that structural violence is frequently a by-product of the historical process of social, economic and political change. The author provided the case of industrialization; most countries have had to industrialize to become wealthier and healthier. However, industrialization has great social and environmental costs. For a start, it is accompanied by urbanization, which often creates a slum population among whom disease is rampant; working conditions for those lucky enough to be employed may be poor; and the industrial process itself may create environmental damage. However, it is unequivocal that most transnational companies owning industries are generating huge profit margins and yet they have not trickled down the benefits to the low cadre workers, thus expanding the level of income inequality between the haves and the have-nots.

2.2 *Socioeconomic Shocks and Structural Violence*

The GPMBR (2020) observes that the last century witnessed numerous developments and innovations that have improved and prolonged lives the world over. However, the same advances have also created unprecedented vulnerability to fast-moving infectious disease outbreaks by fuelling population growth and mobility, disorienting the climate, boosting interdependence and generating inequality.

Illustratively, the report points out the recent outbreak of COVID-19 that has not only caused immediate morbidity and mortality but also strained the provision of services for other health and social concerns. It has reversed economic gains particularly for women, thrown millions into poverty, disrupted education, created food insecurity and generated disunity and distrust from the community level to the global level.

In addition to direct socioeconomic shocks of the health crisis, the pandemic has affected developing countries through global supply chain disruptions, commodity price falls, decreases in remittances by migrants, capital flights and foreign investment decline (Barneveld et al., 2020). As a result, the United Nations Conference on Trade and Development (UNCTD) report (2020) notes that there is a massive loss of income, although this has been disguised somewhat by government support measures in some countries. For this reason, the labour market is modelled assuming fixed wages for unskilled workers, with all the adjustments occurring in the quantity of labour employed. For skilled workers, it is assumed that the adjustment occurs in wage rates, the standard closure. The Organization for Economic Cooperation and Development (OECD) (2020) adds that many emerging-market economies and developing countries face particularly acute macroeconomic policy challenges, with substantial declines in export revenues, particularly from international tourism, compounding the domestic impact of the COVID-19 shock.

The impact of the pandemic has been exasperated by structural violence prevalent in our society, especially among vulnerable and poor groups. The Oxford Committee for Famine Relief (OXFAM) report (2016) highlights that since the turn of the century, the poorest half of the world's population has received just 1% of the total increase in global wealth, while half of that increase has gone to the top 1%. The average annual income of the poorest 10% of people in the world has risen by less than $3 each year in almost a quarter of a century. Their daily income has risen by less than a single cent every year. The analysis elaborates that one of the key trends underlying this huge concentration of wealth and incomes is the increasing return to capital versus labour. In almost all rich countries and in most developing countries, the share of national income going to workers has been falling. This means that workers are capturing less and less of the gains from growth. In contrast, the owners of capital have seen their capital consistently grow (through interest payments, dividends or retained profits) faster than the rate the economy has been growing. Tax avoidance by the owners of capital and governments reducing taxes on capital gains have further added to these returns. This is what we have to address to narrow the rift between the rich and the poor.

The aforementioned situation is further amplified by the recent report by ILO. More than 630 million workers worldwide, that is, almost one in five, or 19%, of all those employed, did not earn enough to lift themselves and their families out of extreme or moderate poverty, which is defined as them earning less than US$3.20 per day in purchasing power parity terms (ILO, 2020). The report further contends that inequalities and widespread decent work deficits not only lead to economic inefficiency but can also undermine social cohesion within countries. Barneveld et al. (2020) add that socioeconomic inequality has been rising globally for over three decades, a consequence of the policies associated with neoliberalism that the donor community and bodies such as the IMF have promoted through aid conditionality. These policies have privileged private markets, corporate wealth and 'flexible' labour markets and weakened long-term community voice. They have created secular declines in labour income share at the expense of obnoxious increases in executive pay packages, fuelling an unprecedented rise in inequality and populist backlash.

The situation seen earlier is likely to be reversed if we have stronger governance locally, nationally, regionally and globally; thus, the benefits of competitive markets could be preserved with clear rules and boundaries and stronger action taken to meet the needs of human development. Governance here means the framework of rules, institutions and established practices that set limits and give incentives for the behaviour of individuals, organizations and firms. Without strong governance, the dangers of global conflicts could be a reality of the 21st-century trade wars promoting national and corporate interests; uncontrolled financial volatility setting off civil conflicts; untamed global crime infecting safe neighbourhoods; and criminalizing politics, business and the police (UNDP, 1999).

On a positive note, the OECD report (2020) has revealed that with incomes held up thanks to government emergency measures and subdued consumer spending, household saving rates rose sharply during the second quarter in many countries, by between 10 and 20 percentage points in the major advanced economies. Household bank deposit holdings have also soared in many European economies. While these suggest there is plenty of scope to finance additional spending, subdued confidence and high uncertainty about the evolution of the virus and labour market developments are likely to keep precautionary saving elevated. Corporate bank deposit holdings have also risen substantially since the onset of the pandemic in many countries, giving scope for stronger spending if demand and confidence improve quickly. However, investment intentions have weakened, suggesting that elevated uncertainty is likely to keep business investment at low levels for some time. Rising unemployment is also likely to worsen the risk of poverty and deprivation for millions of informal workers in emerging-market economies. This has been incensed by the pandemic reinforcing prevailing disparities; for example, well-paid information technology (IT)-skilled persons able to work from home are advantaged over millions of key frontline workers in low-paid retail and service sectors. The fortunes of billionaires linked to digital giants and large pharmaceutical companies have increased many-fold as their stock prices have surged (Barneveld et al., 2020).

The World Bank (2018) has encouraged governments to consider expanding direct cash transfer programs. Cash transfer programmes are progressive and well-targeted so that a large fraction of the benefits is captured by the poor, especially those living in slums. In the COVID-19 era, these programmes are likely to cushion the poor, the devastating shock of the pandemic. However, because of corruption and poor leadership, some of the beneficiaries of these programmes are left out; instead, the programmes end up benefitting the affluent members of the society or become unpredictable in terms of fund distribution. As such, Ozili (2020) has proposed that in the face of a pandemic, governments should consider providing a sustained general safety net for everyone using social and economic policies. There are several ways of doing this, such as providing free electricity to all citizens during the pandemic and making cash transfer payments to all households. He further suggests that policy makers need to also think about measures that will reboot the economy after the coronavirus crisis is over, such as reducing the price of energy products such as fuel and gas and providing bailout relief to small and large businesses so that they will not lay-off workers during the crisis and during the recovery process.

According to the IMF report (2020), effective policies are extremely essential in forestalling worst outcomes. Necessary measures to reduce contagion and protect lives will take a short-term toll on economic activity but should also be seen as an important investment in long-term human and economic health. Economic policies will also need to cushion the impact of the decline in activity on people, firms and the financial system, as well as reduce persistent scarring effects from the unavoidable severe slowdown. The report adds that since the economic fallout particularly reflects acute shocks in specific sectors, policymakers will need to implement substantial targeted fiscal, monetary and financial market measures to support affected households and businesses. Such actions will help maintain economic relationships throughout the shutdown and are essential to enable activity to gradually normalize once the pandemic abates and containment measures are lifted. Alongside this, substantial additional investments in active labour market programmes, including employment services to help jobseekers find a job and enhanced vocational education and training, are needed to create new opportunities for displaced workers, lower-skilled workers and those on reduced working hours. Labour mobility reforms, such as occupational licensing restrictions and housing market rigidities, would also help to facilitate job reallocation and reduce the chances of persistent scarring effects. Moreover, enhanced childcare provision and adequate income protection for vulnerable groups also need to be an integral part of well-designed policy packages to enhance participation, foster reallocation and make the labour market more inclusive (OECD, 2020).

Regrettably, the pandemic has highlighted a number of serious vulnerabilities, including those caused by corruption. In a global pandemic, corruption impedes life-saving resources from reaching people in need. Moreover, it undermines the trust in institutions that is so critical to an effective collective response to such a crisis. As we rebuild towards societies that can be more resilient in the face of the next global challenge, combating corruption, particularly in the health sector, should be a top priority (World Justice Project report, 2020). Thus, to have any chance of curbing corruption, governments must strengthen checks and balances, limit the influence of big money in politics and ensure broad input in political decision making. Public policies and resources should not be determined by economic power or political influence but by fair consultation and impartial budget allocation (Transparency International, 2019).

3. Methodology

This chapter is based on a review of academic and practice-oriented publications throwing light on socioeconomic shocks in the COVID-19 era and its implications for positive peace among the poor and vulnerable communities residing across slums in Kenya. The analysis consulted reputable sources of information such as the World Health Organization (WHO), ILO, Kenya COVID-19 surveys, United Nations organizations, World Economic Forum, OECD, World Bank, journals, Institute for Economics and Peace, government of Kenya's fiscal intervention reports on COVID-19, IMF and information from other public sources. The researcher organized material systematically guided by two approaches as advised by Druckman (2005): simple mechanical word counts and broad-gauged interpretations of themes based on the chapter objectives.

4. Presentation and Discussion of Findings

4.1 *Impact of COVID-19 in Kenya*

The COVID-19 pandemic has had a disruptive effect on the lives of many Kenyans in both the social and economic frontiers. It has caused changes to the education calendar, hindered the free flow of goods and services, increased unemployment rates, caused government revenue shortfalls and affected the socialization of humans due to restrictive measures such as social distancing, movement restrictions, face masking, hand washing and so forth. As such, cases of domestic violence, teenage pregnancies and crimes are on the rise in the COVID-19 era. Development Initiastive (2020) reported that the economic consequences of the pandemic are likely to have a far greater impact on the long-term health, wellbeing and poverty levels of the population as a whole than the predicted fatalities caused directly by the disease; for example, UNDP (2021) and Diop and Asungu (2021) reports revealed a decline in Kenya's GDP growth in 2020. Without COVID-19, the GDP growth was 6%, but with COVID-19 the growth was 1%, although positive compared with 2019. This contraction is a reflection of diminishing household consumption and government expenditure and is likely to have a long-term impact on poverty, public goods and service provision according to the World Bank report (2021); one in five workers in Kenya has lost their jobs since the start of the pandemic. Relatively few firms have resorted to other labour adjustment measures, such as reducing working hours or wages. Firms in tourism and other services have laid off more workers than firms in other sectors. While two-thirds of all businesses are still open, 20% of workers are in businesses that are temporarily closed and 16% in businesses that are only partially open. These findings align with the study of Diop, Asungu and Nnanna (2021), which revealed that the country's vulnerability index stood at 0.174, taking position 111 out of 150 countries studied. Therefore, the country needed more social protection measures to protect vulnerable groups from the devastating impact of COVID-19.

Additionally, an International Finance Corporation (IFC) report (2020) revealed that in 2018, trade accounted for 36% of Kenya's GDP, with agricultural products making up its top five exports. However, with COVID-19 containment measures in place, Kenya's production capacity fell, and there was a sudden decline in flower exports due to compressed air freight capacity, which negatively affected the country's economy, which relies on this industry for approximately $5 billion to $8 billion in foreign income. Furthermore, the development Initiative report (2020) shows that the restriction of movement in and out of the country has dwindled revenues from the tourism and aviation sectors, while delays at borders due to the testing of truck drivers have resulted in losses of profits for business owners. In the long run, the loss of government revenues will continue to have devastating consequences on health, education, service provision and the wellbeing of people in general, indicating a correlation between government measures to contain COVID-19 and economic impact (Asungu, Diop and Nnanna, 2021). This will, in turn, worsen structural violence already existing in slums and other remote parts of the country.

4.2 *Income Inequality and Positive Peace*

According to the recent research by Nyadera and Onditi (2020), the combination of systematic marginalization, poor policies and inadequate planning has left millions of people in Nairobi slums vulnerable to the direct and indirect impacts of the COVID-19 pandemic. These crowded settlements occupy only 5% of the total residential area in the city, and more than 2.5 million people according to Kenya National Bureau of Statistics (KNBS, 2019) call these slums home. The study revealed that economically, the majority of the employed slum dwellers work as casual labourers without health insurance coverage or pension. Those who are self-employed engage in low-paying activities such as waste collection, recycling and street vending, which pose a high health risk.

The nature of jobs here mirrors the level of education of residents. It was found that 44% of residents did not study past primary school, while 11% did not complete secondary schools (TIFA, 2020a). The TIFA survey further revealed that 30% of people lost jobs due to the pandemic, 20% were self-employed now not working, 16% were jobless and not in employment, 13% were self-employed and 5% were full-time employed. Those in employment, 45% of the sample earned less than the minimum wage as set by the Government of Kenya's Regulation of Wages Order, 15% earn between Ksh 1000 and 5000, 55% of those working earn between Ksh 5000 and 20,000 as estimated monthly income. The pandemic has completely exacerbated the inequality and marginalisation experienced by people living in slums. Comparing its impact in the entire country, people living in slums are likely to stay without employment longer, according to the KNBS (2020) survey, in which the proportion of individuals absent from work nationally due to COVID-9-related challenges stands at 61.9%. Of the individuals absent from work, 77.8% were not sure when they would resume. This is likely to widely expand the inequality expeated by slum dwellers.

The loss of income, according to the UNDP report (2020), can also be explained by a lack of market due to the pandemic. The bulk of Kenya's produces are exported to countries that are affected by the COVID-19 pandemic. This has had an adverse effect on export earnings due to weak demand in these markets. The COVID-19 pandemic has already affected the country's exports of horticulture and agricultural goods to Europe, which has some of the hardest-hit cities in France and Italy mainly because of reduced consumer spending as well as shutdowns in major markets. The Agriculture and Food Authority, a horticulture regulator in the country, has indicated that Kenya's earnings from horticulture exports, including flowers, fruits and vegetables, fell by 7% in 2019 to Ksh 142.72 from Ksh 154.7 billion, mainly due to lower prices of flowers at the auction in the Netherlands. Furthermore, the measures instituted internationally to curb the spread of the disease, such as cancellation of international flights and total/partial lockdowns by some countries, had an adverse impact on import-related taxes and sectors such as tourism and hospitality.

Additionally, the Republic of Kenya report (2020b) underlines how the emergence of COVID-19 in Kenya in March 2020 complicated the situation and negatively affected both domestic and import-related revenues, especially in the fourth quarter of FY 2019/2020. The situation became dire when the government could not access medical supplies in foreign markets that would have helped to check the spread of the disease as countries across the world were struggling to deal with the pandemic. Of note, the government quickly reimagined local solutions to deal with the pandemic. Local garment factories were re-engineered to purposely produce personal protective equipment and facemasks to offer protection to frontline medical workers and the populace. This became a blessing in disguise as some more jobs were created, and the country was able to control and manage the spread of the disease. This explains one of the pillars of positive that an agile, innovative, well-functioning government is critical in combating the pandemic, on the one hand, and on the other hand, curbing an economic slowdown.

Another significant finding revealed that the loss of income and repressive virus containment measures have contributed to increasing domestic violence among people living in slums. The survey shows that women are the most affected at 52%, followed by men at 37% and children at 36%. A combination of verbal and physical violence among women leads with 52%, followed by physical violence at 25% and verbal violence at 20%. In men, 39% of the respondents suffered a combination of physical and verbal violence, followed by verbal violence, at 30% and physical violence at 26%. With regard to children, 46% have suffered both physical and verbal violence, followed by physical violence at 28% and verbal violence at 21% (TIFA, 2020b). It is noteworthy in the context of structural violence; a trigger such as COVID-19 potentially transforms the situation into direct violence as seen across the slums. The only solution to this problem occurs when the government ensures that national resources are equitably distributed across the populace.

4.3 Social Safety Nets and Positive Peace

The KNBS (2020) survey asking respondents about information on cash transfers/remittances received by households from relatives or friends after the first case of the coronavirus was reported in Kenya found that, nationally, 18.4% of households reported having received cash transfers/remittances from relatives or friends since the first case of the COVID-19 pandemic was confirmed in Kenya. A higher proportion (22.9%) of female-headed households received cash transfers/remittances from relatives or friends compared to 16.9% of male-headed households. Among the households that received cash remittances, 80.2% reported that the amount received had decreased compared to the period before the COVID-19 pandemic. Of these households, 40.9% reported a large reduction in the amount received. Only 6.7% of the households reported an increase in the amount received. Of note, these resources helped to cushion farmers from the harmful effects of COVID-19.

Similarly, the TIFA (2020a) survey asked people in slums how the government fared on in providing assistance to needy families during the pandemic. There was a widespread agreement that the government had performed better at 'combating the virus' than it had at 'providing assistance to the needy.' Specifically, nearly twice as many felt it had done 'very well' regarding the former as those holding the same view regarding the latter (40% vs. 23%). At the other end of opinion, nearly three times as many felt that the government had done 'not well at all' regarding assistance to the needy compared with combating the virus (17% vs. 6%). The same view is shared by the OXFAM report (2020) that Kenya has responded negligibly to funding social protection and health measures. Tens of thousands of people living in Nairobi's IS and in the countryside have received almost no help from the government and are struggling to feed themselves. Equally, it has been seen in media reports that government agencies misusing COVID-19 funds, Kenya Medical Supplies Authority, senior ministry of health officials and procurement officers have been reported as major culprits. Procurement procedures and guidelines have been mentioned to have been bypassed without proper transparency and accountability mechanisms put in place, citing petty excuses of tackling the health crisis. It must be noted, however, that the government and donors spending seeking to cushion the needy families have supported a better and more equitable economic system.

According to the Republic of Kenya report (2020b), however, the government has made significant achievements in the Social Protection Sector, with financial commitment to the sector remaining at 0.4% of GDP with an annual expenditure of Ksh 26 billion. Over the period, the government further extended cushioning to the poor and vulnerable by linking beneficiaries to complementary programmes such as nutrition, school feeding, agricultural subsidies and health insurance subsidies such as Universal Health Care and NHIF. In other words, UNDP (2020) notes these safety nets, which could be in the form of cash or in-kind transfers accompanied by intervention by health and nutrition officials, because investing in the health and nutrition of vulnerable populations could lower the mortality rate of diseases such as COVID-19, as nutritional level and mortality rates are intricately linked. Social safety nets are also crucial in the postepidemic period to drive "reconstruction" efforts by helping vulnerable members of society better cope with the impact of the COVID-19 pandemic. However, Nyadera and Onditi (2020) advocate for slum-specific policy documents outlining socioeconomic relief measures that are uniquely meant for slum dwellers. For example, providing e-food and e-medical vouchers, leveraging on technology and community health workers to reach out to people deep inside the slums, and mobile clinics with essential stockpiles can be strategically positioned in slums to make up for the few health facilities.

4.4 *Economic recovery and positive peace*

The Government of Kenya has formulated and implemented diverse measures to cushion the poor and the economy from the devastating impact of the COVID-19 pandemic. The Republic of Kenya report (2020b) has uncovered measures such as lowering the value-added tax (VAT) rate from 16% to 14%; reduction of tax rates for both corporate and personal income (PAYE) from 30% to 25%; provision of a 100% tax relief for persons earning a gross monthly income of up to Ksh 24,000; and reduction of turnover tax rate from 3.0% to 1.0% are estimated to cost the exchequer Ksh 172.0 billion in revenue foregone by the government in one financial year. Furthermore, there were allocations to enhance liquidity for SMEs, including Ksh 5.0 billion to fast-track payment of outstanding VAT refunds owed to local businesses, Ksh 5.0 billion for payment of pending bills, and Ksh 3.0 billion seed capital for the SME Credit Guarantee Scheme (Republic of Kenya, 2020a). However, considering the nature of work among people living across Nairobi's IS, as previously highlighted, these measures may not be very helpful.

To address high youth unemployment rates, the government developed a Ksh 10.0 billion '*Kazi Mtaani* Program' targeting 100,000 unemployed youth in the major cities and urban settlements of Nairobi, Mombasa, Kisumu, Nakuru and other major towns to be engaged in fumigation, storm water drainage, cleaning of markets and IS (Republic of Kenya, 2020a). However, this initiative has been confronted with challenges such as corruption, youth demographic bulges and irregularity in terms of payment. As such, Nyadera and Onditi (2020) have suggested that the government should think of long-term post-COVID-19 solutions geared to unique challenges experienced among people in slums. For example, a slum upgrade programme adopting cheaper technology to establish well-organized prefab houses with population limits in an area. By improving the living conditions of slum dwellers through these projects, many social, economic and health-related issues will also be addressed.

5. Concluding Policy Recommendations, Caveats and Future Research Initiatives

The chapter submits that it is pertinent to develop short-term and long-term economic and social policy measures to forestall the worst outcomes of the pandemic among people living in IS. These would include substantial additional investments in active labour market programmes, including employment services to help jobseekers find a job, and enhanced vocational education and training to create new opportunities for lower-skilled workers and those on reduced working hours commonly found in slums as well as boosting efficiency and efficacy of social protection programmes.

In conclusion, this chapter makes the following recommendations:

i. The Government of Kenya, together with the development partners, should initiate a slum upgrade programme adopting cheaper technology to establish well-organized prefab houses with population limits in an area characterized by good sewerage and drainage systems as a way to promote the good health of people in slums.
ii. The Government of Kenya should a establish a pro-poor subsidy programme geared to directly benefit people in the slums. The programme should encompass the provision of e-food and e-medical vouchers and mobile clinics with essential stockpiles strategically positioned in slums to make up for the few health facilities.
iii. The Government of Kenya should strengthen the institutions of governance, especially those handling accountability and transparency, as a way to curb corruption that has become a dragon, swallowing essential resources meant to boost health, physical infrastructure, education and social public good.

In caveats, the study did not focus on the outcomes of COVID-19, such as increased cases of gender-based violence (National Crime Research Centre, 2020), social unrest, homicide and femicide (Standish, 2021) and increasing criminal activities (National Crime Research Centre, 2020). So I suggest a research to happen on violence during COVID-19 and its implication to positive peace in Kenya.

References

Asungu, S., Diop, S. & Nnanna, J. (2021), The Geography of the Effectiveness and Consequences of COVID-19 Measures: Global Evidence. *Journal of Public Affairs*, Vol. 21, p. e2483.

Barneveld, K., Quinlan, M., Kriesler, P., Junor, A., Baum, F., Chowdhury, A., Junankar, P., Clibborn, S., Flanagan, F., Wright, C., Friel, S., Halevi, J. & Rainnie, A. (2020), The COVID-19 Pandemic: Lessons on Building More Equal and Sustainable Societies. *The Economic and Labour Relations Review 2020*, Vol. 31, No. 2, pp. 133–157.

Castro, L. (2015), *Peace Education: Training Manual. Global Partnership for the Prevention of Armed Conflict in Southeast Asia*. GPPAC-SEA.

Development Initiative (2020), *Socioeconomic Impacts of Covid-19 in Kenya*. Nairobi Development Initiative.

Diop, S. & Asungu, S. (2021), *The COVID-19 Pandemic and the New Poor in Africa: The Straw that Broke the Camel's Back*. Forum for Social Economics.

Diop, S., Asungu, S. & Nnanna, J. (2021), *COVID-19 Economic Vulnerability and Resilience Indexes: Global Evidence*. ISSJ-John Wiley and Sons Limited.

Druckman, D. (2005), *Doing Research: Methods of Inquiry for Conflict Resolution*. New Delhi: Sage Publications.

Galtung, J. (1969), Violence, Peace, and Peace Research, *Journal of Peace Research*, Vol. 6, No. 3, pp. 167–191.

GPMB Report (2020), A *World in Disorder. Global preparedness*. Geneva: World Health Organization.

GPMB Report (2021), *From Worlds Apart to a World Prepared*. Geneva: World Health Organization.

IFC (2020), *When Trade Falls Effects of COVID-19 and Outlook*. Washington, DC: IFC.

ILO (2020), *World Employment and Social Outlook: Trends* 2020. Geneva: ILO.

ILO and UNICEF (2020), *COVID-19 and Child Labour: A Time of Crisis, a Time to Act*. New York: ILO and UNICEF.

IMF (2020), *World Economic Outlook*. Washington, DC: IMF.

IMF (2022), *World Economic Outlook: Rising Caseloads, a Disrupted Recovery, and Higher Inflation*. Washington, DC: IMF.

Institute for Economics & Peace (2019), *Global Peace Index: Measuring Peace in a Complex World*, Sydney: IEP. Retrieved from http://visionofhumanity.org/reports.

KNBS (2019), *Kenya Population and Housing Census*. Nairobi: Government Printers.

KNBS (2020), *Survey of Socioeconomic Impact of COVID-19 on Household Report*. Nairobi Government Printer.

National Crime Research Centre (2020), *Protecting the Family in the Time of COVID-19 Pandemic: Addressing the Escalating Cases of Gender-based Violence, Girl Child Disempowerment and Violations of Children's Rights in Kenya*. Nairobi: Government Printer.

Nyadera, I. & Onditi, F. (2020), COVID-19 Experience among Slum Dwellers in Nairobi: A Double Tragedy or Useful Lesson for Public Health Reforms? *International Social Work*, pp. 1–4.

OECD (2020), *Coronavirus: Living with Uncertainty*. OECD Interim Economic Assessment.

Osabuohien, E., Ejemeyovwi, J., Ihayere, O., Gitau, C. & Oyebola, F. (2021), Post-Pandemic Renewable Energy Development in Sub-Saharan Africa. *Sustainability and Climate Change*, 14(3), 183–192. https://doi.org/10.1089/scc.2020.0077

OXFAM (2016), An Economy for the 1%: How Privilege and Power in the Economy Drive Extreme Inequality and How This Can Be Stopped. *OXFAM Briefing Paper*. Retrieved December 1, 2020 from https://www-cdn.oxfam.org/s3fs public/file_attachments/bp210-economy-one-percent-tax-havens-180116-en_0.pdf

OXFAM (2020), *Covid-19 and Vulnerable, Hardworking Kenyans: Why it's Time for a Strong Social Protection Plan*. Oxford: Oxfam GB

Ozili, P. (2020), COVID-19 in Africa: Socioeconomic Impact, Policy Response and Opportunities. *International Journal of Sociology and Social Policy*, 42(3/4), 177–200. https://doi.org/10.1108/IJSSP-05-2020-0171.

Republic of Kenya (2020a), *Stimulating the Economy to Safeguard Livelihoods, Jobs, Businesses and Industrial Recovery*. Nairobi: Government Printer.

Republic of Kenya (2020b), *Budget Review and Outlook Paper*. Nairobi: Government Printers.

Rowson, M. (2012), Violence and Development. In J. Salvage, M. Rowson, K. Melf, and I. Sandøy (Eds.), *The Medical Peace Work Textbook*, 2nd edition (pp. 9–15). London: Medact.

Standish, K. (2021), Suicide, Femicide, and COVID-19. *Peace Review*, Vol. 33, No. 1, pp. 71–79. http://doi.org/10.1080/10402659.2021.1956132

TIFA (2020a), *The Covid-19 Global Pandemic in Nairobi's Low-Income Areas: Health, Socio-Economic and Governance Aspects* Nairobi: TIFA.

TIFA (2020b), *Round 3 Survey on the Covid-19 Global Pandemic in Nairobi's Low-income Areas: Opinion on the Nairobi Area Travel Restriction and Curfew*. Nairobi: TIFA.

Transparency International (2019), *Corruption Perception Index*. Berlin: Transparency International.

Ufua, D., Osabuohien, E., Ogbari, M., Falola, H., Okoh, E. & Lakhani, A. (2021), Re-Strategising Government Palliative Support Systems in Tackling the Challenges of COVID-19 Lockdown in Lagos State, Nigeria. *Global Journal of Flexible Systems Management*, 22, 19–32. https://doi.org/10.1007/s40171-021-00263-z

UNCTD (2020), *COVID-19 and Tourism: Assessing the Economic Consequences*. Geneva: UNCTD.

UNDP (1999), *Human Development Report*. Oxford: Oxford University Press.

UNDP (2019), *Beyond Income, Beyond Averages, Beyond Today: Inequalities in Human Development in the 21st Century*. Human Development Report, UNDP.

UNDP (2020), Articulating the Pathways of the Socio-Economic Impact of the Coronavirus (COVID-19) Pandemic on the Kenyan Economy. *Policy Brief Issue No: 4/2020*. Retrieved November 3, 2020 from https://www1.undp.org/content/dam/rba/docs/COVID-19-CO-Response/Socio-Economic-Impact-COVID-19-Kenya-Policy-Brief-UNDP-Kenya-April-2020.pdf

UNDP (2021), *Analysing Long-term Socioeconomic Impacts of COVID-19 across Diverse African Contexts*. UNDP Regional Bureau for Africa.

World Bank (2018), *Kenya Economic Updates*. Washington, DC: World Bank.

World Bank (2020), *Turbulent Times for Growth in Kenya: Policy Options During the COVID-19 Pandemic*. Washington, DC: World Bank.

World Bank (2021), *Socioeconomic Impacts of COVID-19 in Kenya*. Washington, DC: World Bank.

World Bank (2022), *Global Economic Prospects*. Washington, DC: World Bank.

World Justice Project (2020), *Corruption and the COVID-19 Pandemic*. Washington, DC: World Justice Project.

12 COVID-19 and Poverty Incidence in Sub-Saharan Africa

Evidence from Past Pandemics

Chekwube Vitus Madichie, Franklin Nnaemeka Ngwu, Anne Chinonye Maduka, and Amaka Gertrude Metu

Introduction

Following the declaration of COVID-19 (coronavirus disease 2019) as a global health pandemic by the World Health Organization (WHO) in March 2020, the virus has gained unprecedented relevance, spreading rapidly across different parts of the world in the past four months. As of November 2020, over 48 million cases were reported across 188 countries/regions, with 1.2 million deaths (John Hopkins University [JHU], 2020). Currently, over 500 million cumulative cases and over 6 million deaths have been reported globally (Kaiser Family Foundation [KFF], 2022). In responding to the pandemic, governments around the world took several drastic measures, including national and international lockdowns, stay-at-home policies, school and church closures, social distancing, quarantines, and so on, to contain, as well as curtail, the virus from spreading. While these measures seemed to be effective in mitigating the spread of the virus, their disruptive implications on several existing local and international value chains have been quite severe. The disruption of local and international supply chains resulted in a global economic slowdown while jeopardizing long-term health and food security as countries lost access to critical resources (World Bank, 2020). Demand for goods and services dropped dramatically as a result of the loss of income and concern about the future. International travel restrictions and border inspections have raised the cost of doing business across the globe (Bekkers, *et al.*, 2020). These posed exciting consequences on business operations around the world, as well as unleashing untold hardship on people whose source of livelihood depends on daily economic activities (Osabuohien et al., 2021; Ufua et al., 2021). The International Labour Organization (ILO) estimates that approximately 1.25 billion workers, representing almost 40% of global workers, are employed in sectors with a higher risk of worker displacement. These sectors are equally characterized by a higher ratio of workers in informal employment who have limited access to health services and social protection (ILO, 2020). Trade, investment, growth, and employment have all been adversely affected and the crisis is expected to have an impact on the achievement of the United Nations (UN) Sustainable Development Goals (SDGs), particularly on the goal of ending poverty in all its forms by 2030.

DOI: 10.4324/9781003208358-16

According to the report by PovcalNet (which is an online tool provided by the World Bank for estimating global poverty) on the World Economic Outlook, COVID-19 is likely to have caused the first increase in global poverty since the Asian Financial Crisis in 1998. Due to the COVID-19 pandemic, the percentage share of the world's population living on less than $1.90 per day was projected to increase from 8.2% in 2019 to 8.6% by the end of 2020 and beyond as opposed to the previous projection of decline from 8.1% to 7.8% over the same period using the previous forecast of the World Economic Outlook (PovcalNet: online tool, World Bank). Given the distressed expression of concerns from various quarters, it is not in doubt that COVID-19 will push millions of people into extreme poverty in years to come. In Sub-Saharan Africa (SSA), although the wrath of COVID-19 has been relatively minimal from a health perspective when compared to other regions, the projection by PovcalNet (online tool, World Bank) suggests that the region will be hit hardest in terms of an increase in extreme poverty. It is projected that the pandemic will push 23 million people into extreme poverty in SSA and 16 million in South Asia (PovcalNet: online tool, World Bank). The World Bank attributed the extreme poverty issues in SSA to slower rates of growth, weak institutions, and a lack of resilience. Many countries in SSA have been greatly affected, as most of their households rely on nonlabour income such as remittances, which has been halted as the pandemic equally affects the livelihood of migrants.

To understand the potential impact of COVID-19 on the poverty level in SSA, it is important to draw evidence from past pandemics and major epidemics. Regrettably, despite the growing concerns, as well as the recently renewed global interest in understanding the economic effects of pandemics, there is limited empirical evidence available to explain the potential economic effects of COVID-19, particularly in SSA. Thus, this study relates to two major strands of literature. The first is on the economic effect of COVID-19 and other notable pandemics by Atkeson (2020), Barro (2020), Eichenbaum et al. (2020), Jorda, et al. (2020), Ma et al. (2020), Diop and Asongo (2021), and Diop, Asongo and Nnanna (2021). Specifically, Ma et al. (2020), who examined a similar set of episodes as the current study, reported that, on average, the real GDP is 2.6% lower across 210 countries in the year the outbreak was officially declared. Diop and Asongo (2021), in their study of COVID-19 and the new poor in Africa, reported that the extreme poverty line of US$1.90, the middle poverty line of US$3.20, and the higher poverty line of US$5.5 per day increased by US$0.1, US$0.19, and US$0.32 per day, respectively, while the poverty headcount increased to 35.85% for the US$1.90 poverty line, 57.55% for the US$3.20 per day poverty line, and 76.42% for the higher poverty line (US$5.5 per day). For Diop et al. (2021), in their study of COVID-19 economic vulnerability and resilience indexes, Asia-Pacific and the Middle East are the most economically vulnerable regions to have faced the COVID-19 pandemic, with a value of 0.29, followed by Africa, with a score of 0.26, while Europe is considered the best region for earning the lowest vulnerability index score. The second strand of literature is on how recessions, crises, and pandemics escalate inequality by depressing employment for the most vulnerable group (see De Haan & Sturm, 2017; Furceri et al., 2020).

Thus, this study relies on evidence from past pandemics and/or major epidemics in the past two decades to understand the potential impact of COVID-19 on the poverty level in SSA. It should be noted that even though past pandemics are much smaller in scale, they may have led to an increase in global/regional poverty levels. However, unlike Furceri et al. (2020), who used impulse response functions (IRFs) directly from local projections based on Jorda (2005), this study estimates the IRFs within the framework of the panel structural vector autoregression (SVAR-Panel) developed by Pedroni (2013), which considers responses to both common and idiosyncratic shocks while permitting full cross-section heterogeneity of the response dynamics. Accordingly, this chapter sheds light on the potential impact of COVID-19 on poverty incidence in SSA, drawing evidence from past pandemics and major epidemics.

Stylized Facts on Poverty Incidences Sub-Saharan Africa and Global Pandemic Events

Poverty Incidence in SSA

The World Bank's report entitled "Poverty and shared prosperity: Piecing together the poverty puzzle" documents the tremendous progress the world has made towards ending global extreme poverty by tracking its decline from 1990 to 2015. Specifically, in 1990, approximately 36% of the world's population lived in poverty, defined by a purchasing power parity income of less than $1.90 per day in 2011, and by 2015, only approximately 10% of the world's population lived in poverty (World Bank, 2020). However, relative to the contribution of Latin America and the Caribbean, East Asia and the Pacific and, more recently, South Asia to decreasing global extreme poverty, the much slower battle against poverty in SSA has been unable to equal the success of these other regions. The number of people living in poverty in the SSA region rose from 278 million in 1990 to 437 million in 2020, while the majority of the world's poor are those living in SSA as of 2015 (World Bank, 2020).

SSA's average poverty rate is approximately 41%, and of the 28 poorest countries in the world, 27 are in SSA, all with a poverty rate above 30%. The World Bank's forecasts also show that extreme poverty in SSA shows little or no sign of progress and could prevent countries from ending extreme poverty by 2030 (World Bank, 2020). In part, the problem lies in the slower growth rates in the SSA region, despite recent improvements (Osabohien et al., 2020). The World Bank's report also identifies conflict-related challenges, weak institutions, and a lack of resilience as major obstacles to improving opportunities for the poor in sub-Saharan Africa. The aforementioned scenario is shown in Figure 12.1.

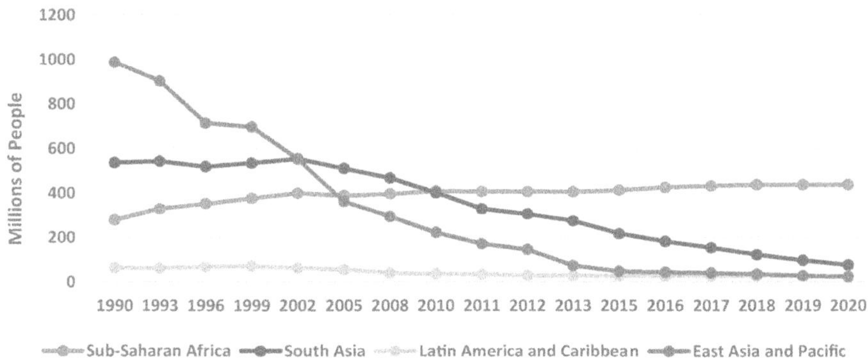

Figure 12.1 People living in extreme poverty in SSA and other regions (millions)
Source: World Bank (2020)

Notable Global Epidemics and Pandemic Events

Our analysis focuses on the major global epidemics and pandemic events. Prior to the 2000s, HIV/AIDS was the most remarkable pandemic event that greeted the world in 1981, with an estimated direct mortality of more than 70 million infections and 36.7 million deaths (Madhav et al., 2017). In 2003, the SARS epidemic was reported to have affected 4 continents and 37 countries, with 8,098 cases and 744 deaths. This was followed by another episode of the pandemic in 2009, when the H1N1 'swine flu' was reported to have affected the world, with mortality ranging from 151,700 to 575,500. In 2012, the MERS epidemic was reported in 22 countries, with 1,879 cases and 659 deaths, while the West African Ebola virus epidemic was reigned in 10 countries in 2014, with 28,646 cases and 11,323 deaths. The year 2016 witnessed another pandemic in the form of the Zika virus in 76 countries, with 2,656 cases of microcephaly or central nervous system malformation. In 2020, the WHO officially pronounced COVID-19 as a global pandemic, having affected 185 countries and territories, with over 48 million confirmed cases and 1.2 million deaths as of November 2020 (JHU, 2020). The global epidemics and pandemic events are summarized in Table 12.1.

Methodology

The Model

The main thrust of this study is to shed light on the potential impact of COVID-19 on poverty level in SSA by drawing evidence from past pandemics and/or major epidemics while unveiling other important determinants of poverty in the region. The study is based on panel data covering 20 SSA countries (see Appendix for the list of countries selected) over the period 1990–2020.

Table 12.1 Summary of Notable Epidemics and Pandemic Events

Year	*Event*	*Geographic Extent*	*Casualties*
1981	HIV/AIDS pandemic	Global	More than 70 million infections and 36.7 million deaths
2003	SARS Epidemic	4 continents, 37 countries	8,098 cases and 744 deaths
2009	H1N1 'Swine flu' Pandemic	Global	151,700–575,500 deaths
2012	MERS Epidemic	22 countries	1,879 cases and 659 deaths
2014	West African Ebola Virus Epidemic	10 countries	28,646 cases and 11,323 deaths
2016	Zika Virus Pandemic	76 countries	2,656 cases
2020	COVID-19	Global (188 countries/ territories)	Over 48 million cases and 1.2 million deaths as of Nov. 2020

Source: Authors' compilation

NB: World Health Organization (WHO): www.who.int/; Madhav et al. (2017); JHU (2020)

The choice of 20 SSA countries is based on the availability of data on variables other than the pandemic/epidemic variable. Even though most of the selected SSA countries were not directly affected by some of the past pandemic/epidemic events, there is a high probability that most of them were economically affected due to globalization and the strength of the global value chain. Therefore, following Ma et al. (2020) and Furceri et al. (2020), this study focuses on six major events – SARS in 2003; H1N1 in 2009; MERS in 2012; Ebola in 2014; Zika in 2016; and COVID-19 in 2020. We, therefore, construct a dummy variable (DUM) for the pandemic/epidemic events, which takes the value of 1 for the years when the WHO declares a pandemic/epidemic for the country and 0 otherwise. Other key variables include poverty rates, economic growth (real gross domestic product), employment rates, foreign direct investment, trade openness, institutional quality, and remittance inflows across the SSA countries.

Unlike Furceri et al. (2020), who used the IRFs directly from local projections, this study estimates the IRFs within the framework of the Panel Structural Vector Autoregression (henceforth, SVAR-Panel) developed by Pedroni (2013), which considers responses to both idiosyncratic and shocks while permitting full cross-section heterogeneity of the response dynamics. Other advantages of the SVAR-Panel include (i) it performs remarkably well at uncovering the properties of the sample distribution of the underlying structural dynamics, even when the panels are relatively short, as illustrated in Monte Carlo simulations, and (ii) these simulations also illustrate that the SVAR-Panel method can be used to improve inference, not only for properties of the sample distribution but also for dynamics of individual members of the panel that lack adequate data for a conventional time series SVAR analysis (Roch, 2019). To estimate the model, we used the heterogeneous SVAR panel because the standard panel methods do not account for heterogeneous dynamics that could result in inconsistent estimation and inference among the panel members (Pesaran & Smith, 1995). In addition, these methods typically neglect the fact that panel members can be linked cross-sectionally through common global shocks. The Pedroni (2013) approach allows for complete variability in the complex responses across the panel's members while also allowing for the cross-sectional dependency due to shocks that are common across the panel's members (Roch, 2019). Additionally, to decompose the shocks into member-specific idiosyncratic shocks and common structural shocks that drive the cross-sectional dependence among members, the algorithm exploits orthogonalities associated with SVAR identification schemes. For each member of the panel, the relative significance of the idiosyncratic versus typical shocks can differ (Pedroni, 2013). In view of the foregoing, we specify the baseline panel SVAR as follows:

$$A_{i0}\, x_{it} = A_i(L)\, x_{it} + \mu_{it} \tag{1}$$

where $A_i(L)$ represents a matrix of polynomials in the lag operator of order q, μ_{it} denotes the structural errors, and x_{it} stands as a vector of variables with country-specific dimension $t = (1, 2,., T)$ for each of the selected SSA members $i = (1,2..., N)$ of the panel represented by the following vector:

$$x_{it} = \begin{bmatrix} POV \\ DUM \\ GDP \\ EMP \\ FDI \\ TOP \\ INQ \\ REM \end{bmatrix} \tag{2}$$

Based on the literature, the main assumption of identifying restriction is that the pandemic dummy (DUM) is an exogenous variable. The exogeneity of DUM suggests that matrix A be restricted as follows: (i) for all $q > 0$, except the first, every other element in the first row of $A_i(L)$ to be 0, and (ii) it is assumed that A_0 be lower triangular with value, 1 on the major diagonal. These assumptions imply that DUM follows a univariate autoregressive process. At this point, the heterogeneous panel SVAR methodology developed by Pedroni (2013) is invoked to estimate the model. The innovation in the Pedroni (2013) approach is the disintegration of orthogonal structural shocks into orthogonal common and idiosyncratic components as follows:

$$\mu_{it} = \Delta_t \bar{\mu}_i + \tilde{\mu}_{it} \tag{3}$$

where μ_{it} represents the composite shock, $\bar{\mu}_{it}$ stands for the common shocks, $\bar{\mu}_{it}$ denotes the idiosyncratic shock, and Δ_i represents a diagonal matrix of the country-specific loadings, reflecting the comparative significance of the common shocks for a specific country. The loading matrix is built by estimating a simple ordinary least squares (OLS) of the composite shock on each country's common shocks, and the composite impulse response is thereafter decomposed as follows:

$$A_i(L) = A_i(L)\Delta_t + A_i(L)(I - \Delta_i\Delta_t')^{1/2} \tag{4}$$

where $\bar{A}_i(L) = A_i(L)\Delta_i$ are the country-specific responses to a common structure shock, $\tilde{A}_i(L) + A_i(L)(I - \Delta_i\Delta_t')^{1/2}$ represents country-specific responses to an idiosyncratic structural shock.

Data

Data relating to poverty rates (POV), employment rates (EMP), foreign direct investment (FDI), trade openness (TOP), and remittance inflows (REM) were obtained from the World Bank (2020), while the real gross domestic product (GDP) and institutional quality (INQ) data were sourced from the African Development Bank ([AfDB], 2020) databases. Further information on the definition and sources of data are summarized in Table 12.2.

Table 12.2 Summary of Variable Definition and Sources of Data

Name	*Abbreviation*	*Definition*	*Source*
Poverty rates (%)	*POV*	Percentage of population living on less than US$1.90 per day.	World Bank database
Pandemic dummy	*DUM*	Binary variable with value 1 for the period of health pandemic events as officially announced by the WHO, and 0 for otherwise.	WHO
Real gross domestic products	*GDP*	The annual total market value of all the final goods and services, expressed in constant basic prices.	World Bank database
Employment rates (%)	*EMP*	Percentage of the population employed.	World Bank database
Foreign direct investment, net inflows (% of GDP)	*FDI*	Foreign direct investment is the net inflows of investment meant to acquire a prolonged managerial interest (up to 10% or more of voting stock) in an enterprise operating in an economy other than the investors.	World Bank database

(Continued)

Table 12.2 (Continued)

Name	*Abbreviation*	*Definition*	*Source*
Trade openness	*TOP*	The ratio of exports plus imports to GDP	World Bank database
Institutional quality	*INQ*	The current structure of the institution and the dissemination of formal and informal rules that govern individuals and organizational behaviours, measured on a scale of 1 to 6, with 1 indicating poor institutional quality and 6 indicating excellent institutional quality.	World Bank database
Remittances (% of GDP)	*REM*	Money sent, often to a person in their home country by a foreign worker.	World Bank database

Source: Authors' compilation

NB: World Health Organization (WHO): www.who.int/; World Bank database (World Development Indicators): www.databank.worldbank.org

Results and Discussion

Cross-Section Dependency Test

The study of the panel residual cross-section dependence test alongside the panel unit root test is the key preliminary test before the estimation of the SVAR-Panel model. For reliability and outcome validity, we used the Breusch–Pagan LM test statistic, as the time coverage in our panel is greater than the number of cross-sections, (i.e., $T=30 > N=20$), and the results are reported in Table 12.3. The value of the Breusch–Pagan LM test statistic is 234.143 and has a probability value of 0.0000 according to Table 12.3. We reject the null hypothesis of cross-section independence and conclude that our panel has cross-section dependencies because the probability value of the Breusch–Pagan LM test statistic is less than 0.05.

Panel Unit Root Tests

The summary of the LLC, IPS, ADFF-χ^2, and PPF-χ^2 panel unit root procedure was used in evaluating the stationary properties of the relevant time-series variables, as well as in establishing their order of integration. From the results of the panel unit root tests shown in Table 12.4, all variables (POV, GDP, EMP, FDI,

Table 12.3 Residual Cross-Section Dependence Test

Test	*Statistic*	*Df*	*Prob.*
Breusch–Pagan LM	234.143	201	0.0000
Pesaran Scaled LM	6.83512		0.0000
Pesaran CD	3.45921		0.0000

Source: Authors' estimation using E-views 10

Table 12.4 Panel Unit Root Test

Variable	*Method*	*Level*	*I(d)*
		Stat. (Prob.)	
POV	*LLC*	−4.41723** (0.0014)	I(0)
	IPS	–3.92089** (0.0001)	
	ADFF-χ^2	78.7276** (0.0001)	
	PPF-χ^2	138.169** (0.0000)	
GDP	*LLC*	−4.50817** (0.0000)	I(0)
	IPS	−4.02126** (0.0001)	
	ADFF-χ^2	88.1132** (0.0002)	
	PPF-χ^2	90.2043** (0.0000)	
EMP	*LLC*	−1.62122 (0.0706)	I(0)
	IPS	−2.51417* (0.0227)	
	ADFF-χ^2	70.4918* (0.0116)	
	PPF-χ^2	69.3413* (0.0281)	
FDI	*LLC*	−4.57218** (0.0000)	I(0)
	IPS	−4.11022** (0.0000)	
	ADFF-χ^2	98.5271** (0.0000)	
	PPF-χ^2	189.980** (0.0000)	
TOP	*LLC*	−3.17438* (0.0128)	I(0)
	IPS	−4.34065** (0.0000)	
	ADFF-χ^2	89.5106** (0.0000)	
	PPF-χ^2	161.028** (0.0000)	
INQ	*LLC*	−3.45213** (0.0011)	I(0)
	IPS	−3.90237** (0.0001)	
	ADFF-χ^2	91.5124** (0.0000)	
	PPF-χ^2	151.210** (0.0000)	
REM	*LLC*	−3.00213** (0.0021)	I(0)
	IPS	−4.29541** (0.0000)	
	ADFF-χ^2	86.2102** (0.0000)	
	PPF-χ^2	132.230** (0.0002)	

Source: Authors' estimation using Eviews 10

**(*) denotes significance at the 1% (5%) level.

TOP, INQ, and REM) are stationary at their level state. This is because most of the unit root test procedures (LLC, IPS, ADFF-χ^2, and PPF-χ^2) have probability values that are less than 0.05 and virtually reject the unit root hypothesis. This indicates that consistent SVAR-Panel model estimates can be generated even though the cointegration test has become unnecessary.

Structural Impulse Response of Poverty Rates to Pandemic Shocks

The responses of the poverty rates to composite, common, and idiosyncratic global pandemic shocks are the core of our analysis in this study. Composite pandemic shocks include common and idiosyncratic shocks emanating from pandemic events. The categorization of these shocks into common and idiosyncratic shocks implies that pandemic shocks have the same or unique effect on different countries. First, composite pandemic shocks, which consist of common and idiosyncratic shocks, relate to the gross effect of the pandemic on all the countries that make up the panel. Second, common pandemic shocks indicate the effects of the pandemic that are similar to all countries in the panel. Third, idiosyncratic pandemic shocks show the effect of the pandemic that is uniquely specific to a particular country within the panel. This is because of the obvious heterogeneity in terms of vulnerability to pandemic shocks alongside the institutional, environmental, welfare, economic, social, and political configurations of countries in the panel setup.

In Figures 12.2, 12.3, and 12.4 (see Appendix), we present the response estimates to composite, common, and idiosyncratic pandemic shocks, respectively. There are similarities in the response of poverty rates to all shocks, meaning that health pandemics have similar effects on poverty levels across countries in SSA. In other words, whether pandemic shocks are viewed from composite, common, or idiosyncratic dimensions, the poverty level in each of the SSA countries will respond similarly to the pandemic. According to the results, poverty rates tend to significantly respond upwardly to the current pandemic in the coming periods. In other words, the results show evidence that poverty incidence in the SSA region will become more pronounced due to the current health pandemic (COVID-19). This upwards response will be particularly sharp and steady during the first four periods and stabilizes through the rest of the periods. This implies that each of the 20 SSA countries will experience a similar poverty rise during the coming years. These responses are statistically significant and quite persistent, as reflected by the confidence intervals. Thus, following past pandemics, it is to be expected that poverty incidence will become more pronounced across all countries in the SSA region due to the current health pandemic (COVID-19). This is particularly expected to prevail within the first four periods after the pandemic event, and thereafter, poverty rates stabilize in the remaining periods. Thus, policymakers and governments across the SSA region should be well informed to take the necessary policy actions ahead of the current pandemic.

Interestingly, the study found that the poverty rate similarly responds negatively and significantly to shocks in real GDP, employment rates, FDI, and remittance inflows across all countries in the SSA region. For instance, poverty rates are expected to respond negatively to real gross domestic product, employment rates, FDI, and remittance shocks at almost the same magnitude across the various shocks (composite, common, and idiosyncratic shocks) within the first four periods, and thereafter, further shock to these variables (GDP, employment rates, FDI, and remittances) will leave the poverty level unchanged. However, trade openness and institutional quality may increase the poverty rate in the first period, and thereafter, poverty declines in the remaining periods. It is important to note that, in the face of any future global health pandemic, sound growth policies, gainful employment policies, remittance attraction policies, attraction of foreign direct investment, free trade flows, and prevalence of strong institutions will help insulate the economy against future poverty incidence in sub-Saharan Africa. These results are reported in the Appendix of this study.

Conclusion

The study investigated the potential impact of the COVID-19 pandemic on the poverty level in the SSA region by drawing evidence from past pandemics from 1990 to 2020. The study estimated the IRFs within the framework of the SVAR-Panel developed by Pedroni (2013), which considers responses to both common and idiosyncratic shocks while permitting full cross-section heterogeneity of the response dynamics.

The results show that pandemic events will similarly exert a significant positive impact on poverty levels in SSA countries. In other words, the poverty level across SSA countries is expected to rise similarly following the current pandemic. This implies that the current COVID-19 pandemic will push more people into poverty in the SSA region. However, the study further reveals that while the current pandemic will exacerbate poverty in SSA, the implementation of sound growth policies, gainful employment policies, remittance attraction policies, attraction of foreign direct investment, free trade flows, and prevalence of strong institutions will serve as good insulators against future poverty influence in the region.

Finally, further studies on COVID-19 and health pandemics are encouraged to further document evidence for policy formulation to mitigate the adverse economic and poverty effects of current and future health pandemics. Thus, we suggest that future studies should focus on variables that identify and explain the health, social, and economic resilience of countries against the current and future health pandemics. Further time-series studies are encouraged to consider pre- and post-health pandemic events using suitable seasonal adjustment modelling frameworks.

Appendix

List of the 20 countries in SSA to be used for the study.

1. Benin	11. Guinea-Bissau
2. Botswana	12. Kenya
3. Burkina Faso	13. Madagascar
4. Cameroon	14. Niger
5. Central African Republic	15. Nigeria
6. Cote d'Ivoire	16. Senegal
7. Equatorial Guinea	17. Sierra Leone
8. Gabon	18. South Africa
9. Ghana	19. Togo
10. Guinea	20. Uganda

Source: The Royal Society – Department for International Development (DfID), Africa Capacity Building Initiative (www.royalsociety.org)

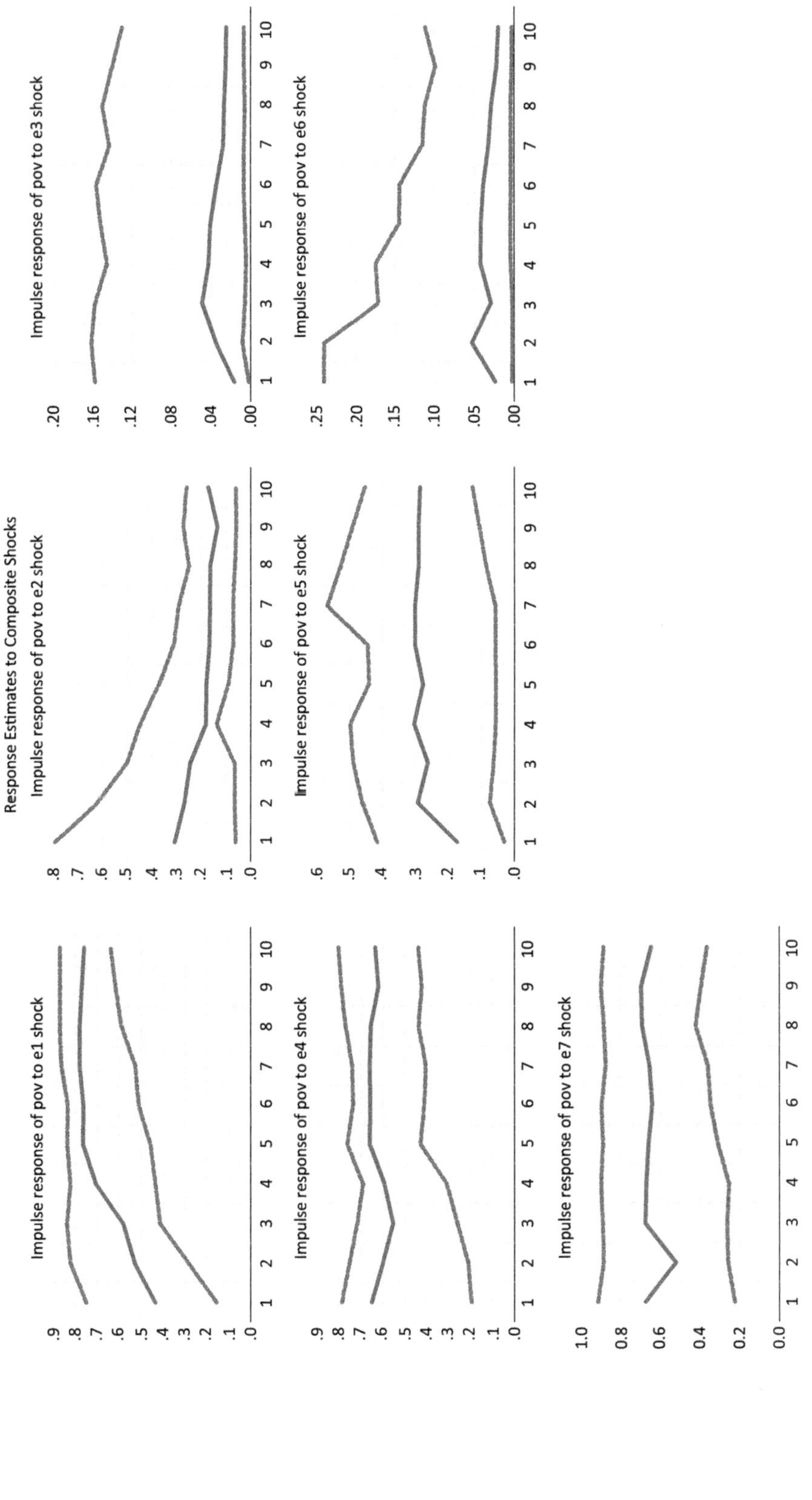

Figure 12.2 Response estimates to composite shocks

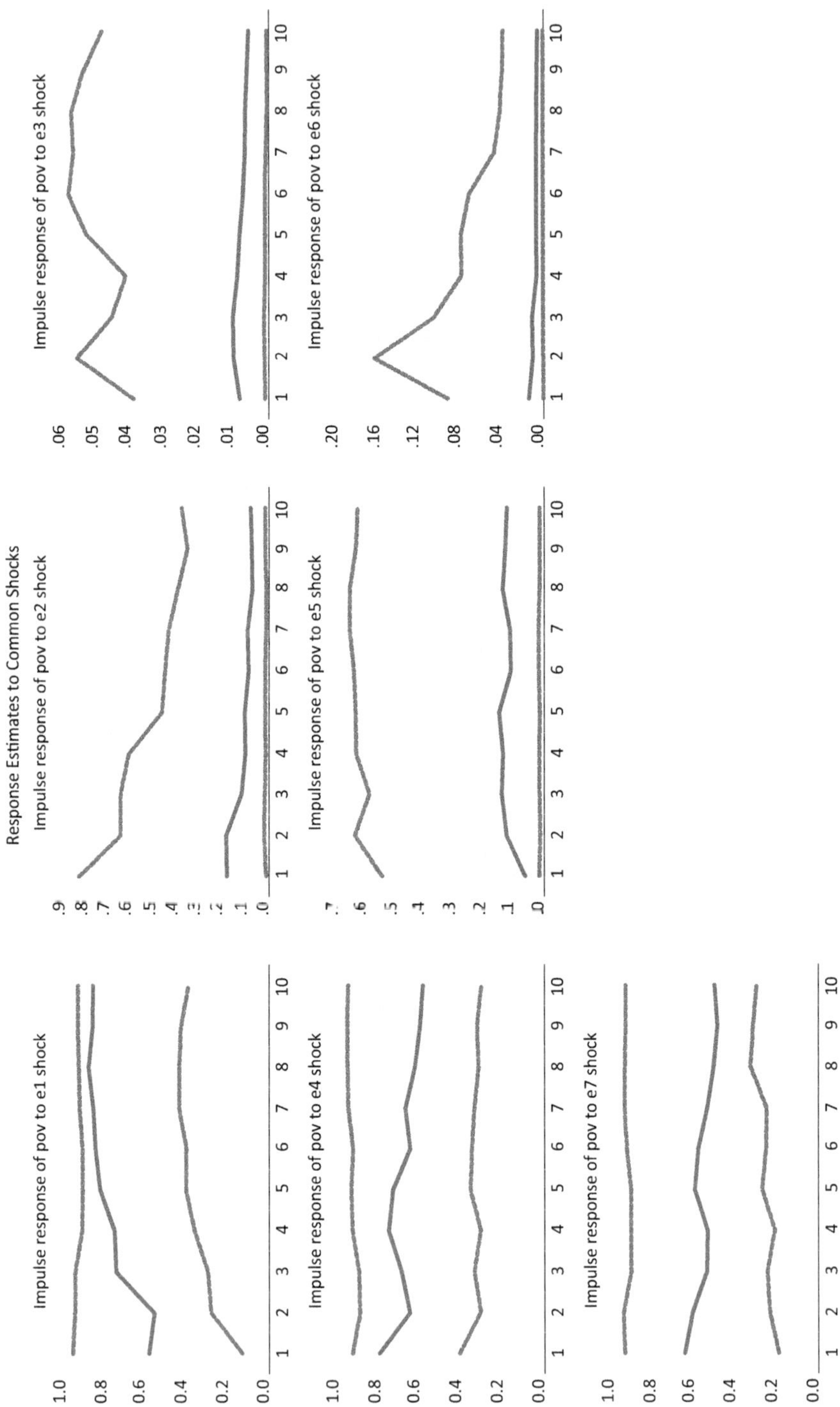

Figure 12.3 Response estimates to common shocks

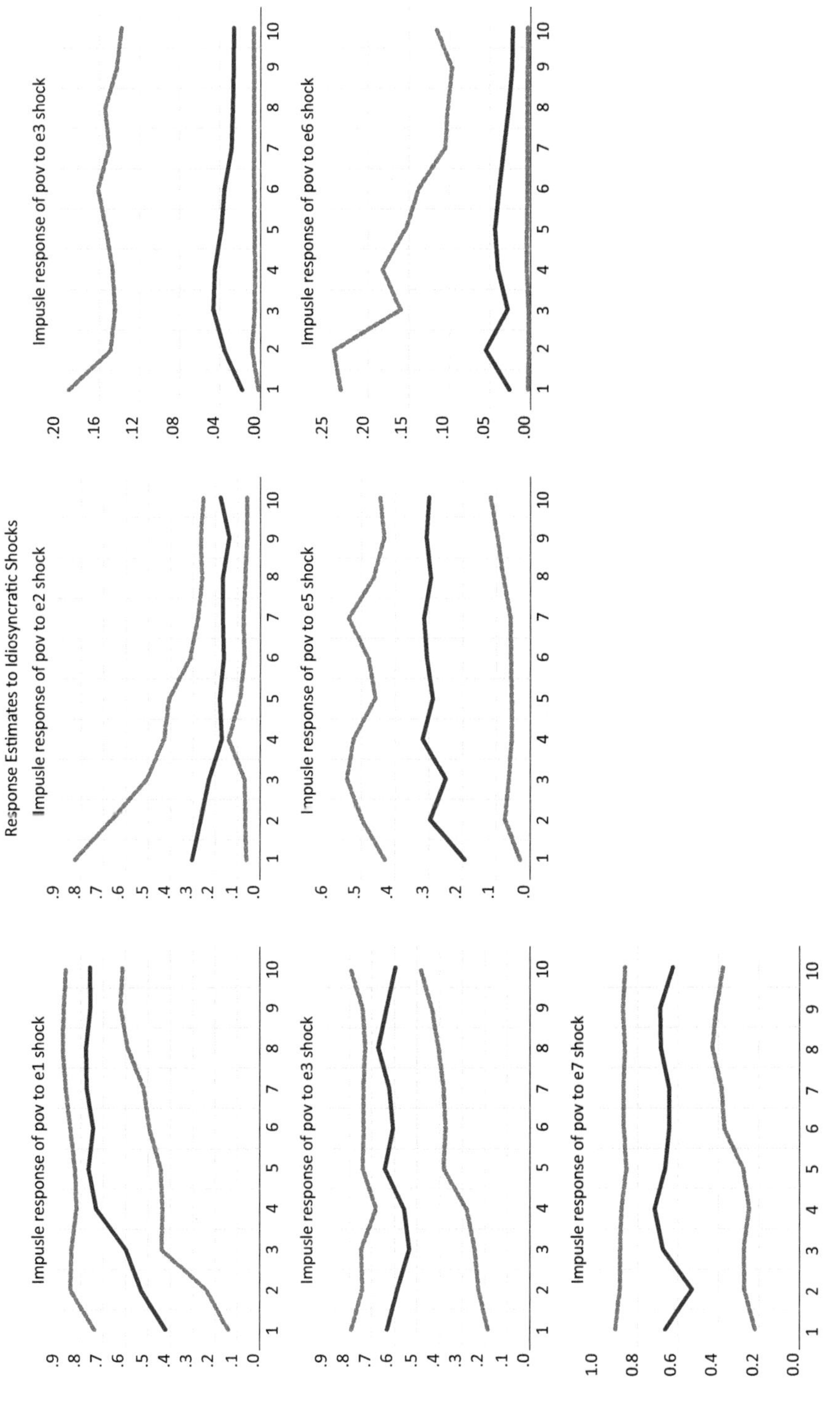

Figure 12.4 Response estimates to idiosyncratic shocks

References

African Development Bank [AfDB] (2020). *Socioeconomic Database 1960–2020*. https://dataportal.opendataforafrica.org/nbyenxf/afdb-socioeconomic-database-1960-2021

Atkeson, A. (2020). What will be the economic impact of COVID-19 in the US? Rough estimates of disease scenarios. *NBER Working Paper No. 26867*. http://www.nber.org/papers/w26867

Barro, R. J., Ursua, J. F. & Weng, J. (2020). The coronavirus and the great influenza pandemic: Lessons from the Spanish Flu for the coronavirus's potential effects on mortality and economic activity. *NBER Working Paper No. 26866*. http://www.nber.org/papers/w26866

Bekkers, E., Keck, A., Koopman, R. & Nee, C. (2020). Trade and COVID-19: The WTO's 2020 and 2021 trade forecast. https://voxeu.org/article/trade-and-covid-19-wto-s-2020-and-2021-trade-forecast

de Haan, J. & Sturm, J. (2017). Finance and income inequality: A review and new evidence. *European Journal of Political Economy*, 50, 171–195. https://doi.org/10.1016/j.ejpoleco.2017.04.007

Diop, S. & Asongo, S. A. (2021). The COVID-19 pandemic and the new poor in Africa: The straw that broke the camel's back. *Forum for Social Economics*. https://doi.org/10.1080/07360932.2021.1884583

Diop, S., Asongo, S. A. & Nnanna, J. (2021). COVID-19 economic vulnerability and resilience indexes: Global evidence. *International Social Science Journal*, 71(S1), 37–50. https://doi.org/10.1111/issj.12276

Eichenbaum, M. S., Rebelo, S. & Trabandt, M. (2020). The macroeconomics of epidemics. *NBER Working Paper No. 26882*. http://www.nber.org/papers/w26882

Furceri, D., Loungani, P., Ostry, J. D. & Pizzuto, P. (2020). Will COVID-19 affect inequality? Evidence from past pandemics. *Centre for Economic Policy Research*, Issues 12, COVID ECONOMICS: CEPR Press. https://www.econbiz.de/Record/covid-economics-vetted-and-real-time-papers/10012208743

ILO – International Labour Organization (2020). *ILO Monitor (2nd ed.): COVID-19 and the World of Work*. https://www.ilo.org/wcmsp5/groups/public/@dgreports/@dcomm/documents/briefingnote/wcms_740877.pdf

John Hopkins University (2020). *Coronavirus Resource Centre*. https://coronavirus.jhu.edu/map.html

Jorda, O. (2005). Estimation and inference on impulse responses by local projections. *American Economic Review*, 95, 161–182. https://doi.org/10.1257/0002828053828518

Jorda, O., Singh, S. R. & Taylor, A. M. (2020). Longer-run economic consequences of pandemics. *NBER Working Paper No*. 26934. http://www.nber.org/papers/w26934

Kaiser Family Foundation (KFF) (2022). Global COVID-19 tracker - Updated as of June 29. https://www.kff.org/coronavirus-covid-19/

Ma, C., Rogers, J. & Zhou, S. (2020). Global financial effects. *Covid Economics*, 5, 56–78. https://www.econbiz.de/Record/covid-economics-vetted-and-real-time-papers/10012208743

Madhav, N., Oppenheim, B., Gallivan, M., Mulembakani, P., Rubin, E. & Wolfe, N. (2017). Pandemics: Risks, impacts, and mitigation. In *Disease control priorities: Improving health and reducing poverty* (edited by Jamison, D. T., Gelband, H., Horton, S., Jha, P., Laxminarayan, R., Mock, C. N. & Nugent, R.), pp.315–345. https://www.ncbi.nlm.nih.gov/books/NBK525302/

Osabohien, R., Matthew, O., Ohalete, P. & Osabuohien, E. (2020). Population-poverty-inequality nexus and social protection in Africa. *Social Indicators Research*, 151(2), 575–598. https://doi.org/10.1007/s11205-020-02381-0

Osabuohien, E., Ejemeyovwi, J., Ihayere, O., Gitau, C. & Oyebola, F. (2021). Postpandemic renewable energy development in sub-Saharan Africa. *Sustainability and Climate Change*, 14(3), 183–192. https://doi.org/10.1089/scc.2020.0077

Pedroni, P. (2013). Structural Panel VARs. *Econometrics*, 2, 180–206. https://doi.org/10.3390/econometrics1020180

https://www.sciencedirect.com/science/article/abs/pii/030440769401644F - !Pesaran, M. H. & Smith, R. (1995). Estimating long-run relationships from dynamic heterogeneous panels. Journal of Econometrics, 68 (1), 79-113. https://doi.org/10.1016/0304-4076(94)01644-F

PovcalNet (online analysis tool). *World Bank. World Development Indicators; World Economic Outlook; Global Economic Prospects; Economist Intelligence Unit*. Washington, DC. https://iresearch.worldbank.org/PovcalNet/

Roch, F. (2019). The Adjustment to Commodity Price Shocks. *Journal of Applied Economics*, 22(1), 437–467. https://doi.org/10.1080/15140326.2019.1665316

Ufua, D., Osabuohien, E., Ogbari, M., Falola, H., Okoh, E. & Lakhani, A. (2021). Re-Strategising Government Palliative Support Systems in Tackling the Challenges of COVID-19 Lockdown in Lagos State, Nigeria. *Global Journal of Flexible Systems Management*, 22, 19–32. https://doi.org/10.1007/s40171-021-00263-z

World Bank (2020). *World development indicators*. Washington, DC: World Bank Group. https://www.worldbankgroup.com

Section 4

Services, Socioeconomic Shocks and Sustainable Development

13 Economic Shocks and Welfare of Nigerian Households

Khadijat Busola Amolegbe, Ebenezer Lemven Wirba, and Gilles Quentin Kane

1. Introduction

Households in Sub-Saharan Africa (SSA) are exposed continuously to various economic shocks due to climate change, food price fluctuations, pests and diseases, and health issues (Di Falco, 2014; Addison et al., 2019; Atake, 2018). However, households employ different strategies such as insurance, borrowing, and realloying resources, to mitigate the effects of shocks (Frankenberg et al., 2003). Each economic shock and the coping strategies employed may have different effects on households. The effects may be positive or negative depending on the household characteristics and prevailing conditions. For example, positive effects of food price fluctuation may result in income gain if the household is a net food seller, while negative effects may lead to loss of income for net food buyers (Arndt et al., 2008; Amolegbe et al., 2021). Hence, understanding the combined effects of each of these shocks on households remains an immediate and important research issue amidst new and emerging threats such as COVID-19 (Saah et al., 2021; Ufua et al., 2021; Amolegbe, 2020; Amu et al., 2021; Diop et al., 2021; Swinnen and Vos, 2021; Kokas et al., 2020; Ibukun and Adebayo, 2021).

A growing body of literature has explored the effects of shocks on households. For example, Amolegbe et al. (2021) studied the effect of unexpected food price shocks on Nigerian households and found that price shocks have negative relationships with household food security status. Ibukun and Adebayo (2021) examined the food security status of households during the pandemic and investigated its determinants using the COVID-19 National Longitudinal Phone Survey. The study revealed that over two-thirds of Nigerian households are threatened by food insecurity due to COVID-19. During the survey, they found that education, income, and wealth status are the main determinants of food security during the pandemic. More generally, COVID-19 has adversely affected household food and nutrition security (Nechifor et al., 2021), as well as the overall welfare of the most vulnerable households, such as the elderly poor (Kokas et al., 2020). Atake (2018) also found that health shocks negatively affect SSA households. The effect of shocks on individuals within households also varies, and females may be disproportionately affected by shocks (Quisumbing et al., 2018). However, the results from these studies are ambiguous, as many of the studies focus on a specific source

DOI: 10.4324/9781003208358-18

of economic shock and do not consider the combined effects of different sources of shocks. The studies also failed to control for the endogenous effects of shocks on households and did not account for households' use of coping strategies to mitigate the effects of shocks.

The study fills the observed knowledge gap by answering the following research question: What is the relationship between economic shocks and household welfare? *That is, which category of economic shock has the greatest effect on a household welfare after controlling for the effects of household characteristics and shock coping strategies?* This study contributes to the literature in four ways. First, we employ a comprehensive household panel survey that allows us to employ a robust empirical strategy. We focus on three waves of the Nigerian Living Standard Measurement Survey (LSMS), and we are also able to control for attrition across the three waves. Second, we focus on the combined effects of all economic shocks faced by households. This is because households are often faced with more than one economic shock at a time, and the ability of the household to mitigate the effects of each shock type varies. Third, we account for the mitigating effects of shock coping strategies employed by the households. Fourth, our focus on Nigeria is also relevant, given Nigeria's broad relevance in SSA. Nigeria has diverse cultural, geographical, and socioeconomic characteristics that are relevant in the context of this study.

The remainder of this chapter is structured as follows. The next section gives a brief review of relevant literature. Section 3 describes the data we employ for this study, and Section 4 briefly presents the empirical strategy we use to answer the research questions. We present and discuss the results in Section 5 and conclude in Section 6.

2. Literature Review

A growing body of literature examines the effects of economic shocks on household welfare and coping strategies in developing countries. In the next paragraphs, we discuss empirical works on the welfare effects of economic shocks. The review will be carried out at the global level, for Africa and then for Nigeria. Using Vietnamese household panel data for 2004–2005 and 2006–2008, Bales (2013) examined the impact of health shocks on household welfare. The results revealed that in Vietnam, poor households witnessed reductions in nonfarm income; meanwhile, rich households witnessed an increase in income. In Indonesia, Frankenberg et al. (2003) assessed the effect of economic shocks on welfare. The results from this study revealed that to respond to the effect of these economic shocks, households adopted a wide array of mechanisms. In this regard, households reduced expenditures on semidurables while maintaining spending on food. For Mexico, Skoufias and Vinha (2013) examined the impact of weather shocks on household welfare. The results of their findings revealed that both the ex-ante and ex-post coping strategies were not able to provide these households with sufficient protection against weather shocks. Another important inference of this study was that weather shocks augment household consumption via a transitory increase in income.

Regarding empirical studies in Africa, Mbegalo and Yu (2016), using Tanzanian household data for 2008–2009 and 2010–2011, quantitatively assessed the impact of food price shocks on household welfare in rural Tanzania. The findings showed that during the crisis, sellers witnessed an amelioration in welfare; meanwhile, buyers suffered welfare losses from the food price hikes. Additionally, the negative impact of the food price shock was more pronounced among the poor than among the non-poor. In Kenya, Wineman et al. (2017) studied the effects of weather shocks on household welfare using three waves of the household panel from 2000 to 2007. Empirical findings from this study revealed that all the different extreme weather shocks affect household welfare, although the effect differs by measures of welfare employed (income and calories). Furthermore, Hangoma et al. (2018), using four waves of Zambian surveys, evaluate the implications of health shocks for household income, medical spending, consumption, and coping strategies. The results showed that households are faced with financial and consumption risks that are expected to reduce household social protection. In Cameroon, Kane et al. (2015) examined the welfare effects of food price volatility using the third Cameroon Household consumption survey and the quadratic almost ideal demand system model. The results indicated that the effect of the food price hike is more severe among poor households and that the welfare losses incurred are a function of the degree of the price hike suffered by the household. This is related to the study by Osabohien et al. (2020a) using panel data as well as Osabohien et al. (2020b) using the LSMS dataset. More recently, Kokas et al. (2020) analysed the impact of COVID-19 on Tunisian household welfare. The lack of adequate access to health insurance, low access to water at home, and overcrowded living conditions make the poor more susceptible to becoming infected by COVID-19. Furthermore, the simulation shows that poverty will increase by 7.3 percentage points and 11.9 percentage points under the optimistic and pessimistic scenarios, respectively.

In Nigeria, Shehu and Sidique (2015) used a nationally representative dataset of rural households to evaluate the effect of idiosyncratic and covariate shocks on welfare proxied with consumption expenditure. The results from this study indicated no significant effect of idiosyncratic and climatic shocks on household consumption; meanwhile, price shocks were found to have a significant negative effect on household consumption. The results also revealed that rich households were able to insure against idiosyncratic and climatic shocks. In contrast, poor households were not able to insure themselves against the impact of economic shocks. Additionally, employing historical food prices and household panel survey data, Amolegbe et al. (2021) assessed the implications of unexpected food price shocks for household food security. The results of their study revealed that food price shocks have a negative effect on household food security measures, with the effect being more pronounced among net buyers. Ibukun and Adebayo (2021), analysing the food security status of Nigerian households during the pandemic and investigating its determinants, showed that socioeconomic variables such as education, income, and wealth status were the main determinants of food security during the COVID-19 pandemic. Furthermore, a huge proportion (two-thirds) of Nigerian households were threatened by food insecurity.

Stemming from the foregoing, studies using Nigeria data to examine the implications of the different shock categories for household welfare are relatively limited, even in the COVID-19 era. Indeed, the effects of the different economic shocks on household welfare in Nigeria are still an empirical issue. The contribution of our present endeavour is largely empirical – using the Nigerian household panel records, pooled OLS, and the random-effects model. We investigated the effects of agricultural shocks, health shocks, financial shocks, weather shocks, and other shocks on household welfare in Nigeria as a whole and by the zone of residency (i.e., rural residency versus urban residency). The study also examined the effects of each of these shocks on food expenditure and on nonfood expenditure. We were also able to account for household characteristics, attrition bias, and the shock coping strategies employed by the households. However, data limitation does not allow us to integrate COVID-19 shock into our analysis.

3. Data

We used the World Bank Living Standards Measurement Study Survey (LSMS) for Nigeria, and we focused only on the first three waves based on the comparability of these three waves. That is, we focused on 2010–2011 (wave 1), 2012–2013 (wave 2), and 2015–2016 (wave 3) surveys to construct our panel dataset that will be used for estimation. The surveys have seasonal variations and are nationally representative covering households in rural and urban areas. The baseline survey consisted of 5,000 households, and we addressed attrition bias across waves. The LSMA data collected on economic shocks are present at the household level. Households were asked to rank the three most significant shocks experienced over time, and dichotomous data were collected based on household responses to the shock-related questions. We focused on the two most severe shocks experienced within the survey year, and we categorized economic shocks experienced by households into five groups.

- *Agricultural shocks* include shocks related to either theft of crops, cash, livestock, or other property, destruction of harvest by fire, pest invasion that caused harvest failure or storage loss, increase in the price of inputs by the government, or fall in the price of output.
- *Financial shocks* include shocks related to job loss, nonfarm business failure, loss of land, or increase in the price of major food items consumed.
- *Weather shocks* are related to poor rains that cause harvest failure, flooding that causes harvest failure, or loss of property due to fire or flood.
- *Health shocks* are related to death or disability of an adult working member of the household, death of someone who sends remittances to the household, illness of an income-earning member of the household, or death of livestock due to illness.
- *Other shocks* include loss of an important contact, departure of an income-earning member of the household due to separation or divorce, departure of

an income-earning member of the household due to marriage, dwelling damaged/demolished, kidnapping, hijacking, robbery, assault, or other shocks that may not have been captured in the other shock categories.

We also accounted for the coping strategies households employ to mitigate the effects of economic shocks. We categorized the coping strategies into six groups.

- *Financial measures* include borrowing from friends and family, taking a loan from a financial institution, purchasing on credit, delaying payment obligations, selling harvest in advance, relying on savings, or taking advance payments from employers.
- *Safety net measures and assistance* employed by households include sending children to live with friends, receiving assistance from friends and family, receiving assistance from nongovernmental organizations (NGOs), and receiving assistance from the government or the use of insurance.
- *Household expenditure cuts* may range from withdrawing children from school, reducing food consumption, or reducing nonfood consumption.
- *Liquidity measures* employed by households to mitigate shocks include selling livestock, land, or other properties.
- Some households also *diversify* by engaging in additional income-generating activities. Households also use *other* shock coping measures, such as migration of a household member for work, and some households may choose to do nothing in mitigating the effects of some economic shocks.

4. Empirical Framework

We employed panel data regression models to answer the research question. That is, we estimated a pooled OLS, fixed effect, and random effect regression model (Wooldridge, 2010). We first explored the effect of each category of shock on household welfare by estimating the following regression.

$$Y_{h,t} = \beta_0 + \beta_1 S_{h,t} + \beta_2 R_{h,t} + \delta H_t + \gamma A_h + e_{h,t} \qquad 13.1$$

where $Y_{h,t}$ is the household welfare indicator (logarithm of per capita consumption, log of food expenditure or nonfood expenditure) of household h at time t. $S_{h,t}$ is a dummy variable that takes 1 if household h experiences a category of shock at time t and zero otherwise. R is a vector of coping strategies employed by household h at time t. These coping strategies include financial, safety net, expenditure cut, liquidity, diversification, and other measures. H_t is a vector of household characteristics that include household structure (polygamous or monogamous), household size, sex of household head, age of household head, number of literate household members, and adult equivalence (Dedehouanou and McPeak, 2020). A_h is the attrition bias, which we constructed using the inverse probability weighting (IPW) methods recommended by Foster and Bickman

(1996), and Verbeek and Nijman (1992). We operationalized the model on the different categories of shocks – agricultural, financial, weather, health, and other shocks – and the impact of each shock evaluated. However, because households simultaneously experience different types of shocks at the same time, we account for the effects of all shock categories by exploring a regression where $S_{h,t}$ is a vector of economic shocks experienced by household h at time t.

Appropriate estimation of panel data requires the two prominent panel data models: fixed-effects and random-effects models. According to Chan and Gemayel (2004), these models can take onboard households and intertemporal differences and control for the effect of unobserved characteristics and missing data. In this regard, panel data modelling can take the following form:

$$Y_{h,t} = \alpha_0 + \alpha_1 S_{h,t} + \alpha_2 R_{h,t} + \rho H_t + \theta A_h + \mu_h + \varepsilon_{h,t} \qquad 13.2$$

where μ_h represents unobserved household-specific effects that are expected to vary with time and constant across households. $\varepsilon_{h,t}$ denotes the random error term. According to Wooldridge (2010), the difference between the fixed effects technique and the random effects technique is based on the assumption we make on the explanatory variables and μ_h. The random-effects model considers μ_h to be random and not correlated with the observed characteristics; meanwhile, the fixed effects models assume that $\mu_h$is not random and that a relationship (correlation) exists between μ_h and observed characteristics. In this regard, in the random-effects model, since μ_h is random, it is lumped into the error term. In practice, the choice between the fixed effects models and the random-effects model relies on the Hausmann test. The Hausmann test is based on the correlation that exists between μ_h and the observed characteristics.

5. Results and Discussion

In this section, we present the descriptive statistics of relevant variables and discuss the results from the empirical analysis. The descriptive statistics are presented overall and by the household zone of residency.

5.1 *Descriptive Statistics*

Table 13.1 shows the descriptive statistics of households with respect to their zone of residency. The descriptive statistics report that the proportion of polygamous households in the rural setting is higher with respect to the urban setting. In terms of household size, descriptive findings show a rural-urban differential. In particular, households in rural areas are found on average to have approximately seven persons per household compared to approximately six persons per household for their urban counterparts.

On average, the percentage of female-headed households was found to be higher among urban dwellers than among rural dwellers. The descriptive results further indicate that in terms of the age of the household head, no significant

Table 13.1 Descriptive Characteristics

	1	2	3	4	
	Total	*Rural*	*Urban*	*Rural-Urban Difference*	
Polygamous household (%)	24.8	28.8	15.2	−0.136***	(−15.49)
Household size (mean)	6.4	6.7	5.7	−0.957***	(−15.94)
Female head (%)	12.7	11.2	16.0	0.0476***	−8.01
Household head age (mean)	5.5	5.9	4.8	−1.072	(−0.10)
Literate members (mean)	3.9	3.8	4.1	0.289***	−5.81
Adult equivalence (mean)	4.9	5.1	4.6	−0.550***	(−11.62)
Shock (%)					
Agricultural	5.0	6.0	2.9	−0.0315***	(−8.16)
Financial	9.5	9.6	9.4	−0.00237	(−0.46)
Weather	6.9	8.9	2.6	−0.0622***	(−13.98)
Health	13.4	14.6	10.8	−0.0378***	(−6.27)
Others	3.7	3.3	4.5	0.0117***	−3.49
Coping strategies (%)					
Financial	10.7	11.3	9.3	−0.0206***	(−3.77)
Safety nets	8.9	9.7	7.3	−0.0241***	(−4.78)
Expenditure cut	7.9	8.3	7.0	−0.0138**	(−2.89)
Liquidate	6.5	8.0	3.3	−0.0465***	(−10.70)
Diversify	1.9	1.9	1.8	−0.00101	(−0.42)
Others	1.7	1.7	1.7	0.000163	−0.07
N	14600	9902	4698	14600	

Note: $^{*}p < 0.1$, $^{**}p < 0.05$, $^{***}p < 0.01$.

Source: Computed by authors using 2010/2011, 2012/2013, 2015/2016 LSMS and Stata 14

differentials exist between households residing in urban areas and households residing in rural areas. However, regarding literacy, the findings reveal that there is a significant rural-urban disparity. On average, households in the urban setting have a higher number of literate members compared to their rural counterparts.

Regarding the different shock types, descriptive statistics report significant rural-urban differences for all the shocks considered in the analysis. Specifically, in terms of households that suffered from an agricultural shock, descriptive statistics reveal that 6% of rural households against 2.9% of urban households were affected by agricultural shocks. Concerning financial shocks, the percentages were 9.6% and 9.4% for rural and urban households, respectively. Meanwhile, 8.9% of rural areas suffered from a weather shock compared to 2.6% of urban households that suffered from the shock. In addition, a greater percentage of rural households suffered from a health shock compared to urban households, which was 14.6% and 10.8%, respectively. For other shocks, we observed that the percentage was somewhat higher among urban households than among rural households.

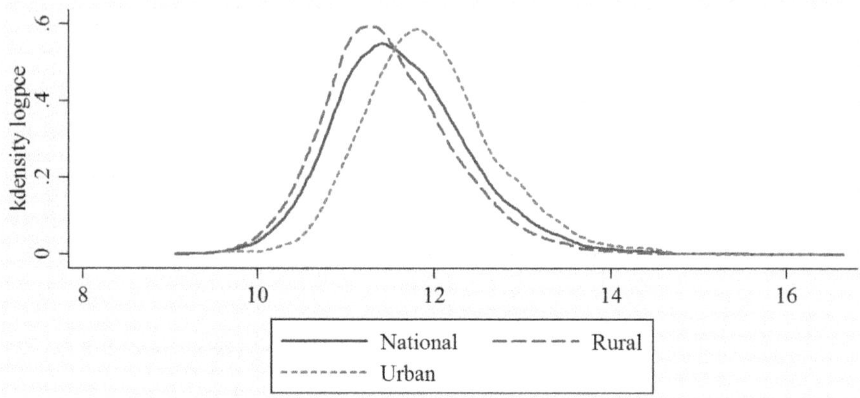

Figure 13.1 Household per capita consumption

Source: Constructed by authors using 2010/2011, 2012/2013, 2015/2016 LSMS and Stata 14

In particular, 4.5% of the urban households were affected by other shocks compared to 3.3% for rural households. The descriptive statistics on the different coping strategies further inform us that there are significant differences in terms of the financial coping strategies, safety nets cuts, expenditure cuts, and liquidity measures. The proportion of households that employ these coping strategies in rural areas was higher than that in urban areas.

Figure 13.1 presents the kernel density estimation of the log of household consumption expenditure per head for the whole sample and by the zone of residency. Comparing the distributions, we observed that the peak of the distribution of the log per capita consumption expenditure for urban households lies to the right of the distribution of the whole sample and rural households. This is a preliminary indication that the welfare of households residing in urban areas is higher than that of rural-dwelling households.

5.2 *Regression Results: Effect of Shocks on Welfare*

The objective of this section is to evaluate the effects of the different shocks on household welfare proxied by per capita consumption expenditure. Table 13.2 displays estimates of the welfare generating function under different assumptions. In particular, Columns 1, 3, and 5 host the estimates of the separate shock categories; meanwhile, Columns 2, 4, and 6 display the estimates in which all the shocks are considered in a single equation. The preferred results for discussion are the pooled OLS and random effects results hosted in Columns 2 and 6.

The results of the pooled OLS and random effects estimation show that the agrocultural shock relates negatively to household welfare. Specifically, the findings of

Table 13.2 Effects of Shocks on Households Per Capita Consumption

Variables	*(1)*	*(2)*	*(3)*	*(4)*	*(5)*	*(6)*
	OLS	*OLS*	*Fixed Effects*	*Fixed Effects*	*Random Effects*	*Random Effects*
Agricultural	−0.108***	−0.108***	−0.00772	0.00125	−0.0489*	−0.0491*
	(0.0303)	(0.0304)	(0.0275)	(0.0277)	(0.0265)	(0.0267)
Financial	0.0340	0.0402	−0.0412*	−0.0282	0.0185	0.0228
	(0.0249)	(0.0255)	(0.0231)	(0.0237)	(0.0220)	(0.0226)
Weather	−0.0964***	−0.0861***	−0.00165	0.00499	−0.0529**	−0.0469*
	(0.0268)	(0.0272)	(0.0251)	(0.0256)	(0.0239)	(0.0244)
Health	0.0356	0.0334	0.0654***	0.0638***	0.0301	0.0287
	(0.0236)	(0.0242)	(0.0223)	(0.0230)	(0.0210)	(0.0218)
Others	0.103***	0.0962***	0.0341	0.0419	0.0357	0.0346
	(0.0364)	(0.0367)	(0.0332)	(0.0335)	(0.0318)	(0.0321)
Shock controls	No	Yes	No	Yes	No	Yes
Coping strategies	Yes	Yes	Yes	Yes	Yes	Yes
Attrition	Yes	Yes	Yes	Yes	Yes	Yes
Constant		12.04***		10.21***		12.03***
		(0.0194)		(0.0767)		(0.0240)
Observations		10,387		10,387		10,387
R-squared		0.162		0.171		
Number of households				3,861		3,861

Source: Computed by authors using 2010/2011, 2012/2013, 2015/2016 LSMS and Stata 14

Note: Standard errors in parentheses.

*p < 0.1, **p < 0.05, ***p < 0.01.

the random effects model revealed that households that suffered an agricultural shock are likely to incur losses in terms of welfare on the order of 0.0491 log points (i.e., approximately 5%) compared to households that never witnessed an agricultural shock. Regarding the effect of financial shock on household welfare, the results indicate that no significant welfare differentials exist between households that were affected by financial shocks and households not affected by financial shocks. These findings are not consistent with those obtained by Mbegalo and Yu (2016) using Tanzanian data, which indicated that a financial shock (food price increase) on average leads to an improvement in welfare among sellers and a loss in welfare among buyers.

Another important inference revealed by the regression results is that weather shocks have a negative effect on household welfare. In particular, the result shows that, on average, households that were affected by a weather shock are expected to suffer welfare losses of approximately 0.0469 log points (i.e., 4.69%) compared to their unfaceted counterparts. This result can be supported by the idea that when households are exposed to extreme weather conditions, this is expected to reduce household farm income based on the hypothesis that a significant proportion of these households depend on agriculture. Wineman et al. (2017) corroborate these findings using Kenyan data by revealing that extreme rough weather negatively affects household welfare. In addition, the results further reveal that health shocks and other shocks are not statistically related to household welfare. Consistent with these findings, Sparrow et al. (2014) also found no significant effect on food and nonfood expenditures even when shocks augment medical expenditures and reduce nonfarm incomes. On the other hand, Khan et al. (2015) indicated that health shocks significantly influence nonfood spending via the income earned.

We explored the effects of economic shocks for rural and urban areas (Table 13.3). Many studies in the literature have noted that economic shocks have varying effects on rural and urban households. The results revealed that weather shocks have a significant negative effect on household per capita consumption of urban households; meanwhile, there was no significant effect of weather shocks on rural households.

We also found that health shocks have a positive effect on the consumption expenditure of rural households, while among their urban counterparts, no significant effect of health shocks was revealed. This could be because when rural households are faced with health shocks such as an illness, they are likely to spend on medications, and this expenditure on medication is expected to soar the household total consumption expenditure per head, which is the proxy for household welfare.

To further explore the effects of shocks on households, we focused on household food and nonfood expenditures. This will enable us to understand the disaggregated effects of economic shocks on households. The disaggregated of total consumption expenditure into food and nonfood expenditure is based on the idea that the different economic shocks are likely to have different effects on food expenditure and on nonfood expenditure.

Table 13.3 Effects of Shocks on Households Per Capita Consumption by Rural and Urban Sectors Using a Random Effect Model

	(1)	*(2)*
Variables	*Rural*	*Urban*
Agricultural	−0.0442	0.0231
	(0.0291)	(0.0600)
Financial	0.0288	−0.0245
	(0.0261)	(0.0420)
Weather	0.00532	−0.169***
	(0.0260)	(0.0627)
Health	0.0611**	0.00913
	(0.0246)	(0.0424)
Others	0.0173	0.0684
	(0.0390)	(0.0530)
Coping strategies	Yes	Yes
Attrition	Yes	Yes
Constant	11.86***	12.61***
	(0.0262)	(0.0466)
Observations	7,330	3,057
Number of households	2,708	1,204

Source: Computed by authors using 2010/2011, 2012/2013, 2015/2016 LSMS and Stata 14

Note: Standard errors in parentheses.

*$p < 0.1$, **$p < 0.05$, ***$p < 0.01$.

Table 13.4 shows the relationship between household economic shock and the logarithm values of household food and nonfood consumption expenditures using the random-effects model. Column 1 focuses on household food expenditure, and Column 2 shows the results for household nonfood expenditure. Regarding the effect of agricultural shocks on household food consumption expenditure and nonfood expenditure, we found that agricultural shocks negatively affect household nonfood expenditure and have no effect on household food consumption expenditure. These findings can be explained by the idea that food is a necessity, and when a household is faced with an agricultural shock, households are expected to reduce the expenditure devoted to nonfood items. Table 13.4 equally indicates that financial shocks have a significant positive effect on household nonfood expenditure. In particular, households that were affected by financial shocks are likely to have a nonfood expenditure that is 0.106 log points (i.e., 10.6%) higher than that of their unaffected counterparts. These findings are economically expected since a financial shock such as price hikes (inflation) is likely to soar the household nonfood expenditure budget. We also found that health shocks have a positive effect on food expenditure while no significant effect is registered on nonfood expenditure.

Table 13.4 Effect of Shock on Food and Nonfood Expenditure Using a Random Effect Model

	(1)	(2)
Variable	*Food*	*Nonfood*
Agricultural	−0.0384	−0.0599*
	(0.0282)	(0.0317)
Financial	0.0225	0.106***
	(0.0238)	(0.0270)
Weather	−0.0404	−0.000461
	(0.0256)	(0.0291)
Health	0.0447*	−0.00483
	(0.0228)	(0.0260)
Others	0.0368	0.0380
	(0.0339)	(0.0382)
Coping strategies	Yes	Yes
Attrition	Yes	Yes
Constant	11.69***	10.58***
	(0.0225)	(0.0328)
Observations	10,387	10,387
R-squared		
Number of households	3,861	3,861

Source: Computed by authors using 2010/2011, 2012/2013, 2015/2016 LSMS and Stata 14

Note: Standard errors in parentheses.

*$p < 0.1$, **$p < 0.05$, ***$p < 0.01$.

6. Conclusion and Policy Implications

This study examined the implications of different economic shocks for household welfare. Specifically, the study assessed the effects of different economic shocks on household consumption expenditure per head for the whole sample and by the zone of residency (urban and rural). The study also evaluated the extent of the different economic shocks on household food consumption expenditure and household nonfood consumption expenditure. To achieve these objectives, we employed three waves of the World Bank LSMS for Nigeria. We focused on the cumulative effects of agricultural, financial, weather, health, and other categories of shocks. We accounted for the mitigating effects of household shock coping strategies and accounted for the attrition effects across survey waves. The random-effects panel model and pooled OLS were further adopted to examine the effects of the different shocks on the various indicators of household welfare.

The results showed that, overall, agricultural shocks and weather shocks negatively affected household consumption per head. That is, households affected by agricultural and weather shocks suffered consumption losses compared to their counterparts that were never affected by these shocks. The study further explored the effect of the different shocks by the zone of residency and found that weather shocks negatively affected the consumption expenditure per head of urban households; meanwhile, health shocks positively influenced the consumption expenditures of rural households. The study also disaggregated the household total consumption expenditures into food and nonfood expenditures and studied the effects of the different shocks on each of the expenditure components. The findings revealed that agricultural shocks negatively affected household nonfood expenditures; meanwhile, health shocks positively affected household food consumption expenditures.

These findings provide essential information for public policy interventions. The implications of these results are in tandem with the wisdom that improving the ability of resource-poor households to resist shocks is vital in the enhancement of household welfare. In this regard, policies aimed at improving household welfare could factor in strategies of mitigating agricultural and weather shocks due to their negative effects on welfare, as depicted by the findings of this study. Specifically, to reduce agricultural shocks, mechanisms aimed at minimizing postharvest losses could be considered in rural development programs.

Future studies can focus on the impact of COVID-19 on Nigerian households when comprehensive and more detailed data are available. Indeed, at the time of conducting this study, there was a lack of sufficiently detailed data on COVID-19. As a result, we were unable to study the welfare impact of this important health shock that may significantly impact households in both the short and long run.

References

Addison, T., Pikkarainen, V., Rönkkö, R. & Tarp, F. 2019. Development and poverty in sub-Saharan Africa. In *Development and Poverty Reduction*. Taylor & Francis.

Amolegbe, K. B. 2020. Hungry birds do not sing: Coronavirus and the school feeding program. *World Development*, 136.

Amolegbe, K. B., Upton, J., Bageant, E. & Blom, S. 2021. Food price volatility and household food security: Evidence from Nigeria. *Food Policy*, 102061.

Amu, B., Osabuohien, E. S., Alege, P. O. & Ejemeyovwi, J. O. 2021. Impact of real shocks on business cycles in selected sub-Saharan African countries. *Cogent Business & Management*, 8, 1875548.

Arndt, C., Benfica, R., Maximiano, N., Nucifora, A. M. & Thurlow, J. T. 2008. Higher fuel and food prices: Impacts and responses for Mozambique. *Agricultural Economics*, 39, 497–511.

Atake, E.-H. 2018. Health shocks in Sub-Saharan Africa: are the poor and uninsured households more vulnerable? *Health economics review*, 8, 26.

Bales, S. 2013. Impact of health shocks on household welfare in Vietnam – Estimates using fixed effects estimation. *Institute of Health Policy & Management (HEFPA) Working Paper*, 18.

Chan, K. K. & Gemayel, E. R. 2004. Risk instability and the pattern of foreign direct investment in the Middle East and North Africa region. *IMF Working Paper, No.139*. Washington, D.C.: International Monetary Fund.

Dedehouanou, S. F. & Mcpeak, J. 2020. Diversify more or less? Household income generation strategies and food security in rural Nigeria. *The Journal of Development Studies*, 56, 560–577.

Di Falco, S. 2014. Adaptation to climate change in Sub-Saharan agriculture: assessing the evidence and rethinking the drivers. *European Review of Agricultural Economics*, 41, 405–430.

Diop, S., Asongu, S. A. & Nnanna, J. 2021. COVID-19 economic vulnerability and resilience indexes: Global evidence. *International Social Science Journal*, 71, 37–50.

Foster, E. M. & Bickman, L. 1996. An evaluator's guide to detecting attrition problems. *Evaluation Review*, 20, 695–723.

Frankenberg, E., Smith, J. P. & Thomas, D. 2003. Economic shocks, wealth, and welfare. *Journal of Human Resources*, 38, 280–321.

Hangoma, P., Aakvik, A. & Robberstad, B. 2018. Health shocks and household welfare in Zambia: An assessment of changing risk. *Journal of International Development*, 30, 790–817.

Ibukun, C. O. & Adebayo, A. A. 2021. Household food security and the COVID-19 pandemic in Nigeria. *African Development Review*, 33, S75-S87.

Kane, G. Q., Mabah Tene, G. L., Ambagna, J. J., Piot-Lepetit, I. & Fondo, S. 2015. The impact of food price volatility on consumer welfare in Cameroon. *WIDER Working Paper 013*. Helsinki: UNU WIDER.

Khan, F., Bedi, A. S. & Sparrow, R. 2015. Sickness and death: economic consequences and coping strategies of the urban poor in Bangladesh. *World Development*, 72, 255–266.

Kokas, D., Lopez-Acevedo, G., El Lahga, A. R. & Mendiratta, V. 2020. *Impacts of COVID-19 on Household Welfare in Tunisia*. Available at SSRN 3755395.

Mbegalo, T. & Yu, X. 2016. The impact of food prices on household welfare and poverty in rural Tanzania. *Discussion Papers, No. 216*. Göttingen: Courant Research Centre – Poverty, Equity and Growth (CRC-PEG).

Nechifor, V., Ramos, M. P., Ferrari, E., Laichena, J., Kihiu, E., Omanyo, D., Musamali, R. & KIRIGA, B. 2021. Food security and welfare changes under COVID-19 in Sub-Saharan Africa: Impacts and responses in Kenya. *Global food security*, 28, 100514.

Osabohien, R., Matthew, O., Ohalete, P. & Osabuohien, E. 2020a. Population – poverty – inequality nexus and social protection in Africa. *Social Indicators Research*, 151, 575–598.

Osabohien, R., Osuagwu, E., Osabuohien, E., Ekhator-Mobayode, U. E., Matthew, O. & Gershon, O. 2020b. Household access to agricultural credit and agricultural production in Nigeria: A propensity score matching model. *South African Journal of Economic and Management Sciences*, 23, 1–11.

Quisumbing, A. R., Kumar, N. & Behrman, J. A. 2018. Do shocks affect men's and women's assets differently? Evidence from Bangladesh and Uganda. *Development Policy Review*, 36, 3–34.

Saah, F. I., Amu, H., Seidu, A.-A. & Bain, L. E. 2021. Health knowledge and care seeking behaviour in resource-limited settings amidst the COVID-19 pandemic: A qualitative study in Ghana. *PLos One*, 16, e0250940.

Shehu, A. & Sidique, S. F. 2015. The effect of shocks on household consumption in rural Nigeria. *The Journal of Developing Areas*, 353–364.

Skoufias, E. & Vinha, K. 2013. The impacts of climate variability on household welfare in rural Mexico. *Population and Environment*, 34, 370–399.

Sparrow, R., De Poel, E. V., Hadiwidjaja, G., Yumna, A., Warda, N. & Suryahadi, A. 2014. Coping with the economic consequences of ill health in Indonesia. *Health economics*, 23, 719–728.

Swinnen, J. & Vos, R. 2021. COVID-19 and impacts on global food systems and household welfare: Introduction to a special issue. *Agricultural Economics*, 52, 365–374.

Ufua, D. E., Osabuohien, E., Ogbari, M. E., Falola, H. O., Okoh, E. E. & Lakhani, A. 2021. Strategizing government palliative support systems in tackling the challenges of COVID-19 lockdown in Lagos state, Nigeria. *Global Journal of Flexible Systems Management*, 1–14.

Verbeek, M. & Nijman, T. 1992. Testing for selectivity bias in panel data models. *International Economic Review*, 681–703.

Wineman, A., Mason, N. M., Ochieng, J. & Kirimi, L. 2017. Weather extremes and household welfare in rural Kenya. *Food security*, 9, 281–300.

Wooldridge, J. M. 2010. *Econometric analysis of cross section and panel data*. MIT Press.

14 Disruptive Effects of COVID-19 and Health Challenges on the Attainment of National Policies and Public Service Provisions in African Countries

Oluwaseyi Ebenezer Olalere

Introduction

The COVID-19 pandemic started at a period when the outlook for many African countries was already improving. Africa has continued its expansion by early 2020, with its growth forecast rising from 2.9% in 2019 to 3.2% in 2020 and 3.5% in 2021 (AfDB, 2020). The annual global gross domestic product (GDP) growth reported by Organization for Economic Cooperation and Development (OECD) is predicted to drop by 2.4% in 2020, from an already weak 2.9% in 2019, as illustrated in Figure 14.1. There is a possibility that growth will be detrimental in the first quarter of 2020 due to global markets plummeting in the foreseeable future (OECD, 2020). With COVID-19, disturbances have arisen in Africa's global supply chains in the face of tumbling oil prices and a decline in global demand for nonoil products from Africa, posing a challenge to the continent's economic stability.[1] Projected losses from oil shocks alone are expected to reduce export revenues in Africa by almost US$101 billion in 2020 (Vaillant, 2020). This decline in oil prices would mainly put resource-dependent countries such as Nigeria, the Democratic Republic of the Congo (DRC), Angola, and other oil-producing African countries at economic and fiscal risk.

Across all scenarios, the economy of African countries appears to be pushed towards a contraction. The oil effect is the largest driver of GDP impact (40% to 70% of the total), and funds 65% of budgeted revenue and 90% of foreign reserves accrual (OECD, 2020). The spread of COVID-19 possibly has a downside risk for sub-Saharan African growth in the short term, particularly in Ghana, Angola, Congo, Equatorial Guinea, Zambia, South Africa, Gabon, and Nigeria, which export an enormous number of commodities to China. This is causing more uncertainty in a continent already struggling with extensive geopolitical and economic instability. However, as the COVID-19 epidemic intensifies, even the more developed nations are overwhelmed by this outbreak's significant health and economic effects. With less than 0.5% of globally confirmed cases in Africa, the continent seems to be primarily spared from the direct health consequences of the COVID-19 pandemic. Nonetheless, the epidemic has already had a destabilizing effect on

DOI: 10.4324/9781003208358-19

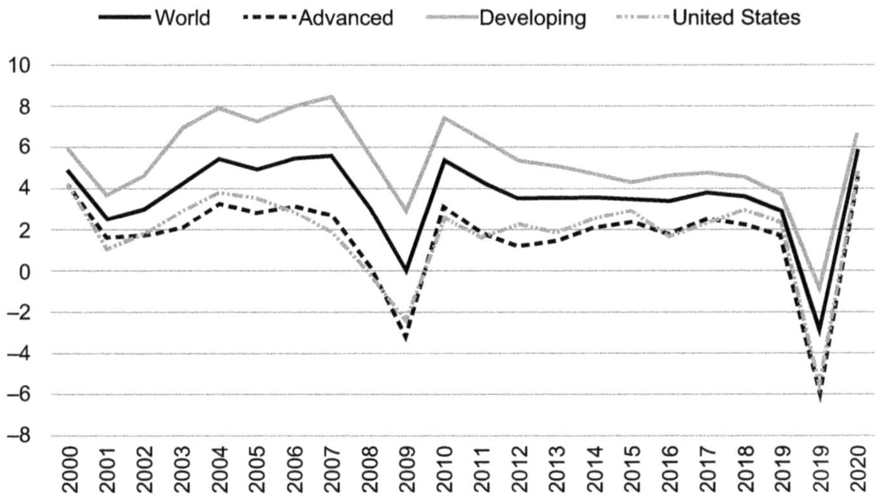

Figure 14.1 Gross domestic product, % change

Note: Data for 2020 and 2021 are estimates.

Source: World Economic Outlook, International Monetary Fund, April 14, 2020

the lives of millions of Africans, with disproportionate and underserved effects on elderly individuals.

Before the COVID-19 epidemic, a large part of health care systems in African countries were underfunded. Currently, 65% of healthcare spending in Africa is made from out-of-pocket spending relative to Europe, where national and regional authorities are legally responsible for the health policies and expenditures of their citizens (Ozili, 2020). Given the quarantine and other steps taken to avoid the spread of COVID-19 in African countries during the COVID-19 pandemic, the number of infected cases continued to grow dramatically. This condition has put immense pressure on public health systems in many African countries. Although the immediate effect on the health system continues to grow, the indirect effects outside health still carry a heavy toll. These include shortages of food, the failure to provide medical aid, income loss and livelihood, problems with implementing physical and sanitary distancing measures, and a potential debt crisis, as well as related political and security threats.

Several African countries are interconnected with affected US and European Union economies. The prices of products such as mineral ores and metals exported from Africa will be severely affected due to a decline in demand resulting from growth deceleration in these significant economies (Yaya et al., 2020; Vaillant, 2020). A conservative report indicates that COVID-19 caused Africa's GDP to fall by 2.1 percent in 2020 alone, with huge economic losses (Jayaram et al., 2020).

To battle the COVID-19 pandemic, various African countries have embraced specific foreign policy patterns such as border closures, stringent migration controls, quarantine declarations, and stay-at-home order compliance (Nantulya & Mavhinga, 2020). These steps represent the dynamic quality of modern-day globalization (Brown & Labonté, 2011). On the one hand, they indicate the rapidly responsive and even dictatorial nature of global knowledge sharing; on the other hand, they accentuate boundaries rather than eliminating them and limit interactions across cultural, political, and technical spheres.

This chapter quantifies the disruptive effects of COVID-19 and health challenges under different possible scenarios. The objective is to delve into health challenges and the disturbing impact of COVID-19 in achieving public service and national policies. It also offers guidance to policymakers on the economic benefits of globally and regionally coordinated policy responses to tame the virus. The paper builds upon related subjects on COVID-19 in African countries, bridging the gap in contemporary literature.

Literature Review

The economic impacts of COVID-19 in developed economies are becoming increasingly widespread (Baldwin & Weder di Mauro, 2020). There is more restricted research focused on developing and emerging countries. The continued uncertainty surrounding the spread of COVID-19 is high, and its influence on Africa is anticipated to be severe, considering the exposure of the continent to China. China has been Africa's major trading partner for a very long period, suggesting that the interdependence between these countries may expose African states to COVID-19. Potential large-scale outbreaks would likely strain the continent's current weakened health systems, and countries in Africa are careful to identify and contain this outbreak quickly. In African countries, identifying the virus may be a problem because of a shortage of laboratory capacity and medical supplies. The WHO has noted that 36 African countries have virus test labs, which helped supply African health workers with personal protective equipment (PPE). Moreover, most countries in Africa set up quarantine centres and shop medicine.

Health care facilities across the continent will experience extreme pressure if the virus takes hold. The global pharmaceutical market was already affected by COVID-19, with prices of pharmaceutical ingredients manufactured in China continuing to increase or not available after extended factory closures and supply chain disruptions. In early March, the Directorate-General for Foreign Trade in India declared that it would limit shipments of 26 pharmaceutical products and chemicals, including paracetamol and antibiotics, leading to a shortage in Africa. India manufactures a significant percentage of generic medicines worldwide.

In recent developments, the Nigerian representatives of the Overseas Pharmaceutical Manufactories reported that COVID-19 impacted Nigerian pharmaceuticals because goods manufactured in China were not shipped before shutting down. As a result, medical supplies and equipment became scarce and hampered due to supply chain problems for medical instruments in Sub-Saharan Africa. For instance, Shadmi et al. (2020) and Yaya et al. (2020) argued that healthcare prices could also decline due to China's role in the international supply chain. However, the demand for medical products, such as masks and anti-infection kits, can help some companies manufacture goods if the requirements for production can be fulfilled and supply chain disruptions from China have not been negatively affected.

There are a few sectors in which investors are likely to receive a very warm welcome. Health care is the most evident. Most African governments have rushed to implement highly destructive locks because they know that under resourced healthcare systems cannot cope with large-scale outbreaks. Health care spending in Africa has been approximately 5% of GDP for several years, relative to a global level of nearly twice that (Fletcher, 2020). Many governments can conclude that a more significant investment in health capacity is a worthwhile investment. Such campaigns are likely to find foreign supporters eager, as COVID-19 has shown how quickly a national outbreak can turn into a global pandemic (see Table 14.1).

Methodology

The chapter analyses the disruptive effects of COVID-19 and health challenges in African countries using discourse analysis and literature research on COVID-19. reports. The chapter uses reliable information extracted from numerous reputable sources, such as the United Nations Educational, Scientific and Cultural Organization (UNESCO), World Health Organization (WHO), International Monetary Fund (IMF), African Development Bank (AfDB), International

Table 14.1 Consequence of COVID-19 in Africa

First-Order Effects		*Second-Order Effects*	*Third-Order Effects*
Economic	GDP drops Trade Balance worsens Job and livelihood losses Wealth depletion Increased health and related spending	Domestic supply chains collapse economic activity stalls Increased nonformal activity	Recession debt crisis Financial distress
Social	Loss of lives Social spending was reduced. Disproportionate impact on vulnerable groups Social services disrupted	Widespread deprivation Social Disaffection Breakdown in Social Services	Increased inequalities and human development losses Vulnerable groups victimized societal unrest
Political	Politicized responses	Erosion of trust Politicization of law enforcement	Political unrest Political violence

Source: UNDP Africa

Labour Organization (ILO), OECD, and United Nations Economic Commission for Africa (UNECA), as well as information from media sources and other public sources. The study focuses on relevant literature that allows us to capture the events occurring currently and identify the role COVID-19 played in the African economy.

Discussion

COVID-19 Health Perspective: Impact on Public Health

In 2015, Africa accounted for less than 2% of the approximately 9.7 billion dollars spent on health worldwide, representing 16% of the world population and 26% of the global disease burden (Watkins, 2020; Oqubay, 2020). Health services are likely to be overwhelmed by the fast spread of the disease. There are several African countries without doctors (0.2 per 1,000 people), hospital beds (1.8 per 1,000) and the health care facilities needed to respond to the epidemic appropriately (Watkins, 2020). Twenty-three countries in Africa are at extreme risk of COVID-19 mortality owing to the paucity of hospital beds (less than 2 per 1,000 people) and extreme levels of mortality from infectious and respiratory diseases (3–8 deaths per 1,000 people), as illustrated in Figure 14.2 (Oqubay, 2020). Given that the COVID-19 pandemic is exacerbating the burden on Africa's

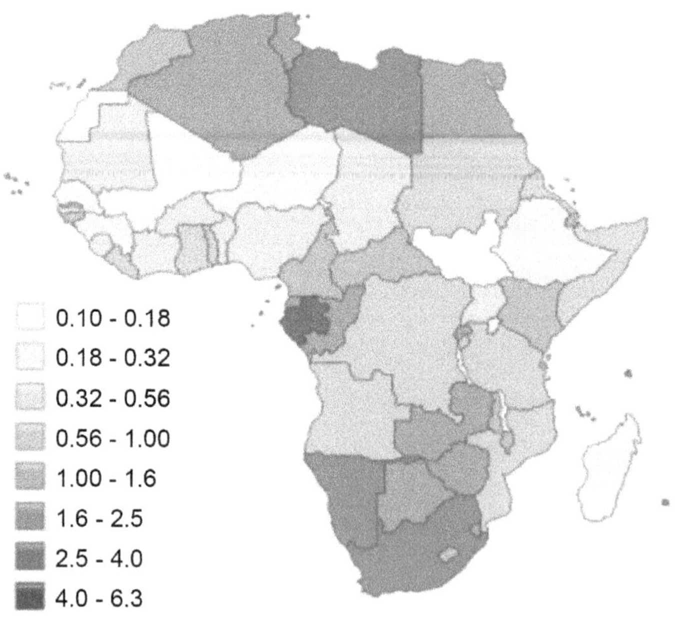

Figure 14.2 Hospital beds per 1,000 population

vulnerable health systems, it is crucial to guarantee that existing healthcare facilities are secured and not just recycled (ECA (2020).

Restricted access to supplies and equipment related to COVID-19 can be daunting to healthcare systems, especially test kits, PPE, fans, and medication products. Disruptions in global supply chains and import tariffs pose a danger as most of Africa's pharmaceutical needs depend on the outside world (94%) (Shadmi et al., 2020). Since 24 April, 80 countries have put export restrictions on vital COVID-19 medical equipment (fans, PPE). Current manufacturing capacities are being transformed into critical equipment. It is essential to encourage Africa's production capabilities so that COVID-19 technologies survive the pandemic and provide the basis for future planning. For the supply of medical equipment, including illumination, cooling, and sterilization, secure access to energy is essential. In the COVID-19 crisis, decentralized technology in renewable energy was demonstrated to be a sustainable, clean, and productive power insulation facility and health facility in Africa.

Public healthcare systems in African countries are fragile and face certain structural challenges. They are highly vulnerable because of their high import dependency on other countries for pharmaceutical products. In addition, over 94% of the total stock of pharmaceuticals is imported and currently does not produce diagnostic tools (UNECA, 2020) (see Figure 14.3). In Africa, healthcare resources, beddings, nursing and midwife personnel, number of inpatient beds and ventilators, and doctors are considerably insufficient than in other regions. The absence of these critical health facilities hurts the continent's preparation for this pandemic. Certain African countries, such as Egypt, South Africa, and Cameroon, to a certain extent, are better equipped with better healthcare facilities than any other country on the continent.

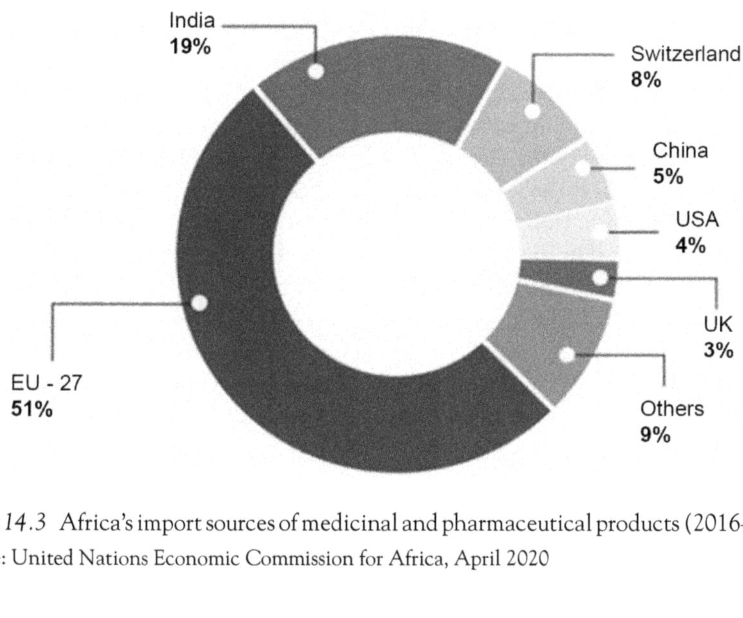

Figure 14.3 Africa's import sources of medicinal and pharmaceutical products (2016–2018)
Source: United Nations Economic Commission for Africa, April 2020

Economic Impact of COVID-19

The COVID-19 pandemic began to significantly impact African economies and, even before hitting the continent's shores, disrupted living conditions. Attributed factors are the declining market for African commodities, capital flight from Africa, the virtual decline of tourism and air transport related to border closures, and local currency devaluation resulting from the worsening current account balance. African nations cannot afford to wait until they are severely affected by the epidemic before implementing socioeconomic assistance programs. A significant number of informal workers in Africa (85.8% of employees) cannot adhere to social and home-stay distances without seriously affecting their lives and lives.[2] Several household employees are forced to decide between the virus and table food. Moreover, nearly 90% of female workers in Africa work without social welfare in the informal sector, making women's households particularly vulnerable.[3]

The African airline industry, which supports 6.2 million people and tourism, has been primarily disrupted since it represents a large share of GDP, especially the Small Island Developing States (SIDS) (ECA, 2020). The crisis was exceedingly catastrophic to tourism and the African aviation sector since the institutional infrastructure that links the region has evolved over the past two decades. Governments, shareholders, and international financial institutions (IFIs) should explore how sustainability and liquidity can be supported by loan guarantees and temporary tax relief in these sectors.

Remittances, which are a crucial source of income or an additional source for many African households, are projected to fall, impacting countries such as Liberia, Gambia, Somalia, and Lesotho, accounting for over 10% of GDP, to a significant extent. The World Bank predicts a 23.1% decrease in cash flows for Sub-Saharan African countries (US$37 billion by 2020). Somalia has undergone substantial reductions in payments of $1.4 billion per annum, representing the largest category of external financial aid. Sub-Saharan Africa currently has an average of 9.1% per transaction, which is among the highest remittance fees.

The crisis's aggregate impact has resulted in the devaluation of exchange rates and a projected decline in Africa's GDP. The UN Economic Commission for Africa (ECA) predicts the growth rate in the best-case situation by 1.1% in 2020 and the 2.6% decline in the worst-case scenario, depriving 19 million people of their livelihoods and in the context of weak structures of social protection within Africa has led to the cumulative impact of the crisis (see Figures 14.4 and 14.5). If crude oil prices continue to fall, countries exporting oil could lose an income of up to US$65 billion.

The global capital flows to emerging markets are anticipated to be disrupted by significant pressure on foreign exchange reserves and exchange rates in African countries. Beyond the dynamics of foreign portfolio inflows, the Nigerian stock market was also affected by the COVID-19 pandemic. There has been a plunge in the primary market indices because of investors pulling out their investments into so-called safe havens such as US Treasury bonds. Barely three weeks after the

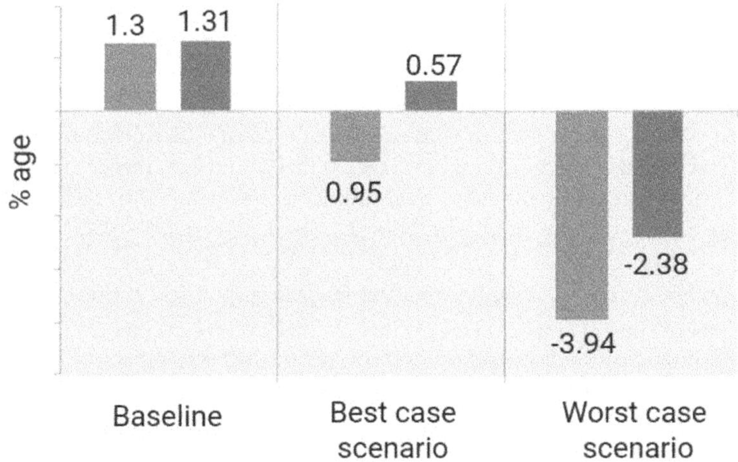

Figure 14.4 Impact of growth decline on poverty and employment generation
Source: ECA (2020)

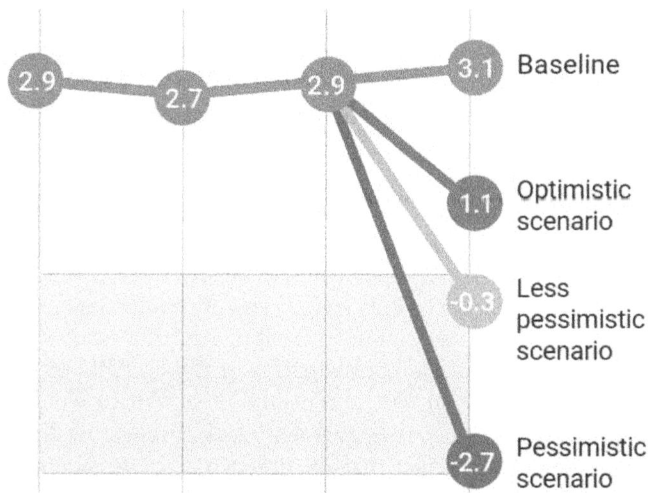

Figure 14.5 Projected decline in real GDP growth
Source: ECA (2020)

The first case of coronavirus was confirmed in Nigeria on 28 January 2020, and stock market investors lost over NGN2.3 trillion (US$5.9 bn) (Ozili, 2021; Fernandes, 2020). The market capitalisation of listed equities, which was valued at NGN13.657 trillion (US$35.2 billion) on Friday, 28 February 2020, depreciated by NGN2.349 trillion to NGN11.308 trillion (US$29.1 billion) on Monday, 23 March 2020 (Ozili, 2021).

Furthermore, the COVID-19 pandemic also affected some other financial markets in Africa. In South Africa, the Johannesburg Stock Exchange Top 40 Index, many of which have exposure to China, slumped 3.7% on 24 February as investors began to consider short-selling strategies (Ozili, 2020). In Kenya, major stocks such as Safaricom and KCB Bank declined by 5.4% and 7%, respectively; on the first day, the first coronavirus case was announced in Kenya (Ozili, 2020). According to its equity trading rules, the Nairobi Stock Exchange (NSE) suspended trading for the NSE 20 index on March 13, 2020, as stock prices continued to plunge on the second day, which requires trading suspension if there was a drop of more than 5%.

Global financial institutions are currently assessing the impact of COVID-19 and reacting to its economic impact, ensuring that they can adjust to new and unprecedented circumstances brought about by the virus. It remains to be seen whether the vast global economic downturn caused by decreased output in China will impact African lenders and compel financial institutions on the continent to be more lenient towards borrowers and cut them some slack. The global impact of the virus has driven down local prices since global economic growth is a crucial driver of commodity prices. The uncertainty of the impact of COVID-19 on local markets is expected to lead to increased risk aversion from investors who are waiting to see its potential impact in Africa. On the plus side, a temporary decline in share prices always provides opportunities for prudent investors.

Asongu et al. (2021) analysed the economic impact of the COVID-19 pandemic, evaluated the effectiveness and relevance of different measures against the pandemic and examined nexuses between the corresponding measures and economic outcomes. The study uses a sample of 186 countries divided into four main regions, notably Asia-Pacific and the Middle East, Europe, Africa, and America. Thirty-four preventive and mitigating measures against the COVID-19 pandemic are classified into five main categories: lockdown, movement restrictions, government and economic, social distancing, and public health measures. The findings show how the effectiveness and consequences of the COVID-19 measures are different across regions. There was a consensus that Africa would be heavily affected by the pandemic due to the continent's lack of robust healthcare systems and corruption, as well as the fact that the absence of safety income nets meant that most lockdown and social distancing measures could not be applied as in more technically advanced countries (Diop & Asongu, 2021).

"Debt Burden – Unprecedented Fiscal Deficits Amidst Already Constrained Budgets"

Africa's average debt -to -GDP ratio rose from 39.5% in 2011 to 61.3% in 2019. The broad annual financing gap of US$68 billion to US$108 trillion for the continent's principal debt is partly due to commercial borrowing, equivalent to approximately 3 to 5% of GDP on the continent (AfDB, 2020). Moreover, most

African countries have insufficient budgetary space to react to the crisis efficiently due to low domestic savings rates, low domestic mobilization of capital, heavy illicit financial outflows, flight of capital, unpredictable oil prices, high fiscal deficits, and sluggish official aid for development (ODA) and FDI flows (see Figures 14.6 and 14.7).

Development partners have been called upon by African Finance Ministers and the African Union to provide US$100 billion, including US$44 billion in debt relief, to support healthcare systems, protect jobs, and ensure a safety net for the most vulnerable.[4] As part of a detailed global response strategy and a global debt standstill, debt sustainability solutions, and structural challenges within an international debt architecture, the "United Nations Secretary-General has called for more than $200 billion" for Africa.[5] Up to $57 billion has been mobilized by official creditors for Africa, including approximately $18 billion from the IMF and the World Bank (IMF, 2020; Ndung'u et al., 2021). The G20 states decided, from 1 May 2020 to the end of the year, to suspend the repayment of debts to low-income countries.[6]

The IMF has supported 19 African countries with debt relief. Moreover, individual nations, such as the EU Member States, the United States, and China, sponsored individual countries or the entire continent. This support is essential; however, substantial additional measures are appropriate, including creditors, which are proportionate to the exceptional nature of the crisis.

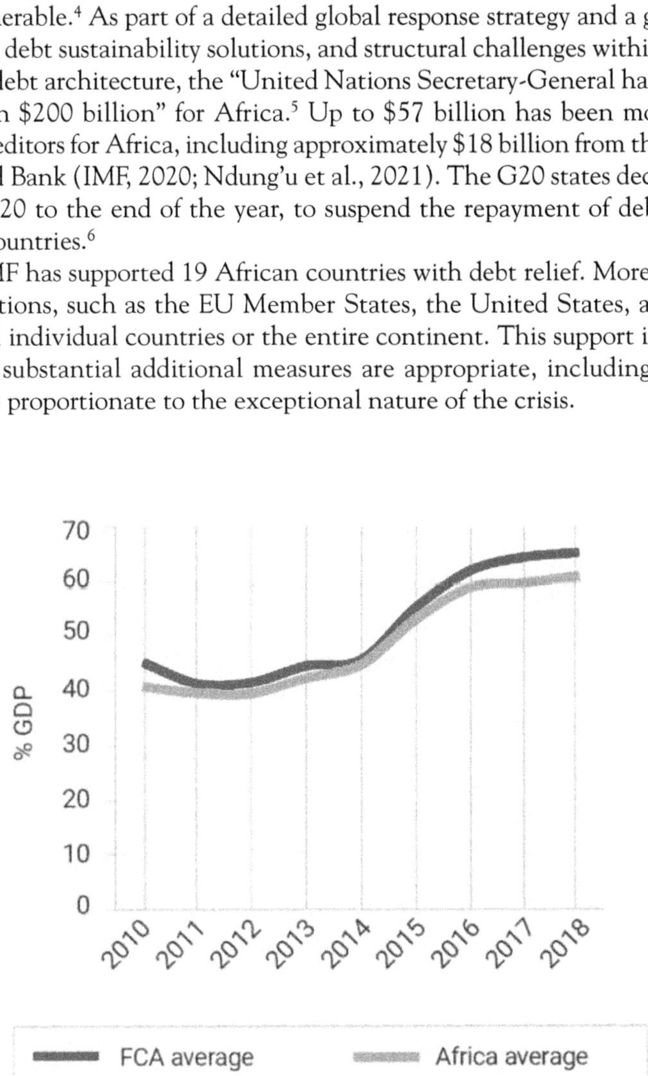

Figure 14.6 Rising external debt to GDP ratio

Source: FCA is Fragile and Conflict Affected Countries

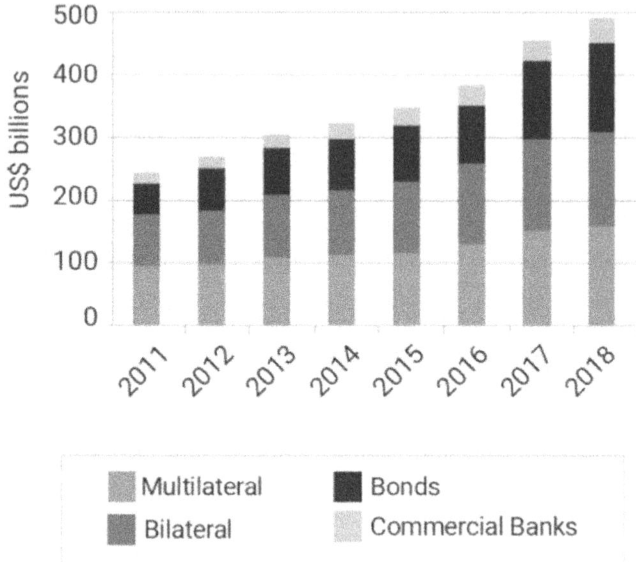

Figure 14.7 Rising share of commercial borrowing
Source: ECA calculations based on World Bank data

The economic forecast revealed how oil-producing countries such as Nigeria would be hit on two fronts: directly due to the reported case in the country and indirectly because of its closeness with – badly hit China, the country's financier of infrastructure and trading partner, and the reliance on global oil prices. The Nigerian government had been grappling with a weak recovery from the 2014 oil price shock before the pandemic, with GDP growth tapering approximately 2.3% in 2019 (McKibbin & Fernando, 2020). The GDP growth rate in 2020 was revised by the IMF from 2.5% to 2% in February due to relatively low oil prices and limited fiscal space. The country's debt profile has been a source of concern for policymakers and development practitioners. The most recent estimate puts the debt service-to-revenue ratio at 60%, which is likely to worsen amid the steep decline in revenue associated with falling oil prices. These constraining factors will aggravate the economic impact of the COVID-19 outbreak and make it more difficult for the government to weather the crisis.

"The Role of Economic Policies and Collaborative Efforts in Mitigating the Effect of COVID-19"

African countries are currently navigating uncertain times, and the global impact of the virus has driven down local prices since global economic growth is a crucial driver of commodity prices. The uncertainty of the impact of COVID-19 on local markets is expected to lead to increased risk aversion from investors who are waiting to see its potential impact in Africa. On the plus side, a temporary decline in share prices always provides opportunities for prudent investors. Global financial institutions are currently assessing the impact of COVID-19 and reacting to its economic impact, ensuring that they can adjust to new and unrecognized circumstances brought about by the virus. It remains to be seen whether the vast global economic downturn caused by decreased output in China will impact African lenders and compel financial institutions on the continent to be more lenient towards borrowers and cut them some slack.

The provision of restricted lending and loan guarantees can improve the involvement of the private sector in continued economic productivity, enhancing the liquidity of small companies and limiting job losses. Through creative methods, African governments may have to provide such financial assistance directly. Groups like the World Bank, the IMF, and the European Investment Bank make money, but primarily as loans, available to Africa. The debt burden already borne by most of these countries would only be increased, as 24 of 47 countries already have current account deficits of over 5% of GDP. Thus, many African countries already have precarious debt profiles, with external debts in six countries reaching 40% of GDP.

African countries' current limited fiscal ability can be strengthened by offering foreign or multilateral financial aid as donations rather than loans. A substantial part of its current debt owing to the financial institutions concerned (e.g., the IMF, development banks, and bilateral donors) may be suspended or cancelled. In April, the G-20 countries decided to suspend debt payments to the poor (mainly in Africa), and the government will free COVID-19 interventions with $20 billion (Ikouria, 2020). This suspension will provide some fiscal space that allows governments to focus on developing economic relief packages that include limited, if any, policy requirements (especially renewed austerity).

Furthermore, this pandemic crisis offers the opportunity to switch to new strategies to diversify Africa's economy by encouraging trade and more regionally (continental) globalization, limiting its dependency on foreign financing (whether loans, grants, or investments). The African Continental Free Trade Agreement (AfCFTA), which was scheduled to begin in July 2020, could be very promising (including 54 out of 55 African Union states only now with Eritrea signing the agreement). AfCFTA's guiding force is to abolish the tariffs on 90% of goods over five to eight years and eliminate tariffs on all goods to facilitate trade in goods and services between African countries.

While the economic benefits of this agreement were overstated (Matheson, 2019), stimulus packages could be positioned to promote cross-border trade across the continent. The AfCFTA is critical of not being fair to all countries on the same continent (Nigeria, South Africa, and Egypt make up over 50% of the continental GDP), and the wider, wealthier continental markets could easily dominate without compensatory social agreement. Past trade agreements indicate that economically elite classes generate benefits, and Africa is already one of the worst economically unfair regions worldwide. To circumvent such undesirable consequences, individual policies need to be designed.

Cross-border trading and cooperation could theoretically retain some funding to help several risky African countries tackle the pandemic, even if a revision of trade agreements is more likely to lead to equal gains and ecological sustainability. In the near term, African countries may join in reducing their tariffs for all COVID-19 supplies and controlling their domestic prices. Member states may sign cost-sharing agreements under the auspices of the African and World Health Organization (WHO) to ensure that deeper financial pockets (or borrowing capacity) in more prominent African countries will not ban smaller, weaker nations.

Conclusion, Policy Relevance, and Future Research Directions

The review of the study revealed that unregulated social policies could influence citizens' social and economic wellbeing. Furthermore, the coronavirus outbreak has shown how a biological crisis can be transformed into a sociological subject. The most significant sociological consequence of the coronavirus outbreak for African citizens is the creation of social anxiety that could affect the attainment of national policies and public service provisions. The outbreak has also demonstrated how susceptible African societies are to facing health hazards. Policy makers could enforce social and national policies that drive the provision of relevant public services.

It is currently difficult to fully understand the duration of the coronavirus outbreak and how many African people will be affected. However, we know that there are far fewer infected people in Africa than in the EU and the USA. While the economic impact is already significant, particularly for oil-dependent African countries, the effects are already significant for African countries that are substantially enjoying a global supply chain. Many African countries have taken significant steps, such as social distancing and lockdown. Most African countries will likely enter an imminent recession once the pandemic ends.

The government has a critical role in the face of real financial and health crises, and monetary measures are perceived to be helpful in resolving public health emergency. Fiscal resources can then provide direct assistance to individuals and companies affected to protect the productive capacities needed when the COVID-19 crisis ends for reviving the African economy. Another indirect action that needs to be taken is to provide everyone with a permanent safety net under social and economic policies during the pandemic. This can be achieved in many ways, including ensuring people have access to basic amenities such as free electricity and relief packages. African policymakers must also focus on actions to reset the economy after the coronavirus crisis has ended, for example, reducing the price of energy goods such as fuel and gas and relieving small and large companies of their bailout so that employees are not dismissed during the crisis and the recovery period.

The apex banks in Africa must find the right balance of monetary-policy incentives to improve economic development. At the same time, fiscal authorities should use the fiscal instruments at their disposal to do the same. Social authorities in African nations should ensure that local citizens have access to reliable communication systems so that community members can communicate with family and friends remotely during the crisis. Effective communication is the most crucial strategy to educate people on the nature of coronavirus infection and the steps they may take to protect themselves.

Finally, this pandemic allows every African nation to reconsider its exposure to the world economy and the disruptive impact on every African country. We must wonder: does globalization's negative consequences outweigh the benefits? Would African countries limit their exposure to international shocks in the future? Will some African countries cut their reliance on oil revenues, such as Angola, Libya, or Nigeria, to decrease their exposure to significant declines in oil prices? While substantial investment in public health and development is required in developed countries, the poorest countries are mostly not excluded. For decades, critical policy intervention has proven significant. Nevertheless, essential players such as politicians and policymakers have continually ignored the scientific evidence on the role of public health as a driver of economic growth and improving the quality of life.

The study's findings suggest the need for extensive research, particularly considering how the COVID-19 pandemic and related health challenges have impacted the implementation of national policies and public service provisions. In so doing, using relevant data with more time-series properties to investigate whether the predictions in this study could be corroborated is worthwhile in future studies. Therefore, focusing on the economic impact of the COVID-19 pandemic and its significant impact on the health sector and overall economic growth will provide valuable insights in most African countries. This will create an opportunity for appropriate and effective measures to be implemented in both high-performing and low-performing countries and regions.

Notes

1 www.bakermckenzie.com/en/insight/publications/2020/03/the-impact-of-covid19-on-key-african-sectors
2 ILO (2018): "Women and men in the informal economy: A statistical picture"
3 ECA (2020). COVID-19 in Africa – Protecting Lives and Economies.
4 www.un.org/sites/un2.un.org/fles/un_policy_brief_on_debt_relief_and_covid_april_2020.pdf
5 UN Secretary-General, 17 April 2020 – Remarks to virtual IMF/World Bank High-level Meeting Mobilizing with Africa (www.un.org/sg/en/content/sg/statement/2020-04-17/secretary-generals-remarks-virtual-imfworld-bank-high-level-meeting-mobilizing-africadelivered)
6 32 https://g20.org/en/media/Documents/G20_FMCBG_Communiqu%C3%A9_EN%20(2).pdf

References

African Development Bank (AfDB). (2020). *African economic outlook: Developing Africa's workforce for the future*. African Development Bank Group: Abidjan, Cote d'Ivoire. https://www.afdb.org/en/documents/african-economic-outlook-2020-supplement

Asongu, S. A., Diop, S., & Nnanna, J. (2021). The geography of the effectiveness and consequences of Covid-19 measures: Global evidence. *Journal of Public Affairs*, 21(4), e2483.

Baldwin, R., & Weder di Mauro, B. (2020). *Economics in the Time of COVID-19*. CEPR Press VoxEU.org.

Brown, G. W., & Labonté, R. (2011). Globalization and its methodological discontents: Contextualizing globalization through the study of HIV/AIDS. *Glob Health*, 7(1), 29.

Diop, S., & Asongu, S. A. (2021). The Covid-19 pandemic and the new poor in Africa: The straw that broke the camel's back. In *Forum for Social Economics* (pp. 1–13). Routledge.

ECA (2020). *Economic Impact of the COVID-19 on Africa*. www.uneca.org/sites/default/files/uploaded-documents/stories/eca_analysis_-_covid- 19_macroeconomiceffects.pdf

Fernandes, N. (2020). *Economic effects of coronavirus outbreak (COVID-19) on the world economy*. Available at SSRN 3557504.

Fletcher, B. (2020). *The economic impact of COVID-19 on sub-Saharan Africa*. https://www.controlrisks.com/our-thinking/insights/the-economic-impact-of-covid-19-on-sub-saharan-africa

Ikouria, E. (2020). *The G20's promise of a debt freeze is not enough for Africa to combat the COVID-19 crisis*. Available from: www.euronews.com/2020/04/20/g20-spromise-of-a-debt-freeze-is-not-enough-for-africa-to-combat-the-covid-19-crisis-view

International Labour Organization (ILO). (2018). *Women and men in the informal economy: A statistical picture*. www.ilo.org/wcmsp5/groups/public/ – dgreports/–dcomm/documents/publication/wcms_626831.pdf

International Monetary Fund (IMF). (2020). www.imf.org/en/News/Articles/2020/04/17/pr20168-world-bank-group-and-imf-mobilize-partners-in-the-fght-against-covid-19-in-africa

International Monetary Fund (IMF). (2020). *Policy Responses to COVID-19*. www.imf.org/en/Topics/imf-and-covid19/Policy-Responses-toCOVID-19

Jayaram, K., Leke, A., Ooko-Ombaka, A., & Sun, Y. (2020). *Tackling Coronavirus in Africa | McKinsey* [Internet]. Available from: www.mckinsey.com/featured-insights/middle-east-and-africa/tackling-COVID-19- in-Africa

Matheson, A. (2019). *The AfCFTA is laudable, but its imminent benefits are overstated* [Internet]. African Arguments. 2019 [cited 2020 May 19]. Available from: https://africanarguments.org/2019/06/26/the-afcfta-is-laudable-but-itsimminent benefits-are-overstated/

McKibbin, W., & Fernando, R. (2020). The economic impact of COVID-19. *Economics in the Time of COVID-19*, 45.

Nantulya, C. K., & Mavhinga, D. (2020). *Africa's COVID-19 Response Should Focus on People's Needs, Rights* [Internet]. Human Rights Watch. 2020 [Internet]. Available from: www.hrw.org/news/2020/04/16/africas-COVID-19-response-should-focus-peoplesneeds-rights

Ndung'u, N., Shimeles, A., & Manda, D. K. (2021). Growing with Debt in African Economies: Options, Challenges and Pitfalls. *Journal of African Economies*, 30(1), 3–13.

OECD (2020). *COVID-19 in Africa: Regional socioeconomic implications and policy priorities*. www.oecd.org/newsroom/global-economy-faces-gravest-threat-sincethe-crisis-as-coronavirus-spreads.htm

Oqubay, A. (2020). *How Africa can fight the pandemic* [Internet]. Project Syndicate. 2020 [cited 2020 Apr 20]. Available from: www.project-syndicate.org/commentary/how-africa-can-fightCOVID-19-by-arkebe-oqubay-2020-04

Ozili, P. (2020). COVID-19 in Africa: socioeconomic impact, policy response and opportunities. *International Journal of Sociology and Social Policy*, (1), 1–24. Doi:10.1108/IJSSP-05-2020-0171

Ozili, P. K. (2021). Covid-19 pandemic and economic crisis: The Nigerian experience and structural causes. *Journal of Economic and Administrative Sciences*, 37(4), 401–418.

Shadmi, E., Chen, Y., Dourado, I., Faran-Perach, I., Furler, J., Hangoma, P., . . ., & Willems, S. (2020). Health equity and COVID-19: Global perspectives. *International Journal for Equity in Health*, 19(1), 1–16.

United Nations Economic Commission for Africa (UNECA). (2020). *Economic Impact of the COVID-19 on Africa*. www.uneca.org/sites/default/fles/uploaded-documents/stories/eca_analysis_-_covid-19_macroeconomiceffects.pdf

Vaillant, A. (2020). *Covid-19 pandemic: African macroeconomic insights from the World Bank*. Available from: www.fasken.com/en/knowledge/2020/04/29-covid-19-pandemic African macroeconomic-insights-from-the-world-bank/.

Watkins, K. (2020). *Africa's race against COVID-19. project syndicate*. Available from: www.project-syndicate.org/commentary/africa-race-against-COVID-19-by kevinwatkins 2020-03

Yaya, S., Otu, A., & Labonté, R. (2020). Globalization in the time of COVID-19: Repositioning Africa to meet the immediate and remote challenges. *Globalization and Health*, 16(1), 1–7.

15 COVID-19 Pandemic and Illegal Oil Refineries in Africa

Evidence from the National Oil Wealth in Nigeria

Olusola Joshua Olujobi

Introduction

The outbreak of the COVID-19 pandemic across the world and the containment measures adopted by the African governments to prevent the spread of the virus, such as total or partial lockdowns, restriction of movements of citizens (Ufua et al., 2021) and how the measures have impacted the efforts to combat illegal oil refineries activities in Africa. This is mainly through the introduction of private partnerships in the establishment of modular oil refineries (Adegbite, 2015; Eboibi and Robert, 2020). The project has been affected since many oil companies have come under severe economic strain threatening their survival and pushing some of them to take drastic measures, putting their workers at risk due to COVID-19. Some oil companies are unable to function and generate revenues, which now makes it difficult to sustain their workforce due to containment measures against the COVID-19 pandemic in Africa (Ardzard and Tali, 2020).

Oil exploration and production activities are currently being affected by illegal crude oil refineries activities. However, the COVID-19 pandemic has impacts on illegal refineries operations since regulatory authorities were not working optimally during the lockdown to combat their illicit activities. In addition, the lockdowns and other containment measures imposed by the African government were compounded by the decrease in crude oil prices, which has affected Africa's economy (Ogbuigwe, 2018).

Nigeria had over 200 million people and a gross domestic product of US$397 billion in 2019 (A Second Voluntary National Review June 2020). Nigeria is the largest economy in Africa, but the COVID-19 pandemic has affected the country's economic policies, thereby resulting in low revenue for the government (Eboibi and Robert, 2020).

In addition, crude oil refining is a chemical engineering process for the conversion of crude oil into valuable products such as liquefied petroleum gas, gasoline or petrol, kerosene, jet fuel and diesel oil. Petroleum refineries have different units and features, such as utility units and storage tanks. A licence to refine petroleum is called Refiner's Licence. Modern refineries turn out to be as many as 800,000 to 900,000 crude oil barrels per day, and some are as low as 100,000 to 150,000 crude oil barrels per day. Illegal oil refineries are booming while the government's refineries

DOI: 10.4324/9781003208358-20

perform below their full capacities and the establishment of private refineries in the sector appear not investment-friendly. The government expends a huge amount in importing fuel that could be refined in the country. This has drained the nation's treasury, deteriorating national growth and petroleum legal framework (Olujobi, 2020a, 2020b).

Nigeria has persistently tried to have its refineries operating efficiently. Notwithstanding having a nameplate refining capacity that surpasses requests, the country is positioned as the third-highest importer of petroleum products in Africa, importing over 80% of petroleum products utilised, thereby creating enormous domestic refining potentials. Despite this challenge, the country's downstream petroleum sector has brighter business prospects for the future (PriceWaterhouseCoopers, 2019).

The Nigeria Natural Resource Charter's 2018 report on crude oil theft in Nigeria also revealed that poverty, corruption and lack of state capacity to enforce its laws are some of the factors facilitating illegal refineries activities due to weak enforcement of environmental laws, overly bureaucratic, and multiple regulatory bodies controlling the industry (Omoregie, 2018; Katsouris and Sayne, 2013).

Nigerian crude oil is stolen daily in commercial quantity, crude oil stolen is exported, and revenues are laundered and expended on properties abroad by militants and some youths in the Niger Delta areas (Katsouris and Sayne, 2013). In addition, the four registered oil refineries in Nigeria have 445,000 barrels per day (bpd), but these refineries only function at 30% of their inaugurated capacities, thereby occasioning a shortage of refined petroleum products to satisfy the local demands. Therefore, there is a need for refining transformation (Akinrele, 2016).

Lack of transparency and poor governance in the industry has encouraged illegal crude oil refineries, as the Federal Government of Nigeria has lost no less than 150,000 barrels of crude oil (bbl), valued at US$6 billion daily, to crude oil theft (Anyio, 2015).

Similarly, the Nigeria Natural Resource Charter 2018 reviewed that organised illicit oil trade has caused Nigeria to lose over 200,000 barrels of oil every day. In addition, over 3.8 trillion Naira were lost by the federal government in 2016 and 2017 to oil thieves. This stolen crude oil from vandalised pipelines gives room for illegal oil refining; absence of quality control of the products and its substandard operations has occasioned environmental and economic harms to biodiversity, aesthetic scenery of the forest, regeneration of plant species, wildlife habitat, water cycle and medicinal plants (Ogbodo and Aigbokhaevbo, 2014).

As crude oil prices remain globally low, revamping Africa's domestic refining capacities is imperative, as lower oil prices mean low-priced crude feedstock and higher refining margins for refiners. A swing from crude production to crude oil refining will make Africa a net exporter of refined petroleum products in the next decade (PriceWaterhouseCoopers, 2019).

There is enormous business potential for refiners in the African market since most African countries cannot meet their current refined petroleum product demands. For instance, Nigeria uses an estimated 39 billion litres daily and if

Nigeria has functioning and adequate refineries with refined petroleum products readily available for local usage and exports; then, there would be the need to establish modular refineries that can bridge the supply of refined petroleum products in African countries.

The study analyses the various legal regimes on oil refineries in Nigeria and advocates that an oil business-friendly environment will promote the establishment and operation of private refineries in Africa. The study further investigates the challenges against tackling illegal refineries operations in Africa to reposition Nigeria's oil refineries to sustain the country's national wealth to guarantee socially, equitable and environmentally sustainable management of the natural resource for the interest of both the present and future generations, which require a paradigm shift from the present inequitable trends of prevalence of illegal oil refineries to sustaining Africa's oil wealth (Oke, 2016).

Literature Review

Refining in the country commenced some years after oil was found in 1956. The Old Port Harcourt Refinery was set up in 1965 with a refining capacity of 38,000 bpd; the country's refining capacity has increased over the years and is ranked the fourth largest in Africa (PriceWaterhouseCoopers, 2017).

In addition, one stream of the literature suggests that the solutions to illegal refiners and corruption are due to a lack of formal legal structures. Another stream of literature focuses more on the inequalities and inequities between public and private sector workers; for instance, public sector officials are at risk of being subjected to corruptive practices due to their economic circumstances. According to Soremi (2020), an illegal oil refinery is a threat to the environment and Nigeria's economy, while Anyio (2015) avers further that oil theft is a social problem, but strengthening the laws will combat the problem.

However, frequent oil thefts, vandalisation of crude oil pipelines and militancy in the oil-producing areas have affected its efficiency in addition to poor equipment maintenance culture in the industry. To combat this menace, the federal government set up the Niger Delta Amnesty Programme to rehabilitate and reintegrate the repented militants (Olujobi and Olusola-Olujobi, 2020), and the Niger Delta Development Commission (NDDC) and the Ministry of the Niger Delta were set up to appease and to develop oil-bearing areas due to environmental degradation occasioned by oil exploration activities. Adamu (2015) argued that militancy is due to the people's need to control their natural resources, but Olujobi & Yebisi (2022) argue that this is a criminal act and economic terrorism that should be punishable with severe sanctions to serve as deterrence to others.

Moreover, Osinibi (2016) asserts that environmental degradation persists in oil-bearing areas due to continued insensitivity to inhabitants' plights, continued pollution of their areas by oil firms and failure to properly clean up oil spills due to nonenforcement and meagre sanctions embedded in some of the relevant environmental laws in Nigeria (Ogbuigwe, 2018).

Nwosu (2020) reiterated in his work "Commissioning of Petroleum Assets: Setting Agenda for an Emerging Subsector in the Nigerian Petroleum Industry" that he believes that flagrant violation of environmental protection laws pertaining to the oil exploration, exploitation and production activities of oil majors in Nigeria is primarily responsible for the harmful, degrading impacts on the environment (Onu, 2020).

Balogun (2015) further argued that the absence of a unified legal regime for combating illegal oil refineries, meagre sanctions and poor implementation is the significant challenge to effective deterrence of this menace. In addition, some scholars (Oke, 2019b; Akinrele, 2016) argued that social, economic and political factors are responsible for militancy activities in the sector; therefore, the government must be proactive to combat the vices.

Additionally, in the view of Usman (2017), it is projected that the demands and utilisation of petroleum products in Nigeria will increase at a rate of 12.8% annually. However, this high growth rate in consumption is not commensurate with Nigerian refiners' capacities. This made petroleum products expensive and unavailable to most Nigerians since they were imported (Usman, 2017). Some legal scholars have argued that the establishment of illegal refineries is due to the government's refusal to satisfy Nigerians' petroleum demands. An illegal oil refinery thrives due to the already available markets for its products, such as diesel (Ekhator, 2016).

In the view of PriceWaterhouseCoopers (2019), licensing modular refineries in oil-producing areas where illegal refineries boomed will combat this menace. Modular refineries have an estimated cost of $250 million with 24,000 bpd refining capacities, contrary to the conventional refinery cost of $1.5 billion for a large refinery with 100,000 bpd capacity. Modular refineries allow structure increments, and the increments would be funded from the funds generated by the modular refineries without being shut down during the increments. It is further argued that modern refineries are simple, efficient, easy and fast in refining at optimal capacity. This study argues that private investors will enter the downstream petroleum sector and build more modular refineries. However, according to Mason (2014), the burning of illegal refineries and their equipment by the Joint Task Force Committee has compounded the environmental problems being a crude method of enforcement of anti-illegal refineries laws and a waste of natural resources (Olujobi et al., 2022).

The current author is of the view that no one can refine crude oil, establish and operate a refinery except under a licence. Therefore, the various refineries operating in the oil-producing areas without a licence are illegal under section 1 of the Hydrocarbon Oil Refineries Act, Cap H5 Laws of the Federation of Nigeria (2004).

However, the outbreak of the COVID-19 pandemic threatened the world into a panic, considering its devastating or infectious nature. When nations were heaving a sign of relief from Ebola virus disease, the coronavirus disease outbreak has infected millions and claimed many lives (World Health Organisation, 2020). This undermined efforts in combatting illegal oil refineries operations in Africa.

The Quarantine Act of 1926 Cap Q2 Laws of the Federation of Nigeria 2004 has been in existence for 95 years, and without any amendments, it has become obsolete and grossly inadequate for combating pandemics such as COVID-19. As a sequel to this, Nigeria's National Assembly introduced the National Health Emergency Bill 2020 to manage public health emergencies in Nigeria (Dan-Azumi, 2021).

The Nigerian oil sector is characterised by a shortage and erratic supply of petroleum products to retailing stations due to recurrent breakdowns of existing refineries and insufficient importation by oil marketers arising from the federal government's regulated pricing. The illegal export of petroleum products such as Premium Motor Spirit (PMS), Dual Purpose Kerosene (DPK), Household Kerosene (HHK) to neighbouring countries at substantial prices to the detriment of Nigerians' fuel demands and the nation's economy (PriceWaterhouseC-oopers, 2017).

The petroleum sector is generating over 70% of the federal government's revenues since oil was discovered. In addition, this has occasioned a shift from agriculture to petroleum due to its massive cash flow from crude oil exports by the Nigerian National Petroleum Corporation (Olujobi and Oyewunmi, 2017). However, the Nigerian oil industry has been in intense public glare due to the persistent smuggling of petroleum products despite insatiable national demands. In addition, this occasioned illegal oil refineries due to the nation's refineries' recurrent shutdowns owing to faulty refineries' equipment and low turnaround maintenance culture in the industry (Ogbuigwe, 2018).

There are four registered refineries in Nigeria. Two are situated in Port Harcourt, each in Kaduna and Warri, exclusively managed by the NNPC with a combined capacity of 445,000 bpd with 30% working capacity, less than the installed capacities. However, this has occasioned the importation of refined petroleum products to satisfy local demands after several failed turnaround maintenance exercises to improve their production capacities but with poor outputs.

However, it is pertinent to note that over 300,000 bbl. Barrels are officially allocated for local refineries to promote the Nigerian Content Act. Nigeria's average daily crude oil production is 1.7 million (Ubani, 2005). The refineries have less than the average of 240,000 bbl per day for local consumption. The domestic refinery capacity was 445,000 bbl per day from 35,000 bbl per day in 1992; due to the bureaucracy of the Warri Refinery constructed in 1978, its processing capacity was increased from 55,000 bbl to 125,000 bbl per day in 1991, and the repair of the Old Port Harcourt Refinery built-in 1964 in Alesa-Eleme with 60,000 bbl per day increased its capacity from 35,000 bbl per day but became burnt in 1988 (Ogbuigwe, 2018). The Kaduna Refinery built-in 1988 with 15,000 bbl per day capacity as an export refinery could not satisfy domestic needs (Asimiea and Omokhua, 2013). The new Port-Harcourt Refinery in Alesa-Eleme could also not meet the growing domestic demands for petroleum products due to low maintenance. The annual growth rate in petroleum product consumption in the country is 12.4%. Average daily premium motor spirit (PMS) local consumption is 30 million litres nationwide, while Lagos is 8 million litres daily (Adamu, 2015).

The refined petroleum product utilisation was projected to be approximately 24 billion liters, and over 80% of Nigeria's refined petroleum products are imported. Thereby, it was creating huge potential markets for local refining businesses for prospective investors in the industry with significant investments potentials in West African countries' energy markets (Olujobi, 2017).

However, this has also occasioned ethnic militias from the Niger Delta areas, who are purportedly fighting injustice occasioned to the areas due to environmental degradation from oil exploration activities. Additionally, the Nigerian National Petroleum Corporation failed to actualise its mandate as a national oil company due to the fusion of regulatory tasks with the formulation of policies and as an oil operator in the industry. The delay in the passage of the Petroleum Industry Act 2021, which could have reformed the sector but weak enforcement of the extant laws on the oil and gas sector, has affected the nation's economy and degenerated by the outbreak of the COVID-19 pandemic (Olujobi, 2021a).

Nigeria's refining capacity should meet its national utilisation projected at approximately 400,000 bpd if proper routine maintenance exercises are executed (Olujobi and Oyewunmi, 2017). Utilising the Joint Military Task Force to engage oil thieves has only compounded the problem as they are often compromised. They are often alleged to offer their escort vehicles to vandals to ensure unrestricted access in moving stolen crude oil to the designated point of delivery (Ogbodo and Aigbokhaevbo, 2014).

The activities of illegal oil refineries and pipeline vandalization caused serious security challenges in the Niger Delta areas and affected Nigeria's economy, as the revenues that are supposed to be accrued to the government go to individual pockets, especially during the lockdown due to the COVID-19 pandemic, which, in turn, affected the development projects in Africa. In addition, these activities of illegal oil refineries and pipeline vandalism caused serious health challenges to the people of the Niger Delta areas, harming their soil and aquatic animals (Abdullahi, 2020). Asongu, Diop and Nnanna analysed the economic impact of the COVID-19 pandemic and evaluated the effectiveness and relevance of different measures against the pandemic. The findings show how the effectiveness and consequences of the COVID-19 measures are different across regions.

Methodology

Using the current literature, the study adopts a conceptual legal research method to apply library-based doctrinal legal research techniques with the conceptual legal research approach. Primary and secondary sources of laws, such as case laws and the Petroleum Industry Act 2021 for combating crude oil thefts in Nigeria, were also considered. Additionally, the provisions of the repealed Hydrocarbon Oil Refineries Act No 17, 1965 Cap., H5, Laws of the Federation of Nigeria, 2004, and the Petroleum Refining Regulations No: 45, 1974 were also assessed. Mixed methods were also utilised based on archival and secondary data sources because these focus on legal doctrines comprised primary sources of law. This approach to legal research is coherent with the law, and it is readily available for verification.

Challenges Against Tackling Illegal Refineries Operations in Africa

One of the various challenges facing refineries operations in Africa is low-capacity utilisation due to poor regulatory governance (Samba and Simplice Asongu, 2021). This has impeded the excellent functioning of the existing refineries. The government, being the sole owner of the refineries, has affected its independence and funding. Applications for finances to execute manufacturing maintenance routines are often delayed due to administrative and bureaucratic procedures associated with the release of funds. Refineries cannot be managed properly in this manner (Olujobi, 2021b). There is a need for machinery upgrades and sound technical know-how to maintain the refineries to sustain their financial and manufacturing capabilities.

However, absolute divestment of the government's substantial equity in the refineries has been preferred as the panacea to this malaise being the best ecological practice globally. Frequent turnaround maintenance should be carried out on the refineries due to regular use, wear and tear, exposure to daily routine and other ecological situations. Undue delays associated with the maintenance of refineries decreased their performance, thereby causing the government to import petroleum products in most African countries, especially Nigeria. This has occasioned a colossal squander of meagre national revenues (Afaha, John et al., 2021). However, this has further contributed to lower capacity utilisation of the existing refineries in Africa (Ogbuigwe, 2018).

Additionally, many of the pipelines supplying crude oil to the various refineries are repeatedly damaged due to agitation for resource management and the consequent rise of militancy in the Niger Delta areas of Nigeria due to environmental degradation of the oil areas by oil firms. Furthermore, theft of crude oil and other petroleum products has occasioned the loss of national revenues to the government (Asimiea and Omokhua, 2013), and this has been made worse due to the ravaging effects of the COVID-19 pandemic on the nation's economy. Therefore, there is a need for the stringent enforcement of oil and gas laws to combat the menace (Occhiali, Giovanni et al., 2020).

There is a persistent regulation of Premium Motor Spirit's (PMS) price by the government, which has occasioned underrecovery of crude cost by oil firms, thereby discouraging investments in the sector. In addition, the government controls the price via regulation of the downstream sector. This makes investments in the refineries unprofitable to investors due to inefficient markets. Thus, it encourages rent-seeking activities and drains the national treasury via a subsidy regime, promoting the smuggling of petroleum products to neighbouring countries for higher profits (Olujobi et al., 2020).

Inadequate local refining capacity to meet the local daily consumption rate, millions of dollars have been spent on turnaround maintenance and other operational costs in many African countries. However, corruption, poor management and poor maintenance of the existing refineries have hampered its efficiency (Olujobi, 2021). In addition, illegal refineries, uncertainties or unrest have caused investors to stay away from the industry (Ayoade, 2009b). Payment of oil subsidies and discrepancies in government policies.

To cushion the high cost of fuel that has occasioned artificially induced fuel scarcity, there is a need for total deregulation of Nigeria's oil and gas sector (Adegbite, 2015). The governments in African countries introduced the various reform programmes to encourage private refineries with incentives to promote investments in the sector and to support long-term economic growth in the industry through transparent privatisation of the existing crude oil refineries through the issuance of a licence to private investors for the establishment of private refineries, Gas Recovery and Processing Plants, as well as Natural Gas and Independent Power Plant Project (Omorogbe, 2003). In addition, privatisation will offer the African government Budgetary relief from certain state enterprises' financial and administrative problems. Thereby, it increases the state's revenues, competition and efficiency in the sector by implementing certain policy objectives, such as Canada, the Philippines, Bangladesh and Chile.

Additionally, the protracted delays associated with the enactment of the Petroleum Industry Act 2021 and the federal government's delay in implementing a comprehensive deregulation policy have discouraged potential investors in the industry (Olujobi, 2021c). This has also occasioned the country losing approximately $15 billion yearly in foreign investments due to regulatory regime uncertainty in the industry (Nigerian Extractive Industries Transparency Initiative (NEITI) Report, 2018).

In addition, the federal government's capacity to earn at least $10 billion or < 4 trillion via marginal fields in the oil and gas sector has been stalled due to uncertainty in the fiscal and legal regime (The Guardian Newspaper Monday 11, 2021). The act made explicit provisions for sustainable development. Section 67 states that the management of petroleum resources shall be conducted under the principles of good governance, transparency and sustainable development of Nigeria (Olujobi, 2020a, 2020b). Section 235 creates the Host Communities Trust Fund (HCTF) to benefit host communities (Aholu and Wifa, 2020), but section 104 allows the Upstream Regulatory Commission to issue exemptions against gas flaring prohibition. This is a major flaw in the act, thereby discouraging a sustainable energy future (Aholu and Wifa, 2020).

Another challenge in the sector is the weak enforcement of laws, insecurity of lives and crude oil infrastructure due to incessant kidnapping, industrial incapacity, crude oil theft, pipeline vandalism and piracy. Crude oil infrastructural damage has affected the supply of crude oil for refining operations in the sector. This is an impediment to growth in the downstream oil sector. These have adversely impacted the refining of crude oil production and occasioned incessant declaration of *force majeure* on crude oil shipments by investors in the industry.

Another significant challenge facing the refining business in Africa is the inappropriate supply of feedstock to the refineries due to inadequate crude oil infrastructure, insecurity, and unstable crude oil production. There is the need for constant access to the feedstock to keep refining productivities at optimum capacities to ensure a constant supply of crude oil to the refineries. There is a significant underutilisation of the Pipelines and Products Marketing Company Limited (PPMC) and private industry capacity due to irregular supply and inconsistent ability to import products independently. As a result, the NNPC imported a large quantity of refined petroleum product supply into the country. The aim is to sell petroleum products at a uniform price in Nigeria via the Petroleum Equalisation Fund. However, corruption, low transportation infrastructure networks, petroleum product supply deficits and illegal exports of refined products to neighbouring countries have affected this laudable objective.

The federal government's frequent modifications of its deregulation policy in the downstream petroleum sector limit access to competitive markets for refined petroleum products in the industry (Olujobi, 2021d). There are also intermittent communal conflicts in oil-producing areas that often affect refineries operations (Ayoade, 2009b).

Furthermore, in 1996, the federal government allotted three Refinery Construction Licenses: Amakpe Refinery with 6,000 bpd capacity, Brass Refinery with 100,000 bpd and Qua Refinery with 100,000 bpd. However, none could make headway due to financial constraints and the nonallotment of crude oil to refine locally (Ubani, 2005).

Lack of genuine dedication on the part of the federal government, the mere fact that the Petroleum Industry Act 2021 was delayed by the legislatures is a pointer to lack of commitment on the government's part to promote sustainable economic growth in the industry (Adejonwo-Osho, 2016).

Funding is a major challenge facing investors in the Nigerian petroleum industry due to the lack of easy accessibility to finances and insufficient access to copious capital on the part of private investors. There is a need for banking reform to support investments in the sector (Etareh, 2006). Additionally, there are inconsistent and unfavourable policy changes by the government's regulatory authorities in the sector that need to be amended (Olujobi et al., 2022).

The Divergencies Between the Quarantine Act 1926, the Control of Infectious Diseases Bill 2020, and the Proposed National Health Emergency Bill 2020 (Public Health Emergency Bill, 2020) for Combating Future Health Emergencies in Nigeria

The Quarantine Act of 1926 empowered the president to prevent the spread and transmission of dangerous and infectious diseases in Nigeria by making regulations to curtail them. In conformity with this, the president made COVID-19 Regulations 2020 that declared COVID-19 a "dangerous infectious disease" and declared lockdown in Lagos, Abuja and the Ogun states.

The Quarantine Act 1926 has eight sections with only six substantive contributions. No provision provides for the direct prevention or control of infectious diseases but delegates the president's power, while the Bill is more comprehensive, with 70 sections.

The Bill makes comprehensive provisions for the prevention and control of the disease. Absence of provision subjecting the legislation to legislative scrutiny. The penalty for contravention of the regulation formulated by the President is 200 or imprisonment for a term of six months or both under section 25 of the act. The minimum fine under the act is 50,000, while the maximum penalty is 2,000,000.00. There is no provision in the act for the disposal of corpses or infected persons. Additionally, there is no provision in the act for dealing with minors infected or who are carriers of infectious diseases. Contrary to its title, the act does not provide quarantine provision but provides robust provision for the isolation of certain persons under the Bill (Abdullahi, 2020).

The act is limited in scope with only eight sections, while the Bill is more comprehensive with 70 sections. Although the act delegates all powers relating to the prevention and control of dangerous infectious disease to the president, the Bill elaborates on prevention and control. While the act vests on the president the power of making wide regulation, the Bill only empowers the president to declare public health emergency, unlike the act, it has no provision for the administration other than the power of making regulations vested in the president, the Bill put the Director-General of the Nigeria Centres for Disease Control in charge of its administration. However, this is a major challenge the Bill faces, given the enormous, unchecked power vested in the Director-General. The act has no provision relating to the peculiarities of minors. However, the Bill has provision to that effect, especially in sections 6(3), 13(3), 14(2).

The enforcement of the COVID-19 regulation occasioned human rights abuses such as extrajudicial killings, torture, degrading and inhuman treatments in violation of the right to human dignity by law enforcement agencies. Upsurge in domestic violence cases in Nigeria and access to justice was impacted as the courts were indefinitely shut. The Quarantine Act of 1926 is archaic and not in conformity with the current economic reality in the country.

The act was repealed and replaced with the Control of Infectious Diseases Bill 2020; the bill has been criticised for contravening the law and constitutional provisions. The Bill grants excessive powers to the Director-General of the Nigeria Centre for Disease and Control and the Minister of Health. Section 15 of the Bill empowers the Minister of Health to declare any premises as an "Isolation Area" and restraint of movement of persons and goods as stated under section 15(3) (a-f) of the Bill. The Minister and Director General are given excess powers under section 20(4), which states that the resolution of the Director-General barring public or social meetings can only be petitioned to the minister, whose verdict shall be conclusive.

Section 58 empowers the police to arrest anyone without a warrant as long he has reason to believe that such a person has infringed Bill's provisions.

Section 20 impedes citizens' constitutional right to freedom of assembly and association by restraining meetings and public and social gatherings. The Bill infringed on the constitutional right to privacy and data safety by authorising mass surveillance and contact tracing under sections 14 and 19 of the Bill. The use of the words "In Good Faith" and "With Reasonable Care" is vague and may be abused. Bill's provisions may be essential to combat the pandemic; however, human rights and the rule of law must not be infringed upon. There is a need for checks and controls to prevent abuses and corruption in combating health emergencies in Nigeria.

Responses of the Federal Government of Nigeria to the COVID-19 Pandemic and Towards Combating Illegal Oil Refineries in Africa

The pandemic outbreak, which started as a minor health issue in Wuhan, China, in 2019, has now become a global health issue forcing the global community to scavenge for solutions (Adesanya). The Presidential Task Force on COVID-19 was set up to coordinate and oversee Nigeria's multisectoral intergovernmental efforts to combat the spread of COVID-19 and mitigate its impacts in Nigeria, including the oil industry. The National COVID-19 Response Centre was established to coordinate multiagency inputs in managing the virus. The Nigeria Centres for Disease Control issues a daily situation report, public health advisory, guidelines, and provisions of equipment and set up facilities and trains the staff to combat the virus. The establishment of the National incident Coordination Centres for outbreak preparedness and response activities enables the Nigeria Centres for Disease Control to gather intelligence reports daily to identify impending public health threats and to ensure that the outbreak responses are well-coordinated and controlled (Nigeria Centres for Disease Control, 2021).

The federal government imposed a lockdown on the Federal Capital Territory and 2 of the 36 states. Other public health measures include the closure of businesses activities, including refineries, schools and international borders. A national curfew was imposed, and subsequently, President Muhammadu Buhari signed the COVID-19 Regulations 2020 by the Quarantine Act sections 2, 3 and 4, Q2 Laws of the Federation of Nigeria 2004. The regulations described COVID-19 as an infectious disease and gave legal backing to combat it. Therefore, there is a need for health security, an essential prerequisite for proactive and reactive measures to minimise the danger and impacts of acute public health in Nigeria (Edozien, 2020). The health sector feels the impact of COVID-19 on not only Nigeria but also the entire African economy, including the refineries. This has occasioned a drop in global oil prices and a decline in oil refineries' production capacities in Africa. Hence, there was a proliferation of illegal refineries activities in Africa because regulatory agencies were not working optimally due to the pandemic. There is a need to upscale health facilities and to put in place sustainable measures to improve the Nigerian public health sector in conformity with the global standard. Many investors may be unwilling to invest in a country's oil refineries where public health is grossly below the global standard considering the adverse effects of the global pandemic on Africa's economy and its citizens' health (Oguche, 2020).

Findings and Discussion

The absence of a stringent legal framework to combat the menace caused by incessant crude oil thefts, pipeline vandalization by the militants, and low maintenance of the existing crude oil refineries has impeded the country's economic growth. The absence of a specific provision on illegal oil refineries in the Petroleum Industry Act, criminalising crude oil theft with stricter penalties for pipeline vandalisation and crude oil theft in Nigeria, is fundamental. The vandalism of crude oil pipelines and the sabotage of oil infrastructure are hurdles to developing Nigeria's oil industry. Therefore, the government needs to reform the industry's various legal regimes and regulations and remedy the various *lacunas* identified in the Act.

Interested investors should invest in proposed modular refineries in Nigeria to meet the current shortfall in Africa refinery capacity since Nigeria supplies petroleum products to neighbouring African countries via illegal channels. Investors should close this gap to meet Nigeria's and other African countries' refined petroleum products' needs by setting up new refineries. For instance, new licences have been awarded to private investors such as the Dangote Group, currently constructing 650,000 bpd refineries in Lekki Free Zone, Lagos. However, more investors are expected to come on board by introducing fiscal incentives on refineries investments to attract more investors. This will increase Africa's refinery capacity, thus creating employment opportunities for Africa's teeming youths, but caution must be exercised to prevent monopolistic tendencies. Furthermore, the host communities in Nigeria, full participation in modular oil refineries and natural resource management and environmental conservation and protection through negotiations, dialogue on agreed terms for collaboration on extractive resources governance and management among investors, host communities and regulatory authorities in Africa are essential to deter the menace of unrestiveness and violence by youths in oil producing countries (Oke, 2019a; Deinduomo, 2009).

The Nigerian Petroleum Regulatory Commission should issue licences, permit to investors in refineries and facilitate crude oil feedstock from upstream petroleum companies. Furthermore, the existing moribund refineries should be transformed, with full capacity utilisation via private sector funding and renovation ingenuity to combat illegal oil refineries and other adverse effects of the COVID-19 pandemic on oil refineries and the Nigerian economy to boost the contribution of Africa to the global economy.

Full deregulation of the downstream petroleum sector will attract private investors to build more refineries and guarantee private funding (Ayoade, 2009a). In addition, the liberalisation of the downstream sector will make the industry free from government control and an unsustainable subsidy scheme, a conduit pipe of corruption (Olujobi et al., 2020).

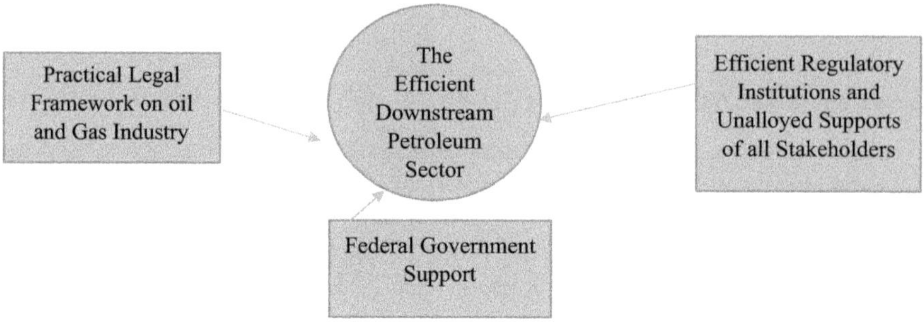

Figure 15.1 Hybrid model for the transformation of Nigeria's crude oil refineries
Source: The author

Hybrid Model for the Transformation of Nigeria's Crude Oil Refineries

Figure 15.1 shows the hybrid model for the transformation of Nigeria's crude oil refineries. The study advocates a hybrid model for transforming Nigeria's crude oil refineries to promote efficiency, deter illegal refineries and ensure the availability and adequate supply of petroleum products.

Recommendations and Conclusion

Recommendations

The outbreak of the COVID-19 pandemic has further delayed the government's efforts in combating the problems of illegal oil refineries in Africa for the sustainability of national oil wealth in the petroleum industry. To achieve this, the following recommendations are made:

- Bailout funds should be deployed to give life support to oil refineries in Africa that may go into insolvency due to the impacts of the COVID-19 pandemic on oil businesses.
- The relevant tax authorities in African countries should defer tax collections from oil firms and other businesses that have been rendered vulnerable by the impact of the COVID-19 pandemic to enable them to recover and stabilise, thereby preventing the loss of businesses.
- African countries should introduce a fiscal stimulus package for the benefits of refineries, small- and medium-sized enterprises and manufacturers to mitigate businesses' vulnerabilities to the adverse effects of the COVID-19 pandemic in Africa.
- By ensuring local communities, full participation in modular refineries and resource and environmental management through negotiations and dialogue

on agreed terms for collaboration in resource governance among the experts, the locals and the regulatory authorities in Africa is critical.

- Complete deregulation of the downstream sector would open the supply and distribution of petroleum products to demands and supply, optimise local refining production from existing refineries and encourage new refineries. There is the need for massive investment in both small- and higher-capacity refineries to meet the domestic sourcing of refined petroleum products, thereby reducing fuel importation in Africa.
- Africa's legislatures need to take a proactive step by enacting laws that will combat oil theft, illegal refining and militancy and other oil-related crimes by criminalising them as terrorism. The proposed law may be referred to as the "Environmental Protection, Oil, Gas Conservation and Terrorism Act, 2022"
- Oil fingerprinting techniques should be utilised to identify and track down stolen crude oil (Olujobi and Yebisi, 2022). In addition, existing oil crime regulations should be amended to make fines more stringent in conformity with the sector's current realities. Stricter enforcement of the laws via prosecution of offenders, tracking and seizure of proceeds will deter illegal oil activities in Africa (Olujobi, 2021).

Conclusion and Policy Implications

The need to repeal the Quarantine Act in Nigeria for modern and comprehensive legislation to combat public health emergencies is long overdue. The Bill is full of inconsistencies with the provisions of the constitution on human rights and to avert future litigation. The study has drawn the attention of the government and the world to the deleterious effects of illegal refineries operations and existing gaps in the supply of refined petroleum products in Africa with solutions by highlighting the sizeable potential for the domestic refining of petroleum products via a modular refinery, an off-the-shelf that is cost-effective, flexible with a short payback duration, making it attractive for investment in the sector.

The impacts of the outbreak of the COVID-19 pandemic have put many oil and gas firms under strain and exposed many to insolvency and liquidation due to dwindling oil prices and illegal refineries operations in Africa. The greater mitigating factor to this impact of the COVID-19 pandemic in the oil and gas sector is robust economic decisions by the government through the introduction of environmental stimuli, bailouts and tax reliefs to oil and gas firms, which would ensure their survival and sustainability in the COVID-19 pandemic era, thereby preventing insolvency and liquidation due to activities of illegal refiners. COVID-19 has threatened the health and lives of millions of people since its emergence. It is a highly contagious disease with the possibility of causing severe respiratory infection prognosis, which has promptly impacted the African sources of revenues from oil and public health systems.

There is a need to improve local refineries' capacities to enhance local production and markets for refined petroleum products and encourage domestic gas utilisation. However, domestic refineries' efficient legal and regulatory framework to employ present and future generations in Africa is the *sine qua non*.

Genetic fingerprinting of crude oil is a viable tool for combating crude oil theft by regulatory authorities and law-enforcement agencies to detect crude oil thieves. In addition, stringent sanctions such as freezing oil thieves' assets, banks accounts, placing them on the blacklist and denying them travelling visas with other stringent measures may combat oil theft and illegal oil refineries in Africa.

A well-designed supply-chain due diligence initiative, such as scrutinising crude oil supplies before purchase, will combat crude oil theft and sanitise global crude oil markets. Additionally, there is a need for maritime security reform and sound security intelligence gathering and analysis. Institution of legal actions against buyers and sellers of stolen crude oil via national criminal laws or civil suits, a conviction for crude oil thieves and their assets seized is another strategy for combating crude oil theft and illegal oil refineries in Africa.

There is a need for unalloyed support for the Extractive Industries Transparency Initiative by all stakeholders in the industry to promote transparency, accountability, proper disclosure and reporting of all transactions in the sector.

Finally, the adoption of a modular refinery model is the best option for Africa to combat the proliferation of illegal refineries and its deleterious effects, being a cost-effective supply option for investors, especially when diesel is the lightest yield. It can be established with a relatively low capital cost, flexible with short payback duration for bank-sponsored facilities, making it distinctly attractive for investors. It will ensure the availability of refined petroleum products, deliver value beyond the traditional oil production business model and build local capacities in the sector, as the quality of human life, survival and country's economy are under colossal danger from the various pollution activities and losses occasioned by the deleterious effects of illegal oil refineries operations in Africa (Olujobi et al., 2022).

There is no misgiving that the COVID-19 pandemic has impacted the petroleum industry, and there is a need to take preemptive measures to strengthen and initiate a sustainable petroleum industry future. Economic diversification and conversion to clean energy are the most sustainable options for Africa or the total deregulation of the downstream petroleum sector. Clean energy necessitates a shift from fossil fuel to green energy for a strong economy. There is a need for a strong regulatory framework and specific human capital development to accommodate this goal in Africa (Asongu et al., 2021).

The study does not provide all answers to the challenges of illegal oil refineries in Africa. However, it has provided insight for combating the menace in Africa's oil and gas sector. Future research can also improve this study by focusing on the empirical view of the topic to further improve oil refineries in Africa to combat fuel scarcity or shortages.

References

Abdullahi, S., (2020), Challenges of Security Enforcement in Nigeria's Maritime Domain. *Port Harcourt Journal of Business Law*, 7(1), 183.

Adamu, K., (2015), Oil Theft and Militancy in the Niger Delta Region of Nigeria: Analysis of the Legal Issues. *University of Maiduguri Law Journal*, 13, 283.

Adegbite, I., (2015), Law, Development and the Nigerian Oil and Gas Refineries. *Nigerian Law Journal*, 18(1), 73–108.

Adejonwo-Osho, O., (2016), Petroleum Industry Bill, Nigeria: Missed Opportunity for Good Governance, Transparency and Sustainable Development? *UNILAG Journal of Public Law*, 3, 56.

Adesanya, O.V., (2020), A Review of the Nigerian Government's Anti-Covid Responses: Issues and Challenges. *Health Law and Policy Journal*, 2(2), 114.

Afaha, J.S., Aderinto, E.A., Oluwole, E.A., Oyinlola, A., Akintola, Y., *Effect of Covid-19 on the Nigerian Oil and Gas Industry and Impact on the Economy*. CPEEL's Covid-19 Volume II Discussion Papers Series. Available at file:///c:/users/dr.%20olujobi%20olusola/downloads/effect-covid-19-nigerian-oil-and-gas-industry-and-impact-economy.pdf (accessed July 3, 2021).

Aholu, O., and Wifa, E.L., (2020), *Regulatory Governance: The Petroleum Industry Bill 2020 and Nigeria's Oil Future* (November 13, 2020). Working Paper Series 001, November 2020. Available at SSRN: https://ssrn.com/abstract=3730659 or http://doi.org/10.2139/ssrn.3730659 (accessed July 2, 2021).

Akinrele, A., (2016), The Current Impact of Global Crude Oil Prices on Nigeria: An Overview of the Nigerian Petroleum and Energy Sector. *Journal of World Energy Law and Business*, 9, 313–345.

Anyio, S.F., (2015), Illegal Oil Bunkering and Oil Theft in Nigeria: Impact on the National Economy and the Way Forward. *Ilimi Journal of Art and Social Sciences*, 1(1), 1–14.

Ardzard, H., and Tali, E., (2020), The Role of the Law in Mitigating Employment Conflicts in Covid-19 Pandemic Era in Nigeria. *Nigerian Institute of Advanced Legal Studies' Health Law and Policy Journal*, 2(2), 181–213.

Asimiea, A., and Omokhua, G., (2013), Environmental Impact of Illegal Refineries on the Vegetation of the Niger Delta, Nigeria. *Journal of Agriculture and Social Research*, 13(2), 121–125.

Asongu, S.A., Diop, S., and Nnanna, J. (2021), The Geography of the effectiveness and Consequences of Covid-19 Measures: Global evidence. *Journal of Public Affairs*, e2483. Available at https://doi.org/10.1002/pa.2483asonguet al.9of9 (accessed February 28, 2021).

Ayoade, M.A., (2009a), *Deregulation of the Downstream Petroleum Sector in Nigeria – Can It Solve the Energy Crisis*. Contributed in Prof. U.O. Umozurike & E.C Ngwakwe (Eds.) 42nd NALT Conference Proceedings.

Ayoade, M.A., (2009b), Nigerian Petroleum Corporation and Prospects for Transparency in the Petroleum Industry Bill. *University of Ado Ekiti Law Journal*, 3, 248–270.

Balogun, T.F., (2015), Mapping Impacts of Crude Oil theft and Illegal Refineries on Mangrove of Nigeria's Niger Delta with Remote Sensing Technology. *Mediterranean Journal Social Sciences*, 6(3), 150–153.

Dan-Azumi, J.D., (2021), *Role of Parliaments in Managing Pandemics: An Evaluation of National Assembly's Response to Covid-19*. Available at file:///c:/users/dr.%20olujobi%20olusola/downloads/roleofparliamentsinmanagingpandemics-anevaluationofnationalassemblysresponsetocovid-19.pdf (accessed July 1, 2021).

Deinduomo, G., (2009), Oil Exploration Activities and Oil-Producing Communities: A Framework for Breaking the Barriers to the Development of Oil Producing Communities. In Emiri F., and Deinduomo, G., et al., *Law and Petroleum Industry in Nigeria Current Challenges*. Essay in Honour of Justice Kate Abiri, 358–377.

Eboibi, F.E., and Robert, E. (2020). *The global legal response to coronavirus (COVID-19) and Its Impact: Perspectives from Nigeria, the United States of America and the United Kingdom.* Commonwealth Law Bulletin, 1–32.

Edozien, L., (2020), Health Federalism: Trials and Triumphs in Nigeria's Response to the Covid-19 Pandemic. *Health Law and Policy Journal*, 2(2), 1–37.

Ekhator, E.O., (2016), Public Regulation of the Oil and Gas Industry in Nigeria: An Evaluation. *Annual Survey of International & Comparative Law, 21*, 43.

Etareh, G.G., (2006), *Financing the Downstream Petroleum Sub-Sector of Nigeria: Options and Challenges, Oil and Gas Financing in Nigeria.* Issues, Challenges and Prospects, Chartered Institute of Bankers of Nigeria, 89–103.

The Guardian Newspaper, Monday 11, 2021, Adekoya, F., & Jeremiah, K., Late PIB passage threatens N4tr marginal fields earnings, pp. 1–2. Available at https://guardian.ng/news/late-pib-passage-threatens-n4tr-marginal-fields-earnings/ (accessed June 29, 2022).

Hydrocarbon Oil Refineries Act Cap H5 Laws of the Federation of Nigeria, 2004, section 1.

Katsouris, C., and Sayne, A., (2013), *International Options to Combat the Export of Stolen Oil, Chatham House* (The Royal Institute of International Affairs). Available at file:///c:/users/hp/desktop/research/nigeria%e2%80%99s%20criminal%20crude_%20international%20options%20to%20combat%20the%20export%20of%20stolen%20oil.pdf (accessed December 28, 2020).

Katsouris, C., and Sayne, A., (2013), *Nigeria's Criminal Crude: International Options to Combat the Export of Stolen, Chatham House.* Available at www.chathamhouse.org/sites/default/files/public/Research/Africa/0913pr_nigeriaoil.pdf (accessed March 4, 2021), 1–68.

Mason, R., (April 19, 2014), *Nigeria Oil Spill Pay-Outs Would Encourage Terrorism Shell Claim.* The Telegraph, Saturday.

Nigeria Centres for Disease Control, (2021), *An Update of Covid-19 Outbreak in Nigeria.* Available at www.ncdc.gov.ng/disease/sitreps/?cat=cat&14&name=An%20update%20of %20Covid-19%20outbreak%20in%20Nigeria (accessed July 26, 2021).

Nigeria Natural Resource Charter, (2018), *NNRC Assess the Impact of Crude Oil Theft on Nigerians.* Available at www.nigerianrc.org/nnrc-assesses-the-impact-of-crude-oil-theft-onnigerians/ (accessed September 29, 2020).

Nigerian Extractive Industries Transparency Initiative (NEITI) Report 2018.

Nwosu, S.E.C., (2020), Commissioning of Petroleum Assets: Setting Agenda for an Emerging Subsector in the Nigerian Petroleum Industry. *The Journal of Jurisprudence, International Law and Contemporary Issues, Faculty of Law, Rivers State University,* 13(1), 31.

Occhiali, Giovanni, et al., (2020), *Overview of the Effect of COVID-19 on Nigeria's Energy Sector.* Chapter 7 (d1wqtxts1xzle7.cloudfront.net).

Ogbodo, S.G., and Aigbokhaevbo, V.O., (2014), Oil Crimes: The Nigerian Dimension, *Journal of Private & Comparative Law. Ahmadu Bello University, Zaria,* 6&7, 329–348.

Ogbuigwe, R., (2018), Ogbuigwe, A. (2018), Refining in Nigeria: History, Challenges and Perspectives. *Applied Petrochemical Research* 8, 181–192. https://doi.org/10.1007/s13203-018-0211-z. Available at https://link.springer.com/article/10.1007/s13203-018-0211-z (accessed March 29, 2022).

Oguche, S., (2020), Towards A Comprehensive Legal Framework for Controlling Dangerous Infectious Diseases in Nigeria: The National Health Emergency Bill 2020 in Perspective, Nigerian Institute of Advanced Legal Studies. *Health Law and Policy Journal,* 2(2), 214–240.

Oke, Y., (2016), *Nigerian Energy and Natural Resources Law (Notes and Materials)*, *Princeton & Associates Publishing Co. Ltd.* 9. Ezekiel Street, Off Toyin Street, Ikeja, Lagos), 1–5.

Oke, Y., (2019a), *Right – Based Approach to Energy Resources Governance in Nigeria, In Nigerian Energy Resources Law and Practice Oil and Gas Law Practice, Cases and Theories.* Princeton & Associates Publishing Co. Ltd, 9, Ezekiel Street, Off Toyin Street, Ikeja, Lagos), 444.

Oke, Y., (2019b), The Law, Practice and Regulation of the Downstream Sector of the Nigerian Gas. In *Nigerian Energy Resources Law and Practice Oil and Gas Law Practice, Cases and Theories*, Princeton & Associates Publishing Co. Ltd, 9, Ezekiel Street, Off Toyin Street, Ikeja, Lagos), 722.

Olujobi, O.J., (2017) Legal Framework for Combating Corruption in Nigeria: The Upstream Petroleum Sector in Perspective. *Journal of Advanced Research in Law and Economics*, VIII, 3(25): 956–970.

Olujobi, O.J., (2020a), Analysis of the Legal Framework Governing Gas Flaring in Nigeria's Upstream Petroleum Sector and the Need for Overhauling. *Social Sciences*, 9(8), 132.

Olujobi, O.J., (2020b), The Legal Sustainability of Energy Substitution in Nigeria's Electric Power Sector: Renewable Energy as Alternative. *Protection and Control of Modern Power Systems*, 5(1), 32.

Olujobi, O.J., (2021a), Combating Insolvency and Business Recovery Problems in the Oil Industry: Proposal for Improvement in Nigeria's Insolvency and Bankruptcy Legal Framework. *Heliyon*, 7, e06123, 1–11.

Olujobi, O.J., (2021b), Deregulation of the Downstream Petroleum Industry: An Overview of the Legal Quandaries and Proposal for Improvement in Nigeria. *Heliyon*, 7(4), e06848, 1–10.

Olujobi, O.J., (2021c), Nigeria's Upstream Petroleum Industry Anti-Corruption Legal Framework: The Necessity for Overhauling and Enrichment. *Journal of Money Laundering Control.* Available at www.emerald.com/insight/1368-5201.htm (accessed June 6, 2021), 1–24.

Olujobi, O.J., (2021d), Recouping Proceeds of Corruption: Are There Any Need to Reverse Extant Trends by Enacting Civil Forfeiture Legal Regime in Nigeria? *Journal of Money Laundering Control.* Available at www.emerald.com/insight/1368-5201.htm (accessed June 2021).

Olujobi, O.J, Olujobi, O.M., and Ufua, D.E., (2020), The Legal Regime on Renewable Energy as Alternative Sources of Energy in Nigeria's Power Sector: The Impacts and the Potentials. *Academy of Strategic Management Journal*, 19(3), 1–19.

Olujobi, O.J., and Olusola-Olujobi, T., (2020), Comparative Appraisals of Legal and Institutional Framework Governing Gas Flaring in Nigeria's Upstream Petroleum Sector: How Satisfactory? *Environmental Quality Management*, 1–14.

Olujobi, O.J., and Oyewunmi A.O., (2017), Annulment of Oil Licences in Nigeria's Upstream Petroleum Sector: A Legal Critique of the Costs and Benefits. *International Journal of Energy Economics and Policy*, 7(3), 364–369.

Olujobi, O.J., Oyewunmi, O.A, and Oyewunmi, A.E., (2018), Oil Spillage in Nigeria's Upstream Petroleum Sector: Beyond the Legal Frameworks. *International Journal of Energy Economics and Policy*, 8(1), 220–226.

Olujobi, O.J, and Yebisi, E.T., (2022), Combating the Crimes of Money Laundering and Terrorism Financing in Nigeria: A Legal Approach for Combating the Menace. *Journal of Money Laundering and Control.* Available at www.emerald.com/insight/content/doi/10.1108/JMLC-12-2021-0143/full/html (accessed February 28, 2022).

Olujobi, O.J., et al. (2022), *Carbon Emission, Solid Waste Management, and Electricity Generation: A Legal and Empirical Perspective for Renewable Energy in Nigeria, International Environmental Agreements: Politics, Law and Economics*. Springer Nature, Netherlands. doi 10.1007/s10784–021–09558. Available online at https://link.springer.com/article/10.1007%2Fs10784-021-09558-z#citeas.

Omoregie, U., (2018), *Nigeria's Petroleum Sector and GDP: The Missing Oil Refining Link*. Available at file:///c:/users/dr.%20olujobi%20olusola/downloads/nigeria%e2%80%99s%20petroleum%20sector%20and%20gdp-%20missing%20oil%20refining%20link%20(uyiosa%20omoregie,%20aug%202018)-2018–08–06t16_59_06.574z.pdf (accessed July 1, 2021).

Omorogbe, Y., (2003), *Oil and Gas Law in Nigeria* (Malthouse Law Series, Lagos), 182.

Onu, K.O.N., (2020), Impacts of the Covid -19 Pandemic on Environmental Protection and Health Care Waste Management in Nigeria. *Health Law and Policy Journal*, 2(2), 241–269.

Osinibi, O.M., (2016) Paper Over Cracks: The Niger Delta Amnesty Programme and the Challenge of Environmental Sustainability in Nigeria. *UNILAG Journal of Public Law*, 3, 104.

PriceWaterhouseCoopers, (2017), *Nigeria's Refining Revolution*. Available at www.pwc.com/ng/en/assets/pdf/nigerias-refining-revolution.pdf (accessed November 30, 2020).

PriceWaterhouseCoopers, (2019), *Refining in Nigeria*. Available at www.pwc.com/ng/en/assets/pdf/nigerias-refining-revolution.pdf (accessed January 1, 2021), 1–15.

Samba, D., & Simplice A.A., (2021), The Covid-19 Pandemic and the New Poor in Africa: The Straw That Broke the Camel's Back. *Forum for Social Economics*. https://doi.org/10.1080/07360932.2021.1884583

Soremi, T., (2020), The Implications of Oil Theft on Social and Economic Development in the Niger Delta. *Global Journal of Social Science*, 19, 1–11.

Ubani, N., (2005), *The Challenges of Building A New Refinery in Nigeria with Limited Energy Infrastructure & Regulated Petroleum Products Market*. Africa Session, Forum 22 paper. Being a Paper presented at the 18th World Petroleum Congress, Johannesburg, South Africa, and September 2005.

Ufua, D., Osabuohien, E., Ogbari, M, Falola, H., Okoh, E., and Lakhani, A., (2021). Re-Strategising Government Palliative Support Systems in Tackling the Challenges of COVID-19 Lockdown in Lagos State, Nigeria. *Global Journal of Flexible Systems Management, 22*, 19–32. https://doi.org/10.1007/s40171-021-00263-z

Usman, A.K., (2017), *Nigerian Oil and Gas Industry: Institutions, Issues, Law and Policies, Malthouse Press Limited, Lagos, 2017*. In Refining Petroleum and Processing of Gas, 383.

A Second Voluntary National Review, (2020), Nigeria, Integration of the SDGs into National Development Planning, available at https://sustainabledevelopment.un.org/content/documents/26308VNR_2020_Nigeria_Report.pdf (accessed June 29, 2022).

Olujobi, O.J.; Yebisi, T.E.; Patrick, O.P.; Ariremako, A.I., (2022), The Legal Framework for Combating Gas Flaring in Nigeria's Oil and Gas Industry: Can It Promote Sustainable Energy Security? *Sustainability* 14, 7626. 2022

World Health Organisation, (2020), Ebola Virus Disease, available on line at, https://www.who.int/health-topics/ebola#tab=tab_1(access June 29, 2022).

16 Remittance Shocks and Poverty Reduction Nexus in Nigeria

Insights from Bootstrap Simulation and Asymmetric Causality Tests

Clement Olalekan Olaniyi and Mojeed Muhammed Ologundudu

1. Introduction

Poverty has continued to be a major socioeconomic problem in countries across the globe. Meanwhile, the incidence of poverty appears to be more severe on some continents than on others. Sub-Saharan Africa (SSA) is more affected by poverty than other continents in the world (Solarin et al., 2021; Ndlovu & Toerien, 2020; Folarin & Adeniyi, 2020; Osabohien *et al.*, 2020; Keho, 2017). It has been discovered that half of the people living in extreme poverty in the world are from SSA (Anetor et al., 2020; Osabohien *et al.*, 2020; World Bank, 2019). It has equally been reported that more than 50.7% of the extremely poor in the world are from countries in SSA (Omar & Inaba, 2020; World Bank, 2016a). The projection has been made that SSA risks being home to 70% of the extremely poor in the world (Koomson et al., 2020; Coulibaly, 2020; Kharas et al., 2018). Additionally, the severity and extremity of poverty vary among countries in SAA. In recent times, among SSA countries, Nigeria has been tagged as the world 'capital poverty' (World Poverty Clock, 2018; Yomi, 2018; Kharas et al., 2018). This is corroborated by the fact that the country has the highest number of people living in extreme poverty across the globe. The statistics in the June report of 2018 by the World Poverty Clock (2018) revealed that 86.9 million Nigerians spend less than $1.90 a day. This further rose to 91 million in 2019. This implies that more than three million Nigerians slipped into extreme poverty (Aderounmu et al., 2021).

Despite the population of India being five times that of Nigeria, it is shocking that Nigeria has more people living in extreme poverty than India (Solarin *et al.*, 2021; Okoi, 2019). It reveals that the incidence of extreme poverty in Nigeria is chronic to the extent that the majority of the populace cannot afford basic needs of life, such as food, clothing, and quality education (Olowookere et al., 2021). To address the problem of extreme poverty in Nigeria, several policies and programmes have been formulated and implemented. Meanwhile, the persistent rise in extreme poverty signals the ineffectiveness of government policies and programmes. It has been reported that the number of people living in extreme poverty in Nigeria increases by six every minute (Fowowe & Shuaibu, 2021; World Poverty Clock, 2018).

DOI: 10.4324/9781003208358-21

The deplorable states of extreme poverty and economic and working conditions in Nigeria have caused many productive working classes to migrate to other countries searching for greener pastures. Most Nigerian youths see migration as a panacea to socioeconomic problems. Thus, Nigeria has become a labour-exporting country (Adeosun & Popogbe, 2021; Oluwafemi & Ayandibu, 2014). This mass exodus of the trained, skilful and professional Nigeria's workforce to foreign countries has made the country attract many remittance inflows from Nigerians in the diaspora to support the livelihoods of poor dependants at home. Presently, Nigeria is the largest recipient of remittance inflows in SSA, and it equally comes sixth in the global ranking (Fowowe & Shuaibu, 2021; Iyemifokhae, 2020; Nwokoye et al., 2020; World Bank, 2016b, 2018).

Remittance inflows to Nigeria remain the second-highest source of foreign exchange earnings after petrol-dollars (Didia & Tahir, 2022; Nwokoye *et al.*, 2020; Urama et al., 2017; Oluwafemi & Ayandibu, 2014). Moreover, remittances are the highest source of unearned foreign capital inflows to the country (Akeerebari, 2022). Paradoxically, it is obvious that both remittance inflows and poverty have been increasing in the case of Nigeria, and it remains a subject of empirical investigation to know whether the surge in remittance inflows catalyses poverty reduction.

Similarly, the issues surrounding the inflows of remittances to Nigeria have taken new twists as a result of the probable devastating socioeconomic effects of the COVID-19 pandemic on the poor. It is on the record that remittances to the country have declined (Abdullahi, 2020; The World Bank, 2021). Amid the COVID-2019 crisis, it is reported that remittance inflows to Nigeria were reduced by 28% in 2020. Specifically, COVID-19 wiped off $5 billion of remittances flows to the country. This might have threatened the stability and economic conditions of the poor in Nigeria. This signals that the fall in remittances to Nigeria might lead to increased poverty and wane access to basic needs by Nigeria's poor (The World Bank, 2022. This indicates that the COVID-19 crisis might have compounded the issues surrounding the extreme poverty and remittance-poverty nexus in Nigeria. Following this murky situation, several studies on Nigeria have investigated the impact of remittances on poverty (Fowowe & Shuaibu, 2021; Olowookere *et al.*, 2021; Iyemifokhae, 2020). It remains unclear whether remittance inflows have been judiciously utilised to catalyse poverty-reducing activities such as productive and entrepreneurial ventures that provide employment opportunities and increase the income and standard of living of the poor (Iyemifokhae, 2020).

A plethora of empirical studies exist on the impact of remittance inflows on poverty in the extant literature (see Acheampong et al., 2021; Azizi, 2021; Fowowe & Shuaibu, 2021; Olowookere *et al.*, 2021; Arapi-Gjini et al., 2020; Iyemifokhae, 2020; Abduvaliev & Bustillo, 2020; Butkus et al., 2020; Musakwa & Odhiambo, 2019; Kumar, 2019; Adams Jr. & Page, 2005), but the outputs of extant studies are mixed and inconclusive. Specifically, the results of these studies fall into three categories. Some studies find a poverty-mitigating effect of remittance inflows, while few others establish a poverty-enhancing effect. A few other studies report the insignificant role of remittance inflows as a catalyst for poverty reduction. Although it should be stressed that most of the extant studies reveal that remittances spur poverty reduction in remittance-receiving countries (Acheampong *et al.*, 2021; Musakwa & Odhiambo, 2021), remittances have a poverty-mitigating effect. The inconclusiveness of the extant studies could be attributed to many factors that include different methodologies, varying measures of poverty, diverse scopes, and the types of regression analyses (cross-sectional, panel and time-series perspectives).

There is rich content in the literature on the impact of remittances on poverty, but empirical studies on the causality between remittances and poverty are still scarce, notwithstanding the significance of its policy dimensions and priorities to government, especially in developing countries (Musakwa & Odhiambo, 2020, 2021). The bulk of extant studies suppress the possibility that poverty could be a causal driver that spurs remittance inflows. It has been explained in existing studies that a high incidence of extreme poverty prompts cause and spur remittance inflows from migrant workers. On the other hand, remittance inflows have been described as catalysts to reduce poverty by supporting the income and consumption of poor dependants in remittance-receiving countries.

Remittance inflows help families in remittance-receiving countries meet increased needs for livelihood support. At the micro-level, remittances tend to improve the welfare of remittance-receiving households by increasing their consumption and income, which eases the capital constraints of the poor. The two perspectives indicate that remittance inflows and poverty can reinforce each other (Hatemi-J & Uddin, 2014). Thus, the relationship could be bidirectional. The nascent empirical literature on the causality between remittances and poverty is contentious and mixed. The results are categorised into four dimensions.

Studies such as Olowookere *et al.* (2021) for Nigeria; Musakwa & Odhiambo (2020) for Botswana; Azam *et al.* (2016) for 39 countries; Sanchez-Loor & Zambrano-Monserrate (2015) for Colombia, Ecuador, and Mexico; Satti et al. (2016) and Yasmin et al. (2015) for Pakistan; Gaaliche & Gaaliche (2014) for 14 emerging and developing countries; and Hatemi-J & Uddin (2014) for Bangladesh found evidence of bidirectional causality between remittance and poverty. Meanwhile, unidirectional causality from poverty to remittance inflows was established in the works of Musakwa & Odhiambo (2021) for South Africa in the short run, Musakwa & Odhiambo (2020) for Botswana. Another strand of studies, such as Siani (2020) for WAEMU countries detected the causal flow from remittance to poverty. A few other studies found evidence of no causal relationship between remittance inflow and poverty reduction (Azam *et al.* 2016; Sanchez-Loor & Zambrano-Monserrate 2015). Mixed results were established in the study by Aloui & Maktouf (2021) for SSA; two-way causality was found in the whole panel of SSA, West, East, and Southern Africa, while unidirectional causality from remittances to poverty was established in the case of Central Africa. Aside from the inconclusiveness of extant studies on the causality between remittance inflows and poverty, there are obvious missing gaps in the body of knowledge that need to be bridged.

All the extant studies assumed linearity and symmetry in the causality between remittance and poverty. This assumption has been questioned and tagged as a mere simplifying assumption in modern advances in empirical analysis and econometrics that are incongruent with realities (Olayeni et al., 2021; Hatemi-J & El-Khatib, 2020; Olaniyi & Olayeni, 2020; Olaniyi, 2019, 2020; Hatemi-J & Mustafa, 2016; Hatemi-J, 2012). Extant studies assumed that the causal impacts of negative and positive shocks between remittance and poverty indicators are equal in absolute terms and magnitudes. Allowance was not made to separate positive shocks from negative shocks in remittance inflows and indicators of poverty. This supposition might be too suppressive, as it rules out the possibility of nonlinearity and asymmetric structure in the data distribution. It has been equally observed that people respond more to negative shocks than positive shocks (Olaniyi, 2020; Granger & Yoon, 2002; Hatemi-J, 2012). This study is a maiden attempt to examine asymmetric causality between remittances and poverty. Symmetric and linear approaches provide limited information and more restricted policy dimensions to guide government and stakeholders.

Asymmetric causality divulges several dimensions of hidden information that are highly advantageous to stakeholders and policymakers. Moreover, asymmetric causality is carried out within the context of bootstrap simulation with leverage adjustments, which produce more reliable and accurate critical values (Olaniyi, 2020; Hatemi-J, 2012; Hacker & Hatemi-J, 2010). The approach equally accommodates variables that are not normally distributed and volatile. Nigeria's data are used to examine asymmetric causality in this study. The trend analyses of remittance inflows and poverty indicators reveal clear evidence of asymmetric structures in the data distribution. Additionally, there are puzzles to unravel about the nexus in the case of Nigeria. Remittance inflows are supposed to catalyse reduction in poverty in Nigeria, but extreme poverty has continued to surge in the country. Thus, there is a need to use a more sophisticated approach to unravel the hidden information on the causal nexus between remittances and poverty in Nigeria.

Aside from the introductory aspect, the subsequent sections are arranged as follows: Section 2 centres on the data description and methodology, while Section 3 addresses the issues relating to the presentation and discussion of empirical findings. The chapter ends with a conclusion and some policy recommendations.

2. Data Description and Methodology

2.1 *Data sources*

This study utilises annual data on Nigeria for the period 1981–2020. Data on all the variables used in this study are gleaned from the World Development Indicators (WDI) of the World Bank. Following the position of extant studies (Musakwa & Odhiambo, 2020, 2021; Hatemi-J & Uddin, 2014), remittance inflow is measured as personal remittances received as a ratio of GDP. Consistent with the definition of the World Bank, personal remittance is the sum of personal transfers and compensation of employees by Nigerians abroad. The per capita consumption is used as a proxy for poverty.

Following the definition of the World Bank, poverty is "the inability to attain a minimal standard of living". Thus, per capita consumption is chosen as a proxy for poverty. The World Bank's definition sees poverty in terms of basic consumption needs. Consistent with previous studies, data on consumption expenditures among the poor are readily available, and it is also more stable than income measures such as per capita income (Odhiambo, 2009a; Woolard & Leibbrandt, 1999; Ravallion, 1992). Scholars have hinted that consumption-based measures of poverty portray welfare better than income-based measures (Koomson et al., 2020; World Bank, 2001). Several studies have used consumption expenditure as a more reliable measure of welfare and a preferred indicator of household living standards (Beegle et al., 2012) because it shows the ability of people to meet and satisfy basic and minimum consumption needs, both food and nonfood components, which is often described as a poverty line (Osabohien *et al.*, 2021; Koomson *et al.*, 2020). Furthermore, many studies have used this measure of poverty. These studies include Das et al. (2021), Solarin *et al.* (2021), Musakwa & Odhiambo (2020, 2021), Akinlo & Dada (2021), Adeleye et al. (2020), Danlami *et al.* (2020), Appiah et al. (2020), Ho & Iyke (2018), Garza-Rodriguez (2018), Sehrawat & Giri (2016a, b), Dhrifi (2015), Uddin *et al.* (2014), Hatemi-J & Uddin (2014), Odhiambo (2009a, b) and Quartey (2005). Recent studies have affirmed that Africa has the lowest household consumption expenditures despite the continent being the second most populous continent in the world (Solarin *et al.*, 2021).

2.2 Model Specification

Following the modelling style of Hatemi-J (2012), data on poverty indicators (per capita consumption) and remittance inflows are decomposed into cumulative positive and negative changes. This idea of data decomposition originated from Granger & Yoon (2002) and was later extended to causality by Hatemi-J (2012). Asymmetric causality is inferred because negative and positive shocks are expected to have different causal impacts. In line with the assumptions that the variables $\left[poverty(pov)\,and\,remittance(rem)\right]$ are integrated of order one $I[1]$, and they observe random walk processes. Given these assumptions, the variables are defined as follows in equations (1) and (2):

$$pov_{1t} = pov_{1t-1} + \varepsilon_{1t} = pov_{10} + \sum_{i=1}^{t} \varepsilon_{1i} \quad (1)$$

and

$$rem_{2t} = rem_{2t-1} + \varepsilon_{2t} = rem_{20} + \sum_{i=1}^{t} \varepsilon_{2i} \quad (2)$$

where $t = 1, 2, \ldots, T$ is the time covered in the study. The pow_{10} and rem_{20} are constant terms at the initial values, while the error terms are defined as $\varepsilon_1 i$ and ε_{2i}. The cumulative positive changes in both *pov* and *rem* are defined as $\varepsilon_{1i}^{+} = \max(\varepsilon_{1i}, 0)$ *and* $\varepsilon_{2i}^{+} = \max(\varepsilon_{2i}, 0)$ *respectively*. While the cumulative negative changes are stated as $\varepsilon_{1i}^{-} = \min(\varepsilon_{1i}, 0)$ *and* $\varepsilon_{2i}^{-} = \min(\varepsilon_{2i}, 0)$ respectively. Hence, ε_{1i} is defined as $\varepsilon_{1i}^{+} + \varepsilon_{1i}^{-}$ while ε_{2i} is also defined *as* $\varepsilon_{2i}^{+} + \varepsilon_{2i}^{-}$. Based on these expressions, it implies that:

$$pov_{1t} = pov_{1t-1} + \varepsilon_{1t} = pov_{1,0} + \sum_{i=1}^{t} \varepsilon_{1i}^{+} + \sum_{i=1}^{t} \varepsilon_{1i}^{-} \tag{3}$$

similarly

$$rem_{2t} = rem_{2t-1} + \varepsilon_{2t} = rem_{2,0} + \sum_{i=1}^{t} \varepsilon_{2i}^{+} + \sum_{i=1}^{t} \varepsilon_{2i}^{-} \tag{4}$$

Subsequently, the positive and negative shocks of the variables are defined in cumulative forms thus

$$pov_{1t}^{+} = \sum_{i=1}^{t} \varepsilon_{1i}^{+} \text{ and } pov_{1t}^{-} = \sum_{i=1}^{t} \varepsilon_{1i}^{-};\ rem_{2t}^{+} = \sum_{i=1}^{t} \varepsilon_{2i}^{+} \text{ and } rem_{2t}^{-} = \sum_{i=1}^{t} \varepsilon_{2i}^{-}$$

where positive shocks are pov_{1t}^{+} and rem_{2t}^{+} while negative shocks are pov_{1t}^{-} and rem_{2t}^{-}. These constructed components are defined as follows: pov_{1t}^{+} is the unanticipated increase in per capita consumption, while pov_{1t}^{-} is the unanticipated decline in per capita consumption. rem_{2t}^{+} is the unanticipated rise in remittance inflows, while rem_{2t}^{-} is the unanticipated fall in remittance inflows. These constructed variables are in cumulative forms.

These derived variables (positive and negative shocks), by construction, are presumed to have an impact on the underlying variable. The causality between these constructed variables is examined. The focus of modelling for causality is on the pair of positive shocks in both poverty and remittance. The causality test is carried out using the vector autoregressive model of order *p*, VAR (p). Testing the causality between cumulative positive shocks' component of pov_{1t}^{+} and rem_{1t}^{+} such as $\left(pov_{1t}^{+}\ rem_{2t}^{+}\right)$. Aside from the pairs of positive shocks in equation (5), all other possible pairs are also considered. The VAR (p) model under the null hypothesis of no asymmetric causality is expressed as follows:

$$\begin{bmatrix} pov_{1t}^{+} \\ rem_{2t}^{+} \end{bmatrix} = \begin{bmatrix} \propto_0 \\ \beta_0 \end{bmatrix} + \begin{bmatrix} \sum_{r=1}^{p} \alpha_{1r} & \sum_{r=1}^{p} \alpha_{21r} \\ \sum_{r=1}^{k} \beta_{1r} & \sum_{r=1}^{k} \beta_{21r} \end{bmatrix} \times \begin{bmatrix} pov_{1t-r}^{+} \\ rem_{2t-r}^{+} \end{bmatrix} + \begin{bmatrix} \varepsilon_1^{+} \\ \varepsilon_2^{+} \end{bmatrix} \tag{5}$$

Following the proposition of Toda & Yamamoto (1995) and Hatemi-J (2012), to account for the unit root process, an unrestricted extra lag is included in equation (5). An optimal lag is chosen following an innovative lag-based Hatemi-J Information Criterion which is specified as follows:

$$\text{HJC} = \text{In}\left(\left|\hat{B}_r\right|\right) + r\left(\frac{n^2 InT + 2n^2 In\left(InT\right)}{2T}\right), \qquad r = 0,\ldots,p. \tag{6}$$

$\left|\hat{B}_r\right|$ is the determinant in the VAR model in equation (5) of the estimated variance-covariance matrix of the error terms with lag order r, n is for the number of equations in the VAR model and T is the number of observations. The null hypothesis that rem_{1t}^{+} does not cause pov_{2t}^{+} and that pov_{2t}^{+} does not cause rem_{1t}^{+} are formulated as follows:

$$H_0 : \alpha_{21_r} = 0, \forall r, \tag{7}$$

and

$$H_0 : \beta_{21_r} = 0, \forall r, \tag{8}$$

where $r = 1,\ldots,p$. Consistent with the works of Hatemi-J (2012) and Hatemi-J & El-Khatib (2016), the null hypotheses are examined through the modified Wald test which is compared to bootstrapped critical values. Evidence of causality is affirmed if the value of the Wald test statistic is above the bootstrapped critical value at the conventional levels. Otherwise, evidence of causality is rejected. The Wald test statistics and bootstrapped critical values are obtained via 10,000 iterations in the GUASS code provided by Hacker & Hatemi-J (2010). Data decompositions of poverty and remittance into cumulative positive and negative changes are implemented in the GUASS code supplied by Hatemi-J (2014).

3. Discussion on Empirical Findings

3.1 *Data Decomposition*

Data on the poverty reduction indicator (proxy by per capita consumption, *pov*) and remittance inflows (*rem*) are decomposed into cumulative negative and positive changes via the GUASS codes supplied by Hatemi-J (2014), and it is an offshoot of the earlier GUASS codes provided by Hatemi-J (2012). The collection of graphs in Figure 16.1 indicates clear evidence of an asymmetric structure in the data distribution. The graphical illustrations of raw data of per capita consumption and remittance inflows and their respective positive and negative shock components affirm the need to capture asymmetric structures in the causality between remittances and poverty reduction in Nigeria. The data equally display evidence of unit root processes in the data distribution.

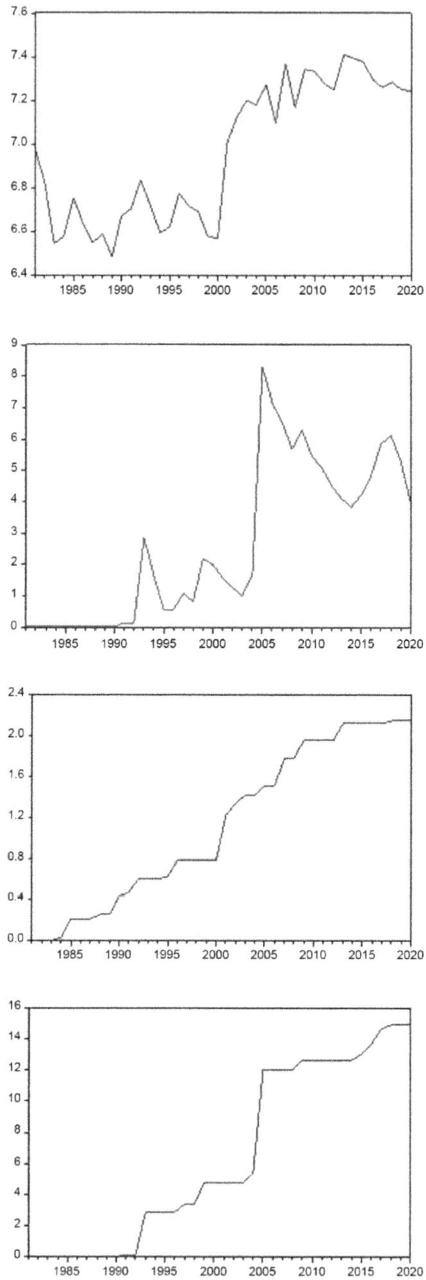

Figure 16.1 The time plots of the poverty indicator and remittance inflows

Note: The time plots of the poverty indicator and remittance inflows as well as their positive and negative cumulative sums *pov* represent the poverty indicator, while *rem* denotes remittance inflows. The cumulative positive sum of each variable is denoted by +, and the cumulative negative sum is denoted by −.

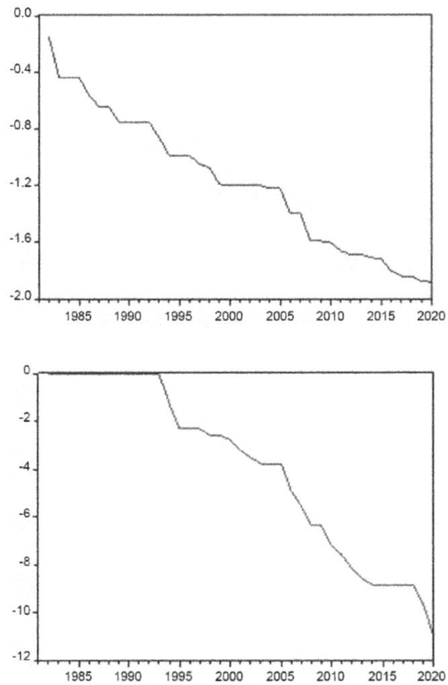

Figure 16.1 (Continued)

3.2 *Unit Root Tests*

Testing for stationarity properties of the underlying variables is a prerequisite to the use of the asymmetric causality approach of Hatemi-J (2012). This method is built around Toda & Yamamoto (1995), which requires the addition of extra lag in the vector autoregressive model. The unit root processes of the variables determine the number of extra lags to be included. Thus, augmented Dickey-Fuller (ADF) and Phillips–Perron approaches of unit root tests are utilised to determine the extra lags.

The results of unit root tests are presented in Tables 16.1 and 16.2. It is obvious from the results that most of the variables and their respective shock components attain stationarity at first difference. Only raw data of the poverty indicator and its negative shock components attain stationarity at the level in the results for intercept and trend. These results are confirmed in both the ADF and PP tests. This finding suggests the robustness of the decisions from the unit root tests. The unit root tests affirm the existence of unit root processes in the variables and their components. Thus, an extra one lag must be included in the Hatemi-J approach of causality, which accounts for bootstrap simulations with leverage adjustment for robustness and high precisions. It is important to hint that the results of cointegration tests are not reported in this study, which is premised on the fact that the cointegration

Table 16.1 Unit Root Test (Augmented Dickey-Fuller, ADF)

Variables	*Level*		*First Difference*	
	Intercept	*Intercept and Trend*	*Intercept*	*Intercept and Trend*
pov	−1.202	−3.503**	−7.005***	−6.925***
rem	−1.731	−2.792	−6.238***	−6.156***
Pov+	−0.819	−1.794	−6.743***	−6.736***
Rem+	−0.298	−2.580	−5.980***	−5.910***
Pov ⁻	−1.993	−4.912**	−8.885***	−8.815***
Rem ⁻	1.722	−2.357	−3.531**	−3.930**

Note: *** and ** stand for 1 and 5 percentage levels of significance

Table 16.2 Unit Root Test (Phillips–Perron, PP)

Variables	*Level*		*First Difference*	
	Intercept	*Intercept and Trend*	*Intercept*	*Intercept and Trend*
pov	−1.074	−3.515**	−7.584***	−7.470***
rem	−1.575	−2.821	−7.272***	−7.346***
Pov+	−0.837	−1.812	−6.777***	−6.813***
Rem+	−0.154	−2.635	−6.071***	−5.992***
Pov –	−2.261	−4.903**	−10.004***	−10.800***
Rem –	1.447	−2.007	−3.159**	−3.405*

Note: ***, **, and * represent the 1, 5, and 10 percentage levels of significance

test is not a prerequisite to testing causality between integrated variables within the VAR framework as long as extra unrestricted lags are added (Olaniyi, 2020; Hatemi-J, 2012; Toda & Yamamoto, 1995).

3.3 *Linear causality tests*

To ensure the robustness of the result, we first follow the study of Hatemi-J & Uddin (2014), which examined the linear causality between remittances and poverty in Bangladesh. This is done within the bootstrap simulations with leverage adjustment as proposed by Hacker & Hatemi-J (2010). The result of linear bootstrapped causality is reported in Table 16.3. The findings of linear and symmetric causality reveal that there is no causal relationship between remittance inflows and poverty in Nigeria.

The result implies that persistent inflows of remittances to Nigeria have not led to a significant reduction in poverty. This may suggest that the bulk of the money received by the households in Nigeria is expended on things that are not poverty mitigating in nature. On the other hand, the result of linear causality from poverty to remittance inflows reveals that a high incidence of extreme poverty might not be the reason migrant workers (Nigerians in diaspora) are sending money home. It

Table 16.3 Linear (Symmetric) Bootstrap Causality with Leverage Adjustment

Null Hypothesis	*Wald Test Statistics*	*Bootstrap Critical Value at 1%*	*Bootstrap Critical Value at 5%*	*Bootstrap Critical Value at 10%*	*Lag Order*
rem≠>pov	0.153	7.622	4.141	2.844	1
pov ≠>rem	0.994	7.703	4.105	2.866	1

equally suggests that remittances sent home by Nigerian migrants do not spur poverty reduction by improving their living standards. Although these outcomes appear surprising because Nigeria is a high remittance-receiving country, it is less shocking in the sense that extreme poverty has been increasing in recent times. This result stands incongruent with the study by Hatemi-J & Uddin (2014), which adopted the same approach in the case of Bangladesh and obtained bidirectional causality between remittances and poverty. Meanwhile, the findings corroborate the results of studies by Azam *et al.* (2016) and Sanchez-Loor & Zambrano-Monserrate (2015). These studies found evidence of no causality between the two variables, which implies that they are independent of each other. Thus, policy dimensions on both remittance inflows and poverty reduction in Nigeria can be formulated and implemented independently of each other. Meanwhile, this approach might not be rich in the content, as nonlinearity and asymmetric structures are not accounted for. Thus, asymmetric causality is examined and discussed in the subsequent section.

3.4 *Asymmetric Causality Tests*

This subsection extends the frontier of knowledge on the causal relationship between remittances and poverty by incorporating asymmetric structure and nonlinearity. The results of asymmetric causality within the framework of bootstrap simulations with leverage adjustment are presented in Table 16.4. All the possible combinations of pairs of shock components (positive and negative) are carefully considered. The results indicate that there is clear evidence of causality in the nexus between remittance inflows and poverty in Nigeria. The pair [rem^- pov^-] of negative shocks in both poverty and remittances reveals that there is a bidirectional causality. From one side, the result shows that a decline in remittance inflows to Nigeria [rem^-] spur and triggers an increase in poverty [pov^-].

In practical applications, this implies that persistent falls in remittance inflows cause corresponding declines in the per capita consumption and welfare of the poor in Nigeria. The asymmetric causality divulges hidden information that linear and symmetric causality fail to detect. This re-emphasises the significance of incorporating an asymmetric structure in the causality between remittances and poverty. This finding implies that a drop in remittances from Nigerian migrants in the diaspora will aggravate the extremity and burdens of poverty in the country. On the other side of the coin, it is reported that a persistent increase in poverty [pov^-], that is, a fall in per capita consumption, causes a decline in remittance inflows [rem^-] to Nigeria.

Table 16.4 Asymmetric (Nonlinear) Bootstrap Causality with Leverage Adjustment

Null Hypothesis	*Wald Test Statistics*	*Bootstrap Critical Value at 1%*	*Bootstrap Critical Value at 5%*	*Bootstrap Critical Value at 10%*	*Lag Order*
rem+ ≠> pov+	0.003	15.558	4.081	2.375	1
pov+ ≠> rem+	0.276	19.538	4.839	2.713	1
rem – ≠>pov –	11.073**	14.194	3.997	2.446	1
pov – ≠> rem –	4.002**	12.235	3.800	2.401	1
rem+ ≠> pov –	0.750	16.845	4.112	2.413	1
pov – ≠> rem+	0.222	18.031	4.553	2.416	1
rem – ≠> pov+	6.273**	13.337	4.149	2.507	1
pov+ ≠> rem –	0.471	12.463	4.049	2.553	1

Notes: ** denotes 5 percentage level of significance; Bootstrapped critical values are obtained via 10,000 iterations

This result implies that if the extent of extreme poverty continues to rise despite the continued rise in inflows of remittances to support the livelihoods of the dependants at home, Nigerian migrants might be discouraged from sending more money home. This is inferred because migrants might be disincentivised to support the poor at home since their conditions remain unchanged and the remittances have no poverty-mitigating effects. Additionally, asymmetric causality from a fall in remittance inflows [*rem–*] to an increase in per capita consumption [*pov*$^{+}$], a fall in poverty, is detected. This suggests that if remittance inflows are pruned to reduce spending on frivolities and unproductive activities, they might not yield more employment opportunities and better income for the extremely poor. This process may give the poor more access to more funds that will spur an improvement in their welfare. Alternatively, it suggests that if the remittance inflows are transferred to the rich instead of the poor, it may end up causing and worsening extreme poverty in Nigeria. Another perspective is that a persistent fall in remittance inflows could force poor Nigerians to be more innovative, creative, and productive to engage in activities that will make their lives better off. This study has successfully introduced a new dimension into the studies on the causal relationship between remittance and remittance by establishing the necessity of incorporating nonlinearity and asymmetric structures, which previous studies have neglected.

4. Summary and Conclusion

There are a plethora of studies on the impact of remittance inflows on poverty reduction in high remittance-receiving countries in the extant literature. The bulk of these studies assumed that there is no feedback effect from poverty on remittance inflows. Meanwhile, the research outcomes of a few studies that examined the causality between remittances and poverty are mixed and inconclusive.

Aside from the inconclusiveness of existing studies, these studies assumed symmetry and linearity in the causal relationship between remittances and poverty.

This assumption has been faulted in recent advances in econometrics, and it appears not to be consistent with economic realities. Thus, the present study deviates from the existing studies by introducing asymmetric structures and nonlinearity into the causal nexus between remittances and poverty in Nigeria for the period 1981–2020. This approach follows the method of Hatemi-J (2012), which is carried out within the framework of robust bootstrap simulations with leverage adjustments. Nigeria's data are adopted due to peculiar situations and puzzles surrounding the remittance inflows and extremity of poverty in the country. Moreover, there are asymmetric structures and nonlinearity in the trend analysis of remittances and per capita consumption, a proxy for poverty reduction. Thus, utilising the asymmetric causality approach is of utmost importance.

The findings from linear and symmetric causality reveal no evidence of causality, which indicates an independent relationship between remittance inflows and poverty in Nigeria. Meanwhile, clear cases of hidden causality are detected when an asymmetric approach within the framework of bootstrap simulations with leverage adjustment is utilised. Bidirectional causality is established between the pair of negative shock components in remittances and poverty. On one side of the coin, it reveals that the declines in remittance inflows (negative shocks in remittance) spur and cause an increase in poverty (negative shocks in per capita consumption) in Nigeria. This implies that extreme poverty tends to increase in Nigeria if there is a persistent drop in the inflows of remittances. On the other hand, a rise in poverty tends to cause a decline in remittance inflows. This shows that Nigeria's migrants in the diaspora might be discouraged from sending money back home if it is clear that remittances do not improve the living standards of poor dependants at home. Last, it is found that a drop in remittance inflows to Nigeria propels a fall in poverty. This implies that if remittances are not forthcoming again, it would create an incentive to work hard in the poor, and this will open the eyes of the poor to opportunities and innovative ventures that could trigger an improvement in their living standards.

This study has contributed to the extant literature by incorporating asymmetric structure and nonlinearity into the causal relationship between remittances and poverty. The Stakeholder and government agencies are encouraged to monitor the asymmetric structures in the dynamics of remittances and poverty in Nigeria. Additionally, the attention of stakeholders should be shifted to the sensitivity of declines in remittance inflows to poverty reduction in Nigeria. It is important to stress that this study specifically considered the case of Nigeria, and other scholars are, therefore, encouraged to consider incorporating asymmetric structures in the causal nexus between remittance inflows and poverty for other countries.

References

Abdullahi, A. (2020). Examining the linkage between migrant remittances, entrepreneurship development and Covid-19 in Nigeria. *Gusau International Journal of Management and Social Sciences*, 3(1), 118–134.

Abduvaliev, M., & Bustillo, R. (2020). Impact of remittances on economic growth and poverty reduction among CIS countries. *PostCommunist Economies*, 32(4), 525–546.

Acheampong, A. O., Appiah-Otoo, I., Dzator, J., & Agyemang, K. K. (2021). Remittances, financial development and poverty reduction in Sub-Saharan Africa: Implications for post-COVID-19 macroeconomic policies. *Journal of Policy Modelling*, 43(6), 1365–1387. https://doi.org/10.1016/j.jpolmod.2021.09.005

Adams Jr, R. H., & Page, J. (2005). Do international migration and remittances reduce poverty in developing countries? *World Development*, 33(10), 1645–1669.

Adeleye, B. N., Gershon, O., Ogundipe, A., Owolabi, O., Ogunrinola, I., & Adediran, O. (2020). Comparative investigation of the growth-poverty-inequality trilemma in Sub-Saharan Africa and Latin American and Caribbean Countries. *Heliyon*, 6(12), e05631.

Adeosun, O. T., & Popogbe, O. O. (2021). Human capital flight and output growth nexus: Evidence from Nigeria. *Review of Economics and Political Science*, 6(3), 206–222. https://doi.org/10.1108/REPS-07-2020-0088

Aderounmu, B., Azuh, D., Onanuga, O., Ogundipe, O., Bowale, E., & Azuh, A. (2021). Poverty drivers and Nigeria's development: Implications for policy intervention. *Cogent Arts & Humanities*, 8(1), 1927495.

Akeerebari, T. J. (2022). Dynamic modelling of the influence of diaspora cash remittance on macroeconomic stability in Nigeria. *European Journal of Social Sciences Studies*, *7*(2), 76–100. http://doi.org/10.46827/ejsss.v7i2.1221

Akinlo, T., & Dada, J. T. (2021). The moderating effect of foreign direct investment on environmental degradation-poverty reduction nexus: evidence from sub-Saharan African countries. *Environment, Development, and Sustainability*, 23, 15764–15784. https://doi.org/10.1007/s10668-021-01315-1

Aloui, Z., & Maktouf, S. (2021). The impact of foreign direct investment and international remittances on poverty: Evidence from Sub-Saharan African Countries in 1996–2017. *Transnational Corporations Review*, 1–12.

Anetor, F. O., Esho, E., & Verhoef, G. (2020). The impact of foreign direct investment, foreign aid and trade on poverty reduction: Evidence from Sub-Saharan African countries. *Cogent Economics & Finance*, 8(1), 1737347. https://doi.org/10.1080/23322039.2020.1737347

Appiah, M., Frowne, D. I., & Tetteh, D. (2020). Re-examining the nexus between financial development and poverty reduction: Evidence from emerging economies. *Applied Economics Journal*, *27*(2), 125–144.

Arapi-Gjini, A., Möllers, J., & Herzfeld, T. (2020). Measuring dynamic effects of remittances on poverty and inequality with evidence from Kosovo. *Eastern European Economics*, 58(4), 283–308.

Azam, M., Haseeb, M., & Samsudin, S. (2016). The impact of foreign remittances on poverty alleviation: Global evidence. *Economics & Sociology*, 9(1), 264–281.

Azizi, S. (2021). The impacts of workers' remittances on poverty and inequality in developing countries. *Empirical Economics*, 60(2), 969–991.

Beegle, K., De Weerdt, J., Friedman, J., & Gibson, J. (2012). Methods of household consumption measurement through surveys: Experimental results from Tanzania. *Journal of Development Economics*, 98(1), 3–18. https://doi.org/10.1016/j.jdeve co.2011.11.001

Butkus, M., Matuzevičiūtė, K., & Raupytė, K. (2020). Effects of remittances on poverty: Evidence in CEE countries. *Organisations and Markets in Emerging Economies*, *11*(1), 69–82.

Coulibaly, B. S. (2020). *Foresight Africa: Top priorities for the continent 2020 to 2030*. Africa Growth Initiative, Brookings Institute. https://media.africaportal.org/documents/ForesightAfrica2020_2030.pdf

Danlami, I. A., Hidthiir, M. H., & Hassan, S. (2020). Evidence of inflation-poverty causality in Nigeria based on the Toda-Yamamoto dynamic causality test. *Journal of Business and Social Review in Emerging Economies*, 6(1), 277–286.
Das, P., Paria, B., & Firdaush, S. (2021). Juxtaposing consumption poverty and multidimensional poverty: A study in Indian context. *Social Indicators Research*, *153*(2), 469–501.
Dhrifi, A. (2015). Financial development and the "growth-inequality-poverty" triangle. *Journal of the Knowledge Economy*, 6(4), 1163–1176.
Didia, D., & Tahir, S. (2022). Enhancing economic growth and government revenue generation in Nigeria: The role of diaspora remittances. *The Review of Black Political Economy*, English (United Kingdom). https://doi.org/10.1177%2F00346446211025647
Folarin, O., & Adeniyi, O. (2020). Does tourism reduce poverty in sub-Saharan African countries? *Journal of Travel Research*, 59(1), 140–155.
Fowowe, B., & Shuaibu, M. (2021). Impact of international remittance inflows on poverty in Nigeria. *The Journal of Developing Areas*, 55(1).
Gaaliche, M., & Gaaliche, M. Z. (2014). The causal relationship between remittances and poverty reduction in developing country: using a nonstationary dynamic panel data. *Atlantic Review of Economics: Revista Atlántica de Economía, 1*(1), 1–12.
Garza-Rodriguez, J. (2018). Poverty and economic growth in Mexico. *Social Sciences*, *7*(10), 183. https://doi.org/10.3390/socsci7100183
Granger, C. W., & Yoon, G. (2002). Hidden cointegration. *U of California, Economics Working Paper*, (2002–02). https://dx.doi.org/10.2139/ssrn.313831
Hacker, R. S., & Hatemi-J, A. (2010). *HHcte: GAUSS module to apply a bootstrap test for causality with endogenous lag order*. Statistical Software Components G00012, Boston College Department of Economics.
Hatemi-J. A. (2014). *ASCOMP: GAUSS module to transform data into cumulative positive and negative components*. Statistical Software Components G00015, Department of Economics, Boston College.
Hatemi-J, A. (2012). Asymmetric causality tests with an application. *Empirical Economics*, 43(1), 447–456. http://doi.org/10.1007/s00181-011-0484-x
Hatemi-J, A., & El-Khatib, Y. (2016). An extension of the asymmetric causality tests for dealing with deterministic trend components. *Applied Economics*, 48(42), 4033–4041.
Hatemi-J, A., & El-Khatib, Y. (2020). The nexus of trade-weighted dollar rates and the oil prices: an asymmetric approach. *Journal of Economic Studies*, 47(7), 1579–1589. https://doi.org/10.1108/JES-06-2019-0266
Hatemi-J, A., & Mustafa, A. (2016). *A MS-Excel module to transform an integrated variable into cumulative partial sums for negative and positive components with and without deterministic trend parts*. MPRA Paper No. 73813. https://mpra.ub.uni-muenchen.de/73813/
Hatemi-J, A., & Uddin, G. S. (2014). On the causal nexus of remittances and poverty reduction in Bangladesh. *Applied Economics*, 46(4), 374–382.
Ho, S. Y., & Iyke, B. N. (2018). Finance-growth-poverty nexus: a reassessment of the trickle-down hypothesis in China. *Economic Change and Restructuring*, *51*(3), 221–247.
Iyemifokhae, O. (2020). The impact of remittances on household poverty. *International Journal of Business and Economic Development (IJBED)*, 8(2), 49–73
Keho, Y. (2017). The impact of trade openness on economic growth: The case of Cote d'Ivoire. *Cogent Economics & Finance*, 5(1), 1332820. https://doi.org/10.1080/23322039.2017.1332820
Kharas, H., Hamel, K., & Hofer, M. (2018). Rethinking global poverty reduction in 2019. *Blog. Future Development at Brookings, 13*.

Koomson, I., Villano, R. A., & Hadley, D. (2020). Effect of financial inclusion on poverty and vulnerability to poverty: Evidence using a multidimensional measure of financial inclusion. *Social Indicators Research*, *149*(2), 613–639.

Kumar, B. (2019). The impact of international remittances on poverty alleviation in Bangladesh. *Remittances Review*, *4*(1), 67–86.

Musakwa, M. T., & Odhiambo, N. M. (2020). Remittance inflows and poverty nexus in Botswana: A multivariate approach. *Journal of Sustainable Finance & Investment*, 1–15. https://doi.org/10.1080/20430795.2020.1777786

Musakwa, M. T., & Odhiambo, N. M. (2021). The causal relationship between remittance and poverty in South Africa: A multivariate approach. *International Social Science Journal*, *71*(239–240), 37–48.

Musakwa, M. T., & Odhiambo, N. M. (2019). THE impact of remittance inflows on poverty in Botswana: an ARDL approach. *Journal of Economic Structures*, 8(1), 1–13.

Ndlovu, G., & Toerien, F. (2020). The distributional impact of access to finance on poverty: Evidence from selected countries in Sub-Saharan Africa. *Research in International Business and Finance*, *52*, 101190.

Nwokoye, E. S., Igbanugo, C. I., & Dimnwobi, S. K. (2020). International migrant remittances and labour force participation in Nigeria. *African Development Review*, *32*(2), 125–137.

Odhiambo, N. M. (2009a). Finance-growth-poverty nexus in South Africa: A dynamic causality linkage. *The Journal of Socio-Economics*, *38*(2), 320–325.

Odhiambo, N. M. (2009b). Financial deepening and poverty reduction in Zambia: An empirical investigation. *International Journal of Social Economics*, *37*(1), 41–53.

Okoi, O. (2019). The paradox of Nigeria's oil dependency. *Africa Portal*. *January*, *21*, 2019.

Olaniyi, C. O. (2020). Application of bootstrap simulation and asymmetric causal approach to fiscal deficit-inflation nexus. *Global Journal of Emerging Market Economies*, *12*(2), 123–140.

Olaniyi, C. O. (2019). Asymmetric information phenomenon in the link between CEO pay and firm performance: An innovative approach. *Journal of Economic Studies*, 46(2), 306–323.

Olaniyi, C. O., & Olayeni, O. R. (2020). A new perspective into the relationship between CEO pay and firm performance: Evidence from Nigeria's listed firms. *Journal of Social and Economic Development*, *22*(2), 250–277.

Olayeni, R. O., Tiwari, A. K., & Wohar, M. E. (2021). Fractional frequency flexible Fourier form (FFFFF) for panel cointegration test. *Applied Economics Letters*, *28*(6), 482–486.

Olowookere, J. K., Olowo, S. O., Mabinuori, O. T., & Aderemi, T. A. (2021). Foreign capital inflows and poverty reduction in Nigeria: An implication for sustainable development. *EuroEconomica*, *40*(1), 33–41.

Oluwafemi, A., & Ayandibu, A. O. (2014). Impact of remittances on development in Nigeria: Challenges and prospects. *Journal of Sociology and Social Anthropology*, 5(3), 311–318.

Omar, M. A., & Inaba, K. (2020). Does financial inclusion reduce poverty and income inequality in developing countries? A panel data analysis. *Journal of Economic Structures*, 9(1), 1–25.

Osabohien, R., Wiredu, A. N., Nguezet, P. M. D., Mignouna, D. B., Abdoulaye, T., Manyong, V., . . . & Awotide, B. A. (2021). Youth participation in agriculture and poverty reduction in Nigeria. *Sustainability*, *13*(14), 7795. https://doi.org/10.3390/su13147795

Osabohien, R., Matthew, O., Ohalete, P., & Osabuohien, E. (2020). Population – poverty – inequality nexus and social protection in Africa. *Social Indicators Research*, *151*, 575–598.

Quartey P. (2005). *Financial sector development, savings mobilisation and poverty reduction in Ghana*. UNU-WIDER research paper no. 2005/71, United Nations University, Helsinki.

Ravallion, M. (1992). Poverty comparisons. Living Standard Measurement Study Working Paper, 88.

Sanchez-Loor, D. A., & Zambrano-Monserrate, M. A. (2015). Causality analysis between electricity consumption, real GDP, foreign direct investment, human development and remittances in Colombia, Ecuador and Mexico. *International Journal of Energy Economics and Policy*, 5(3), 746–753

Satti, S. L., Hassan, M. S., Hayat, F., & Paramati, S. R. (2016). Economic growth and inflow of remittances: Do they combat poverty in an emerging economy? *Social Indicators Research*, *127*(3), 1119–1134.

Sehrawat, M., & Giri, A. K. (2016a). Financial development and poverty reduction in India: an empirical investigation. *International Journal of Social Economics*, *43*(2), 106–122.

Sehrawat, M., & Giri, A. K. (2016b). Financial development and poverty reduction: Panel data analysis of South Asian countries. *International Journal of Social Economics*, 43(4), 400–416.

Solarin, S. A., Gil-Alana, L. A., & Gonzalez-Blanch, M. J. (2021). Fractional persistence in income poverty in Africa. *Social Indicators Research*, *155*(2), 563–581.

Siani, J. (2020). International remittances, poverty and growth into WAEMU countries: Evidence from panel cointegration approach. *Economics Bulletin*, 40(2), 1446–1456.

Toda, H. Y., & Yamamoto, T. (1995). Statistical inference in vector autoregressions with possibly integrated processes. *Journal of Econometrics*, 66(1–2), 225–250.

Uddin, G. S., Shahbaz, M., Arouri, M., & Teulon, F. (2014). Financial development and poverty reduction nexus: A cointegration and causality analysis in Bangladesh. *Economic Modelling*, 36, 405–412.

Urama, N. E., Nwosu, E. O., Yuni, D. N., & Aguegboh, S. E. (2017). International migrant remittances and labour supply in Nigeria. *International Migration*, 55(1), 37–50.

Woolard, I., & Leibbrandt, M. (1999). *Measuring poverty in South Africa*. DPRU Working Papers No. 99/33 (October), Development Policy Research Unit, University of Cape Town.

World Bank. (2001). *World development report 2000–2001: Attacking poverty*. Retrieved on 4/16/2021 from World Bank Group. New York: Oxford University Press website: https://openknowledge.worldbank.org/handle/10986/11856

World Bank (2021). World development indicator. https://data.worldbank.org/indicator/BX.TRF.PWKR.CD.DT?locations=NG

World Bank (2016a) *Poverty and shared prosperity 2016: taking on inequality*. World Bank Group, Washington, DC. https://openknowledge.worldbank.org/bitstream/handle/10986/25078/9781464809583.pdf

World Bank (2016b), *Migration and remittances factbook 2016, World Bank*. Washington, DC.

World Bank (2019). *Poverty overview*. The World Bank. www.worldbank.org/en/topic/poverty/overview

World Bank. (2021). *Defying predictions, remittance flows remain strong during COVID-19 Crisis*. www.worldbank.org/en/news/press-release/2021/05/12/defying-predictions-remittance-flows-remain-strong-during-covid-19-crisis

World Poverty Clock (2018). *The percentage of Nigerians living in extreme poverty could increase by 2030*. https://worldpoverty.io/headline

Yasmin, I., Hussain, Z., Akram, W., & Yasmin, N. (2015). Bidirectional causality between remittances and poverty: An empirical evidence from Pakistan. *Journal of Economics and Sustainable Development*, 6(24), 176–183.

17 Reshaping the Educational System for Post-COVID-19 Schooling in a Developing Country

Flora Olubukola Olaniyi

Introduction

Earlier in 2020, the whole world woke up to the biting effect of a new virus that began ravaging the People's Republic of China in December 2019. The coronavirus disease that was eventually tagged COVID-19 became pandemic when the World Health Organization (WHO) announced the arrival of the virus in all continents of the world. Hence, countries of the world were all caught unaware, and everyone has to close up both internal and external borders to contain the virus from further spread. The effect was felt in all aspects of human life, including the education system, since all schools from the elementary to the tertiary had to shut down to curb further spread. As a matter of fact, the academic session has been grossly disrupted to the extent that both federal and state governments could not agree yet on how to resuscitate the already battered school system knowing well that if the virus comes in contact with children and young adults, it will surely have a devastating effect on all. How then can the school move forward was the question everyone has been asking since the world health body has announced that the disease will live with us for a long time.

Since issues of teachers' development are not new, a shift in what teachers need becomes a subject for debate. The challenges of COVID-19 have brought forth the need for teachers to improve on the mode of disseminating educational information especially in developing nations since they are countries with no appreciable industrial development (Ndoma, 2010). However, the traditional pedagogy of didactic teaching methods that teachers are used to have made it difficult for them to be able to impact education using ICT. This has, in turn, become a debacle for the growth of technological innovation in education. To this end, it will be of paramount importance to investigate the most used teaching platforms that were engaged during the period of the COVID-19 lockdown in selected public and private schools in the Ibadan metropolis and the challenges of the teachers who taught during the period. School owners as well as teachers of private schools within the study areas were contacted, while the director of school programmes in the Ministry of Education was also contacted for opinions concerning the public schools' mode of academic information dissemination during the pandemic.

DOI: 10.4324/9781003208358-22

Conventional teaching pedagogy has to do with formal learning environments and classroom-based learning as teachers' intervention (Watkins & Mortimore 1999). The concept of pedagogy is related to support for children's development through care and education. Pedagogy includes active listening, arguing and discussing through reflection and interpretation that supports children's involvement and participation. There are many arguments on whether traditional or modern teaching is better. Either way, schools are starting to get an earful from parents on how their children are learning. In traditional teaching, teachers control what the students are doing from the four walls of a classroom. Students put pencil to paper instead of typing on computers. Teachers stand on the front of the classroom, give lectures and have the students take notes (Jayalaxmi, 2016). Conventional teaching also requires a student to come class early if he/she is to be seen and known to be a serious type. Some teachers even prefer some set of students to sit in a particular place in the class. All of these classroom dynamics have been successfully threatened by the arrival and the corresponding shocks that came with the virus. Students are no longer coming to receive this conventional method in schools, and school management is not making revenue to pay the teacher's salary. In the long run, both the teachers and the schools have found themselves in a great economic shock due to the shift in the paradigm. The question is, will the conventional teaching technique survive this shift that is eminent in the present-day information sharing environment? Only time will tell!

The COVID-19 Challenge for the Education Sector

Coronavirus disease 2019 (COVID-19) officially entered Nigeria through the Murtala Mohammed International Airport on 27 February 2020. An Italian expatriate was the culprit (Ogunode et al., 2020). As of 3 December, Nigeria had tested over 620,000 persons with confirmed cases up to 67,000; 67,960; a total discharged of 63,839, while the number of deaths recorded stood at 1177 with Lagos State the epicentre with a total of 23,439 that had been confirmed to have the virus. In the wake of the pandemic, all educational facilities (tertiary, secondary, primary and preprimary) were put under lock and key in a bid to stop any further spread. COVID-19 caused by the novel virus SARS-CoV-2 (WHO, 2020) brought about unprecedented times where every individual had to practice some nonpharmaceutical measures, such as social distancing, wearing face masks and coughing into the elbow, to cut the spread. How easy this will be with children of school age was a great concern and thus made schools to be brought under locks and keys. The challenges posed by COVID-19 are massive for the school system since the traditional model of person-to-person educational didactics, chalk talks and lectures had to be compromised. The novel coronavirus is a new strain that has not been previously identified in humans. Therefore, little was known about it until recently, when scientists studied it slightly better and developed vaccines to prevent it (WHO, 2020; Ogunode et al., 2020).

Data from the United Nations Educational, Scientific and Cultural Organization (UNESCO) show that the preprimary, primary, secondary and tertiary students were all affected and that approximately 87% of these students were affected as of March 2020 in more than 180 countries of the world. Ogunode et al. (2020) identified the reduction of international education, disruption of the academic calendar across the board, cancellation of local and international conferences, teaching and learning gaps, loss of the workforce in educational institutions and a cut in the budget of higher education as some of the challenges the education system has to cope with for a while. However, a great concern that the stakeholders are expected to be mindful of should be how the teachers would survive the change and at the same time we need to be concerned of the political will of the governments of the developing nations especially if they are willing to support the new normal that is ravaging the whole culture of schooling in the world.

ICT and Emerging Technologies for Educational Advancement

In a recent study carried out by the United Nations Educational, Scientific and Cultural Organization (UNESCO), approximately 9.8 million students in the African region as a whole are experiencing disruption in their education due to the effect of the emergence of the COVID-19 pandemic and lockdown owing to school closures (UNESCO, 2020). For the fear of possible contact with the disease, many institutions have to move their courses to different online platforms. Research has shown that approximately 76% of Africa's population does not have access to internet, the frequent electricity disruption in the areas that have, coupled with high cost of data in a poverty endemic society, and poor connectivity are impeding factor changes that are sweeping the entire world of academy (Mahler, Montes & Newhouse, 2019; Obana, 2020). However, some universities in some parts of Africa have decided to take up this challenge by making their presence visible via the internet. Unfortunately, no Nigeria university can boast of having approximately 50% of its programs online.

Emerging technology could be seen as ambiguous and confusing since it has always been used loosely. The technology has been called by so many other names, such as information and communication technologies (ICT), technologies in education, digital technologies and emerging technologies (ETs), in recent years (Andrés-Sosa-Neira et al., 2017). However, in this study, the conceptualization of the term indicates technologies that are adaptable, disruptive, evolving, innovative, ubiquitous, complementary and generate a degree of uncertainty. It is always associated with catchy terms and acronyms such as i-learning, student 2.0 and education 3.0, which traverse innovations (Veletsianos & Kleanthous, 2009).

WhatsApp is one of the technologies that has been adopted by many in passing out both educational and noneducational information. It is a free instant messaging and voice over internet protocol service invented by Brian Acton and Jan Koum in 2009 but presently owned by Mark Zuckerberg of Facebook (Ansari & Tripathi, 2017; Purkayastha & Chanda, 2018). Research conducted showed that

WhatsApp has over 1.3 billion daily users, over 55 billion messages are sent in a day, over 4.5 billion photos and over 1 billion videos are shared per day with over 60 languages supported (Purkayastha & Chanda, 2018).

The Zoom app is another innovation useful in video conferencing. It is also suitable for multiple participants, audio and video sharing, screen sharing, working on a whiteboard and recording, which has been very useful in education especially during the COVID-19 shock we are experiencing (Odularu et al., 2022). This later became popular among both students who missed the lectures and those who wanted to refresh and reinforce the lesson plan. The opportunities in these applications are expected to be leveraged for African nations to redirect their educational policies, especially for a post-COVID-19 era.

The Future Is Now

Despite the disruption in the education system due to the COVID-19 lockdown, the education system has tried to evolve from the traditional method to the new age of digital technology that will enhance teaching and learning (Almarzooq et al., 2020; Ufua et al., 2021; Odularu et al., 2022). However, many developing countries had no plans for an alternative to the present model of the teacher-student approach of teaching since innovations in these lines are always being frustrated by educational policies that are supposed to have been repealed and re-enacted to allow for improvements. The pandemic has also exposed so many of these countries as they have to shut schools for a long time while they were thinking of the way forward. The time has come for these nations to be proactive and remedy the devastating situation of the pandemic as created by implementing the various policies on digitalising the education that have been adopted by other countries if they cannot develop their own (Ndoma, 2010).

However, the inequality in access to the internet will continue to be a debacle to the achievable future until something drastic is made in terms of investment. There are still digital divides in developing countries such that exist between schools within the same country where some are better equipped than others. The truth is that the COVID-19 pandemic and lockdown have made schools look in the option and opportunities that are embedded in the internet facility, but do they have the capability to access the opportunities? Schools, especially higher institutions, should begin to look in the direction of massive open online courses (MOOCs), but do they have the capacity to deliver such programmes online? Cahapay (2020) is of the opinion that reduced content is essential in developing a curriculum. The suggested range of integration models in curriculum development developed by Fogarty and Stoehr (1991) is still relevant today. Since it is no longer didactic, the content that goes online is expected to be concise but informative.

Methodology

Data were collected primarily using in-depth interviews with the principals of the selected private schools and key informant interviews with the director of the school programme whose opinion represents that of the public schools in the state. A questionnaire was adopted for the teachers. Three local government areas of Ibadan North, Ibadan Northwest and Ibadan Northeast were considered out of the five within the metropolis. A total of 15 principals and 442 teachers were sampled in the study areas. Inclusion criteria for the teachers included participation in the online teaching process. The data generated were analysed through SPSS version 20 and qualitatively via content analysis. Descriptive statistics of simple percentages and frequency counts were employed in describing the positions of the teachers, while verbatim quotations were used for the positions of the school director and the principals.

Results

Private School Model of Teaching During the Lockdown

Private schools in Nigeria were the first to think it through and came up with the solution of an online teaching platform that could replace the old pedagogy. After approximately two months into the lockdown, some private schools were already frustrated with the federal government directives of the total lockdown of schools and were ready to return to teaching. The only option that was available was the online teaching platform. This mode of teaching and the associated challenges were the driving forces for this research.

Proprietors were asked of their ideas on what they consider as an online teaching platform; the investigation revealed that the majority of them had an understanding since they were able to state that it had to do with teaching via an online medium. For instance, a participant is of the opinion that "it is teaching and dissemination of academic materials and information using the internet". In the same vein, another participant takes the understanding further by adding that "it has to do with teaching and passing across information using virtual means". The participant was probe further on what virtual is, and he said "situation of teaching where both the teacher and the student will have the opportunity of seeing and hearing each other instantaneously". These, among others, drive home the understanding and awareness that the researcher is seeking to determine.

Participants from private schools were then asked to mention some of the online teaching platforms they know in a bid to ascertain their awareness of the availability of these teaching platforms and the most preferred online teaching platform they engaged in during the lockdown. Responses here differ since there were a whole lot of them that the users engaged in. Some even had to change from one to another in an attempt to maximize the opportunity in the technology. From Zoom, Blackboard, Microsoft Teams, Dropbox paper to Google Team, Google Hangout, House Mate, Floop, WhatsApp, Slack, Eventbrite, Schoology and so on. Participants claimed they listen to the opinions of their ICT directors to know the most suitable online teaching platform to use. Investigation, however, revealed that the engagement of any of the online teaching platforms is dependent on factors such as internet connectivity, funds for data, smart devices and technical know how. However, some platforms were still favored over others. It was also found that most of the schools had never made use of the online teaching platform until the COVID-19 lockdown.

Further investigation of those who were in charge of the OTP in the schools visited shows that the work of the ICT director was to set up the platform that is preferred while the teachers were the ones taking the students in each of the subjects. The majority of the subjects were thought by the subject teachers, but there was a rescheduling of the time table to suit the condition of learning at home. There was no intense training for the teachers on how to handle this new innovation. In most of the schools, the ICT directors mainly showed them what to do and asked them to call for attention should any problem arise. On the cost incurred, school management bears the burden, although the majority of them charged the parents for online teaching, and any student whose parent does not pay will not be given access to the virtual class or added to the group where educational materials are being shared. In most of the schools visited, it was discovered that they were not using any virtual classroom rather, the management preferred to use the WhatsApp platform to send assignments to students. After completing the assignment, the students will send it back to the platform where the teacher will harvest them for grading. On the other hand, some schools restricted the WhatsApp platform so that only the admin could send assignments to parents that had been added on behalf of their children; thus, they did not expect feedback from this channel. In this type of arrangement, most of the schools did not ask the parent to pay for the service but was only doing it for the sake of their students. However, participants stated that some other types of challenges they faced included failure in connectivity, poor connectivity, epileptic power supply and parents not knowing how to handle the platform, while some parents who refused to enrol their children technically set back the children.

Public School and the Mass Media Option

On the part of the public schools within the Ibadan metropolis, the director of school at the Ministry of Education was interviewed on the specific role the ministry played concerning continuous learning during the lockdown and the teaching model that was the most preferred and adopted and possible challenges they faced. For instance, he was asked about the type of teaching platform they engaged in during the lockdown and he said:

> We only engaged the mass media for the dissemination of educational information for our students, and we made use of the state-owned Broadcasting Corporation of Oyo State (BCOS) and the state radio stations. However, it was not only the ministry that ran school on the air program during the time of the lockdown; other private organizations, individuals and companies also sponsored other private radio and television stations to run school on the air program.
>
> (KII/Director of School/15/10/2020)

The informant was further asked what informs the usage of mass media as a platform for teaching during the lockdown and he explained that they had to consider students who are from poor socioeconomic backgrounds in the decision because the mass media is easy to connect with and since it costs almost nothing to hear from it. He further added that if they had to use any other means, such as the online teaching platform or WhatsApp, some students would not be able to connect since their parents' level of education and exposure may hinder them from enjoying the benefits. For instance, some of them might not have smartphones and devices, and it will not be nice for us to put them in any form of burden again. Moreover, we did not collect any money from them, and it was our sole responsibility to take care of our students.

In the same vein, the study probe for the qualification of those who are handling the teaching and the informant claimed they are experienced and good teachers in the subjects they were asked to take. He further added:

> "Although the teachers were not trained since the COVID-19 pandemic caught everybody unaware, we were so sure of the ones we called upon since we already have their curriculum vitae with us". Additionally, since the teachers were just to teach and they do not have anything to do with the recordings of the lessons, the training was not needed. The studio manager will only give the teacher the instruction on when to start so there was no serious need for training except maybe for some teachers that may be camera shy anyway. The studios were set up within our building here at the secretariat, and the teachers are familiar with the ministry so there was no reason for any of the teachers to fidget, although we still had one or two of them anyway.
> (KII/Director of School/15/10/2020)

The informant also made us understand that principals of public schools were not involved in the programme since they do not have any role to play in the whole recording and dissemination of the teaching. On the issue of the type of arrangement that is between the ministry and the mass media organizations concerning airing the school on the air programme, the researcher intends to know where the funding came from, how they manage the time and selection of the subjects that were taught. The investigation then revealed that the Universal Basic Education Commission (UBEC) gave the ministry some funds in support of the programme, but the ministry spent its own money before the support was received. The teachers were appreciated with a small amount of money, but state-owned mass media organizations such as the BCOS, Oluyole FM, Ajilete FM and the Oke-Ogun FM did not collect any money for airing the programmes. They only did it for us as part of their own social responsibility. In many situations, the programme runs for 25 minutes. Therefore, the informant was also asked if there was any form of feedback that the ministry received from the public and from their students; he said:

> We received so much feedback from our parents, students and the general public. We had parents and members of the public get in touch with

> us and telling us how they have learnt from the program. We also had complaints from the Oke-Ogun axis of the state calling our attention to the loss of signal from the television station. It was highly impactful because it covered so many grounds and we were able to complete the curriculum during the period. Additionally, teachers who were not teaching were able to gain from their colleagues. The topics that were not well understood by them that their colleagues took made them understand it better. It also allowed students to learn from another teacher aside their own school teachers, while parents and other members of the public wanted the program to be back on air. Although all the teachers cannot be selected for the program, it should be a wake-up call for them to be the best in the areas they have chosen as a carrier.
>
> (KII/Director of School/15/10/2020)

From the aforementioned perspectives, everyone has to decide on the model of teaching that suits them the most, and the mass media seems to be the most suitable for public schools since the population of students in public schools is larger. It is also pertinent to note that the location of students may not support the use or connectivity of the internet. The socioeconomic status of parents is also a strategic factor that needs to be considered before the decision on the kind of teaching platform that is to be used. We can then assume a position of the fact that the public school model of information dissemination could be better in reaching a larger percentage of students. However, information as well as education is not complete without feedback, which is not realistic with the use of the mass media platform (Kapur, 2018).

Coping Strategy of Teachers with Online Teaching Platforms

Since the role of teachers in the new and modern pedagogy cannot be downplayed, the research took into account the kind of challenges they are expected to face and how they are coping with the new normal. To this end, teachers were asked if they presently have either a smartphone or a laptop or both since these devices are believed to be very useful in connecting the internet for online teaching purposes. It was discovered that 82% (349) of them have smartphones, 37% (157) own a laptop, and 45% (191) have both a smartphone and a laptop. Furthermore, teachers were asked about the type of online teaching platform they were familiar with out of the listed options. It is not surprising to see that all the teachers (100%) were familiar with the WhatsApp platform for teaching, while 56.4% (240) were those familiar with the Zoom platform while Google Hangout came third with approximately 46% (196). The data collected revealed that the most preferred online platform by the teachers was the messaging application since 61.6% (262) of them said so compared to 38.4% (164) who preferred the virtual online platform although the onus lies with the school management. It was also discovered that respondents were not specially trained on how to handle the platforms the schools have chosen order than the idea they personally have while using their personal social media platforms (Chan, Joshi, Lin and Mehta, 2015; Topps et al., 2013).

In the same vein, 82% (349) of the respondents claimed not to have any problem using the adopted platform except for the challenges of internet disruptions. One major challenge that respondents faced was the fact that they had to come to the school premises before they could teach their students since the school was the one responsible for the cost of the internet facility. The majority of them amounting to 83% (354) were in this category, while only 17.3% (74) of the teachers said they do connect with their students from home since the school has shared data with them and allows for such arrangements. Respondents were further asked if they think the socioeconomic status of students could have an effect on the way and manner students assimilate educational instructions, especially when teaching is done online. Responses show that 48.7% of teachers deferred in their opinions (207) of them answered in the affirmative, while 44.8% (191) did not think socioeconomic status of students' parents has anything to do with online learning. However, the remaining 6.5% (27) of respondents were indecisive of the effect of socioeconomic status on student online listening ability.

Teachers were further asked if they usually encounter any form of distraction from students while teaching is ongoing. Furthermore, 93.5% (398) of respondents said most of the students are always distracted when teaching is ongoing, but an exception was made to the time when parents monitor the children while teaching is ongoing. Concerning the way respondents monitor their students while teaching is going on, teachers who are using virtual online platforms to disseminate information and educational materials seem to be able to monitor the students better than those using other means, such as messaging applications. These and many other variables were revealed from the data collected via the questionnaire used.

The essence of these data is meant to show the coping strategy of teachers when using online platforms.

Discussion of Findings

From the empirical findings, school owners said they depend primarily on the opinion of their ICT directors concerning the platforms to be used. This is definitely a right step in the right direction. However, the knowledge of the ICT director also needs to be enhanced through training and retraining since the knowledge of information technology is not static (Ogbomo, 2011). This is also because discovery shows that messaging application was better favoured than the virtual application does not make it better, but the amount of data that the virtual uses were a major reason for these figures. The quality of internet service from the providers can also encourage messaging applications other than virtual. This finding is in agreement with that of Fasiku et al. (2020).

In the case of public schools, especially the way they are managed in Nigeria, it may be difficult to achieve a total shift from the traditional pedagogy to the digital way of teaching. Many of the schools are located in the suburbs and remote areas where internet facilities have not reached. The mass media is therefore the only way to reach such students. It will, however, be good if the government, private organizations, individuals and companies can encourage telecom companies to provide facilities in the areas, as Oznacar and Dagli (2016) concluded that students use knowledge gained in all fields of life. From the discussion with the director of the school, 25 minutes of teaching each day is not good enough. How much can a pupil gain in 25 minutes of learning per day? The time should have been increased to at least approximately 4 hours per day. Pupils usually spend between six and seven hours in school before the pandemic. Why then reduce the time? Last, for the fact that the teachers were able to cope in teaching with the new method means they will continually do well if properly trained and capacity increased. Whatever will then discourage the teachers and hamper their interest should first be removed. The active use of innovative teaching methods by teachers is a necessity in the digital generation and must be encouraged greatly, which was concurred by Mynbayeva, Sadvakassova and Akshalova (2018) and Revathi, Elavarasi and Saravanan (2019).

Conclusion and Recommendation

The emergence of COVID-19 was a great shock to the educational sector. The crisis has been successful in destabilizing the old pedagogy of educational didactic and person-to-person teaching, thus bringing about the need for an immediate but far-reaching solution. It is therefore wise to expect that online teaching platforms will be the next phase of disseminating educational information by schools all over the world. It is also envisaged that students will prefer the online teaching platforms as they will be having it in the comfort of their homes, while the teachers feel that online teaching will not be as effective as when students are in the four corners of the classroom. While the debate is ongoing, it will be wise enough for schools (in all categories) to begin to think in the direction of online teaching platforms since data that are the bedrock of the internet have been described as oxygen and life by major telecom operators in Nigeria. It is therefore chiefly important that we begin to consider the expansion of subject pedagogies, environmental approaches to teaching, the digital generation and the changing taking place in the whole world, as well as the innovation in teaching for us to be able to serve this age of digital generation. Thus, the renewal of teaching methods is a compulsion.

From the foregoing, it will be meaningful based on the field experience generator in the course of this research to recommend that there is the need for government through the Nigeria Communication Commission (NCC) to encourage telecom operators to improve the quality of their internet services and make data accessible at a lower rate. Since the application of the innovation method is major individualistic, teachers need to be encouraged to adopt the new and innovative methodological competence and pedagogical skills they will use in impacting knowledge to their students. This task, however, needs the teacher to be trained in actualising the goal. School management and the Ministry of Education also need to encourage the new system by providing the necessary facilities for the actualization of the dream. There is the need to start working on the process of repealing and re-enacting those policies that are not digital generation friendly. Policies are made for humans and not the other way round. Since students are greatly influenced by their teachers, teachers should try as much as possible not to be parochial in their thinking and readiness to accept the change when it finally done on them. As much as the internet and digitalisation are useful, there should be a follow-up scheme that will ensure both students and teachers are making proper use of the digital platforms at the right time.

References

Almarzooq, Z., Lopes, M., & Kochar, A. (2020). Virtual learning during the COVID-19 pandemic: a disruptive technology in graduate medical education. *Journal of the American College of Cardiology*. https://doi.org/10.1016/j.jacc.2020.04.015

Andrés-Sosa-Neira, E., Salinas, J., & Crosetti, B. (2017). Emerging Technologies (ETs) in education: a systematic review of the literature published between 2006 and 2016. *International Journal of Emerging Technologies in Learning* 12(5):128. https://doi.org/10.3991/ijetv12i05.6939

Ansari, M.S., & Tripathi, A. (2017). Use of WhatsApp for effective delivery of library and information services. *Journal of Library and Information Technology* 37(5):360–365.

Cahapay, M. B. (2020). Rethinking education in the new normal Post-COVID- 19era: a curriculum studies perspective. *Aquademia Journal* 4(2). https://doi.org/10.29333/aquademia/8315

Chan, T., Joshi, N., Lin, M., & Mehta, N. (2015). Using Google Hangout on air for medical education: a disruptive way to leverage and facilitate remote communication and collaboration. *Journal of Graduate Medical Education*. 7(2): 171–173. http//doi.org/10.4300/JGME-D-14-00545-1

Fasiku, B. B., Awoleye, M. O., & Oyebisi, T. O. (2020) Assessment of quality of internet service delivery in selected Southwestern Universities in Nigeria. *International Journal of Computer Application*, 177(34): 27–33.

Fogarty, R., & Stoehr, J. (1991). *Robin Fogarty's models of integrating curricular with multiple intelligences: teams, themes, and threads*. Palatine, IL: Skylight Publishing, Inc. https://learning.arpdc.ab.ca/pluginfile.php/odresource/content/Fogartys.Model.Intergration.pdf

Jayalaxmi (2016). Importance of innovative teaching methods an evaluative study of traditional and modern reaching techniques – a survey. *International Journal of Current Research and Modern Education* 1(1):250.

Kapur, R. (2018). *Role of media in the development of education*. Retrieved from www.researchgate.net/publication/323725768_Role_of_Media_in_the_Development_of_Education

Mahler, D. G., Montes, J., & Newhouse, D. L. (2019). Internet access in sub-Saharan Africa. Poverty and Equity Note. *World Bank Group*. http://documents.worldbank.org/curated/en/518261552658319590/Internet-Access-in-Sub-Saharan-Africa

Mynbayeva, A., Sadvakassova, Z., & Akshalova, B. (2018). *Pedagogy of the twenty-first century: innovative teaching methods*. London: IntechOpen.

Nasir, M. (2013). Role of media in a developed society. *Interdisciplinary Journal of Contemporary Research in Business* 5(2):407–415. Retrieved from http://journal-archives33.webs.com/407-415.pdf

Ndoma, I. (2010). How rich countries got rich and why poor countries stay poor. *Journal of Contemporary Asia* 40(4):690–693. http://dx.doi.org/10.1080/00472336.2010.507069

Obana, J. (2020). Could educational technology be a 'holy grail' amid Covid-19 crisis? *The Manila Times*. Retrieved from www.manilatimes.net/2020/03/18/business/columnists-business/could-educational-technology-be-a-holy-grail-amid-covid-19-crisis/704202/

Odularu, G., Osabuohien, E., Ufua, D., & Osabohien, R. (2022). Conclusion: COVID-19 and pandemic preparedness in a digital age. In Osabuohien, E., Odularu, G., Ufua, D. and Osabohien, R. (Eds.) *COIVD-19 in the African Continent: Sustainable Development and Socioeconomic Shocks* (pp. 351–356). Bingley: Emerald Publishers Limited. https://doi.org/10.1108/978-1-80117-686-620221033

Ogbomo, E. F. (2011). Issues and challenges in the use of information communication technology (ICTs) in education. *Journal of Information and Knowledge Management* 2(1). https://www.ajol.info/index.php/iijikm/article/view/144579

Ogunode, N. J., Abigeal, I., & Lydia, A. E. (2020). Impact of COVID-19 on the higher institutions development in Nigeria. *Electronic Research Journal of Social Sciences and Humanities*, 2:126–135.

Öznacar, B., & Dagli, G. (2016). The impact of mass media tools on students at the high school level. *Anthropologist* 23(1):152–162.

Purkayastha, N., & Chanda, A. (2018). WhatsApp as a means of sharing information among LIS professionals of North-East India: a study. *International Journal of Research in Applied, Natural and Social Sciences* 6(9):69–82.

Revathi, G., Elavarasi, S., & Saravanan K. (2019) Innovative methods of teaching and learning for education. *Journal of Emerging Technologies & Innovative Research* 6(5), 159-163.

Rotolo, D. (2015). What is an emerging technology? *Research Policy* 44(10):1827–1843. https://doi.org/10.1016/j.respol.2015.06.006.

Topps, D., Helmer, J., & Ellaway, R. (2013). YouTube as a platform for publishing clinical skills training videos. *Academic Medicines: Journal of the Association of American Medical Colleges* 88(2):192–197. https//doi.org/10.1097/ACM.0b013e31827c5352

Ufua, D., Osabuohien, E., Ogbari, M, Falola, H., Okoh, E., & Lakhani, A. (2021). Restrategising government palliative support systems in tackling the challenges of COVID-19 lockdown in Lagos State, Nigeria. *Global Journal of Flexible Systems Management* 22:19–32. https://doi.org/10.1007/s40171-021-00263-z

United Nations Educational, Scientific and Cultural Organization. (2020). 2020 Global Education Meeting: extraordinary session on Education post COVID-19. *Background Document*. Retrieved from www.gem2020-extraordinary-session-concept-note-en.pdf

Veletsianos, G., & Kleanthous, I. (2009). A review of adventure learning. *The International Review of Research in Open and Distributed Learning* 10(6):84–105. https://doi.org/10.19173/irrodl.v10i6.755.

Watkins, C., & Mortimore, P. (1999). Pedagogy: what do we know? In Mortimore, P. (Ed.) *Understanding Pedagogy and its impact on Learning*. London: Paul Chapman/Sage.

World Health Organization. (2020). *Coronavirus disease (COVID-2019) situation reports*. Geneva. Retrieved from www.who.int/emergencies/diseases/novel-coronavirus-2019/situation-reports

18 Effect of COVID-19 on Small- and Medium-Scale Enterprises in Nigeria

Which Sector Is Mostly Affected?

Maria Chinecherem Uzonwanne, Amaka Gertrude Metu, Kingsley Chidera Adonike and Francis Chukwudi Onyedibe

Introduction

All over the world, economies and businesses are enduring a staggering downturn amid the spread of the coronavirus disease (COVID-19) pandemic which has unfolded with tremendous speed and affected markets in unprecedented ways (Kurmann, Lale & Ta, 2020). According to the World Health Organization (2020), COVID-19 is an infectious disease caused by a newly discovered coronavirus.

In Nigeria, the first confirmed case was announced on February 27, 2020, when an Italian citizen tested positive for the virus. A second case of the virus was identified on March 9, 2020, in a Nigerian citizen who had contact with the Italian citizen (Maclean, & Dahir, 2020; Nigerian Centre for Disease Control [NCDC], 2020). COVID-19 has spread to the states in the country infecting people and as of May 5, 2021, the country had a total of 2,133,061 samples tested, 166,730 confirmed cases, 2,029 active cases, 162,584 discharged cases and 2,117 deaths (NCDC, 2021). As the virus spreads, societies, economies and businesses are being affected. A Deloitte survey conducted among over 1,000 firms showed that the epidemic will adversely affect sales volume and cash flows as well as the ability to serve consumers and manage businesses (International Labour Organization [ILO], 2020a). Significant risks also include ensuring the safety of employees returning from vacations and business trips, difficulties related to the supply of raw materials, and lack of tools for organizing remote work. Many public health systems and other public services and administrative bodies have reached a breakpoint and millions of jobs and businesses are being affected around the world. The labour markets are being profoundly hit by this invisible threat, while the public service is reaching the limit of their capacities and alleviating actions are of utmost urgency. Disruptions to production have now spread to supply chains across the world. All businesses, regardless of size, are facing serious challenges, especially those in the aviation, tourism, and hospitality industries, with a real threat of significant declines in revenue, insolvencies, and job losses in specific sectors (International Labour Organization, 2021c). Sustaining business

DOI: 10.4324/9781003208358-23

operations will be particularly difficult for small- and medium-scale enterprises (SMEs) especially food system firms in lower- and middle-income countries such as Nigeria which are suffering financial hardship because of the pandemic and related control measures (GAIN, 2020).

Sustaining business operations will be particularly difficult for SMEs. Following the Nigerian government's policy on the restriction of movement, travel bans, border closures and quarantine measures, entrepreneurs and workers in SMEs may lose a substantial proportion of daily income and wages, particularly informal and casually employed workers (Salem, 2020). These losses may represent a degradation of their daily subsistence living. The potential adverse effect and effective corrective measures have become a source of concern, as the Nigerian government's palliative measures, in the form of cash transfers, focus on the consumption needs of the absolute poor and vulnerable in society. These palliatives do not explicitly protect SMEs, entrepreneurs and workers from their potential losses in income and wages.

COVID-19 has a different impact depending on the type of business (Price, 2020). The smaller the business, the harder the hit; companies with fewer than 20 employees are most affected as a result of low cash flow and capital. Those companies were the first to reduce hours for employees or lay off employees. However, the Nigerian Labour Act protects income for workers and allows people to do their business to also protect their income, therefore, it implies that those in the public sector receive their salary (ILO, 2020b). However, those in informal sectors depend solely on the day-to-day economic activities to earn their income and given this economic slowdown which was positioned to affect their businesses and income earnings. The majority of informal sectors are largely SMEs, and with the slowdown in economic activities, a huge loss of income may be accumulated leading to a dead loss.

Given the effect of lockdown in terms of income source deprivation for these SMEs and at the same time, an increase in the price of goods as well as reductions and/or shifts in demands and consumption patterns is expected because many SME operators in the country source their inputs from China which further serves as the epicenter of the pandemic (Chinedu et al., 2020). It is expected that similar interruptions in supply chains will translate into reduced income for not only retailers in the textiles, pharmaceuticals, automotive, food processing, leather, and footwear industries, but also money changers, transporters, and other people operating in different parts of these chains. On this basis, the researchers examined the effect of COVID-19 on SMEs in Nigeria as well as the SME sector that is mostly affected by the coronavirus pandemic.

Review of Related Literature

Coronavirus Pandemic in Nigeria

On February 27, 2020, Nigeria recorded her first case of the dreaded coronavirus disease through an Italian citizen who travelled into the country (NCDC, 2020). This reality awakened the federal and state government to protect Nigerians, has recognized the fast rate of morbidity and mortality of the virus among other nations. Civil societies and government agencies embarked on enlightenment campaigns for good hygiene and social distancing in public places while the NCDC in partnership with state governments implemented mechanisms for case detection, contact tracing and patient isolation/quarantine (Nwosu, Marcus, & Metu, 2020; Musa, & Aifuwa, (2020). To further prevent the spread of the virus, the Federal Government of Nigeria on March 30, 2020 closed all national borders and airspaces, schools, worship centres and other public centres, with Abuja the Federal Capital, Lagos and Ogun states being placed on total lockdown for 14 days (Olapegba, Ayandele, Kolawole & Oguntayo, 2020). The partial/total lockdown was later extended to May 3, 2020, due to high rate of infection and spread. COVID-19 testing laboratories were set up in Lagos, Irrua in Edo State and the FCT and state governments opened isolation centres and imposed dusk to dawn curfews in their territories. Aifuwa, Musa and Aifuwa (2020) admitted that these drastic decisions or measures taken by the federal government had negative impacts on the economy. These coerced people to stay at home; businesses and offices were closed, excluding essential goods providers such as health care, food and agricultural items. On the bright side, the decision and measure have yielded a high compliance rate from citizens, as they frequently engage in hand washing, practice social distancing and self-isolation and avoid going to work, schools or crowded areas (Olapegba et al., 2020). Moreover, many religious leaders in the country went ahead to stop large gatherings, barred handshaking and directed their members to pray at home (Makinde, Nwogu, Ajaja &Alagbe, 2020; Olatunji, 2020).

Notwithstanding the strides achieved over a brief period, the cases of COVID-19 continue to multiply exponentially across the country as displayed in Table 18.1.

The recent increase in the number of cases was attributed to the increased capacity for testing (NCDC, 2020). However, there is growing concern that not all citizens are adhering to the guidelines on COVID-19 laid down by the NCDC. This was conspicuously witnessed in states such as Kano, Bauchi and Jigawa, where hundreds of mysterious deaths were recorded in a short time, accompanied by an increase in the number of confirmed cases (NCDC, 2020; Salem, 2020).

Coronavirus Pandemic and SMEs in Nigeria

The benchmarks for describing the scale of an enterprise differ from country to country and in Nigeria, their operations cover economic activities within all sectors. Igbanugo, Uzonwanne and Ezenekwe (2015) noted that the definition of SMEs is a significant issue for policy development and implementation and depends primarily on the purpose of the classification. Although most countries have disaggregated definitions of SMEs, Nigeria has a unified operating definition for SMEs. The National Policy on SMEs adopts a classification based on dual criteria of assets and employment (Metu, 2017). The asset base lies between ₦5 million and ₦500 million, and the staff strength is between 10 and 100 employees (Igbanugo et al., 2015; Adonike, 2015).

Table 18.1 COVID-19 Update for Nigerian States (May 5, 2021)

States Affected	*No. of Cases (Lab Confirmed)*	*No. of Cases (on Admission)*	*No. Discharged*	*No. of Deaths*
Lagos	59,178	732	57,990	456
FCT	19,871	595	19,110	166
Kaduna	9,094	24	9,005	65
Plateau	9,063	1	9,005	57
Rivers	7,271	37	7,133	101
Oyo	6,857	2	6,731	124
Edo	4,908	0	4,723	185
Ogun	4,683	3	4,630	50
Kano	3,997	23	3,864	110
Ondo	3,311	28	3,219	64
Kwara	3,129	6	3,068	55
Delta	2,629	1	2,556	72
Osun	2,578	6	2,520	52
Enugu	2,464	200	2,235	29
Nasarawa	2,383	0	2,344	39
Katsina	2,103	17	2,052	34
Gombe	2,056	13	1,999	44
Ebonyi	2,037	40	1,965	32
Akwa Ibom	1,913	16	1,879	18
Anambra	1,909	64	1,826	19
Abia	1,693	2	1,669	22
Imo	1,661	4	1,620	37
Bauchi	1,549	14	1,518	17
Benue	1,366	15	1,327	24
Borno	1,337	99	1,200	38
Adamawa	1,130	12	1,086	32
Taraba	1,001	0	977	24
Niger	935	5	913	17
Bayelsa	888	2	860	26
Ekiti	876	3	862	11
Sokoto	775	0	747	28
Jigawa	532	4	512	16
Yobe	460	16	435	9
Kebbi	450	42	392	16
Cross River	394	0	376	18
Zamfara	244	3	233	8
Kogi	5	0	3	2
Total	**166,730**	**2,029**	**162,584**	**2,117**

Note: Nigeria Centre for Disease Control (2021)

The Small and Medium Enterprise Development Agency of Nigeria (SMEDAN) as cited in Abdullahi, Abubakar, Aliyu, Umar, Umar, Sabiu, Naisa, Khalid and Abubakar (2015) describes SMEs based on the following criteria: small-scale enterprises are businesses with 10–49 people with an annual turnover of N5 million to N49 million naira, while a medium-scale enterprise has 51–199 employees with a yearly turnover of N50 million to N499 million naira. Thus, following the diverse descriptions, this study adopts the meaning of SMEs from the point of view of SMEDAN (2005) as cited in Abdulahi et al. (2015). According to SMEDAN (2013), these SMEs are spread across sectors such as Accommodation and Food Services Activities, Mining and Quarrying, Construction, Water Supply; Sewerage, Waste Management and Remediation, Wholesale and Retail Trade Manufacturing, Repairs of Motor Vehicles and Motor Cycles, Agriculture, Forestry, Fishing and Hunting, Transport and Storage, Information and Communication, Administrative and Support Services Activities, Other Services Activities, Hotel and Restaurant, Education, Art Entertainment and Recreation.

SMEs have been affected by several factors such as fiscal, monetary, social, and economic, etc., arrangements across the globe with few expectations from the angle of health (pandemic). Previous experience with diseases of similar or lower scale such as severe acute respiratory syndrome (SARS), shows that when these types of epidemics rage, the devastation is not only on human life but also on sources of livelihood (Gerald, Obianuju & Chukwunonso, 2020). Coronavirus was declared a pandemic by the World Health Organization (WHO) on March 11, 2020, and since then, it has become a world emergency, given its effect on the world's businesses and economy. This has forced many countries to adopt preventive protocols including restrictions on the transportation of people and goods which reduced the flow of supply of goods, personnel and services needed to keep the economy and businesses buoyant. The restrictions on movement for Nigeria include a ban on mass gatherings of people, a ban on interstate travel (except those on essential duties) and closure of markets, worship centres, offices, social gatherings, schools, and so on.

All these measures put in place were to limit the spread of the virus from one state to another and to limit community transmission of the disease (Chinedu et al., 2020). Several SMEs across different sectors (textiles, pharmaceuticals, education, automotive, food processing, hospitality, information and communication technology (ICT) and e-commerce, leather, footwear, etc.) in the economy felt the impact differently. To some SMEs, the restriction of movement may have led to shortages in supply; to others, it may have led to the disruption of transportation of finished products thus leading to decreased sales and difficulty in paying staff. For developing countries such as Nigeria, SMEs may have had to deal with anxiety over uncertainties that might characterize the aftermath of the pandemic, which may include challenges with cash flow, customer retention, and disruption in essential operation processes. Households and SMEs are prone to be hard hit by the effect of the pandemic as businesses are ground to a halt. SMEs constitute approximately 90% of all businesses in Nigeria (Bako, 2020).

Theoretical Framework

This study is anchored on the Dynamic Capabilities Theory as propounded by David Teece, Gary Pisano and Amy Shuen, in their 1997 paper titled Dynamic Capabilities and Strategic Management. According to Teece, Pisano and Shuen (1997), the theory explains dynamic capability as the ability of a firm to adapt rapidly to continually changing situations in a business environment. This is the firm's ability to integrate, build and reconfigure internal and external competencies to address rapidly changing environments (Teece et al., 1997). Dynamic capability theory gives insight into the relationship that links a firm's resources and product markets to competitive advantage and organizational survival. It helps to show how firms achieve sustainable competitive advantage and survive in a business environment that is ever-changing and full of uncertainties (Gerald et al., 2020).

Teece et al, (1997) highlighted three fundamental assumptions on which the theory is premised. The first is the capacity to identify and shape opportunities. The second is to use these opportunities and the third is to sustain competitiveness through reconfiguring the enterprise's assets. The main assumption of this framework is that an organization's basic competencies should be used to create short-term competitive positions that can be developed into a longer-term competitive advantage, although, several scholars have criticized this theory as being vague and tautological (Wheeler; 2002; Wang, 2007). While the theory remains very helpful when addressing how to respond to the changing business environment, it may fail to describe exactly how to further specify, develop, and identify those capabilities.

Despite these shortcomings, the theory still comes in handy for this study, as it helps to explain firms' (SMEs) behaviour amid uncertainties (COVID-19 pandemic). SMEs can be said to be strategically agile organizations when they sense changes and seize the opportunity to maintain a competitive advantage whereas the opposite is the case for non-strategically agile organizations that may not be able to stay afloat amid the pandemic.

Empirical Literature

A plethora of studies have been conducted to evaluate the impact of the coronavirus on the activities of SMEs in and around the world. Winarsih, Indriastuti and Fuad (2020) studied the impact of COVID-19 on the digital transformation and sustainability of SMEs to develop a framework for the sustainability of SMEs. The study found that the implementation of social distancing in the country makes people limit activities outside their homes, thus decreasing sales turnover. As an implication, SMEs need to change their mindset in running their businesses using technological inputs.

In another related study, Chinedu et al., (2020) investigated the impact of COVID-19 on the survival of Igbo-owned businesses in Nigeria and found a relationship between restrictions on movement and business sustainability. The study also showed that 96% of changes in the sustainability of Igbo-owned businesses are accounted for by changes in restrictions on interstate movement. The study recommends that the government provides various business incentives such as tax rebates, suspended loan repayment and interest-free loans and other stimulus packages to SMEs to keep them afloat while the pandemic persists.

The effect of the COVID-19 outbreak on the performance of private businesses in Nigeria was carried out by Aifuwa, Musa and Aifuwa (2020). The survey showed that coronavirus adversely affected both the financial and non-financial performance of privately owned firms in Lagos state and Nigeria in general. The study concludes that the COVID-19 pandemic harms firm performance in Nigeria and recommends, among other things, that the government consider private firms in its palliative programmes or stimulus packages.

Gerald, et al. (2020) assessed the strategic agility and performance of SMEs in the phase of the coronavirus pandemic using 306 business owners in Anambra state. Data were analysed using the simple regression technique and the results showed that strategic agility has an impact on the performance (captured by competitive advantage) of SMEs. They concluded that COVID-19 will not have a huge effect on SMEs that are quick enough to identify what was happening in other countries and made provisions for changes to their business operations. The study submits that SME owners should always be on the alert for likely changes in the business environment and prepare for them.

Falokun (2020) examined the impact of, the coronavirus on micro, small and medium-sized enterprises (MSMEs) in Nigeria. Participants in the survey involved 1674 MSMEs comprising 69% females and 31% males with experience sharing online sessions with 42 other leaders of MSMEs. The SMEs cut across sectors such as agriculture, fashion, manufacturing, education, retail and health. Other sectors represented include beauty/cosmetics, information technology, social services, media and transportation. The results showed that MSMEs are count losses in terms of income as recorded by most businesses. The study recommends an urgent need for economic policies that can safely lead to the revival of the MSMEs.

Yusufu and Olawaseun (2020) investigated the effect of the COVID-19 pandemic on the performance of small businesses in Ogun state. The sample for the study was some selected micro and small businesses in Abeokuta, Ogun state. The findings of the study revealed that the low demand due to the lockdown policy of the government drastically reduced the sales volume of the micro and small-scale businesses. The result also showed that the lowering of the buying behaviour also affected the supply of goods and services as well as the general performance of micro and small enterprises. The authors recommend that the government review the lockdown policy to enable the country to return to normalcy to facilitate effective economic growth and development through SMEs.

Fairlie (2020) examined the impact of coronavirus on small business owners in the first three months after social distancing restraints were implemented in the United States. Adopting nationally representative data from April 2020, the Current Population Survey (CPS), findings revealed that the drop in active business ownership was the largest on record. Additionally, losses to business transactions were seen across almost all industries. African American businesses were the worst hit hard by experiencing a 41% decline in business activity, Latinx business owner activities fell by 32%, while Asian business owner activities dropped by 26%.

In another related study, Seth, Ganaie and Zafar (2020) conducted research on the impact of the COVID-19 pandemic on SMEs in Pakistan using 920 businesses as the sample. The study highlighted the issues faced by SMEs during the lockdown and their effect on employment generation and production. The findings revealed that SMEs have identified areas for government support to maintain and sustain their businesses and mitigate the impact of the coronavirus. These include SME-specific support measures such as tax relief, financial packages, guarantees and grants, relaxation in payments of utility bills, easing conditions for loan repayments and support in paying salaries.

Following a gap in the literature on how the COVID-19 pandemic has affected SMEs operating in various sectors in Nigeria, this study is put forward to fill the research gap by investigating the impact of the COVID-19 pandemic on SMEs in Nigeria. This was done with a keen interest in identifying the SME sector that is most hit by the pandemic in Nigeria.

Methodology

Sampling

Using the Yamane (1967) formula for sample size determination $[N/\{1+N(e)^2\}]$ where $N = 1{,}737$ (total SME population in Anambra state) and $e = 0.06$ (error margin) a sample size of 240 respondents was obtained. A quota sampling technique was employed to distribute the questionnaire. This was achieved by dividing the SMEs into ten different groups (sectors) and each sector was allocated with 24 copies of the questionnaire as shown in Table 18.2.

Table 18.2 Sample Clusters

Clusters	*SME Type*	*Respondents*
A	Textile, Leather and Footwear	24
B	Pharmaceuticals	24
C	Automotive and Engineering	24
D	ICT and E-commerce	24
E	Transport	24
F	Education	24
G	Retail and Wholesale	24
H	Food Processing and Agriculture	24
I	Hospitality	24
J	Construction	24
Total		**240**

Note: Authors' compilation

Due to the Nigerian government's social distancing rules and curfew/lockdown enforcement, travelling interstate to assess all SMEs in the country was not feasible at the time of the study. Additionally, online promotion of the survey was not considered because SME owners are relatively those in the lower ebb of the socio-economic stratum whose coping strategies, amid the pandemic, may not include mobile data subscriptions for any online survey. However, for wider coverage, the entire 1,737[1] SMEs in Anambra state formed the population for the study. Anambra state was however selected because it has the highest number of SMEs in Nigeria and houses the largest markets for all Nigerian SME products in the country (Uzoatu, 2019; Metu, 2017; Ujumadu, 2012).

Data Collection

The study employed primary data for the analysis which were obtained from 240 copies of a structured questionnaire administered on an equal basis (24 copies per sector[2]) to the participants who are mostly SME owners in their domain (Onitsha Main Market and Nkwo Nnewi Market[3]). The face and content validity of the instruments were performed by two experts in the Faculty of Social Sciences at Nnamdi Azikiwe University, Awka, Nigeria. Each of the instruments had a total of 16 items. The questionnaires were divided into two sections (Section A and Section B). Section A contains questions on the demographic features of the respondents whereas Section B contains questions that are aimed at answering the research questions posed to the study. Sequentially, a total of 185 copies of the questionnaire with a 77.1% rate of return were retrieved and used for the analysis.

Data Analysis

The analysis of data was carried out by using simple percentages in analysing options structured in the following order strongly agree, agree, and disagree. The analysis here is based on relative frequency using simple percentages, with a threshold of acceptance of 50% and above. Here, "strongly agree" and "agree" are grouped as acceptance while "disagree" is grouped as rejection. This implies that any questionnaire item with a 50% and above should be accepted as playing out in the firm of the respondents while the ones with less than 50% are rejected as not being true.

Results and Discussion

Table 18.3 contains the demographic data of the respondents. A higher proportion of males (55.1%) than females (44.9%) participated in this study. For the age of the SME operators, the majority of them (49.2%) were aged between 26 and 33 years. Additionally, the table indicates that a majority (48.1%) of the respondents have secondary school education whereas a significant percentage (43.3%) of them are degree holders, which further depicts their readiness for entrepreneurship despite

Table 18.3 Demographic Characteristics of the Respondents

S/N	*Variables*	*Categories*	*Frequency*	*Percentage (%)*
1	Age	Below 18years	27	14.6
		18–25 years	39	21.1
		26–33 years	91	49.2
		Above 33 years	28	15.1
2	Gender	Male	102	55.1
		Female	83	44.9
3	Educational qualification	No formal education	4	2.2
		O Level	89	48.1
		Diploma	12	6.5
		Degree	56	30.3
		Higher degree	24	13.0
4	Number of employees	0–15	65	35.1
		16–35	76	41.1
		36–49	21	11.4
		50–65	13	7.0
		66–85	10	5.4
		Above 86	nil	nil
5	Marital status	Single	56	30.3
		Married	93	50.3
		Divorced/Separated	7	3.8
		Widowed/Widower	29	15.7
6	Ethnic nationality	Igbo	57	30.8
		Yoruba	33	17.8
		Hausa/Fulani	28	15.1
		Others	67	36.2

Source: Authors' compilations from Field Survey

their high level of education. Most of the respondents (30.8%) were of Igbo ethnic nationality and more than 50% of the respondents were married. Based on the number of employees, further demographic information shows that 87.6% of the firms selected are small-scale firms with 12.4% of them on the medium-scale implying that there are more small-scale enterprises in Nigeria than medium-scale enterprises.

Table 18.4 shows the respondents' responses to the effect of COVID-19 on SMEs based on respective questionnaire items. Evidence from the analysis shows that questionnaire item 8 was rejected by the respondents, by showing a 58.9% disapproval of the item, while questionnaire items 7, 9, 10, 11, 12, 13, 14, 15 and 16 are considered true as their percentages are above the threshold of 50%. By implication, the result shows that the SME owners rejected that they witnessed difficulty in paying their staff amid the increased operational cost. This implies that the remuneration of their staff has been from the reserves of the affected firms. Additionally, the respondents agreed that following the restriction of movement protocols of the government, it became difficult for them to access input, and most workers found it difficult to come to work, thus affecting cash flows. The

Table 18.4 Effect of COVID-19 on SMEs (Frequency and Percentages)

S/N	*Effect of COVID-19 on Your Business*	*Strongly Agree*	*Agree*	*Disagree*	*Total*	*Decision*
7	Decrease in sales and revenue because of low patronage	145 78.4%	12 6.5%	28 15.1%	185 100%	Accept
8	Difficulty in paying staff	54 29.2%	22 11.9%	109 58.9%	185 100%	Reject
9	Difficulty in accessing inputs	105 56.8%	5 2.7%	75 40.5%	185 100%	Accept
10	limited financial reserves	109 58.9%	19 10.3%	57 30.8%	185 100%	Accept
11	Closed retail and sales outlets	99 53.5%	15 8.1%	71 38.4%	185 100%	Accept
12	Difficulty with staff coming to work	173 93.5%	2 1.1%	10 5.4%	185 100%	Accept
13	Loss of business contracts	167 90.3%	8 4.3%	10 5.4%	185 100%	Accept
14	Increased operational costs	92 49.7%	9 4.9%	84 45.4%	185 100%	Accept
15	Downsizing of staff to meet operational cost	116 62.7%	12 6.5%	57 38.8%	185 100%	Accept
16	Cash flow shortages	84 45.4%	34 18.4%	67 36.2%	185 100%	Accept

Note: Authors' compilations from the Field Survey

respondents further agreed that the COVID-19 pandemic has reduced their financial reserves which are not unconnected to the unavoidable lockdown of their retail and sales outlets around the country. This finding agrees with that of Aifuwa, et al. (2020) posit that the COVID-19 pandemic negatively affects both the financial and non-financial performances of private businesses in Nigeria.

In Figure 18.1, hospitality (92%), education (90%) and transport (81%) are the three most affected SME sectors by the COVID-19 pandemic in the studied area. This implies that the hospitality sector which includes firms such as recreation centres, hotels and bars are the worst hit by the pandemic. The top three least affected SMEs are those in ICT and e-commerce, food processing and agriculture, and pharmaceuticals as they polled a percentage negative response of 50.77%, 50.38% and 48.15% to the questionnaire items. These may be attributed to the essential nature of the food and agricultural processing firms and the pharmaceutical firms to society; they were exempted from total shutdown during the peak period of the pandemic. ICT-related firms took advantage of the internet to continue operations amid the pandemic. Other relatively fewer sectors affected by the pandemic are the construction sector (69.89%), retail and wholesale sector (73.05%), textile, leather, and footwear (65.24%), as well as the automotive and engineering sector (60.97%). The policy implication of this result indicates that the operations of firms that have an online presence such as ICT

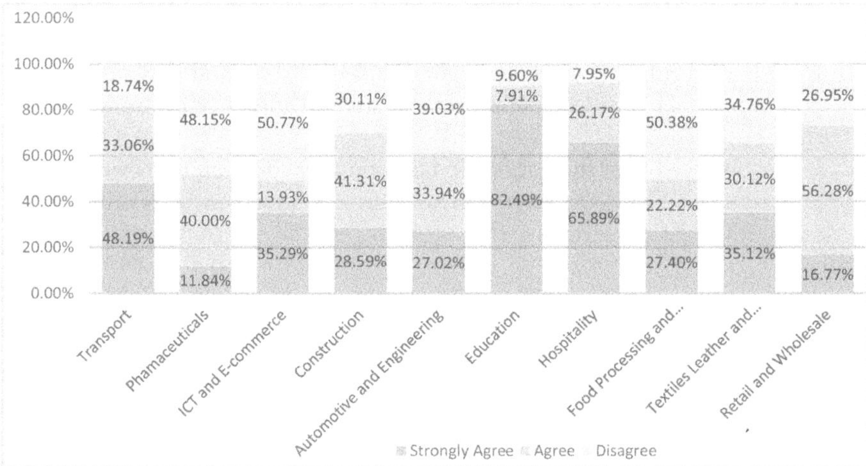

Figure 18.1 Distribution of respondents according to sectors (%)

Note: Authors' compilations from the Field Survey

and e-commerce businesses are usually immune to physical lockdown and movement restrictions. This could form the new normal for firms that hitherto have not taken advantage of the internet to do so.

Conclusion and Policy Implications

The COVID-19 pandemic brought severe hardship and losses to properties around the world, as a result of the different measures put in place to contain the spread. This study investigated the effect of COVID-19 pandemic on SMEs in Nigeria to identify the sector that is most affected by the pandemic. The study found that measures such as restrictions on movements, forced shutdown of business operations, regulations on opening and closing time for businesses, adversely affected sales, cancellation of business contracts, closing of sales outlets, reduction in cash flows, downsizing of staff, loss of financial reserve and difficulty in assessing material inputs. Furthermore, findings from the study show that the SMEs in the hospitality sector are the most affected by the pandemic followed by those in the education and transport sectors. The least affected SME sectors are those operating in ICT and e-commerce, food processing and agriculture, and the pharmaceutical firms.

Considering the importance of SMEs to the economic recovery of Nigeria, some policy recommendations are proffered. These include:

i. First, since the education sector is among the sectors most affected by COVID-19, the government at all levels is advised to provide interest-free loans for school owners and administrators so that they could manage their enterprises after the lockdown.

ii. Second, following the gradual ease of lockdown, the government at all levels is advised to grant tax cuts, especially to SMEs in the hospitality and transport sectors. This will help cushion the adverse effects of the pandemic on their businesses.

iii. It was observed that the pandemic had minimal effect on firms with online presence, and SMEs are advised to key into e-commerce which will help the facilitation of transactions with customers regardless of their locations.

Notes

1 SMEDAN (2013) estimates the number of SMEs in Anambra state to be 1,737

2 The selected sectors are as follows: 1. Textile, Leather and Footwear (2 copies were not returned); 2. Pharmaceuticals; 3. Automotive and Engineering; 4. ICT and E-commerce; 5. Transport; 6. Education; 7. Retail and Wholesale; 8. Food Processing and Agriculture; 9. Hospitality; and 10. Construction

3 The Onitsha Main Market is the biggest market in Nigeria while the Nkwo Nnewi Market is the largest spare markets in Nigeria

References

Abdullahi, M. S., Abubakar, A. Aliyu, A. L., Umar, K., Umar, M. B. Sabiu, I. T., Naisa, F. U. K., Khalid, S. S., & Abubakar, L. S. (2015). The nature of small and medium scale enterprises (SMEs): Government and financial institutions support in Nigeria. *International Journal of Academic Research in Business and Social Sciences*, 5(3), 525–537

Aifuwa, H. O., Musa, S., & Aifuwa, S. A. (2020). Coronavirus pandemic outbreak and firms' performance in Nigeria. *Management and Human Resource Research Journal*, 9(4), 15–25

Bako, Y. A. (2020). *Effect of global pandemic virus (COCID-19) on small businesses in Ogun state: Experience from Abeokuta South local government, Ogun State Nigeria*, Available at https://www.researchgate.net/project/effect-of-global-pandemic-virus-covid-19-on-small-businesses-in-ogun-stateexperience-from-abeokuta-south-local-government-ogun-state-nigeria (accessed 18/09/2020)

Chinedu, O. F., Dennis, M. O., & Chikwuemeka-Onuzulike, N. (2020). Impact of COVID-19 on the survival of Igbo-owned businesses in Nigeria: The nexus. *International Journal of Financial, Accounting, and Management*, 2(2), 121–130

Fairlie, R. W. (2020). The impact of COVID-19 on small business owners: The first three months after social-distancing restrictions. *NBER Working Paper No. w27462*, Available at SSRN: https://ssrn.com/abstract=3673693 (accessed 16/09/2020)

Falokun, L. (2020). *Impact of COVI-19 on micro, small and medium-sized enterprises in Nigeria*. Available at https://smetoolkit.ng/articles/17096-impact-of-covid-19-on-micro-small-and-medium-sized-enterprises-in-nigeria (accessed 18/09/2020)

GAIN- Global Alliance for Improved Nutrition (2020). *Impacts of COVID-19 on small and medium-sized enterprises in the food system: Results of an online survey*. Geneva: GAIN

Gerald, E., Obianuju, A., &Chukwunonso, N. (2020). Strategic agility and performance of small and medium enterprises in the phase of COVID-19 pandemic. *International* Journal of Financial, Accounting, and Management, *2*(1), 41–50. Available at https://doi.org/10.35912/ijfam.v2i1.163 (accessed 18/09/2020)

https://www.anambrastate.gov.ng/news?r=anambra-wins-again,-this-time-for-supporting-small-businesses&hs=1fd31d366130d335fcef14babbcb9aaf (accessed 17/09/2020)

https://www.pmnewsnigeria.com/2020/03/09/breaking-nigeria-records-second-case-of-coronavirus/ (accessed 17/09/2020)

Igbanugo, I. C., Uzonwanne, M. C., & Ezenekwe, R. U. (2015). Small and medium scale enterprises in an African setting: The place of women. *International Journal of Economics, Commerce and Management*, 4(3), 762–778

International Labour Organization (2020a, March 18). ILO monitor: COVID-19 and the world of work. 1st edition. *ILO Briefing Note*. Available at https://www.ilo.org/global/about-the-ilo/WCMS_738753/lang--en/index.htm (accessed 17/09/2020)

International Labour Organization (2020b). *Nigeria labour act 1974*. Available at https://www.ilo.org/dyn/natlex/docs/WEBTEXT/42156/64980/E74NGA01.htm (accessed 18/09/2020).

International Labour Organization (2020c, April 23). Video: Impact of COVID-19 on employment and the labour market in the Kyrgyz Republic. Results of the rapid assessment. *ILO News*. Available at https://www.ilo.org/moscow/news/WCMS_782862/lang--en/index.html (accessed 05/06/2021)

Kurmann, A., Lale, E., & Ta, Lien (2020). *The impact of COVID-19 on small business employment and hours: Real-time estimates with home base data*. Available at https://www.mcgill.ca/popcentre/files/popcentre/hbdraft_0612.pdf (accessed 16/09/2020)

Maclean, R., & Dahir, A. L. (2020, February 28). Nigeria responds to the first coronavirus case in sub-Sahara Africa. *New York Times*. Available at https://www.nytimes.com/2020/02/28/world/africa/Nigeria coronavirus.html (accessed 17/09/2020)

Makinde, F., Nwogu, S., Ajaja, T., & Alagbe, J. (2020, March 22). COVID-19: Adeboye, Oyedepo, Okonkwo, Adeyemi, and others hold online services. *The Punch*. Available at https://punchng.com/covid-19-adeboye-oyedepo-okonkwo-adeyemi-others-hold-onlineservices/ (accessed 18/10/2020)

Metu, A. G. (2017). Challenges of accessing finance by female micro-entrepreneurs in Anambra state. [Unpublished doctoral dissertation] Nnamdi Azikiwe University Awka Nigeria.

Musa, S. & Aifuwa, H. O. (2020). Coronavirus pandemic in Nigeria: How can small and medium enterprises (SMEs) cope and flatten the curve. *European Journal of Accounting, Finance, and Investment*, 6(5), 55–61.

Nigeria Centre for Disease Control (2020). *COVID-19 Nigeria*. Available at https://covid19.ncdc.gov.ng (accessed 18/10/2020)

Nigeria Centre for Disease Control (2021). *Confirmed cases by state*. Available at https://covid19.ncdc.gov.ng (accessed 05/06/2021)

Nwosu, C. A., Marcus, S. N., & Metu, A. G. (2020). COVID-19, lockdown, supply disruptions and inflationary pressure in Nigeria. Socialscientia Journal of the Social Sciences and Humanities, Thematic, 5(4T), 84–95. Availabe at https://journals.aphriapub.com/index.php/ss/article/view/1226 (accessed 05/06/2021)

Olapegba, P. O., Ayandele, O., Kolawole, S. O. & Oguntayo, R., Gandi, J. C., Dangiwa, A. L., . . . Iorfa, S. K. (2020). *COVID-19 knowledge and perceptions in Nigeria*. Available at https://doi.org/10.31234/osf.io/j356x (accessed 18/09/2020)

Olatunji, H. (2020). *Coronavirus: Catholic Church in Lagos suspends sprinkling of 'holy water', and handshakes during mass*. Available at https://www.thecable.ng/coronavirus-catholic-church-in-lagos-suspends-sprinkling-ofholy-water-handshakes-during-mass (accessed 18/10/2020)

PM News (2020). *Nigeria records a second case of coronavirus*. Available at https://www.pmnewsnigeria.com/2020/03/09/breaking-nigeria-records-second-case-of-coronavirus (accessed 18/10/2020)
Price, L. (2020). *Impact of COVID-19 on small businesses – Where is it worst?* Available at https://smallbiztrends.com/2020/04/impact-of-coronavirus-on-small-businesses.html (accessed 15/09/2020)
Salem, T. (2020). Reps call for enforcement of interstate lockdown. *Vanguard Newspaper*, Available at https://www.vanguardngr.com/2020/05/reps-call-for-enforcement-of-inter-state-lockdown (accessed 18/09/2020)
Seth, N. J., Ganaie, M. A. & Zafar, F. (2020). *Impact of COVID-19 (Coronavirus) on small and medium enterprises (SMEs) in Pakistan*. SME Development Authority Ministry of Industry and Production Government of Pakistan: Lahore
SMEDAN (2013). *SMEDAN and National Bureau of Statistics collaborative survey: Selected findings* (2013). Available at file:///C:/Users/HP/AppData/Local/Temp/SMEDAN%20 2013_Selected%20Tables-1.pdf (accessed 19/09/2020)
Teece, D. J., Pisano, G., & Shuen, A. (1997). Dynamic capabilities and strategic management. *Strategic Management Journal*, *18*(7), 509-533
Ujumadu, V. (2012). *Anambra has the highest number of SMEs in Nigeria*. Available at: https://www.vanguardngr.com/2012/07/anambra-has-highest-number-of-smes-in-nigeria-aganga (accessed 18/09/2020)
Uzoatu, U. M. (2019). *Anambra wins again this time for supporting small businesses*. Available at https://www.anambrastate.gov.ng/news?r=anambra-wins-again,-this-time-for-supporting-small-businesses&hs=1fd31d366130d335fcef14babbcb9aaf (accessed 18/09/2020)
Uzonwanne, M. C., Ezenekwe, U., Nzeribe, G., Mathew, N. & Adonike, K. C. (2020). Impact of transportation cost on prices of consumable commodities in Anambra State. *Journal of Economic Studies*, *17*(2), 195–204.
Wang, C (2007). Dynamic capabilities: A review and research agenda. *International Journal of Management Reviews*, 9(1), 31–51.
Wheeler, B. C. (2002). NEBIC: A dynamic capabilities theory for assessing net-enablement. *Information Systems Research*, *13*(2), 125–146.
Winarshih, Indriastuti, M. & Faud, K. (2020). Impact of COVID-19 on digital transformation and sustainability in small and medium enterprises (SMEs): A conceptual framework. In: Barolli, L., Poniszewska-Maranda, A., Enokido, T., (eds) *Complex, intelligent and software-intensive systems*, *1194*. Springer, Cham. Available at https://link.springer.com/chapter/10.1007/978-3-030-50454-0-48 (accessed 15/09/2020)
World Health Organization (2020). *WHO Director-General's opening remarks at the media briefing on COVID-19 - 11 March*. Available at https://www.who.int/dg/speeches/detail/who-director-general-s-opening-remarks-at-the-media-briefing-on-covid-19-11-march-2020 (accessed 19/10/2020)
Yamane, T. (1967). *Statistics: An introductory analysis*. *2nd edition*. Harper and Row, New York.
Yusuf, A. B. & Oluwaseun, J. O. (2020). *Effect of global pandemic virus (Covid-19) on small business in Ogun state: Experience from Abeokuta South local government, Ogun state Nigeria*. Available at https://asatechconsult.com/wp-content/uploads/2020/05/effect-of-global-pandemic-virus-covid-19-on-small-business-in-ogun-state.pdf (accessed 19/10/2020)

Conclusion

Socioeconomic Shocks, Pandemic Responsiveness, and Platonic Policies Revisited

Gbadebo Odularu, Daniel Ufua, Evans Osabuohien, and Romanus Osabohien

Introduction and Rationale

As public and environmental health policymakers watch for new virus variants, COVID-19 has become increasingly endemic in an environmentally endangered ecosystem with a greater frequency of desertification, drought, Giga wildfires, heatwaves, and floods. However, the two largest economies – the US and China – have huge joint responsibilities to decarbonize the world in the face of their deepening geopolitical rivalry. In a slightly similar vein, COVID-19 has exposed the pre-pandemic and inherently stark fragilities, ethnic inequities, and unsustainable socioeconomic practices prevalent in most low- and middle-income countries (Odularu, 2020c; Odularu, Osabuohien, Ufua and Osabohien, 2022). With most economies struggling to exhibit skin-in-the-game characteristics, COVID-19 adversely impacted every industry with the expectation that more people would be engaged in virtual working, shopping, schooling, and watching electronic devices from home, thereby scaling the need for instant virtual connections and a huge data demand (Odularu, 2020a; Odularu, 2020b).

Based on the practical vastness, research applicability, and socioeconomic relevance of every chapter, the policy recommendations in this book represent excellent tools for improving African governments' knowledge of critical interventions for overcoming socioeconomic shocks such as the COVID-19 pandemic (Odularu, Osabuohien, Ufua and Osabohien, 2022). In addition, these strategically articulated chapters deploy sustainable development politics and policies as significant determinants of outcomes, and this fundamental understanding remains the foundational tool for public health practice in the 21st century. Thus, this concluding chapter discusses the importance of scaling and accelerating the global delivery of vaccines towards vaccine gap closure in Africa, thereby deploying a-Platonic policies to overcome the socioeconomic shocks generated by the pandemic.

DOI: 10.4324/9781003208358-24

Africa's Responsiveness to Stemming SARS-CoV-2: Lessons from the US's Collaborative Strategy

When the COVID-19 virus struck in 2019, it spread rapidly to all countries and triggered significant shifts across many facets of our lives. Consequently, governments responded by taking measures such as school closings; travel restrictions; bans on public gatherings; social welfare provisions; vaccination campaigns; contract tracing; emergency investments in healthcare facilities; and greater investment in research, development, and innovation (Hale et al., 2021; Khan, 2020). For instance, Millipore Signa alone supplied materials for more than 50 vaccine candidates, 35 diagnostic testing solutions, and 20 therapies for COVID-19 (Genetic Engineering & Biotechnology News, July 2021).

More specifically, recalling that a core component of the American Rescue Plan, a $1.9 trillion economic stimulus bill, was signed into law by President Joe Biden in March 2021 to accelerate the country's socioeconomic recovery from the COVID-19 pandemic and the ongoing recession. These countries also called for rapid research interventions from their governments and their related agencies. For instance, the US National Institutes of Health, National Science Foundation, Patient-Centered Outcomes Research Institute (PCORI), and other donor nonprofits such as Rockefeller Foundation, Pfizer, and Johnson and Johnson, are shifting national discourse and innovative strategies, procedures, and collaborations towards overcoming the biggest challenges to better prepare for the next major socioeconomic and public health emergency or pandemic.

Innovative solutions to socioeconomic shocks such as the COVID-19 pandemic are more non-linear than we think, and scientists would like to think. From a technological viewpoint, the rapid acceleration of mRNA vaccines at the forefront of stemming COVID-19 spread speaks to the power of non-linear, disruptive innovation born from step-function changes in technologies (Genetic Engineering & Biotechnology News, July 2021). However, technology may be way ahead of the regulatory environment in this increasingly complex and dynamically digital business ecosystem where digital assets, digital currencies and digital opportunities expand as the global community acquires knowledge around digitalization (Odularu et al., 2022; Ufua et al., 2021; Kashyap, 2019).

According to Airfinity, a provider of life-sciences data, as children's vaccination expands, more adults will take booster jabs in 2022. The Global Dashboard on Vaccine Equity[1] analysis on per capita GDP growth rates from the World Economic Outlook shows that richer countries vaccinate quicker and recover economically faster from COVID-19. In comparison, poorer countries may not achieve pre-COVID-19 levels of growth until 2024. All these dynamic interactions, from COVID-19 vaccine discovery to vaccine hesitancy and the production of new antiviral pills, show the power of non-linearity at work (Odularu et al., 2022; Sharpe and Faden, 1998). Afterwards, one may not be too surprised that from the Federal Research Act of 1913 to the CARES Act of 2020, Conti-Brown and Feinstein (2021) revealed that at the congressional authority frontiers, there were no patterns of responding to crises or logic of grand design.

The deleterious effects of COVID-19, as a socioeconomic shock, will linger among most African economies partly because of limited financial resources for more inclusive safety net programmes and subsequently because approximately 1% of Africans are well vaccinated compared to approximately 75% of their counterparts in the North. According to the Gates Foundation, one of the world's largest charities, 90% of households will attain their pre-pandemic average incomes in wealthy countries, compared with only one-third of low- and middle-income countries, mostly in Africa. By implication, it is highly critical that urgent interventions to boost supply and make vaccines more affordable and accessible to Africa, Furthermore, the Global Dashboard on Vaccine Equity insights reveals that vaccine equity is very imperative to saving African lives and driving a fairer and faster recovery from the pandemic. More specifically, COVID-19 vaccine programmes are expected to cost low-income countries an additional 56.6% of health budgets, compared with 0.8% of wealthy countries' health expenditures.

Although Africa has solidified its vaccine production plans in the last quarter of 2021, many of its countries will remain unvaccinated for much of 2022, mainly due to both demand- (vaccine hesitancy) and supply-side (value chain capacities) challenges. Unfortunately, these vaccine demand and supply dynamics will result in higher rates of illness and hospitalizations and slower rates of bringing African economies back better.

With all this evidence, it has become compellingly clear that certain risks of COVID-19 vaccination far outweigh its uncertain risks. Furthermore, from a more probabilistic perspective, Daniel Bermoulli (1971) could be adapted to understand whether uncertain benefits outweigh certain COVID-19 vaccination risks. One of the basic assumptions is that the probability p of contracting COVID-19 (or its variants like the *Delta* and *Omicron*) during a year (if the subject is not immune) remains the same at every age, as does the probability q of dying from COVID-19, once contracted.

If $r(t)$ is the total population in Africa who survives to age t, let $c(t)$ be the number of people who survive to age t without COVID-19 infection. One considers what happens between the age of t and $t + \delta t$, where δt is small, which could both be represented as follows:

$$\delta r = r\,(t + \delta\, t) - r(t);$$

and

$$\delta c = c\,(t + \delta\, t) - c(t).$$

Between the ages of t and $t + \delta t$, the probability that someone who has survived to age t without having COVID-19 will be infected with the virus is approximately $p\delta t$, the probability that they will die of COVID-19 is $pq\delta t$, and the probability that they will die of some other diseases is approximately $u(t)\delta t$ for some unknown $u(t)$. The calculation of δr requires the number of deaths from other diseases among both immune and non-immune patients and the number of those who died from COVID-19 during the period. Bernoulli's formula contains two constants p and q, in which the death rate varies between epidemics but (in agreement with others who had studied the available statistics) takes $q = \frac{1}{8}$ as a reasonable number. The latest costs of vaccines show an average of US$15.80, and without global financial support, low-income countries' health costs could soar by more than half to fully vaccinate a target of 70% of their populations. The High-income countries would increase their health spending by just 0.8% to achieve the same results.

However, the selected socioeconomic development agenda in Africa suffers from platonicity. Policy Platonicities occur when socioeconomic programmes and policies (agenda) over-or underestimate their understanding of the subtle changes that constitute the world and what weight needs to be imparted to each such sustainable development process (Markey-Towler, 2018; Taleb, 2007). According to Taleb (2007), a Platonic fold is an explosive boundary where the Platonic mindset enters into contact with messy reality. The gap between the Sustainable Development Goals (SDGs) that African economies achieve and the SDGs that the economies think they know becomes dangerously wide. 'Platonicity' makes us think that we understand more than we do. In other words, it makes economies think that they have attained greater development goals than their real socioeconomic circumstances By adaptation, when models, programmes, and policies are incorrect in some specific applications, (i) policy designers do not know beforehand where the policies will be wrong, (ii) nor do they know that the socioeconomic models are potential medicines that pose random but very devastating side effects on the political economy, and (iii) these mistakes result in severe socioeconomic catastrophes. Most African economies, especially in the post-COVID-19 period, may continue to suffer from policy platonicity, in which their socio-economies are driven by a platonic blueprint that seems to 'make sense', rather than focusing on messier and less tractable structures.

Policy platonicities and inverse problems are evident in Africa when we mechanically import selected socioeconomic development theories to solve post-pandemic development challenges. From Platonicity's rationalist argument, any socioeconomic development policy that presents secondary usefulness, and one does not pay for, will present an extra opportunity should a heretofore unknown application emerge, or a new ecosystem appears (Taleb, 2007). In other words, a policy intervention with the largest number of secondary benefits will gain the most from environmental randomness and epistemic opacity (Kreuzer and Parsons, 2019)!

At this juncture, it is pertinent to introduce bleedingness as a socioeconomic derivative, and the relationship between the variables is convex rather than linear – the more convex the curve, the more amplified the random outcomes will be. By implication, convexity is the primary mechanism that generates bleeding. According to Taleb (2007, 2008), convexities result in serious socioeconomic fragilities. This justifies the need to interpret bleeding within the 'epistemic' context of leveraging it to understand the socioeconomic effects of the pandemic and the probable human behavior based on the four forecasting quadrants posited by Taleb (2004a, 2007, 2008). Effective socioeconomic institutions reduce the fragility and bleedingness that constrain Africa from leapfrogging its continental economy towards attaining sustainable economic cooperation and transformation (Odularu et al., 2022; Acemoglu and Robinson, 2012).

The socioeconomic system's capacity exhibits anti-bleeding characteristics if it delivers societal expectations and grows when a global shock occurs (Odularu et al., 2022; Ufua et al., 2021). Within this scope, it is essential to note that micro-level bleeding is not necessarily harmful to a trading system, but individuals and firms in the trade ecosystem exhibit antifragile behavior (Taleb, 2004b; Odularu et al., 2022).

More socioeconomic empowerment-related and public infrastructure should be built to connect underserved and vulnerable communities at the state and local levels. For instance, the Nigerian Basic Health Care Provision Fund (BHCPF)[2] should develop and implement a COVID-19 or public health emergency health equity dashboard, an interactive tool providing disparity data to local governments across the country. The dashboard provides information in a transparent and useful way to guide localized responses to not only the epidemic infection and vaccination patterns but also sensitizes arms of government to increase BHCFP allocation in a timely manner (HCDN, 2021).

Policy a-Platonicity and Increasingly Dynamic Socioeconomic Future

In today's increasingly complex socioeconomic and politically dynamic environment, regulations, science, technology, policy, and law significantly impact shock-responsive government interventions, thereby enhancing public health programmes and health outcomes. Africa's post-pandemic and socioeconomic development agenda should focus squarely on how to swiftly transition from policy Platonicity (a top-down, formulaic, closed-minded, self-serving, and commoditized) approach to an a-Platonic (bottom-up, open-minded, skeptical, and empirical) socioeconomic development trajectory (Taleb, 2008). Despite the policy platonicity peculiarities within its socioeconomic development space, as one observes how the future of the pandemic evolves in Africa, the differential gap between the recommended policies and naturally effective policy interventions is widening by the day. In that sense, the past may be misleading in predicting the dynamic future of Africa. In view of this, emerging and future research should focus on the efficiency of government agencies to successfully manage policy platonicity and what set of key takeaways to help policymakers plan a formidable preparedness path forward for mitigating future pandemics:

- According to IMF *F&D Magazine* on 'Quantum Computing's Possibilities and Perils', quantum computing has the potential to accelerate scientific discovery and innovation, revolutionize socioeconomic development modeling, and empower machine learning and artificial intelligence. However, the computing power of these mighty quantum machines could also threaten modern cryptography and undermine financial stability. For instance, in 1981, the late Caltech professor, Richard Feynman (a Nobel Prize co-winner for his work with quantum electrodynamics) noted that 'Nature isn't classical, dammit, and if you want to make a simulation of nature, you'd better make it quantum mechanical, and by golly, it's wonderful problem because it doesn't look so easy.'

- Enhancing Policy Antifragility: The pandemic presented an unprecedented need for reliable, data-driven insights to navigate collapsing socioeconomic ecosystems, support struggling businesses, and design nudges to incentivize vaccination, especially among seemingly unreluctant people. Thus, transforming socioeconomic systems require a compelling evidence base along with fintech, trade technology, innovations, and digitalization. More specifically, the United Nations Research Roadmap for the COVID-19 Recovery[3] provides a workable framework for leveraging the power of science to foster stronger socioeconomic recovery and a more equitable, resilient, and sustainable future. However, vaccine inequity seems to be one of the world's biggest obstacles to ending this pandemic and recovering socioeconomically from its devastating effects. In other words, it appears logical that the massive provision of vaccines will curb the spread of COVID-19 in the global south in a linear and positive correlation. A globally united effort would consolidate the already-sparked breakthroughs that disrupt the traditional ways we research, develop, produce, and deliver towards multiplying these outcomes to combat other devastating global health challenges. Thus, for future policies, some African development partners have proposed 'rapid socioeconomic recovery, renewal and resilient' (3Rs) policies. However, most of these 3R policies will become beautifully platonified in most African communities that are currently chronically undervaccinated (Taleb, 2007, 2008). Instead, antifragile policies are beyond resilience or recovery towards leveraging socioeconomic shocks for Africa's survival and development agenda.
- Mobile position data contact tracing[4] is crucial for epidemic control if it complies with relevant data privacy regulations. Thus, data-driven innovation and artificial intelligence (AI) systems offer the potential to better understand the role of genetic factors in health and wellbeing and deliver more efficient therapies and diagnostics. In other words, we want to leverage digitalization (AI systems) to show and implement the role of the bioeconomy in community health and wellbeing. Currently, there is a need for data combination and sharing across organizational boundaries to have comprehensive data to deploy advanced computational methods for training the types of algorithms and conducting AI-driven studies that allow Africa to better respond with policy interventions to bring its economies back better. However, based on how African countries are deploying mobile positioning data technology to reduce the spread of COVID-19, there is an increasing need

to enforce digital contact tracing while adhering to the guidelines provided by the National Data Protection Regulation (NDPR).

- Healthcare is experiencing a digital transformation globally that continually enables consumers to demand convenience, while businesses exhibit digital behavior by leveraging artificial intelligence, innovation, automation, and advanced analytics. This global trend became more pronounced due to the COVID-19 era. Thus, the post-pandemic future of healthcare in Africa should adopt, apply, and utilize the integration of Industry 4.0 technologies such as artificial intelligence, blockchain, digital health, and the Internet of Medical Things (IoMT) (Ow, 2021). This is more evident as the global tech ecosystem transitions from 3G- and 4G-enabled technologies, which launched transformative changes in audio and video communications, to 5G-enabled technologies, which enable transformative changes in a broader array of environments encompassing communication, transportation, health care and industrial production.
- Every community, country, and continent's COVID-19 pandemic experiences and policy responses are geographically different and diverse from one another. and Africa's socioeconomic shock-responsive policy interventions should take a more interdisciplinary and experimental approach in preparing Africa for the pandemic (Osabuohien, Ejemeyovwi, Ihayere, Gitau and Oyebola, 2021). For instance, we still remember that in October 2019, Abhijit Banerjee, Esther Duflo, and Micheal Kremer jointly won the 51st Sveriges Riksbank Prize in Economic Sciences in Memory of Alfred Nobel for their experimental 'randomized control trials (RCTs)'[5] approach in alleviating global poverty. The interdisciplinary nature of these regional shock-absorbing policies should look beyond the epistemological, political and ethical differences underlying many of the interdisciplinary disagreements and encompass a wide range of other subjects.

Concluding Remarks

With the increasing diversity of healthcare delivery platforms, more African countries are strategically strengthening their public health information systems in response to the vastness of stakeholders' interests, need for data security, the privacy of data, and Universal Health Coverage and Prevention of Non-Communicable Diseases. Thus, as these tools evolve, this chapter focuses on the constantly evolving nature of socioeconomic shocks and the need for technologically driven scientific a-Platonic policies that are well-evidence-based and embedded towards advancing our health and wellbeing.

In conclusion, it is critically imperative that Africa's policy interventions and preparedness strategies for the future of the COVID-19 pandemic place emphasis on the a-Platonic spectrum of public health programs while analyzing the correlation between scalability science and socioeconomic development outcomes in the face of the current knowledge and practice gaps in Africa.

Notes

1 The Global Dashboard on Vaccine Equity is a joint initiative from United Nations Development Programme (UNDP), the World Health Organization (WHO), and University of Oxford's Blavatnik School of Government, which combines the latest COVID-19 vaccination information with the most recent socioeconomic data. Global Dashboard on Vaccine Equity launched, featuring data from COVID-19 tracker | Blavatnik School of Government (ox.ac.uk)
2 In 2014, the Federal Government (FG), through the enactment of the National Health Act (NHAct), committed to providing the (Basic Minimum Package of Healthcare Services (BHPHS) to all Nigerians using at least 1% of the Federal Government Consolidated Revenue Fund (CRF) and 25% counterpart funding.
3 UN Research Roadmap for the COVID-19 Recovery | United Nations
4 JMIR mHealth and Health – COVID-19 Mobile Positioning Data Contact Tracing and Patient Privacy Regulations: Exploratory Search of Global Response Strategies and the Use of Digital Tools in Nigeria
5 RCTs are considered the gold standard for the evaluation of anti-poverty and shock responsive policy interventions, especially in health, gender, politics, schooling, credit, and gender case studies.

References

Acemoglu, D. M. and J. A. Robinson. 2012. *Why Nations Fail: The Origins of Power, Prosperity, and Poverty*. Crown Books.

Bermoulli, D. 1766. De la mortalite cause par la petite verole, et des avantages de l'inoculation opur la prevenir. *Mem, Math, Phys. Acad. R. Sci. Paris*. 72(1–45), 1766. There is an English translation by L. Bradley in Smallpox Inoculation: An Eighteenth-Century Mathematical Controversy published by the Adult Education Department, Nottingham, 1971.

Conti-Brown, Peter and Brian D. Feinstein, 2021. The Contingent Origins of Financial Legislation. *Washington University Law Review*, Forthcoming. Available at SSRN: https://ssrn.com/abstract=3778189 or http://doi.org/10.2139/ssrn.3778189

Hale, Thomas, Jessica Anania, Noam Angrist, Thomas Boby, Emily Cameron-Blake, Martina Di Folco, Lucy Ellen, Rafael Goldszmidt, Laura Hallas, Beatriz Kira, Maria Luciano, Saptarshi Majumdar, Radhika Nagesh, Anna Petherick, Toby Phillips, Helen Tatlow, Samuel Webster, Andrew Wood, Yuxi Zhang. 2021. "Variation in Government Responses to COVID-19" Version 12.0. Blavatnik School of Government Working Paper. 11 June 2021. Available: www.bsg.ox.ac.uk/covidtracker

Human Capital Development Network (HCDN). 2021. *Implementation of the Basic Health Care Provision Fund (BHCPF) in Nigeria*. HCDN Advocacy Brief February. Available https://options.co.uk/sites/default/files/bhcpf_advocacy_brief.pdf

Kashyap, R. 2019. The Economics of Enlightenment: Time Value of Knowledge and the Net Present Value (NPV) of Knowledge Machines. *B.E. Journal of Economic Analysis and Policy*, 20(2), 2019–0044. Available SSRN: https://ssrn.com/abstract=3282967 or http://doi.org/10.2139/ssrn.3282967

Khan, Naushad, Shah Fahad, Mahnoor Naushad, Shah Faisal and Quarantine Role in the Economic Development of the World Society. 2020 April 14. Available SSRN: https://ssrn.com/abstract=3576189 or http://doi.org/10.2139/ssrn.3576189

Kreuzer, Marcus and Craig Parsons, Epistemological and Ontological Priors: Varieties of Explicitness and Research Integrity. 2019 February 12. *American Political Science*

Association Organized Section for Qualitative and Multi-Method Research, Qualitative Transparency Deliberations. Working Group Final Reports, Report I.1–1 (August 2018), Available SSRN: https://ssrn.com/abstract=3332846 or http://doi.org/10.2139/ssrn.3332846
Markey-Towler, B. 2018 February 26. *Antifragility, the Black Swan and Psychology: A Psychological Theory of Adaptability in Evolutionary Socioeconomic Systems*. Available: http://doi.org/10.2139/ssrn.3130038
Odularu, G. 2020a. The Primer: Bracing Nigerian Trading Ecosystem for the Future. In: Odularu, G. (ed), *Strategic Policy Options for Bracing Nigeria for the Future of Trade*. Cham: Palgrave Macmillan. https://doi.org/10.1007/978-3-030-34552-5_1
Odularu, G. 2020b. Conclusion and Policy Recommendations. In: Odularu, G. (ed), *Strategic Policy Options for Bracing Nigeria for the Future of Trade*. Cham: Palgrave Macmillan. https://doi.org/10.1007/978-3-030-34552-5_8
Odularu, G. 2020c. *Digital Pathways for Fostering PostCOVID-19*. Available www.afronomicslaw.org/2020/07/18/digital-pathways-for-fostering-post-covid-19-trade-outcomes/?fbclid=IwAR2FOS9d9U6epp8ItvrqhRlJkfmevHPbITuPmdaXRqt0ed9X12oYEH6U5Fk
Odularu, G.O.A., E. Osabuohien, D. Ufua and R. Osabohien. 2022. Conclusion: COVID-19 and Pandemic Preparedness in a Digital Age. In: *Osabuohien, Odularu, Ufua and Osabohien, 2022. 'COVID-19 in the African Continent: Sustainable Development and Socioeconomic Shocks*. Bingley: Emerald Publishing Limited. https://cseaafrica.org/building-businesses-back-better-amid-covid-19-pandemic-in-africa/
Osabuohien, E., J. Ejemeyovwi, O. Ihayere, C. Gitau and F. Oyebola. 2021. Post-Pandemic Renewable Energy Development in Sub-Saharan Africa. *Sustainability and Climate Change*, 14(3), 183–192. https://doi.org/10.1089/scc.2020.0077
Sharpe, V.A. and A.I. Faden. 1998. *Medical Harm: Historical, Conceptual and Ethical Dimensions of Iatrogenic Illness*. Cambridge: Cambridge University Press.
Taleb, N.N. 2004a. Bleed or Blow-up? Why Do We Prefer Asymmetric Payoffs? *Journal of Behavioural Finance*, 5(1), 2–7.
Taleb, N.N. 2004b. *Fooled by Randomness: The Hidden Role of Chance in Life and the Markets*. New York: Random House, 24.
Taleb, N.N. 2007. *The Black Swan: The Impact of the Highly Improbable*. London: Penguin.
Taleb, N. N. 2008. *The Fourth Quadrant: A Map of the Limits of Statistics*. Unpublished Manuscript. www.edge.org/3rd_culture/taleb08/taleb08_index.html
Ufua, D.E, Emielu, E.T. Olujobi, O.J., Lakhani, F., Borishade, T.T., Ibidunni, A.S. and Osabuohien, E. (2021). Digital Transformation: A Conceptual Framing for Attaining Sustainable Development Goals 4 and 9 in Nigeria. *Journal of Management and Organisation*, 27(5), 836–849. https://doi.org/10.1017/jmo.2021.45
Ufua, D., E. Osabuohien, M. Ogbari, H. Falola, E. Okoh and A. Lakhani. 2021. Re-Strategising Government Palliative Support Systems in Tackling the Challenges of COVID-19 Lockdown in Lagos State, Nigeria. *Global Journal of Flexible Systems Management*, 22, 19–32. https://doi.org/10.1007/s40171-021-00263-z

Index

Note: Page numbers in *italics* indicate a figure and page numbers in **bold** indicate a table on the corresponding page.

www.ingramcontent.com/pod-product-compliance
Ingram Content Group UK Ltd.
Pitfield, Milton Keynes, MK11 3LW, UK
UKHW020145200926
475702UK00005B/925
* 9 7 8 1 0 3 2 0 7 6 9 3 5 *